CARL VAN VECHTEN
150 WEST FIFTY-FIFTH STREET

Langston

Dear Langston, You are

VAN VECHTEN
ONE CENTRAL PARK WEST
NEW YORK 23, N. Y.

June 2 1964

Dear Langston. Thank
you for your letter &
the inventory. You have
done a lot for the
Collection and for
one am grateful.

December 6 1962

affections
Carlo

VAN VECHTEN
FIFTY-FIFTH STREET

Dear Langston,
Can you get over for a party for Paul Morou
I am giving Sunday night — I hope so. He is
here only for a few days on his way home to
Paris from the Orient.

I hope you are the same!
Carlo.

Essie Robeson also is going to have a baby. Ha
is growing.

and MORE MONEY o you!

MONEY o you!

REMEMBER ME TO HARLEM

REMEMBER ME TO HARLEM,

*The Letters of Langston Hughes
and Carl Van Vechten,
1925–1964*

EDITED BY EMILY BERNARD

Alfred A. Knopf  New York 2001

THIS IS A BORZOI BOOK
PUBLISHED BY ALFRED A. KNOPF

Copyright © 2001 by Emily Bernard and the Estate of Langston Hughes

*All rights reserved under International and Pan-American Copyright Conventions.
Published in the United States by Alfred A. Knopf, a division of
Random House, Inc., New York, and simultaneously in Canada
by Random House of Canada Limited, Toronto.
Distributed by Random House, Inc., New York.*

www.aaknopf.com

*Knopf, Borzoi Books, and the colophon are registered trademarks
of Random House, Inc.*

*All text and photographs credited to Carl Van Vechten are reprinted here by permission
of the Carl Van Vechten Trust. All rights reserved.*

*Library of Congress Cataloging-in-Publication Data
Hughes, Langston, 1902–1967.
Remember me to Harlem : the letters of Langston Hughes and Carl Van Vechten,
1925–1964 / edited by Emily Bernard. — 1st ed.
p.   cm.
Includes bibliographical references and index.
ISBN 0-679-45113-7
1. Hughes, Langston, 1902–1967 — Correspondence.   2. Van Vechten, Carl,
1880–1964 — Correspondence.   3. Novelists, American — 20th century —
Correspondence.   4. Authors, American — 20th century — Correspondence.
5. Music critics — United States — Correspondence.   6. Photographers — United
States — Correspondence.   7. Afro-American authors — Correspondence.
8. Harlem Renaissance.   I. Van Vechten, Carl, 1880–1964
II. Bernard, Emily, 1967– III. Title.
PS3515.U274 Z598 2001
818'.5209 — dc21
[B]   00-062929*

*Manufactured in the United States of America
First Edition*

For Clara Jean Jefferson Bernard, poet, mother, friend
and
for Bruce Kellner, thank you

CONTENTS

Appendixes

ACKNOWLEDGMENTS

This book exists because of the insight, generosity, and guidance of many remarkable people. I am grateful to Harold Ober Associates, lawyers for the Langston Hughes Estate, for granting me permission to reprint the letters of Langston Hughes. Donald Gallup and Joseph Solomon, former literary trustee and executor, respectively, for the Estate of Carl Van Vechten, were enthusiastic about this project from the start. Bruce Kellner, successor literary trustee of the Carl Van Vechten Estate, and Arnold Rampersad, executor of the Langston Hughes Estate, provided incalculable assistance and tremendous support. To them, I am forever indebted.

I thank the National Endowment for the Humanities for providing me with the support that enabled me to complete this book. Smith College generously granted me a leave so that I could devote myself to this project. I am particularly grateful to President Ruth Simmons and Provost John Connolly for their attention to the details that made my year away from Smith a smooth and efficient one. While at Smith, I could always depend upon the support of colleagues Brenda Allen, Ann Ferguson, Elizabeth V. Spelman, and Marilyn Schuster. Smith colleagues Dan and Helen Horowitz provided me with shelter and fabulous evenings in Cambridge during my time away from Smith. I spent my year off at the W. E. B. Du Bois Institute at Harvard University, and it became my sanctuary. I thank Henry Louis Gates, Jr., and Richard Newman, particularly, for their generosity and encouragement during that memorable year. Nina Kollars, Evelyn Hurley, and Kevin Rabener were staff members at the Du Bois Institute whose skill and humor made every day I spent there a pleasure. I am grateful to the faculty and staff at Penn State Harrisburg for their support of this project in its final stages.

I am grateful to the administrators and staff of the Beinecke Rare Book and Manuscript Library at Yale University, where most of the correspondence of both Langston Hughes and Carl Van Vechten can be found in the James Weldon Johnson Collection, which is part of the Yale Collection of American Literature. Patricia Willis, curator of the Collection of American Literature, is a dear friend upon whose encouragement and example I have come to depend. The staff at the Beinecke Library became a surrogate family during my numerous visits. I thank Steve Jones, Maureen Heher, N'gadi Kponou, and Alfred Mueller for their skill, patience, and unwavering hospitality.

At the New York Public Library, Manuscripts and Archives Division, where the Carl Van Vechten papers are housed, I was lucky to have the support of staff members like Angie Sierra and Ben Alexander. At the Harry Ransom Humanities Research Center at the University of Texas at Austin, I was guided through the Alfred A. Knopf papers by a talented and helpful staff. The Schomburg Center for Research in Black Culture contained helpful written material and photographs.

Last but far from least among the institutions I would like to acknowledge is Yale University, in whose classrooms I first learned about the friendship between Langston Hughes and Carl Van Vechten. Yale College Dean Richard Brodhead, Linda Watts, Candace Waid, Carla Kaplan, Robert B. Stepto, Hazel V. Carby, and Jean-Christophe Agnew were teachers during my undergraduate and graduate years at Yale from whom, gratefully, I continue to learn.

I am indebted to my editor, Judith Jones, for putting her faith in me and guiding this project to completion. Her guidance and care were remarkable. Her skillful assistant, Ken Schneider, is a friend and an advocate. I thank the copyeditor, Kate Scott, for her diligence as well as her interest in this book. I am grateful for the expertise of Rita Madrigal, the production editor.

My agent, Faith Hampton Childs, is a mentor and a champion. I thank her for believing in this project and its editor from the very beginning.

I am grateful to Richard Avedon for his generous support of this project.

I am pleased to thank the many people who contributed to the research required to complete this project. Elizabeth Barnes, Jaime Castle, Jessica Eldridge, Kemi Illesamni, Bryna McClane, Emily Musil, Alana Samuels, and Shanté Smalls were brilliant research assistants whose commitment to their work delighted and inspired me. Laura Yow contributed her extraordinary research skills to this project as well as her patience and support to its editor. I thank Warren Bernard for his knowledge and skill in both photography and computers. Elizabeth Alexander, Mia Bay, A'Leila Bundles, George Chauncey, Farrah Griffin, George Hutchinson, Amy Kaplan, Carla Kaplan, Pete Miller, Honor Moore, Jill Nelson, Richard Newman, Robert O'Meally, Kathleen Pfeiffer, Darryl Pinckney, Barbara Rodriguez, David Roessel, Steven Watson, and Tom Wirth provided invaluable support through their writing or conversation—often both.

I thank Davida Pines for telling me I could do this book. Elizabeth Alexander, Noël Alicea, James Bernard, Warren Bernard, Lisa Collins, Casey Greenfield, Miranda Massie, Martha Nadell, Sandhya Shukla, Michelle Stephens,

Heidi Tinsman, Mike Vasquez, and Sarah Weir are all friends and family who counseled, comforted, and sometimes cajoled, until the book was done. John Gennari I thank for his immeasurable love, faith, and patience.

Finally, I am honored to thank, in particular, Bruce Kellner and Arnold Rampersad, whose professional accomplishments and personal generosity set a humbling example. Both of these men read countless drafts and entertained even more countless questions. They cheered me when I was on a productive path and righted me when I strayed, doing both with a benevolence that I will always seek to emulate. I simply could not have done this book without the scholarship, counsel, and contributions of both of these extraordinary men.

INTRODUCTION

Langston Hughes and Carl Van Vechten met at a benefit party in Harlem on the evening of November 10, 1924. "Kingston" was the name Van Vechten heard and recorded in his diary; maybe he was distracted by the commotion surrounding his new acquaintance. Hughes had returned that day from a ten-month stay in Europe, where he had made his way through Paris and Italy working and writing poetry. From abroad, he had dazzled black Harlem literati with his work, and now everyone was eager to meet the celebrated newcomer. He was twenty-two years old. At forty-four, Van Vechten was long used to public curiosity. For nearly twenty years, he had enthralled New York with his opinionated dance and music criticism, as well as with several novels. He was equally famous for his personal flamboyance. The *New York Times* chronicled his social life and fashion peccadilloes with a breathless fascination typically reserved for movie stars. But on that night in 1924, Carl Van Vechten was just another onlooker, drawn to Harlem because of the cultural movement blossoming there. The movement would become known as the Harlem Renaissance. Even during its first stirrings, Langston Hughes was understood to be one of its most promising talents. Months later, the two men would meet again at another Harlem event and embarked on a friendship that would endure until Van Vechten's death almost forty years later.

Photographs from around 1924 reveal a large, imposing Van Vechten, with thin graying hair and generous lips that barely reached over a

famously protruding pair of front teeth. His odd looks were comple-
mented by a one-of-a-kind wardrobe that included jade bracelets, ruffled
blouses, and silk lounging robes. The whole effect was irresistible for
popular caricaturists of the era such as Ralph Barton and Miguel Covarrubias. By contrast, Langston Hughes was the definition of handsome in
1924, slender and elegant, with the dreamy looks befitting a poet. These
surface differences hint at more substantial contrasts that would seem to
make a friendship between them unlikely. Van Vechten's privileged Mid-
western background had nothing in common with the nomadic, neglect-
ful upbringing Hughes had endured. Poverty had shaped Hughes's life
the same way that material comfort was taken for granted in Van
Vechten's. For all of his financial hard luck, however, Hughes never developed anything more than a casual attitude about money. He had a hard
time asking for it even when it was owed to him, and it never stayed in his
pockets long once he got it. Van Vechten wanted Hughes to take a more
deliberate attitude toward his finances. Hughes in turn wished Van
Vechten would take the relationship between art and politics more seriously. Their ideas on the subject clashed while their friendship was still
young, and remained one of the most tender points of disagreement
between them. On top of all of these differences, there was race.

Blacks in 1920s Harlem were generally of two minds about downtown
white interest in uptown happenings. The same white money that kept
most Harlem activities afloat also pushed black people out of their own
establishments. In a 1927 essay called "The Caucasian Storms Harlem,"
the black writer Rudolph Fisher described the situation common in most
Harlem cabarets: "I am actually stared at, I frequently feel uncomfortable
and out of place, and when I go out on the floor to dance I am lost in a sea
of white faces." Some Harlem clubs, like the famous Cotton Club, barred
black patrons altogether. Black resentment grew quietly. "They didn't say
it out loud," Langston Hughes wrote in his 1940 autobiography, *The Big
Sea,* "for Negroes are practically never rude to white people." Harlem
blacks understood all too well the bottom-line importance of white
investment in Harlem. Still, blacks resented being treated "like amusing
animals in a zoo," to use Hughes's words, by whites whose interest in
black culture lasted only until the bartender's last call. "Rent parties,"
thrown ostensibly to raise rent money for the host, became an important
way for blacks to congregate privately, away from the curious gazes of
white people.

Initially, Carl Van Vechten's interest in black culture seemed to be an
exception to the general shallowness of white voyeurism uptown. His signature Harlem tours were rites of passage for white sophisticates, but Van
Vechten's fascination with black culture far outdistanced the curiosity of

those he shepherded to Harlem. He wrote articles for *Vanity Fair* and other mainstream magazines extolling the virtues of spirituals and the blues, arguing for their recognition as authentic American art forms. He threw parties as a way of introducing struggling black artists to influential whites. These parties became legendary in black circles and were written up regularly in the society pages of the *Amsterdam News.* Van Vechten loved his nights at the Savoy, but he was also a dedicated and serious patron of black arts and letters.

Things changed after August 1926, when Carl Van Vechten published his notorious novel *Nigger Heaven.* After that, his name became synonymous with white exploitation of black culture; the association still holds today—that is, when he is remembered in connection with the Harlem Renaissance at all. Most of the time, Van Vechten's name generates more blank stares than disapproving frowns. But during the heyday of this cultural movement, Van Vechten was, in the words of the late historian Nathan Huggins, "the undisputed downtown authority on uptown night life."

❧❧❧

Scholars argue about the exact dates of the Harlem Renaissance, or the New Negro Renaissance, as it was called then, but nearly all agree that the term itself is misleading. For one thing, there was never exactly a "renaissance." What took place during the 1920s was not a rebirth but just another stage in the evolution of black American art that had begun in the 1700s. In addition, black intellectual and cultural activities during the early part of the twentieth century were by no means limited to New York's Harlem. Literature, music, and politics also flourished in cities like Detroit, Chicago, Philadelphia, and Washington, D.C., all of which were prominent destinations for the quarter-million black migrants fleeing Southern poverty and racial violence during the period known as "the Great Migration." The promise of jobs in these cities gave migrating blacks the last reason they needed to leave the South. Post–World War I economic prosperity all over the country was the grease that kept the wheels of the Harlem Renaissance in motion. But although the bulk of Harlem Renaissance activity shut down with the crash of 1929, many black artists didn't produce their best-known works until after the New Negro Movement had more or less closed up shop.

There are, of course, practical reasons for the centrality of Harlem to the movement. For literary hopefuls like Langston Hughes, Harlem was important because of the recent establishment of New York as the center of the publishing industry. But practical reasons aside, Harlem was simply a mythical place, the stuff of fantasy. "I'd rather be a lamppost in Harlem than Governor of Georgia," went a popular folk saying. The activity on and off the streets was constant. Inside cabarets, buffet flats, speakeasies, and ballrooms, each dancer, singer, and musician was more ingenious than the one who came before her. "Harlem . . . isn't typical— but it is significant, it is prophetic," philosophized one of the godfathers of the movement, Alain Locke. The two-mile section of northern Manhattan was known as the "black Mecca," and claimed two hundred thousand black residents by 1928, the year the Renaissance was in full bloom.

The Harlem Renaissance had almost as many philosophers as cabaret dancers. No one articulated the vision of the movement more precisely than W. E. B. Du Bois, an intellectual of international prominence whose career would span two generations. Du Bois was the founder of *The Crisis,* the official magazine of the National Association for the Advancement of Colored People (NAACP), an organization Du Bois also helped to found. *The Crisis* was the most important forum for black news and culture, and every black writer dreamed of getting published in its pages. Other magazines carried weight; *Opportunity* and the *Messenger* were also important vehicles of black thought. But none of the other journals could boast a leader as impressive as Du Bois. *The Crisis* was his pulpit. His editorials were passionate lectures about racial uplift. In an April 1920 issue, he identified the arts as the path for black salvation: "A renaissance of American Negro literature is due; the material about us in the strange, heart-rending race tangle is rich beyond dream and only we can tell the tale and sing the song from the heart." No word was published in *The Crisis* that didn't meet Du Bois's standards. Because art had the potential to liberate black people from social bondage, Du Bois believed, it should be approached with gravity, even reverence. Every time a writer put pen to paper, he was taking the future of the race in his hands.

While writers, painters, and philosophers contemplated the significance of this unique historical moment, most other Harlemites struggled to find work and to survive the racism they found in their new Northern homes. The experience of this majority barely exists in contemporary stories about the Harlem Renaissance, and that's the way the movement's architects wanted it. Du Bois himself believed that the social status of blacks could best be achieved through the efforts of a very small fraction of blacks and whites. This "talented tenth" would pull "all that are worthy of saving up to their vantage ground." Influenced by the Victorian morality of their youth, Du Bois and other movement leaders were motivated by a "politics of respectability," and were always mindful of the derogatory beliefs the white world held about them.

So, effectively, several different "renaissances" took place during the

1920s. Those who sought leadership from Du Bois had little use for the pageantry of the black political leader Marcus Garvey, and probably neither constituency wanted anything to do with those who heard salvation in the baritone of the cross-dressing blues singer Gladys Bentley. Though all of black America was energized by the social and political changes, only a very few were interested in the debates taking place in the parlors of Striver's Row, a nickname for one of Harlem's most elite neighborhoods. As Langston Hughes put it in *The Big Sea,* "The ordinary Negroes hadn't heard of the Negro Renaissance. And if they had, it hadn't raised their wages any."

Cynical by 1940, Hughes virtually swooned the first time he set foot in Harlem in 1924. He wrote wistfully in *The Big Sea:* "I was in love with Harlem long before I got there." Harlem was Hughes's first home, at least in symbolic terms. Born in 1902 in Joplin, Missouri, to Carrie and James Hughes, he came from a distinguished line of black radicals: his maternal grandmother's first husband had died fighting with John Brown at Harper's Ferry. This venerable ancestry did not translate into a blessed childhood for young Langston, however. His parents' unhappy marriage effectively ended when he was still a boy, and Hughes spent the majority of his childhood shuttling from relative to relative while his mother, Carrie, struggled to establish herself in a variety of careers. She loved her son but was simply unable to provide him with any stability. She married again and gave Langston a stepbrother, Gwyn Clark, whom he always looked after, as he did his mother. Carrie would depend on Langston in his adulthood, expecting him to provide for her. Sometimes Van Vechten would get involved and give Carrie financial help when Hughes was unable to do so.

Hughes may have resented his mother, but he hated his father. James Nathaniel Hughes was a difficult man to like. "My father hated Negroes," Hughes explained in *The Big Sea.* He also thought his son's literary ambitions were a waste of time, although Langston didn't realize the full extent of their differences until he went to visit his father in Mexico during his seventeenth summer. Langston suffered during that visit; his hatred for his father made him physically ill. The visit changed him, but it also helped him shape an image of himself in opposition to his father. More importantly, it was during this trip that he wrote one of his most famous poems, "The Negro Speaks of Rivers." Still, he would revisit that painful summer again and again in later years, using it like a barometer to measure other difficult experiences against it. His childhood would provide material for his poetry, plays, and a novel, *Not Without Laughter.*

By contrast, Carl Van Vechten's childhood was so stable that he found it stifling. He was born in Cedar Rapids, Iowa, in 1880 to Charles Duane and Amanda Fitch Van Vechten. Like Hughes, Van Vechten was descended from political radicals: his mother was a suffragist who kept company with abolitionists and his father's donations helped establish the Piney Woods School for free black children at the turn of the century. The elder Van Vechten instructed his children to address with respect the blacks who worked on their property. Young Carl expanded upon the lesson when he was a college student at the University of Chicago, and became a regular in the city's black entertainment night spots, as well as its black churches.

By the time the Harlem Renaissance was born, Carl Van Vechten's interest in black culture was already intense. But it wasn't until the mid-twenties that this interest exploded into an "addiction," as he himself later called it.

It started with a book. Walter White's searing novel about the Atlanta race riots, *Fire in the Flint,* moved Van Vechten to ask their mutual publisher, Alfred A. Knopf, for an introduction to the author. Within days, Van Vechten knew "every important Negro in Harlem," or so he claimed. It was White who escorted Van Vechten to the historic NAACP event at Happy Rhone's cabaret on November 10, 1924, where both men met Langston Hughes.

Van Vechten told his biographer, Bruce Kellner, that he and White "got on like a house afire," which was lucky, considering how useful the friendship was for each of them. As secretary of the NAACP, White was eager for access to Van Vechten's world of downtown connections. Van Vechten didn't disappoint him. Not only did he facilitate individual meetings for White, he gave parties at which powerful whites met black artists on the most intimate of terms. Countless unions were forged at these events. His parties created Harlem legends, such as the one in which Mrs. Astor is greeted too familiarly by a porter at Union Station. "How do you know my name, young man?" she asked. "Why, I met you last weekend at Carl Van Vechten's," he responded. White wasn't the only one who came to identify Van Vechten's tony address as the "downtown office of the NAACP." Van Vechten's ingenious brand of "social work" was one of his greatest contributions to the Harlem Renaissance.

Van Vechten's next deed was what many consider the least of his contributions to the Harlem Renaissance: *Nigger Heaven.* In three breathless months, Van Vechten composed this banal story of a thwarted love affair between Mary Love, a librarian at the Harlem branch of the New York Public Library, and Byron Kasson, a would-be writer. The novel would have disappeared like most 1920s potboilers were it not for a few off-color scenes and its title. Van Vechten's representations of black sexuality offended those who believed that black uplift should be achieved through the politics of respectability. With his title, he had violated the unwritten law that forbade a white man's using the word "nigger."

What complicated Van Vechten's case was that he knew the law. As a footnote to the first appearance of "nigger" in the book, Van Vechten cautioned: "While this informal epithet is freely used by Negroes among themselves, not only as a term of opprobrium, but also actually as a term of endearment, its employment by a white person is always fiercely resented." He even added a final directive: "The word Negress is forbidden under all circumstances."

So why did Van Vechten call his book *Nigger Heaven* when he knew better? He claimed the title was ironic. He also must have believed that he was entitled to use the term. Friends like Zora Neale Hurston had crowned him an "honorary Negro." One of his favorite portraits was a Miguel Covarrubias cartoon of himself in blackface titled "A Prediction." Van Vechten took all of this literally. A combination of naïveté and arrogance led him to believe he was unique, a white man who had transcended his whiteness.

Van Vechten's choice was also inspired by his keen commercial sensibilities; he saw African American culture in terms of potential book sales. "The squalor of Negro life, the vice of Negro life, offer a wealth of novel, exotic, picturesque material to the artist." This was Van Vechten's own response to a questionnaire he anonymously composed for *The Crisis,* called "The Negro in Art: How Shall He Be Portrayed?" and published six months before the release of *Nigger Heaven.* Writers from every corner of American literature were solicited for responses. In his own response, Van Vechten waved away black "sensitivity" to sensationalistic depictions as bad business sense. "Are Negro writers going to write about this exotic material while it is fresh," he wrote, "or will they continue to make a free gift of it to white authors who will exploit it until not a drop of vitality remains?"

The boldness with which he asserted his right to the "exotic material" of black culture had a lot to do with the swift condemnation that followed on the heels of the book's publication. The black press denounced *Nigger Heaven* and the "Negro pseudo-intellectuals" who had abetted the white author in its creation. Those who had been suspicious of Carl Van Vechten all along now had the evidence they needed to condemn him. It seemed to many that Carl Van Vechten had had hidden motives, that he had ruthlessly exploited Harlem for his material gain.

The book had its black defenders, however, many of them, not surprisingly, Van Vechten's close friends. "No book could possibly be as bad as *Nigger Heaven* has been painted," Langston Hughes wrote in the *Pittsburgh Courier* in 1927, gently sidestepping the question of the novel's literary qualities. Even when Hughes returned to the controversy nearly fifteen years later in *The Big Sea,* he never tried to base a defense on the book's merit. Instead he sympathized with those who felt alienated by the racial epithet in the title but insisted that readers put the whole thing in perspective. "The critics of the left, like the Negroes of the right, proceeded to light on Mr. Van Vechten, and he was accused of ruining, distorting, polluting, and corrupting every Negro writer from then on," Hughes remembered.

Of all his black associates, Van Vechten was most often accused of corrupting Langston Hughes, particularly when Hughes's second book of poetry, *Fine Clothes to the Jew,* was published in 1927, even though Hughes had composed most of the poems before he met Van Vechten. *Fine Clothes* drew as much fire for its title and sensual content as did *Nigger Heaven.* In defending Van Vechten, then, Hughes was essentially defending his own artistic decisions.

Hughes allowed that Van Vechten's title may have been "an unfortunate choice." In 1926, he was one of several people—including Van Vechten's own father—who tried to dissuade Van Vechten from using it. But whatever discomfort he felt never interfered with his support for the book. In fact, when Van Vechten was threatened with a lawsuit for using popular song lyrics in the book without permission, he turned to Hughes, who was then a student at Lincoln University in Pennsylvania. Hughes jumped on the first train and replaced the borrowed lyrics with originals in a night-long session at Van Vechten's apartment.

Hughes's generosity was inspired, at least in part, by gratitude for the man who had arranged his first book contract. Several months passed before Hughes and Van Vechten caught sight of each other again after their initial encounter on November 10, 1924. But when they met again on May 1, 1925, they formed one of the most enduring bonds of their lives. An awards dinner sponsored by *Opportunity* magazine brought them together this second time. Langston Hughes walked off with a first prize for his poem "The Weary Blues." Again, Van Vechten found himself in the crush of people trying to congratulate the young poet. But this time around, the two men discovered one of their many common interests, and spent the evening together doing what they both loved: prowling the nightspots of Harlem.

Hughes visited Van Vechten's apartment on West Fifty-fifth Street the next day, where he explored the lavish rooms and read some of his poetry. Van Vechten, or "Carlo," as his intimates called him, insisted that Hughes leave his manuscript of poems overnight. When Hughes came back to claim it, Van Vechten had suggestions and a title. What did Hughes think of calling the book *The Weary Blues?*

He had a publisher in mind as well. Van Vechten quickly made arrangements to have lunch with his friend and editor, Alfred A. Knopf, whose firm was only ten years old in 1925. Within three weeks, Hughes had his first book contract. Van Vechten also arranged for *Vanity Fair* to publish a selection of poems from the manuscript.

In his first letters to Van Vechten, Hughes marvels at his older friend's attention and generosity. Van Vechten's influence at Alfred A. Knopf, Inc., was at its height in those days. He had been a Knopf author since 1916, when the publisher, with his year-old company, had convinced Van Vechten to compose a book for him, a collection of essays called *Music and Bad Manners*. Van Vechten continued to produce a book of essays every year for Knopf that were reviewed well but sold poorly. Then, he struck gold with his first novel, 1922's *Peter Whiffle*, a fictional biography that went through eight printings in the first year. He had discovered himself as a writer several years before, after a friend remarked that his letters made better reading than his published material: "After that a change came over my writing. It was true; I had been excluding personality from my work. I had not been expressing myself, and writing which is not self-expression . . . is entirely useless." With *Peter Whiffle*, Van Vechten's experiments with self-expression had finally paid off, and Knopf began dominating the best-seller lists with a redoubtable trio of writers: H. L. Mencken, Joseph Hergesheimer, and Carl Van Vechten.

Van Vechten had considerable muscle to flex at Knopf when he decided to help Langston Hughes, who dreamed of a similar kind of literary success. Hughes had impressed the black literati with his early poems, but none of his Harlem mentors had the power to get Hughes published. Van Vechten's one lunch date with Alfred Knopf meant that Hughes could quit his tedious day job doing research for the African American historian Carter G. Woodson. Soon, Van Vechten was hard at work helping other black writers get published at Knopf. Nella Larsen's novels *Quicksand* and *Passing*, the 1927 reissuing of James Weldon Johnson's *Autobiography of an Ex-Colored Man*, as well as many of the significant works of Langston Hughes all came about as the direct result of Van Vechten's influence.

Although Hughes certainly felt a debt to Van Vechten, who would serve as his de facto editor and agent for years to come, gratitude hardly covers the range of feelings Hughes and other blacks felt for Van Vechten. What they saw in Van Vechten was more than a useful contact; he was a fellow champion of free expression in black arts and culture.

By 1926, a conflict had split the Harlem literati in two. Old school writers like Du Bois still believed that blacks should use literature as a way to put their best foot forward, to produce an image that challenged the racist manner in which white people most often portrayed them. But a younger group of new school writers loved the very features of black culture that old school writers found embarrassing. As a leader of the new school, Langston Hughes articulated the views of this group in his powerful 1926 essay, "The Negro Artist and the Racial Mountain": "Let the blare of Negro jazz bands and the bellowing voice of Bessie Smith singing Blues penetrate the closed ears of the colored near-intellectual until they listen and perhaps understand." Hughes found the anxieties of the "smug Negro middle class" boring. He was energized by the way the black majority lived their lives while the elite worried about appearances: "These common people are not afraid of spirituals, as for a long time their more intellectual brethren were, and jazz is their child." Like Van Vechten, he had an eye on the market: "They furnish a wealth of colorful, distinctive material for any artist because they still hold their own individuality in the face of American standardizations." But mainly, he celebrated artistic freedom: "We younger Negro artists who create now intend to express our individual dark-skinned selves without fear or shame."

Hughes's words became a rallying cry for black writers who rankled at the constraints imposed upon them by both white expectations and the agendas of black taste-makers like Du Bois. And after *Nigger Heaven* was published, Van Vechten became something of a poster boy, a perfect case in point, for black writers who wanted to change the rules about black art. The fact that their work provoked their stuffy mentors was a pleasing side effect to their revolution.

Like Hughes, Van Vechten loved "the low-down folks," as Hughes called the black working class. But for many blacks his whiteness raised questions about his motivations. The black poet Countee Cullen— Hughes's rival for the affections of Harlem poetry lovers—never forgave Van Vechten for the title *Nigger Heaven.* Du Bois's scathing review of the book ended with the suggestion that readers "drop the book gently in the grate." Even whites found his affiliations with blacks suspicious. "Sullen-mouthed, silky-haired author Van Vechten has been playing with Negroes lately," *Time* magazine remarked cattily in 1925.

Black friends mounted a defense. In his autobiography, *Born to Be,* the black singer Taylor Gordon called Van Vechten, the man who had discovered him, "the Abraham Lincoln of Negro Art." Zora Neale Hurston once said, "If Carl Van Vechten were a people instead of a person, I could then say, these are my people." Nella Larsen proclaimed Van Vechten "the best thing that ever happened to the Negro race." But none of this was enough to salvage Carl Van Vechten from his present-day fate of virtual erasure.

Nigger Heaven does not really explain Van Vechten's disappearance from the history of the Harlem Renaissance. Nor does the fact that he was a white man whose influence in this black movement was sometimes unwelcome. Almost every black artist had to negotiate white patronage in some form or another. But no white patron has been disdained as intensely as Carl Van Vechten. Why? Because Van Vechten was a gay white man active in a black movement whose homosexual overtones are still controversial. By virtue of both race and sexual orientation, Van Vechten's motives have always been doubly suspect.

Van Vechten was married for over forty years to Fania Marinoff, a Russian actress, who was "simply the only satisfactory person alive," he wrote in a 1928 diary entry. But Van Vechten had various sexual interests; posthumous records further confirm this fact. In the 1950s, Van Vechten willed nearly twenty mysterious scrapbooks to the James Weldon Johnson Collection at Yale's Beinecke library; his instructions were that they not be opened until twenty-five years after his death. In 1989 they were opened and were found to reveal homoerotic photographs, cartoons, and drawings. The images are deliberately tongue-in-cheek, so to speak, but the scrapbooks also contain more serious articles, such as news clippings about gay bashings, drag balls, and scandals about individuals caught performing "perverse acts."

Van Vechten did not make a particular secret of his sexual interests. On the other hand, Langston Hughes's sexual orientation continues to cause a lot of public speculation. In the course of working on this book, I have been asked many times whether the two men were lovers (they were not). Anyone looking to this book for confirmation that Hughes was gay will be disappointed. In fact, anyone seeking information about Hughes's romantic life at all will be frustrated. Hughes was famously secretive about his private life. In his youth, he wrote excitedly to Van Vechten about the same few women he describes in his autobiographies. At least in his letters, Hughes never shared with Van Vechten any more about his love life than he committed to public record.

Van Vechten himself rarely refers in these letters to his interest in men. The men with whom he had three successive long-term relationships—Donald Angus, Mark Lutz, and Saul Mauriber—appear in these letters as dear friends of Carlo's, which they all would become. Van Vechten had several other short-term affairs and even more brief flings with other men. Hughes would have been aware of Van Vechten's extramarital activities—as was Fania—but they do not play a part in the friendship the two shared in letters.

Sex isn't the only thing the two men never discussed. Hughes had a complex relationship with his white patron, Charlotte Mason. When she dropped him, he experienced the most profound heartbreak of his life. But you won't see any reference to this episode in his letters. In addition,

Van Vechten never discusses with Hughes the confusion and sadness he felt when *Nigger Heaven* was excoriated by the black press.

What these letters do reveal are many of the important changes that took place in American culture during the first half of the twentieth century. Their correspondence is an unusual record of entertainment, politics, and culture as seen through the eyes of two fascinating and irreverent men. Hughes and Van Vechten gossip about the antics of the great and the forgotten. And what is between the lines is often just as meaningful. As Carlo wrote to Langston in a June 4, 1925, letter: "There are so many things that one can't talk about in a letter."

∘ ∘ ∘

"What letters you write! Maybe I do too. Sometimes I wonder if OUR letters wont be the pride of the Collection!" Carl Van Vechten wrote to Langston Hughes on August 16, 1943. Carl refers here to the James Weldon Johnson Memorial Collection of Negro Arts and Letters, which had become his new obsession by the early 1940s. All of Harlem was devastated when Johnson was killed in a car accident in 1938, and Van Vechten more than most. The two had been close since the 1920s, having met at the same 1924 party that had brought Hughes and Van Vechten together. They shared a common birthday, June 17, along with Alfred A. Knopf, Jr., and the three of them celebrated it together every year, along with their families. Van Vechten was an honorary pallbearer at his friend's funeral.

Within a year of Johnson's death, Van Vechten was trying to raise funds for a memorial statue to be erected in the middle of Harlem to honor Johnson, but when the war broke out, the necessary materials became scarce and the project proved too expensive. In the meantime, Johnson's widow, Grace Nail Johnson, had been approached by the Library of Congress for her husband's papers. Van Vechten was inspired. He approached Bernhard Knollenberg, head librarian at Yale University, and together they established the James Weldon Johnson Memorial Collection of American Negro Arts and Letters at Yale, which may well be the greatest contribution made by Carl Van Vechten to the cause of black arts and letters.

"It seemed most appropriate to couple the name of my friend James Weldon Johnson with material of which his advice had been so important an element in its selection. My love and respect for the dead poet actually demanded that I do so," Van Vechten wrote in a 1942 essay for *The Crisis*. The decision was also practically motivated. Van Vechten knew that if the collection was in his own name, black writers and artists might not donate their work. Finally, Van Vechten loved the idea of donating black materials to a white institution. He would reverse the order when he established the George Gershwin Memorial Collection of Music and Musical Literature at Fisk University in 1947.

Archival work was Van Vechten's fourth career. He had given up writing novels when his last effort, *Parties,* published in 1930, proved a failure. He promptly turned his attention to photography, an interest he had nurtured since childhood. From 1932 until his death in 1964 he took portraits of every well-known African American who would sit for him. Not everyone would. Sidney Poitier was "exceptionally rude" to him, as Van Vechten would tell Hughes in a 1959 letter, and Ralph Ellison rebuffed his offers altogether. By some blacks, Van Vechten would never be forgiven for *Nigger Heaven.* For others, the simple fact of this white man's fascination with blackness was too peculiar to stomach.

Others were perhaps put off by the way Van Vechten talked about his photography. He himself referred to the act of taking pictures as a way of "capturing" people. Carlo had been an ardent collector since he was a child watching his mother tend to her precious tin trunk of heirlooms. He describes those moments as having generated his own interest in the act of collecting in "The Tin Trunk," an essay in his 1932 collection of autobiographical essays, *Sacred and Profane Memories.* Van Vechten's proprietary attitude about his photographs extended increasingly to his feelings about black culture in general, particularly as he got older and even bad press about him was hard to find.

By the 1950s, the James Weldon Johnson Collection was virtually the only thing he discussed in his correspondence with Hughes, one reason that fewer letters from that period are included in this collection. Another reason is that Hughes was simply too busy to write as often as he did in the early years. "Everybody else seems to hear from you but me," Carlo complained to Langston on December 6, 1942. Van Vechten would never have made such a comment fifteen years earlier when Hughes was writing so frequently that Van Vechten noticed if a day went by without a letter from him. But things had changed. Hughes was in demand all over the world. By the late 1940s, he had to hire an assistant just to help him keep up with his correspondence. Meanwhile, Van Vechten was not the star he had been. He would never find out what happened when Hughes approached his editor at Knopf about the possibility of Van Vechten's contributing the foreword to his latest edition of poems. "I certainly do not think that at this time it would be a good idea to ask Carl Van Vechten to write one," was his editor's answer.

By the 1950s, Van Vechten was pestering Hughes constantly about going through the materials in his basement to be sent to Yale. Finally, on October 11, 1959, he wrote Langston these lines: "Perhaps I did not make myself clear to you last night about the way I feel about the JWJ Memorial Collection of Negro Arts and Letters. For the past ten years I have devoted at least fifty per cent of my waking hours to this perpetuation of the fame of the Negro and it saddens me to realize how few Negroes realize this and how still fewer make any attempt to assist the collection."

Van Vechten signed the letter "yrs, with too much impatience and some faint hope, Carlo, the Patriarch," something he'd taken to calling himself in jest in his old age. Perhaps his gentle sign-off was meant to soften the tone of his accusations. But Hughes was probably used to Van Vechten's bitterness by then. That wasn't the first time Van Vechten had complained to Hughes about his erasure from black cultural history. His deeds were being passed down but his name wasn't. If this letter reverberates with a patronizing sting, it also sags with the frustration of an old man forgotten by time and the culture he helped to nurture.

I remember when I first read this letter as a college student, preparing to write my senior thesis. A year before, I had learned about Carl Van Vechten; at first I simply had to find out more about the white man who had had the audacity to call a novel *Nigger Heaven*. Then I became interested in the dynamics of his relationships with Harlem Renaissance writers, especially Hughes. The more I read the more questions I had. What was the story of their friendship? Was it built only on gratitude? Did Hughes privately resent Van Vechten? What was the secret that kept their friendship alive?

I discovered the secret when I happened to glimpse a note Hughes had hand-written on the envelope: "CVV at a ripe old age." Langston loved him. He loved the bitter old man as he had loved the younger, famous version who had gotten him published. He hoped that future readers would understand Carlo's angry lines through the lens of his own fondness, respect, and compassion.

Hughes wrote back the very next day. He made fun of Van Vechten's attitude and teased him about the ugly undercurrents of his professed benevolence. He ended his letter with a final dig at Van Vechten's new penchant for lamenting "the faults of the race." Hughes included an addendum: "I was so glad to see you the other night. I guess absence makes the heart grow fonder."

•••

This book is a story about two people, one famous, one formerly famous but now mostly unknown, who lived during an extraordinary period in American history. Between the two of them, they knew *everyone,* and nearly all of those people come to life in the pages that follow. Langston

Hughes and Carl Van Vechten helped make the movement we know as the Harlem Renaissance, and for that reason their story is meaningful. But the most important story in this book is about a friendship—one complicated by race, power, and money. Like most friendships, it endured its share of ups and downs. But unlike most friendships, this one thrived because of difference, not in spite of it.

A NOTE ON THE TEXT

This volume represents a mere fraction of the nearly one thousand five hundred letters exchanged by Langston Hughes and Carl Van Vechten between 1925 and 1964. The letters I have chosen were selected both for their liveliness and for the stories they tell. My decisions were guided largely by significant episodes in the friendship between the two men.

Hughes and Van Vechten dated most of their letters, but sometimes they identified them only by the day of the week on which they were written. Often I found the undated letters contained information that enabled me to assign them an exact date. When this wasn't possible, I approximated dates as precisely as I could.

Every letter in this volume appears in its entirety. In order to present each writer's voice faithfully, I deleted nothing. The few misspellings and errors in grammar or punctuation that I judged to be accidental and potentially distracting to the reader I corrected. The misspellings and errors in grammar that remain reflect the spontaneous nature of the letter and the idiosyncrasies of the author. For instance, Hughes often spelled Van Vechten's wife's name "Fannia" instead of the correct "Fania." Both Langston Hughes and Carl Van Vechten sometimes invented spellings for words when conventional spellings seemed to them insufficient. In these cases, editorial corrections would have actually compromised the unique qualities of their correspondence. The same is true in the case of Van Vechten's punctuation. Sometimes he wrote entire letters without a single period, using only dashes and dots as punctuation. I let these letters stand as they are because, again, polishing them meant jeopardizing their essential spontaneity. I did, however, reorder some of the marginal material that appears in several letters. Often a type-written letter from either man would be framed by handwritten scribbles, meant either to clarify or embellish points made in the letter. In these cases, I tried to remain as true as possible to the form of the original letter while still heeding typesetting constraints. Editorial intrusions are indicated in brackets, including the rare moments when either man's handwriting proved impossible to decipher. The use of *sic* has been generally avoided.

This "Note on the Text" is followed by a list of friends and acquaintances [dramatis personae] who appear often in the correspondence and played significant roles in the lives of Van Vechten or Hughes. A symbol ($\ddagger$) appears next to the first mention of the name of a person identified in the list. I hope readers will enjoy reading these letters in sequence, so I haven't included bracketed surnames after first names subsequent to the first mention of a person who appears frequently. For instance, it will quickly become clear that "Walter" is always Walter White, "Nora" Nora Holt, "Eddie" Eddie Wasserman, "Harold" Harold Jackman, and "Dorothy" Dorothy Peterson. Several others who are mentioned in the correspondence only rarely I identify in footnotes. A few people I simply could not identify. Other names are common enough to make identification unnecessary.

The bibliography lists the works I consulted in order to prepare this volume as well as titles of books about the remarkable period known as the Harlem Renaissance. In the acknowledgments I give the locations of the original letters that are printed here.

DRAMATIS PERSONAE

MARIAN ANDERSON (1902–1993) became the first African American to sing at the Metropolitan Opera in New York City, in 1955. She had become a phenomenon in Europe after a debut recital in Berlin in 1932.

DONALD ANGUS (1899–1990) was the stage manager for the 1925 *Revue Nègre* in Paris, which featured Josephine Baker. He and Carl Van Vechten met in 1919 and began an affair that eventually segued into a long-term friendship.

RICHMOND BARTHÉ (1901–1989) was a prominent African American sculptor who worked in clay, marble, and bronze. He began painting at the age of six, entered the Chicago Art Institute in 1924, and graduated in 1929. His career spanned sixty years.

GLADYS BENTLEY (1907–1960) was a powerful singer and outrageous cabaret performer. She was openly bisexual and usually outfitted herself for her act in a bow tie and tails. In *The Big Sea,* Hughes reminisced about the days when Bentley would play her piano from ten in the evening until dawn the next morning, "an amazing exhibition of musical energy."

ARNA BONTEMPS (1902–1973), a librarian and writer, moved from Los Angeles to Harlem in 1924, when he met Langston Hughes. The two became lifelong friends and collaborators. Bontemps's first novel, *God Sends Sunday,* was published in 1930. In 1943 he began a twenty-two-year career as head librarian at Fisk University.

BENJAMIN BRAWLEY (1882–1939) was a critic, teacher, and author of several literary studies, one of them being *The Negro in Literature and Art in the United*

States (1919). Brawley was outspoken in his belief that Harlem Renaissance writers represented the race poorly when they used vulgar themes in their work.

STERLING A. BROWN (1901–1989) was among the most formidable poets, folklorists, and literary critics of his generation. He was the author of *Southern Road* (1932), a collection of poetry, and of studies of African American literature, such as *The Negro in American Fiction* (1937). He taught at Howard University for forty years.

CHARLES CHESNUTT (1858–1932) was the first modern African American fiction writer. His short stories captured black Southern vernacular speech and were published in *The Atlantic Monthly* in the 1880s and '90s. The NAACP awarded him a Spingarn Medal for his literary achievements in 1928.

MIGUEL COVARRUBIAS (1904–1957) was born in Mexico and emigrated to the United States in 1923 with the help of Carl Van Vechten. He immediately became one of the most sought after caricaturists and illustrators in New York. His work regularly appeared in *Vanity Fair* and *The New Yorker,* among other magazines.

COUNTEE CULLEN (1904–1947) was Hughes's friendly rival for the title of Harlem's poet laureate, although they had very different styles. Modeling his work on the English Romantics, Cullen published his first book of poetry, *Color,* in 1925 while he was still a graduate student at Harvard. He never shook his suspicion that Van Vechten was "coining money out of the niggers," as he wrote to the teacher and intellectual Harold Jackman on October 7, 1925.

NANCY CUNARD (1897–1965) was a member of the Cunard shipping family. She was an editor by trade and a staunch Communist by conviction. Her family was scandalized by her passions, including her live-in relationship with the African American musician Henry Crowder. Cunard's greatest contribution to the Harlem Renaissance was her massive anthology, *Negro,* published in 1934.

MABEL DODGE. See MABEL DODGE LUHAN.

AARON DOUGLAS (1898–1979) was one of the most highly regarded painters of his generation. He moved to Harlem in 1925 and met Winold Reiss, a German portrait artist whose work influenced a number of young black painters. He illustrated the advertisements for *Nigger Heaven* and contributed work to periodicals like *The Crisis, Vanity Fair, Theatre Arts,* and *American Mercury.*

MURIEL DRAPER (1886–1952), a friend of Van Vechten's, was famous for the salon she presided over at her London residence, Edith Grove. Harlem Renaissance figures were regulars in its New York equivalent during the 1920s. Draper wrote the introduction to Taylor Gordon's 1929 autobiography,

Born to Be, to which Carl Van Vechten wrote the foreword and the artist Miguel Covarrubias contributed the illustrations.

W. E. B. DU BOIS (1868–1963) was among the twentieth century's greatest visionaries. He was the author of the remarkable 1903 work *The Souls of Black Folk* and was a founder and director of the NAACP from 1910 to 1934. He also established *The Crisis,* the most influential journal of the Harlem Renaissance. He believed Harlem Renaissance artists should take responsibility for the political and social implications of their work. He became dissatisfied with the integrationist philosophy of *The Crisis* and the NAACP and parted ways from both in 1934, when his interest shifted to more radical and global concerns. In 1961, he formally joined the Communist party and took up residence in Ghana. By the time he died he had written twenty-one books and edited fifteen others.

MAX EWING (1903–1934) was a writer and a musician who contributed music regularly for the Greenwich Village Follies. He was famous for the "art gallery" in his home, floor-to-ceiling displays of celebrities. Van Vechten designated Ewing one of the "Famous Beauties of the XXth Century," a title he bestowed on men he admired. Ewing's 1933 novel, *Going Somewhere,* satirizes New York social life in the 1920s. He killed himself in 1934.

JESSIE REDMON FAUSET (1882–1961) is sometimes called one of the "midwives" of the Harlem Renaissance. She was the literary editor at *The Crisis* from 1919 to 1926, as well as the author of four novels about the black bourgeoisie. Fauset was the first editor to appreciate the genius of Langston Hughes. She also helped nurture the work of George Schuyler, Jean Toomer, Countee Cullen, and Claude McKay.

RUDOLPH FISHER (1897–1934) moved to Harlem in 1925, where he established outstanding careers in both literature and medicine. He published short fiction in the *Atlantic Monthly, The Crisis,* and *Story* magazine throughout the 1920s. At the same time, he developed a successful practice as an X-ray specialist. His first novel, *The Walls of Jericho* (1932), is a satiric look at Harlem society. Hughes called him "the wittiest" of the "New Negroes of Harlem."

EMMANUEL TAYLOR GORDON (1893–1971) was both a singer and a writer who teamed up with the composer John Rosamond Johnson for a series of concerts of spirituals in the United States and Europe. Gordon's 1929 autobiography, *Born to Be,* included an introduction by Van Vechten, who helped nurture his career.

PORTER GRAINGER (?–?) was an actor, a writer, and a musician. He appeared in many shows during the twenties and contributed the scripts to several of them, including *Get Set* with Donald Heywood in 1923 and *Lucky Sambo* with Freddie Johnson in 1925. Grainger sometimes accompanied Bessie Smith at private parties. In the 1930s, Grainger slipped into obscurity.

WILLIAM CHRISTOPHER ("W. C.") HANDY (1873–1958) was a composer who became known as "the father of the Blues." He played the cornet and the organ and cofounded a music publishing company with Harry Pace in 1907. He may be best known for his 1914 song "St. Louis Blues."

ROLAND HAYES (1887–1976) was a tenor who began his musical career with the Fisk Jubilee Singers in 1911. His phenomenal success in Europe won him American recognition in 1923. He became a leading interpreter of German lieder in the United States.

CHESTER HIMES (1909–1984) was a novelist and autobiographer who captured the attention of Carl Van Vechten with the manuscript of his novel *Yesterday Will Make You Cry*, which would not be published until 1998. In 1960, Van Vechten called Himes's 1947 novel *Lonely Crusade* "the best novel ever written yet by a Negro." Himes moved to Paris in 1953, in part because his novels failed to achieve the critical recognition in the United States that they received in Europe. In Paris, Himes was part of the African American expatriate community that included Richard Wright and James Baldwin.

NORA HOLT (1890–1974) was the first black woman to receive a master of music degree from the Chicago Music College, in 1918. During the Harlem Renaissance she was a celebrated nightclub performer. One of Van Vechten's constant companions, she was one of the most glamorous Harlem Renaissance personalities. Holt was the model for Lasca Sartoris, *Nigger Heaven*'s femme fatale.

ZORA NEALE HURSTON (1891–1960), a folklorist, playwright, essayist, and fiction writer, was born in Notasulga, Alabama. Hurston had her first story published in the Howard University literary magazine while she was an undergraduate there from 1918 to 1919. By 1925, Hurston was in New York, where she studied anthropology with Franz Boas at Columbia University. She graduated from Barnard College with a bachelor of arts degree in 1928. Her published works include her 1937 novel, *Their Eyes Were Watching God*, and her 1942 autobiography, *Dust Tracks on a Road*.

HAROLD JACKMAN (1900–1960) was a schoolteacher in Harlem, a well-respected intellectual, and a close friend of both Hughes's and Van Vechten's. He founded the Countee Cullen Memorial Collection at Atlanta University in 1947. Jackman was the physical model for Byron Kasson, the protagonist in *Nigger Heaven*.

CHARLES S. JOHNSON (1893–1956) was, along with Jessie Fauset and Alain Locke, one of the three "midwives" of the Harlem Renaissance, according to Langston Hughes. As executive director of the National Urban League, Johnson founded *Opportunity: A Journal of Negro Life* in 1923, the official publication of the Urban League and a complement to *The Crisis* magazine. *Opportunity* published creative writing and also sponsored literary competitions, which helped to publicize new black talent. Johnson "did more to encourage and develop Negro writers during the 1920s than anyone else in America," wrote Hughes in *The Big Sea.*

HALL JOHNSON (1888–1970), a choral director and composer, organized the Hall Johnson Choir in Harlem in 1925, whose program of spirituals was in great demand in the United States and abroad. Johnson was appointed choral director for the 1930 play *The Green Pastures,* by Marc Connelly, and his choir appeared in the 1936 film version. Johnson wrote the book and score for the 1933 folk play *Run, Little Chillun,* which ran for 126 performances in New York and whose cast included Langston Hughes's mother.

JAMES WELDON JOHNSON (1871–1938) was an author, diplomat, song-writer, lawyer, educator, and civil rights advocate. He held appointments as U.S. consul to Venezuela (1906–1908) and Nicaragua (1909–1912). He published the novel *The Autobiography of an Ex-Colored Man* anonymously in 1912. At Van Vechten's urging, Knopf reissued the novel with Johnson's name attached in 1927. He held high-ranking positions in the NAACP until 1930, when he resigned in order to accept a teaching appointment at Fisk University. Van Vechten established the James Weldon Johnson Collection of Negro Arts and Letters at Yale University in 1941 to honor Johnson, one of his closest friends, who died in a car accident in 1938.

JOHN ROSAMOND JOHNSON (1873–1954)—known by his middle name—was James Weldon's brother and composing partner. Together, they wrote numerous songs, including "Lift Every Voice and Sing," otherwise known as the "Black National Anthem." They collaborated on two collections of spirituals, *The Book of American Negro Spirituals* (1925) and *The Second Book of Spirituals* (1926). The brothers teamed up with Bob Cole to write the musicals *Shoo-Fly Regiment* (1906) and *The Red Moon* (1908).

ALFRED A. KNOPF (1892–1984) founded the publishing house that bears his name in 1915, at the age of twenty-three. The same year he published Van Vechten's second book, *Music and Bad Manners,* and the author and the publisher developed a lifelong friendship. In the late teens, the literary trio of Van Vechten, Joseph Hergesheimer, and H. L. Mencken helped turn the firm into one of the most important publishing houses in the country.

BLANCHE KNOPF (1894–1966), Alfred's wife and partner, served as Hughes's primary editor until the 1940s. She was the primary contact for Harlem Renaissance writers like Hughes, Nella Larsen, and Walter White, who published with the firm. She frequently served as editor for Van Vechten, and he was an informal literary scout for her, keeping her abreast of the black American literary scene.

NELLA LARSEN (1893–1963), the author of two well-respected novels, *Quicksand* and *Passing,* was one of the most important writers of the Harlem Renaissance. She considered Van Vechten one of her most trusted confidants and corresponded with him about the most intimate details of her life.

ALAIN LOCKE (1886–1954) was another "midwife" of the Harlem Renaissance. Having received his B.A. from Harvard, he became the first black American Rhodes Scholar in 1907. He studied in Berlin and Paris, and received his Ph.D. from Harvard. Locke was the chair of the Philosophy Department at Howard University when he was invited to edit a special Harlem issue of *Survey Graphic* called *Harlem: Mecca of the New Negro* in 1925. The phenomenal success of this issue—it was the most widely read in the history of the magazine—encouraged Locke to expand on the idea and assemble *The New Negro* eight months later. A collection of poetry, essays, and fiction, *The New Negro* was the definitive anthology of the Harlem Renaissance.

MABEL DODGE LUHAN (1879–1962) and Van Vechten became friends in 1913. Initially, Luhan found him strange, "with eyes full of good-natured malice and teeth that made him look like a wild boar," she wrote later in her memoir *Movers and Shakers* (1963). Van Vechten called her his first real mentor, the major influence on his aesthetic sensibilities. She married Tony Luhan, a Taos Pueblo Indian, in 1923.

FANIA MARINOFF (1887–1971), a Russian émigrée and an actress, was Van Vechten's wife for over fifty years. They met in 1912 and became close instantly, despite the fact that they "quarrelled almost incessantly about important and unimportant matters," as Carl told the Columbia Oral History Project in 1960. Marinoff began acting at eight years old and enjoyed a steady career on the stage until the 1920s.

ROSE MCCLENDON (1884–1936) was a prominent black actress of the stage and an acting teacher. She received acclaim for her role in *Deep River* (1926) and for her performance the same year in Paul Green's Pulitzer Prize–winning play *In Abraham's Bosom*. McClendon received outstanding reviews for her leading role in *Mulatto*, the 1934 play by Langston Hughes. In 1946 Carl Van Vechten presented to Howard University the Rose McClendon Memorial Collection, a collection of one hundred photographs of black artists and writers.

CLAUDE MCKAY (1889–1948), born in Jamaica, was enabled by a Jamaican government program to come to the United States in 1912 so that he could pursue an agricultural education at Tuskegee Institute in Alabama. McKay wanted to become a writer, however, and moved to Harlem in 1914. He became enchanted with communist politics in the late teens and served for a year as associate editor of the radical magazine *The Liberator.* He eventually lost faith in communism, and was converted to Roman Catholicism by the end of his life. Du Bois linked McKay's 1928 novel, *Home to Harlem,* and Van Vechten's *Nigger Heaven* in a review for *The Crisis,* and the association held for years, much to McKay's frustration.

FLORENCE MILLS (1895–1927) was a singer and dancer who began her performing career at the age of five, when she won several dance contests. By the time she was eight years old, she had her first stage appearance as Baby Florence Mills. She formed a singing trio with her sisters and eventually teamed with Ada "Bricktop" Smith and Cora Green as the Panama Trio. Her first big role was in the 1921 musical comedy *Shuffle Along.* She had another leading role in the musical comedy *Blackbirds of 1926,* which had phenomenal runs in New York, Paris, and London. Mills was an international star when she died suddenly of appendicitis. At her spectacular Harlem funeral, a flock of black-birds was released from a plane, an homage to her theme song, "I'm a Little Blackbird Looking for a Bluebird."

ABBIE MITCHELL (1884–1960), along with Rose McClendon, was one of the finest black actresses of her generation. She began her career at the age of fourteen when she auditioned for *Clorindy: The Origin of the Cakewalk,* by Will Marion Cook, whom she later married. Mitchell studied voice in Paris and gave concerts in Europe and the United States. In 1926, she appeared in *In Abraham's Bosom* with McClendon.

RICHARD BRUCE NUGENT (1906–1987), born into the black upper class in Washington, D.C., was a writer, painter, and would-be actor who was best known for his wit, good looks, and flamboyant style. Nugent became enam-ored of Hughes when they met in 1924, calling him a "made-to-order Hero for me." Nugent became a fan of Van Vechten, too, and modeled himself on Peter Whiffle, the main character in Van Vechten's 1922 novel of the same name.

LOUISE THOMPSON PATTERSON (1901–1999) was an educator and a labor organizer. Thompson made the acquaintance of Langston Hughes in Harlem in the late 1920s, when they were under the aegis of the same patron, Char-lotte Osgood Mason. She worked for a short time as secretary to both Hughes and Zora Neale Hurston while they collaborated on their ill-fated 1931 play, *Mule Bone.* Thompson dedicated herself to political work not long after her stint as a typist, and in 1933 began fifteen years of service to the International Workers Order. Thompson, who had married Wallace Thurman in 1929 and filed for divorce shortly afterward, married the lawyer William Patterson in 1940. He had been a lawyer for the Scottsboro case of 1930, in which Thompson was deeply involved.

DOROTHY PETERSON (1897–1978) was a teacher, librarian, and sometime actress who appeared in the 1930 play *Green Pastures* and was active in little theater groups in Harlem. Van Vechten based his lead female character in *Nigger Heaven* on Peterson. They were very close friends, corresponded often, and accompanied each other to social events. Peterson was a librarian at the Harlem branch of the New York Public Library and later a teacher at the Wadleigh School for Girls in Harlem. She worked closely with Van Vechten on establishing the James Weldon Johnson Memorial Collection of American Negro Arts and Letters at Yale.

PAUL ROBESON (1898–1976) was among the most famous black performers of the twentieth century. He began his stellar career at Rutgers University, where he earned twelve varsity letters and made Phi Beta Kappa in his junior year. After graduating from the law school at Columbia University, he took his first stage role in 1921. Among his many memorable roles were leads in *The Emperor Jones, Porgy, Showboat,* and *Othello.* Van Vechten admired Robeson greatly, and the two met in 1925.

GEORGE SCHUYLER (1895–1977) was an iconoclastic journalist and satirist and an editor of the radical black magazine *The Messenger* from 1923 until 1928. At the same time, he was a columnist for the *Pittsburgh Courier,* one of the most widely read black newspapers of its day. Schuyler didn't believe that anything distinguished African American culture from Western European culture, as he argued in his June 16, 1926, essay in *The Nation,* "The Negro-Art Hokum." In 1931 he wrote his best-known work, *Black No More,* a novel that lampoons both black and white racial attitudes.

BESSIE SMITH (1894–1937), later known as "empress of the Blues," left her Chattanooga, Tennessee, home in 1912 to join a traveling show. She toured with various revues and tent shows until she signed with Columbia Records in 1923, quickly becoming their best-selling blues artist. Van Vechten was enchanted when he saw her live performance in 1925, and wrote about the experience in a May 1926 essay for *Vanity Fair* called "Negro 'Blues' Singers." In "Memories of Bessie Smith," a 1947 essay in *Jazz Record,* he remembered a performance she once gave at his apartment: "This was no actress; no imitator of women's woes. . . . It was the real thing: a woman cutting her heart open with a knife until it was exposed for us all to see."

ARTHUR SPINGARN (1878–1971) was a lawyer and a lifelong advocate for black people. Spingarn served the NAACP in several capacities: he was its lawyer in 1909, its vice president in 1911, and its president from 1940 until his retirement in 1966. Spingarn's brother, Joel, a writer, and his sister-in-law, Amy, a philanthropist, were also deeply committed to the progress of African Americans. Arthur Spingarn was also an art and book collector who donated all of his materials relating to African Americans to Howard University. He provided legal counsel for Langston Hughes throughout Hughes's career.

NOËL SULLIVAN (1890–1956) was a member of a prominent San Francisco family and a dedicated patron of the arts. He admired Hughes's work and gave him a writing sanctuary at Hollow Hills Farm, his estate in Carmel, California. There, Hughes wrote his first collection of short stories, *The Ways of White Folks* (1934). Sullivan eventually became friendly with Van Vechten as well.

PRENTISS TAYLOR (1907–1991) was a painter and a lithographer. Van Vechten introduced him to Hughes in 1931, and the three founded a short-lived publishing company called Golden Stair Press. He designed the book jacket for Van Vechten's 1932 book, *Sacred and Profane Memories.*

LOUISE THOMPSON. See LOUISE THOMPSON PATTERSON.

JEAN TOOMER (1894–1967) wrote *Cane* (1923), a montage of poetry and prose that is generally considered to be the first significant work of the Harlem Renaissance. Toomer's mixed racial heritage was always a source of inner conflict for him. In 1931, he refused to be included in the second edition of James Weldon Johnson's *Book of American Negro Poetry,* claiming in a letter to Johnson to be "simply an American."

A'LELIA WALKER (1885–1931) was a socialite who inherited the fortune of her mother, Madame C. J. Walker, the empress of black hair-care products. Guests of all types were welcome at A'Lelia's famous parties, which she held in all of her three homes. In 1928, she established The Dark Tower, a salon for black writers, at her 136th Street home. Van Vechten, a frequent companion of Walker's, modeled a prominent *Nigger Heaven* character, Adora Boniface, on the heiress.

EDDIE WASSERMAN (?–?) and Van Vechten socialized together for years. An heir of the Seligmann banking family, Wasserman (who changed his name to Waterman) would become over the course of his life both an art dealer in Paris and a drug addict.

ETHEL WATERS (1896–1977) had a career as a singer and actress that spanned more than fifty years. Waters spent her childhood on the streets of Chester, Pennsylvania, and, in her early twenties, she began touring the South playing vaudeville and tent shows as Sweet Mama Stringbean. She gave memorable performances in the 1927 musical *Africana* and the 1933 show *As Thousands Cheer.* Van Vechten wrote about her several times, beginning with his 1926 *Vanity Fair* essay "Negro 'Blues' Singers," in which he called her "superior to any other woman stage singer of her race."

DOROTHY WEST (1908–1998) was a Boston-born fiction writer who published her first short story in 1926 in *Opportunity.* She and Hughes were part of a group of twenty-two black Americans chosen to travel to Russia to represent the United States in an ill-fated film project in 1931. During the 1930s, she edited *Challenge,* later *New Challenge,* a magazine that attempted to keep the work of young black writers in print.

WALTER WHITE (1893–1955) was a civil rights activist and a writer whose first novel, *The Fire in the Flint* (1924), was the major source of inspiration for Van Vechten's interest in African American culture. White became the assistant executive secretary of the NAACP in 1918. When James Weldon Johnson retired in 1930, he assumed the position of executive secretary. In 1960, Van Vechten remembered that, a week after meeting White, "I knew practically every famous Negro in New York because Walter was a hustler."

REMEMBER ME TO HARLEM

1925–1926

When the correspondence between Carl Van Vechten and Langston Hughes began, Van Vechten was in New York, tirelessly cultivating an expertise on Harlem life. Hughes was in Washington, D.C., living with his mother and working as a personal assistant for the "father of Negro history," Carter G. Woodson, who founded the Association for the Study of Negro Life and History in 1915. Hughes performed secretarial chores and worked on Woodson's massive study, Free Negro Heads of Families in the United States in 1830.

After hours, Hughes would head for Seventh Street, where he found "sweet relief." There, "ordinary Negroes . . . played the blues, ate watermelon, barbecue, and fish sandwiches, shot pool, told tall tales, looked at the dome of the Capitol and laughed out loud," he recalled in his 1940 autobiography, The Big Sea. The life there inspired his poetry. "I tried to write poems like the songs they sang on Seventh Street—gay songs, because you had to be gay or die; sad songs, because you couldn't help being sad sometimes. But gay or sad, you kept on living and you kept on going. Their songs—those of Seventh Street—had the pulse beat of the people who keep on going."

During his time in Washington, Hughes wrote and published more poetry than he had since he started writing at the age of thirteen.

CARL VAN VECHTEN TO LANGSTON HUGHES, MAY 6, 1925

Dear Langston,

I haven't heard from you since your return;[1] I hope you haven't forgotten that you promised to send your book[2] back as soon as it is rearranged. I shall do my best to get it published, and that should be easy because it is a beautiful book. Also, please don't forget the Frankie song[3] (if it was a Frankie song), and you spoke of a better book about Hayti[4] than the one I have: can you dig out the name of it for me? I trust that it will not be very long before you visit New York again: you must know that I like you very much.

sincerely

Wednesday

1. *After his visit to Van Vechten's home on Sunday, May 3, Hughes returned to Washington. This is Van Vechten's first letter to Hughes.*
2. *Hughes's manuscript would become his first published collection of verse,* The Weary Blues *(1926).*
3. *Van Vechten refers to the legendary ballad, "Frankie and Johnny," about a St. Louis prostitute who shoots her unfaithful lover.*
4. *Once common spelling of Haiti, now obsolete.*

LANGSTON HUGHES TO CARL VAN VECHTEN, MAY 7, 1925

1749 S Street, N.W.
Washington, D.C.

May 7, 1925

Dear Carl,

What a delightful surprise, your letter! I didn't think you would write me first as I've had you in mind all week for a note. I typed "Frankie Baker" for you on Monday but have been waiting for a chance to write a few explanations about it. I've been busy.

Perhaps you have heard "Frankie" before. It's a very old song, and is supposed to have originated in Omaha after Frankie Baker, a colored sporting-woman famous in the West, had shot her lover, Albert. The whole song runs to a blues tune, the chorus very blue, but the tune of each verse varies slightly, better to express the sentiment; the last two verses are sung like a blues dirge. And Bruce, the giant one-eyed cook in Paris, used to give elaborate characterizations of the bar-tender, Frankie, and the judge, while I kept the hot cakes turning.[1] He was as much an entertainer as a cook, and had been everywhere bumming and sailing. He knew all kinds of "rounders" tunes and "low-down" Negro songs.[2] There was a particularly good one celebrating the sexual charms of a certain worthless rounder who was

A total loss
But a sweet _____ from Henrico.

And another lament called "Sugar-babe,—you don't love me now." You ought to be able to find some old-timer around Harlem to sing "Frankie" for you. It has a number of versions,—some more interesting (and dirtier) than the one I remember. Obscenity doesn't stick in my head, though.

No, I didn't say anything concerning a book about Hayti. I just said I would like to go there this summer. (And I may go yet if the index to "Free Negro Heads of Families" continues to bore me as it did today).

I am going to rearrange the book Sunday. I can work on poetry only when it amuses me, and this week it didn't amuse me: I was too sleepy.

I do want to come up to New York again soon. And remember your promise: a whole day to look at your beautiful things. And talk with you.

Sincerely,
Langston Hughes

1. *In late February of 1924, Hughes deserted his ten-week old job as a messboy on a ship called the* McKeesport *as soon as it reached Holland. He caught the night train for Paris, "a dream come true," he recalled in* The Big Sea. *Bruce was famous as the cook at Le Grand Duc, a Parisian nightclub where Hughes worked as dishwasher and learned to become a jazz poet. He stayed in Europe until the end of November.*
2. *A "rounder" is a narrative song in which each verse is rounded off with a repeated line. A rounder can also be a ne'er-do-well, a wastrel.*

LANGSTON HUGHES TO CARL VAN VECHTEN, MAY 10, 1925

1749 S Street, N.W.
Washington, D.C.

May 10, 1925

Dear Friend,

I am mailing my book to you in the morning. It has been rearranged and thirty poems have been taken out. It can stand even more cutting but I can't decide myself which others to take out; however, if you'd like to remove some more for the betterment of the book, go to it. I hope you'll like the new arrangement. Tell me about it when you write.

Did you get the Frankie song? And have you been to Harlem this week? I met Rudolph Fisher‡ again at a little party over here and he shows no traces of conceit. He is a most interesting young fellow, talks and sings well, and can entertain a whole room full of company. Clarissa

Scott¹ was there, too,—that charming young lady I told you about. And she asked all sorts of questions about you.

I got one poem at least out of my New York trip,—the To a Black Dancer in the "Little Savoy." (It's in the book.) There was a perfectly divine black girl there one night drunk on joy (and gin, too, perhaps.) If you've never been to the Little Savoy, don't go, though.² It's a rummy place frequented by Jew-boys and clerks who don't have a good time. I just happened to run into adventure that once. A lady pianist from another cabaret known as "Piano-playin' Miss Viola" dropped in and sat down beside me. I bought her a drink, and immediately she declared that she loved me and insisted on paying for all the following drinks,—bottle after bottle of gin! Two or three other colored fellows and a high-yellow girl came to our table and at five in the morning we were having such a gay time that everybody else gathered around to look on. And then some-one started a fight. And if you've never seen a fight in one of those little cabarets, you've missed some excitement! I missed the piano-playin' lady so the party broke up.

The Blind Bow Boy has a most interesting beginning,³ but I am anx-ious to see what happens to Harold under his sophisticated new tutor. That ought to be entertaining. I haven't had a chance to read anything this week.

I like your letters. Write to me again.

Sincerely,
Langston

1. *A poet, educator, and essayist.*
2. *A popular Harlem speakeasy.*
3. The Bind Bow-Boy *was Carl Van Vechten's second novel, published in 1923.*

CARL VAN VECHTEN TO LANGSTON HUGHES, MAY 13, 1925

Your letters are so very charming, dear Langston, that I look forward every morning to finding one under the door. I have been lucky during the past week! The poems came this morning and I looked them over again. Your work has such a subtle sensitiveness that it improves with every reading. The poems are very beautiful, and I think the book gains greatly by the new arrangement and the title. Knopf‡ is lunching with me today and I shall ask him to publish them and if he doesn't some one else will. Would you permit me to do an introduction? I want to.

Frankie came, and thank you. I know the song, but with different words. There are, I suppose, two thousand versions. This is a good one. It's too bad that you didn't take down every syllable that fell from the lips of that holy cook.

I'm glad you liked The Blind Bow-Boy. I think you'd better read Peter Whiffle next,[1] if you really want to read any more; I'll send it to you.

Of course, I got the Gulf Coast Blues at once. I'm doing a paper about the Blues for Vanity Fair and anything you know about them, or if you even know the names of any other good ones, will help.[2]

I've never even heard of the Little Savoy; I wish I had been with you that night. I have never, in my experience of twenty-five years, seen a fight in a Negro cabaret; on the other hand I've never been in a white place when there wasn't one. The difference, I suppose, is that white people almost invariably become quarrelsome when they are drunk, while Negroes usually become gay and are not inclined to fight unless they want to kill some one. I'm going on a Harlem party tonight; if you were here we'd take you with us.

ALFRED A. KNOPF, PHOTOGRAPH BY
CARL VAN VECHTEN, 1935

I hope to meet Rudolph Fisher some time. I read Ringtail and found it full of picturesque detail,[3] but not as good, on the whole, as The City of Refuge.[4]

You will find your name, by the way, in the note I have written about Countee Cullen‡ in the June Vanity Fair, not yet out.[5]

Will you do something for me? I want you, if you will, to write me out the story of your life—detailing as many of your pregrinations and jobs as you can remember. Is this too much to ask?

I'll let you know about your book as soon as possible. In the meantime, please don't forget

Carl Van Vechten

Wednesday

---

1. *Van Vechten's first novel, published in 1922.*
2. *Van Vechten was a friend of Vanity Fair's editor Frank Crowninshield, which accounts for the magazine's early interest in African American music. Van Vechten said that Vanity Fair "was the first of the better magazines to publish Negro material repeatedly."*
3. *Fisher's story "Ringtail" was published in the May 1925 Atlantic Monthly.*
4. *Fisher's first short story, published in the Atlantic Monthly in February 1925. It won the 1925 Crisis short story contest.*
5. *Van Vechten arranged to have a selection of poems by Cullen published in the June 1925 Vanity Fair. His note of introduction claimed: "All his poetry is characterized by a suave, unpretentious, brittle intellectual elegance." He praised Cullen for being "able to write*

stanzas which have no bearing on the problems of his own race." Van Vechten mentioned Hughes in a list of young black writers, musicians, actors, and dancers "sufficiently earnest of what the 'gift of the black folk' (to employ Dr. Du Bois's poetic phrase) will be in the immediate future."

CARL VAN VECHTEN TO LANGSTON HUGHES, MAY 14, 1925

No letter came from you this morning, dear Langston, just as I was getting used to finding one daily under the door! My news is this: that I handed The Weary Blues to Knopf yesterday with the proper incantations. I do not feel particularly dubious about the outcome: your poems are too beautiful to escape appreciation. I find they have a subtle haunting quality which lingers in the memory and an extraordinary sensitivity to all that is kind and lovely. "Sweet trumpets, Jesus!" The request for your biography was no idle one.¹ I hope you will take it seriously. When the book is done I shall need it . . . and please make it as long as possible. Did you tell me, by the way, that you had been photographed by Nik Muray?² I can get one from him with no trouble, and from any one else with very little. Yesterday I sent you Peter Whiffle and The Tattooed Countess³ . . . So now you have all my novels. One Clara Barnes appears in both these books.

Laurel and Bayleaves to <u>you</u>!⁴

Carlo

Thursday

1. *Van Vechten refers here to his request in the previous letter for a biography of Hughes.*
2. *Nickolas Muray was a celebrity photographer and a frequent guest at Van Vechten's parties.*
3. *Van Vechten's The Tattooed Countess was published by Knopf in 1924. It is a sardonic look at its author's adolescence in Cedar Rapids, Iowa.*
4. *This is the first time Van Vechten shares with Hughes his penchant for customizing salutations. The Van Vechten biographer Bruce Kellner wrote: "He loved to sign his letters fancifully, occasionally at the expense of good taste but never at the expense of good humor." Most of the sign-offs in these letters Van Vechten invented expressly for Hughes.*

LANGSTON HUGHES TO CARL VAN VECHTEN, MAY 15, 1925

1749 S Street, N.W.
Washington, D.C.

May 15, 1925

Dear Friend,

I would be very, very much pleased if you would do an introduction to my poems. How good of you to offer. I am glad you liked the poems in the new arrangement and I do hope Knopf will like them, too. It would be great to have such a fine publisher!

About your paper on the Blues,—Sunday I am going to type some old verses for you that I used to hear when I was a kid, and that you may or may not have heard. You probably have. On the new records I think the Freight Train Blues (one of the many railroad Blues) is rather good, and Reckless Blues, and Follow the Deal on Down. Did you ever hear this verse of the Blues?

> I went to the gypsy's
> To get my fortune told.
> Went to the gypsy's
> To get my fortune told.
> Gypsy done told me
> Goddam your un-hard-lucky soul!

I first heard it from George, a Kentucky colored boy who shipped out to Africa with me,—a real vagabond if there ever was one.[1] He came on board five minutes before sailing with no clothes, nothing except the shirt and pants he had on and a pair of silk sox carefully wrapped up in his shirt pocket. He didn't even know where the ship was going. And when somebody on board gave him a suit he traded it in the first port to sleep with a woman. He used to make up his own Blues,—verses as absurd as Krazy Kat and as funny.[2] But sometimes when he had to do more work than he thought necessary for a happy living, or, when broke, he couldn't make the damsels of the West Coast believe love worth more than money, he used to sing about the gypsy who couldn't find words strong enough to tell about the troubles in his hard-luck soul.

I did like the Blind Bow-Boy. I hope you will send Peter Whiffle. Do you know any Negro Pauls in Harlem—those decorative boys who never do any work and who have some surprisingly well-known names on their lists?[3] In a really perfect world, though, people who are beautiful or amusing would be kept alive anyway solely because they are beautiful or amusing, don't you think?

About the story of my life,—I don't know what you want it for, and for me to sit down seriously and think about it and write it would take a long, long time. I mean,—to show cause and effect, soul-pregrinations, and all that sort of thing.* But I will send you an outline sketch of external movements; an essay I did for the Crisis contest on the Fascination of Cities;[4] and a semi-autobiographical poem I did for the Crisis, but which I don't think they're publishing. Out of all that junk you'll perhaps get something. And then if you would know more, just ask me, and I'll be glad to answer.

COUNTEE CULLEN, C. 1925

I'm having some pictures taken here, but they may not be as good as the Muray ones, so perhaps you'd better get him to give you one of his if you wish one.

I am anxiously awaiting the June Vanity Fair. I like the magazine, and Countee does such lovely things. What's become of John Peale Bishop?[5] I liked his work and I don't believe I've read anything of his lately. And Nancy Boyd's clever essays?[6]

  Remember me to Harlem.

    Sincerely,

    Langston

*How serious it sounds!

1. *Hughes made his first trip to Africa in the summer of 1923 by taking a job on the* West Hesseltine, *a freighter bound for Africa. Hughes remembered his first glimpse of the continent in* The Big Sea: *"My Africa, Motherland of the Negro peoples! And me a Negro! Africa! The real thing, to be touched and seen, not merely read about in a book." He visited Nigeria, Sierra Leone, and the Cameroons before returning to the United States in October.*
2. *George Herriman started the famous comic strip "Krazy Kat" in 1914.*
3. *Affected and elegant, Paul Moody is one of the main characters in Van Vechten's* The Blind Bow-Boy.
4. *Hughes's autobiographical essay, "The Fascination of Cities," won second place in the August 1925* Crisis *essay competition. It was published in the January 1926 issue of* The Crisis.
5. *Bishop was a poet, a fiction writer, and an essayist. He was also an editor at* Vanity Fair *in 1922.*
6. *Pseudonym for Edna St. Vincent Millay.*

CARL VAN VECHTEN TO LANGSTON HUGHES, MAY 17, 1925

Dear Langston,

I hope you eventually received the telegram I sent you yesterday.[1] Western Union telephoned me several times that there was no one home to sign for it but I instructed them to keep on trying. I wanted you to know immediately that Knopf was publishing your book. He will write you and send you a contract. I think it is a little late for the fall list but you will probably appear in January 1925.[2] I shall write the introduction[3] and the cover design will be by Covarrubias.‡ I hope you are happy about this, because I am.

Also, I have spoken to Vanity Fair about you and they are extremely desirous of seeing your work. I am almost certain that after seeing it they will publish some of it. Please, therefore, send twenty or thirty poems, so that she can make a selec-

tion, to Miss Margaret Case, Vanity Fair, 19 West Forty-fourth Street, New York City. Of course, don't send anything that has been printed before, and send as many jazz and cabaret things as you happen to have on hand. But you know Vanity Fair and you will know what best will suit them.

MIGUEL COVARRUBIAS AND CARL VAN VECHTEN, C. 1925

And now you must know why I asked for biographical data. I felt convinced that these things, and others, would happen and I wanted to be prepared. Don't bother about anything "psychological" (unless it is important and easy for you to set down) but send me a chronological list of the places you have lived (including date and place of birth), the schools you have been to (and how long), and your jobs. And you'd better send me one of your new Washington photographs, even if I secure the New York one.

Lilacs and pansies to you!
Carlo

Sunday

1. *Van Vechten's ecstatic telegram read:* LITTLE DAVID PLAY ON YOUR HARP.
2. *Van Vechten meant 1926.*
3. *Reprinted in Appendix I, page 329.*

LANGSTON HUGHES TO CARL VAN VECHTEN, MAY 17, 1925

Sunday

Dear Carl,

I am sending you today the poem that I promised, The Fascination of Cities, and some old verses of the Blues. I hope you will find them all interesting. You will excuse me for sending you a carbon of Cities. I wanted to copy it for you but time moved faster than I did and I had to meet an engagement. Do you get the bull fight I am trying to describe in Mexico? By the way, I wish I'd have known you two years ago. I had a very beautiful pair of banderillos that I left in my room at Columbia when I went to sea. They might have gone well with the Spanish fan in your apartment. They were special ones that Gaona, the great Mexican matador, used in a festival fight at Easter. They were burnt orange, with tiny fruits of silk and tinselled gold. He had them made to contrast with his suit of mauve-grey. I got them while the blood was still fresh on them, with bits of the bull's hair stuck to the hilt. They were beautiful things to torture an animal with.

I know very little to tell you about the Blues. They always impressed me as being very sad, sadder even than the spirituals because their sadness is not softened with tears but hardened with laughter, the absurd, incongruous laughter of a sadness without even a god to appeal to. In the Gulf Coast Blues one can feel the cold northern snows, the memory of the melancholy mists of the Louisianna low-lands, the shack that is home, the worthless lovers with hands full of gimme, mouths full of much oblige, the eternal unsatisfied longings.[1]

There seems to be a monotonous melancholy, an animal sadness running through all Negro jazz that is almost terrible at times. I remember hearing a native jazz-band playing in the Kameroon in Africa while two black youths stamped and circled about a dance hall floor, their feet doing exactly the same figures over and over to the monotonous rhythm, their bodies turning and swaying like puppets on strings. While the two black boys, half-grinning mouths never closed, went round and round the room, the horns cried and moaned in monotonous weariness, — like the weariness of days ever coming, going; like the weariness of the world moving always in the same circle, — while the drums kept up a deep-voiced laughter for the dancing feet. The performance put a damper on the evening's fun. It just wasn't enjoyable. The sailors left and went to a French whorehouse.

Perhaps the reason the Blues seem so melancholy to me is that I first heard them sung as a child by a blind orchestra that used to wander about the streets of the slums and the red-light district in Kansas City, singing for nickels or pennies, a fish sandwich, or anything one chose to give. The ribald verses, the music that seemed to cry when the words laughed, the painted girls from the houses of ill-fame in their gingham dresses, and the invariable verse about

> Goin' to the river
> And sit down

made me feel that there was no music in the world sadder than the Blues. But I was a kid then.

I wish that I could write you every day if it meant getting your delightful notes in return. Thank you very much for the books. I liked your lovely first chapter on Paris in Peter Whiffle. I am sorry I didn't first see Paris as you saw it. I caught only the gloomy coldness of it. When I arrived I had come down from the North a chill grey morning in February. It was snowing as the train passed the Belgian frontier, and the snow had turned to rain in Paris. And it seems to me that it rained steadily the whole seven months I was there! And I was never quite warm until July . . . But I did have one perfect week in Venice and, later, one glorious time in Catania.[2]

(Request: Could you find out for me the name of that Italian song they sing after the fiesta in Pauline Lord's "They Knew what they Wanted?"[3] I want to get it on a record.)

The Blind Bow-Boy again. I knew a colored girl, a cabaret singer in Paris, almost exactly like Zimbule.[4] I had thought of writing a story about her and calling it The Golden Creature. That last chapter of the Bow-Boy is delightful. Oh! That adorable Campaspe.[5]

I am afraid it is going to take me a long time to write you a "biography." Not that there is anything so intricate, or interesting, or deep about it. But I hate to think backwards. It isn't amusing. Today I sat half the morning wondering what the difference in me would have been had my father brought me up in Mexico instead of my aunt and grandmother in Kansas. And I wrote nothing. Wouldn't you be satisfied with an outline? I am still too much enmeshed in the affects of my young life to write clearly about it. I haven't yet escaped into serenity and grown old yet. I wish I could. What moron ever wrote those lines about "carry me back to the scenes of my childhood"?

Jessie Fauset[‡] wrote me about the little dinner and the pleasant evening with you. Has she introduced you to her cat, Stevie? I know him better than I do Sch . . . arazade.[6] (Can't spell it.) You ought to meet my most ordinary kitten,—Mutt.

As 'tis said in Spanish,—Hasta luego. Vaya usted con dios,—some happy god I hope.

Sincerely,
Langston

1749 S Street, N.W.
Washington, D.C.

1. *"Gulf Coast Blues" was a hit for Bessie Smith in the spring of 1923.*
2. *After returning from Africa in October 1923, Hughes spent less than two months stateside before taking the messboy job on the* McKeesport *on December 8.*

3. *Actress Pauline Lord played the lead in this 1924 play by Sidney Howard.*
4. *In* The Blind Bow-Boy, *Zimbule O'Grady is not only a sixteen-year-old snake handler, she is "a girl . . . for whom God had determined to do his best."*
5. *The author describes his character Campaspe Lorillard as "about thirty, intensely feminine, intensely feline."*
6. *Van Vechten named one of his cats Scheherazade after he edited the memoirs of Rimsky-Korsakov for Knopf.*

CARL VAN VECHTEN TO LANGSTON HUGHES, MAY 17, 1925

Dear Langston, Apparently—I judge from your letter this morning—you did not receive my telegram on Saturday. I am sorry, because I wanted you to hear the news at once—but you will learn it all from my letter which I mailed you yesterday. You will also understand better what I mean by your biography. I want only the facts at first—as many as possible—we'll fill in the psychology later. I'll probably ask lots of questions—at present I am interested in a new phase of you. I discover from your letters—and a paper in the new number of <u>The Crisis</u> which just arrived this morning—that you have a very great talent as a writer of prose. I want you to play with this talent. In the first place you can treat many subjects in that form that you cannot treat in verse—in the second place you can make more money,—already you write fluently. Your sense of character is extremely picturesque. You describe accurately—and <u>with your own eyes</u>. Of course, you have enough material in the back of your head to write forty books once you get started. At first it is difficult to co-ordinate all one's qualities, but I am sure you can. Perhaps, for all I know you have already. I am only judging these fragments. What you write me about the Blues, for example, is so extraordinary that I want to incorporate it into my article—with due credit to Langston Hughes, poet and charming fellow. Muray is trying to find your plates. He says they were taken a long time ago before they began to make systematic records. Were you already famous when they were taken?[1] I have been very slow in finding out about you, but I am doing my best to make up for that. I regret the BANDERILLOS, I almost wish you hadn't written me about them!

I have been signing sheets for the large paper copies of Firecrackers all the morning.[2] This afternoon I go to the dentist. It is not a pleasant day. In between I am trying to write a paper for the Mercury on Breakfasts.[3]

bien à toi—

Carl Van Vechten

I am trying to find some paper of an extremely appropriate design to bind your Weary Blues. We want to make it as beautiful a book as possible.

I'll find out what the Italian song [is] for you as soon as possible—and let you know, I haven't seen the play myself.

1. *Hughes got his first professional photographs made at the insistence of Jessie Fauset in May of 1923. He wasn't famous at that point, but he had made a tremendous impression on the black literati by becoming a very important poet at* The Crisis *at the age of nineteen. Jessie Fauset was the first person to appreciate Hughes's genius when he sent three poems to the* Brownie's Book *in September 1920. Fauset was literary editor of this magazine for young readers, which was founded by W. E. B. Du Bois in 1919.*
2. *Van Vechten's fourth novel, published in 1925.*
3. *Published by Alfred Knopf, the periodical* American Mercury *was edited by the curmudgeonly journalist H. L. Mencken and the theater critic George Jean Nathan.*

LANGSTON HUGHES TO CARL VAN VECHTEN, MAY 18, 1925
(TELEGRAM)

**THANKS IMMENSELY THE SILVER TRUMPETS ARE BLOWING
LANGSTON HUGHES**

LANGSTON HUGHES TO CARL VAN VECHTEN, MAY 18, 1925

Monday

Dear Carl,

I am very happy about the book, and surprised! How quickly it's all been done! Bravo to you! When I brought the manuscript up to New York I imagined I'd be all summer at least looking for a publisher,—if I ever found one. You're my good angel! How shall I thank you?

Unfortunately, now that I have a chance to sell poetry (I've had a note from The Nation, too,) I have nothing at all good on hand. And I can't write poetry to order. But perhaps I can get together a dozen or so poems among which Vanity Fair might find a few interesting. I certainly hope so. Never in my wildest dreams had I imagined a chance at Vanity Fair.

I am glad Covarrubius is going to do the cover. I like his work and it should go well with the book. And with your introduction,—what more do I need? As the old folks say: I'll have to walk sideways to keep from flying! All this is very fine of you.

You shall have the life outline as soon as possible. And a picture from here when they're finished.

It was charming of you to send a telegram,—but I got your letter first?!? Funny, wasn't it. But it's all right for

I am very happy,
Langston

ughes wanted Van Vechten to believe he was thrilled with his introduction. "Humming-birds and bright flowers in a marsh, — that's the way your introduction strikes me. Full of color and different, I've seen no other introduction like it, that's why it pleases me so much," he wrote in an August letter not included in this volume because, aside from this line, it contains only a list of manuscript corrections he wanted Van Vechten to make. In fact, Hughes had reservations about the introduction, which he shared with his trusted friend and fellow poet, Gwendolyn Bennett, who tried to reassure him in a letter from late 1925: "Never you mind about the colored people [not] liking the Covarrubias cover nor the Van Vechten introduction . . . you're not writing your book only for colored people. And if they who chance to have a kinship of race with you don't like your things . . . well, let them go hang!"

CARL VAN VECHTEN TO LANGSTON HUGHES, JUNE 4, 1925

Dear Langston,

The histoire de ta vie was so remarkable both as regards manner and matter that I hesitated for some time before deciding what should be done with it.[1] It seemed absurd for me to write a preface about you when you had written such a beautiful one yourself, but another idea has dawned which seems even better. I have discussed the matter with Mrs. Knopf[‡] and she agrees with me fully. As I wrote you before I think you are a topnotch writer of prose: in this biography you have an amazing subject. Treat it romantically if you will, be as formless as you please, disregard chronology if you desire, weaving your story backwards and forward, but however you do it, I am certain not only that you can write a beautiful book, but also one that will <u>sell</u>. There will be in it not only exciting incident, vivid description of character and people and places, but something more besides: the soul of a young Negro with a nostalgia for beauty and colour and warmth: that is what I see in all your work. Now this is why the book will have an enormous appeal, because hundreds of young people of whatsoever color, nay thousands, have this same nostalgia but they do not know how to express it, but they react to it emotionally when it is expressed. What I want you to do, therefore, is to write this book. It may be as long or as short as you please. I know it is hard to write a book with all the other things you have to do, but I am sure you can do it. What I am going to suggest to you is that you make yourself write a little every day: say 300 words. You will find this method hard at first and very easy after a week or two. In fact, some days you will want to write 2,000 words, but however many words you have produced on a certain day make yourself write the stipulated 300 on the next. You might read a few personal biographies, Sherwood Anderson's A Story Teller's Story (which is all fiction), for example, or Edwin Bjorkman's The Soul of a Child (which is all fact). This may serve to give you more confidence to go ahead, but after you have learned their way, disregard it to any extent and do your book in your way. I shall be very happy when you write me that you have begun this book. Be as digressive as you please — when anything reminds you of something else, another experience, another episode, put it down. Try to be as frank as possible, but when your material runs a little thin, don't be afraid to imagine better material or to put down some one else's experience as your own. I am infinitely obliged to you for your assistance in regard to the Blues . . . Zora Neale Hurston[‡] and W. C. Handy[‡] have given me further material; in fact I feel soon that I could write a book on the subject. Bessie Smith[‡2] is promised me for an evening soon. By the way, I think her rendering of the "Weepin' Willow Blues" on the Columbia is almost the best of all.

I hope Vanity Fair will like your poems as much as I did; but if they don't, remember that that will not destroy their beauty. I can recall the time, not so very long ago, when a paper of mine would come wandering back refused by eight or ten magazines. Off I would shoot it to another and eventually it would usually be accepted. You have caught the jazz spirit and the jazz rhythm amazingly; some of them ought to be recited in stop-time!

Firecrackers is my new novel. In it appear characters from all the old ones. I hope soon to start work on my Negro novel, but I feel rather alarmed. It would be comparatively easy for me to write it before I knew as much as I know now, enough to know that I am thoroughly ignorant!

There are so many things that one can't talk about in a letter — I think a long conversation would be advantageous to both of us. Perhaps, a little later, you can run over for a couple of days and talk and look at my books and make yourself as comfortable as you can chez moi.

pansies and marguerites to you!

Carl

Thursday

Apparently, there are three songs used in the second act of They Knew What They Wanted: (1) La Donna è Mobile from Rigoletto (2) Funiculì, Funiculà (3) Maria, Marì. The last two are famous Neapolitan popular songs and easy to get in any form.

1. *"L'histoire de ma vie" was Langston's answer to Van Vechten's persistent requests for an autobiography. Essentially, it is an extensive outline of the places and people important to Hughes up until 1925. Hughes never published "L'histoire de ma vie" but it did provide the foundation for his 1940 autobiography* The Big Sea.
2. *Both Van Vechten and Hughes were lifetime fans of the singer Bessie Smith, who gave a memorable performance of a different sort at one Van Vechten party. When Fania Marinoff ‡ attempted to kiss Smith good-bye, the Blues empress shoved her, shouting, "I ain't never heard of such shit!"*

LANGSTON HUGHES TO CARL VAN VECHTEN, JUNE 4, 1925

Thursday

Dear Carl,

I have been thinking about what you said concerning the histoire de ma vie and the making of a book out of it. I would rather like to do it and yet there are a number of reasons why I wouldn't like to do it. The big reason is this: There are so many people who would have to be left out of the book, and yet they are people who have been the cause of my doing or not doing half the important things in my life, but they are or have been my friends, for that reason I couldn't write them up as I would like to. Besides most of them are still very definitely connected with my life in a negative or positive way. So you see, unless I showed effects without causes, or else fictionalized a good deal (which might be interesting) the book wouldn't be all that it ought to be. Do you get me? And then I'm tired. I've had a very trying winter and don't feel like doing anything all summer except amusing myself. And writing prose isn't amusing after a day of reading censuses in an office. I can't be bored both night and day and I don't want to be driven back to sea from sheer boredom. I ought to give college another trial.¹ Besides, I think I will like Howard.²

I've just discovered a number of little bars here frequented by southern Negroes where they come to play the banjo and do clog dances. There may be a chance to pick up some new songs and one certainly sees some interesting types.

When you mentioned Bessie Smith you reminded me that I once

wrote a Blues for her and never did anything with it. It's nothing unusual but I'm sending it to you. If you see her ask her if she likes it. She used to be quite amusing when she was doing her old act in small-time houses. And when she sang He May Be Your Man at the big anniversary performance of Shuffle Along in New York (were you there?) she was a "riot," but the last time I saw her she didn't seem so good. But I like her records,—and speaking of Blues, have you heard Clara Smith sing If You Only Knowed? It's a real, real sad one! Do hear it. But I believe our tastes in Blues differ. You like best the lighter ones like Michigan Waters and I prefer the moanin' ones like Gulf Coast and Nobody Knows the Way I Feel This Morning. Have you seen one Ozzie McPearson?[3] She does a low-down single that is really good, but I expect she'll cut half the rough stuff when she plays New York and then she won't be so funny. When will your paper on the Blues appear? And is Campaspe in Firecrackers? I hope so.

I believe Vanity Fair is using some of my stuff. They sent me a telegram for some more. Otherwise I haven't heard from them. I'm glad if they liked some of it.

Zora Neale Hurston is a clever girl, isn't she? I would like to know her. Is she still in New York?

What a magnet New York is! Better to be a dish washer there than a very important person in one's own home town seemingly. A young student friend of mine from Mexico has finally arrived there,—to work in a hotel. And yesterday a letter came from Africa, from a boy in Burutu, saying that he intends to stowaway for New York the first chance that offers! And half the Italian boys I knew in Dezenzano[4] swear that in a few years they will all be waiters at the Ritz!

Thanks for telling me what the songs are in They Knew What They Wanted. And for the suggestions toward writing the book.

I sent you one of the new pictures. Out of four poses I am not sure it is the best, but perhaps you will like it. It looks somewhat like me anyhow. But to relieve the seriousness I am enclosing some snapshots taken with the office girls here.

I would like to come up to New York again but can't make it for at least two months yet. My expenditures are always ahead of my income and my monthly check is gone before it comes. But I am going to exercise economy, as I have been so advised, if I can find anything to exercise it on. Being broke is a bore. That's one reason why I like the sea,—the old man always advances money in port and at sea one doesn't need any, but on land one needs money all the time and I don't believe I've ever had enough at any one time to last me more than a day. If it's a quarter it goes, if it's fifty dollars it goes just the same, and the next day . . . one looks for some more.

Today is only the fourth yet my pockets show no signs of having received anything on the first. And June is a long month. All months are.

Write to me soon.

I send pansies and marguerites to you, too,

Sincerely,

Langston

1. *Hughes's first college trial was at Columbia in 1921. He lasted a year. He was alienated from the virtually all-white student body, and his father's unpredictable financial help made the situation even worse. Still, Columbia helped him accomplish his true goal. "I had come to New York to attend Columbia," he wrote later, "but really why I had come was to see Harlem."*
2. *Alain Locke, editor of the groundbreaking 1925 anthology* The New Negro, *encouraged Hughes to consider his own alma mater, Howard University. Hughes had decided he wanted to go to a traditionally black college, to the amazement of a few Harlem literati who considered such schools anachronistic and declassé. Jessie Fauset put it frankly in an October 23, 1925, letter to Hughes: "You'd get just the mere formal 'book-larnin' and no contacts to speak of." She wanted him to apply to Harvard.*
3. *Ozzie McPhearson was popular in the touring revue* Ebony Follies.
4. *Hughes spent August 1924 in Desenzano in northern Italy at the home of a friend, Romeo Luppi, a waiter at the Grand Duc.*

CARL VAN VECHTEN TO LANGSTON HUGHES, BEFORE JUNE 24, 1925

Dear Langston,

I think it has finally been arranged that you are to appear in the September number of Vanity Fair. I have already done a note about you, and I think they are using Muray's photograph of you. Thank you, by the way, for the new photograph. I do not like it as well as Muray's but it is very good. My paper on the Blues, which I think is fairly interesting, will appear in the August number of Vanity Fair.[1] I have quoted extensively from you with such effect that the editor is very enthusiastic about your prose. I have an article about Spirituals in the July number.[2] You are wrong about my preference in Blues. The sadder they are the better for me too. My favourite just now is the Weeping Willow Blues, sung by Bessie Smith. W. C. Handy has presented me with an old Black Swan[3] record of My Man Rocks Me With One Steady Roll, an old whore house song, which goes like this:

My Man rocks me with one steady roll,
There ain't no slippin' when he once takes hol',
I looked at the clock an' the clock struck one,

I said to daddy, ain't we got fun,
While he was rockin' me with one steady roll.

How they got away with it, I don't know. I had a wonderful party here last night. Paul Robeson‡ and Lawrence Brown sang.[4] Cissie Loftus[5] gave her imitation of Bert Williams.[6] I wish you had been here. As for your book, I didn't mean for you to start it today or tomorrow, but I wanted you to think about it, and do it as soon as you can. Don't worry about the personalities. You will find this a problem in any novel, if you ever write novels. Characters tend to resemble people in certain ways and the trick is to make them enough different so that they won't be recognized. Another way of disguising a friend is to change his name, and then have him appear somewhere else in the book under his own name, so that he will not be connected with the character that really represents him. I hope you will do this book; I know that you can, and I feel sure that you will grow enthusiastic over it yourself as soon as you begin to work on it. Yes, Campaspe is very prominent in Firecrackers. I'll send you a copy soon. But you should not read it until you have read my other novels, as characters from all of them appear in it.

It is very hot again. I am in pyjamas, reading proofs.

bien à toi,
Carl Van Vechten

1. *He called it "The Black Blues."*
2. *Titled "Folksongs of the American Negro."*
3. *Black Swan, the first record label owned and operated by blacks, was cofounded by Henry Pace and William C. Handy in 1921.*
4. *The concert pianist Lawrence Brown collaborated with Paul Robeson for thirty-eight years, until Robeson's death.*
5. *The actress Marie Cecilia Loftus had a well-known talent for mimicry.*
6. *A popular minstrel performer, comedian, and actor.*

LANGSTON HUGHES TO CARL VAN VECHTEN, JUNE 24, 1925

1816 Twelfth Street, N.W.
Box 308, Washington, D.C.

June 24, 1925

Dear Friend,

I liked your article on the Spirituals in Vanity Fair and I think I shall enjoy the one on the Blues even more. Have you heard Bessie Smith's newest release: "The Soft Pedal Blues"? It's a wonderful reproduction of the atmosphere of a buffet flat at four in the morning.[1]

I'll be all ready for Firecrackers when it comes out. I liked the Tattooed Countess, but it isn't nearly so different as The Blind Bow-Boy, nor so beautiful. I'm reading Peter Whiffle now. One critic in a college paper says that after the downfall of The Bow-Boy you get up again with the Countess. How do they get that way? But which of your novels do you yourself like best?

Did your ancestors ever happen to live in Catskill County in New York?[2] In the census of 1830 I've discovered a whole family of free Negroes named Van Vechten living there. They must have descended from or once belonged to a white family of that name, so perhaps you have colored relatives.

I've met a couple of interesting fellows about my own age,—one a pianist and the other an artist, and we have been amusing ourselves going downtown to the white theatres "passing" for South Americans, and walking up Fourteenth Street barefooted on warm evenings for the express purpose of shocking the natives. The artist boy has had some of his sketches taken by Harper's Bazaar. They are not at all Negro but very good for one who has had so little training. I'd like to have you meet him. He has some amusing ideas for a Negro ballet and some clever ideas for short stories if he weren't too lazy to write them. Like myself—But I am going to try to do the book because you want me to.

I hope to see you again by August anyway. Perhaps Ricardo[3] will come up then, too.

Sincerely,
Langston Hughes

1. *The buffet flat was a roving Harlem institution "where varied and often perverse sexual pleasures were offered cafeteria-style," according to David Levering Lewis, author of* When Harlem Was in Vogue. *Buffet flat parties were also known for their Southern food.*
2. *There is no Catskill County. Hughes probably meant "Catskill country," which was given its name by one of Van Vechten's ancestors.*
3. *Nickname for Richard Bruce Nugent.*‡

CARL VAN VECHTEN TO LANGSTON HUGHES, JUNE 29, 1925

[Handwritten] Countee Cullen's book comes out early in September, <u>before</u> the anthology.

Dear Langston,

Every time you write you send me the titles of wonderful Blues. I hope you will keep this up, because I want to have the largest collection available. The "Soft Pedal Blues" is very amusing, especially the war whoop. I played it for Paul Robeson last night.

I certainly had relatives in Catskill Country in 1830. My ancestors landed here in New Amsterdam in 1638, and the record distinctly mentions "two Negro servants." Perhaps these are their descendants. Perhaps . . . Anyway if you can trace their present whereabouts it would amuse me.

Your adventures en espagnol entertain me vastly. I hope Ricardo will come with you in August.

Alain Locke‡ was here last week and came to see me. He showed me the contents of his Negro Anthology. The announcement of your contribution was a little disturbing. Of course, you know that you cannot publish in book form anything included in your own book without permission from Mr. Knopf. I think there could be no objection to using the poems in the Survey Graphic, but Locke had a further section labeled "Jazzonia," and I think it would be a decided mistake to publish any of the jazz poems in book form before your book appeared.[1] You see, this anthology will appear a good three months before your book appears; everybody will buy it and if it contains a sufficient number of your best poems it will take the edge off the sale and reviews of your own book. If it were coming out after your book there could be no such objection. Even so, it is the part of wisdom to be sparing in contributions to anthologies. However, this is merely personal advice. Mr. Knopf's opinion in the matter is the final one. He and Mrs. Knopf are now in Europe, but perhaps you have settled on the question with him already?

bien à toi,
Carl Van Vechten

June 29, 1925

1. *Locke's 1925 anthology* The New Negro *contains a music section with two Hughes poems, one of which is "Jazzonia."*

<hr>

LANGSTON HUGHES TO CARL VAN VECHTEN, AUGUST 23, 1925

Sunday

Dear Carl,

Forgive me for not having written you sooner. I had such a good time in New York that it has taken me the entire week to rest up. Now I am engaged in answering my unanswered correspondence, letters from six days to six months old. I'm a very impolite person about writing promptly. And today is such a glorious day that I'm afraid no one will be written to but you.

Because you want me to write my autobiography, I am going to enjoy doing it. Otherwise, I wouldn't. I hope you will like it when it's finished. I think I shall write it in great detail and then perhaps you will help me cut out the uninteresting parts. I am going to get a new job, a new room, and a new typewriter and see what devoting one's life to one's art is like.

I am going to read some of my poems at the Penguin Club, some down-town white place, on Thursday.[1] First time I ever did such a thing but I might like it. I hated to turn down their invitation a second time. And I suppose I'd better begin to learn to read in public anyway.

I enjoyed seeing you in New York.[2] Saturday night after we left you we had supper with Abbie Mitchell‡ at Eddie's. Then Hall Johnson‡ and I went to Leroy's and Small's. Aren't the dancers strange under that blue light at Leroy's? Then on Sunday I spent half the morning making necessary calls, a couple of delightful hours with Walter White,‡—Jane[3] sang for me and Walter talked about his novel and sprinkled his conversation with the first names of famous people whose last names would come to me about thirty seconds later than their first. I'm not used to hearing the great spoken of so intimately,—Carl, and Paul, and Roland, and Conrad, and Haywood, and Ruth.[4] It was fun keeping up with him. In the late afternoon at Hall's studio, Marguerite Avery, like Walker a real African type, sang my "Mother to Son" for me and one Service Bell did an amusing imitation of Jean Starr singing "Everybody Loves My Baby."[5] Hall Johnson has done, I think, a very sympathetic and beautiful setting for my song. Because you know about music, I'd like you to hear it. You might find Hall interesting. He's very tall, very ugly, and has fifty Negro spirituals which have never been heard up North. Bell sang one of them for me: I've been 'buked and I've been scorned, which I thought very good. Hall is working on a setting for my Blues now and I've just written some additional verses. . . . Then came afternoon tea with Jessie Fauset. We talked about your Tattooed Countess. . . . Then the concert at the Stadium where I heard the Fire-Bird music of Stravinsky. . . . After that a little party in a tiny studio built on the roof six stories above Harlem. . . . Then the one o'clock train for Washington.

Death in Venice is terribly well done. A friend of mine has just loaned me your Red to read.[6] It's not dull. . . . I suppose you've heard Chicago Bound Blues[7]. . . . That was delicious soup you had for dinner that night. I hope your maid comes back.

Vanity Fair is having an unprecedented sale in the colored colony here in the last few months. Colored shop keepers who had never heard of the magazine a short while ago are displaying it now and I've already autographed no less than six copies on the page containing my poems. I like that cover this month, and that drawing of the Pagagaly.[8]

Remember me to your wife. I hope she is no longer ill.

Sincerely yours,

Langston

1816 Twelfth Street

Box 308

Washington, D.C.

1. *This was Hughes's first reading for a white audience.*
2. *Hughes went to New York for the* Crisis *awards ceremony on August 14. He won two awards: a third place in Poetry and a second place in Essays for his "The Fascination of Cities." After the ceremony, he had dinner at Van Vechten's. Ricardo, or Richard Bruce Nugent, joined them later. Afterward, Hughes and Nugent left to explore the Harlem night spots described by Hughes above.*
3. *Jane White, daughter of Walter and his wife, Gladys.*
4. *Hughes refers to Paul Robeson, probably the singer Roland Hayes, the journalist Heywood Broun, and his wife, the writer Ruth Hale. Carl is, of course, Van Vechten, and Conrad remains unidentified.*
5. *Hughes compares the singer Marguerite Avery to A'Lelia Walker.‡ Service Bell was a little-known actor and Jean Starr, a well-known jazz composer and musician.*
6. *Red is a 1925 collection of reprints of Van Vechten's writings about music.*
7. *Recorded by Bessie Smith in 1923.*
8. *A world-famous cabaret in Budapest.*

LANGSTON HUGHES TO CARL VAN VECHTEN, SEPTEMBER 7, 1925

Sunday

Dear Carl,

That's glad news about my book going to press. I didn't know it would go so soon. I didn't tell you either that I had decided to take out that bloody Sunset poem that you never liked, but it can be taken out in the proof and the order of one or two things changed in that section, no? Boy, I'm anxious to see the proofs of my own first book!

I intended to mention Aaron Douglas‡ to you in my last letter. I'm glad you've met him. His work is certainly more unusual than that of any other colored artist I know. I hope he becomes known.

Thanks for the Jezebel Pettyfer.¹ I shall carry it around under my arm for the next six days. It's more than good.

This has been some week-end for me. It started with a polite party that bored me to incivility. I left. Then on Saturday night the police came and took away the most likeable room-mate I've had since I've been working at a summer hotel and it seems that when he left half the earthly belongings of the guests in residence there left with him. But he wore their clothes beautifully. When I build my jail I'm going to put all the good people in and leave the bad ones out. Surely then the world would be amusing. And tonight a man died in front of me at the theatre. Heart failure, caused doubtless by having to hear, for the ten thousandth time, "Everybody Loves My Baby." He died during a rendition of that song. I don't blame him.

Tomorrow I am going to move. My new address will be my old one again: 1749 S Street, N.W. Write me there.[2]

I got along fine with my Penguin Club reading. At least, the people said I did. I met a former cabinet minister and a friend of Sara Teasdale's[3] and a few other important humans. There was quite a crowd and if I had not been the center of attraction I would have been amused. But if doing it over again will bring me to New York, all right. Let's go.

The Vanity Fair people haven't sent me any check yet. Are they supposed to? And I wonder if they would send me a couple of copies of the September number. I want to send one or two to Europe and am too broke to buy them. (I just bought this typewriter.) . . . And I got a card from a Frenchman in France who says he likes my poetry.

I've just sent Hall a lot of extra verses for my Blues that I made up. Some of them are:

> Arms in the wash-tub,
> Feet in rusty shoes.
> Arms in the wash-tub,
> Feet in rusty shoes.
> I'm a wash-board baby
> Rubbin' my wash-tub blues.
>
> Want a buy me a rose bud
> And plant it at my back door.
> Buy me a rose bud
> And plant it at my back door,
> So's when I'm dead
> Won't need no flowers from de store.
>
> Goin' up in a tower
> Tall as a tree is tall.
> Goin' up in a tower
> Tall as a tree is tall.
> Gonna think about my man
> And let my fool-self fall.

Not wonderful but blues-like enough.

What is Excavations about?[4] Is
Covarrubias back? When are you
going abroad? I wish you weren't
going. When are you coming
back? You might meet Bruce,
though, and they say the Grand
Duc is booming again. All the
theatre and cabaret people go
there in the late hours of the
early morning. And you can see
them perform to better advantage
than you can in their own working places. And if you see Bruce
buy him a drink of Jamaican rum
and ask him if he remembers
Jimmy (that's me) and if he
chooses to talk to you he will, and
if he don't he won't.

"A PREDICTION": CARL VAN VECHTEN,
BY MIGUEL COVARRUBIAS, 1926

C'est tout.

> Sincerely,
> Langston

1. *Haldane MacFall's* The Wooings of Jezebel Pettyfer *was published by Alfred A. Knopf
   in 1925. It describes turn-of-the-century black life in Barbados.*
2. *Hughes had taken a room at the YMCA temporarily, but shrinking finances forced him to
   move in with his mother.*
3. *An American poet.*
4. *Published by Knopf in 1926,* Excavations *is a book of essays about musical and literary
   personages.*

Friday

Dear Carl,

I have been trying to write you for the last two weeks. I have a new job
now working in a hotel.[1] The hours are longer but I have the whole afternoon off. Almost every day some one comes in, tho, so I get nothing done.
I wished I lived in an apartment like you with a hall boy so I could get a
telephone down: Nobody home. . . . When one gets real famous one must
have to be bored with a lot of uninteresting people,—no?

A few days ago I sent you some new Blues. I want to dedicate the best one to you, if any of them are ever published, — and if you like it. I think the Po' Boy Blues is the best and if you know anyone who would like to do music for one or two of them, please hand them over to them. I've got any number of verses, but haven't been able to put anything together that I think The Mercury would like. I wish I could. I don't think they'd want just a plain song like I sent you, do you?

Jessie Fauset was down here for a week-end a short time ago. She is enthusiastic about your book on cats.[2] Says it's the best thing of yours she has read. Everybody here likes your article on the Negro theatre in Vanity Fair, too.[3] Locke wishes he could have it for his book. I like your suggestions for improving the revues, especially the one about the choruses: why they don't use black choruses for a colored show, I don't know. They can usually sing better and certainly work harder than the yellow girls. A cabaret scene would be a scream, too, if they'd do it right. Irvin Miller[4] did have one in one of his shows once. Did you see it, where a black man kept following a high yellow girl around the cabaret floor until his shoes wore out?

The autobiography is coming. I believe it is going to be interesting. I want to have it ready by the first of the year. What's the news about my other book, do you know? And your Negro novel? . . . Are you still thinking of going abroad? . . . How did Hotsy-Totsy go in Paris?[5]

Would Knopf object to my reading The Weary Blues over the radio? There's a bare chance of my getting an engagement at a rate that would be more than a month's salary at the hotel. The man has asked to see my poetry and is thinking of arranging a Blues accompaniment for The Weary Blues, so I have been told.

Your article with my poetry in Vanity Fair has brought me a number of letters from the various places where I used to live. And there was quite a piece in the Lincoln, Ill. paper about me, followed later by a letter from one of my former teachers telling about how well she remembered me and what a bright boy I was in her classes. You'd think I was famous already! Lots of people seemed to like the Fantasy in Purple.

Did I tell you in my last letter that Hall Johnson had done the music for a new show that they hope to put on Broadway? I believe it is ready for rehearsals now.

Today is pay-day so I must go back to work early before the money runs out. Last time I left half my pay in my locker and somebody stole it. This time I shall not be so stupid. I shall buy some new Blues records and pay my rent. . . . The place I work is quite classy. There are European waiters and it caters largely to ambassadors and base-ball players and ladies who wear many diamonds. It is amusing the way they handle food.

A piece of cheese that everybody else carries around in his hands in the kitchen needs two silver platters and six forks when it is served in the dining room.

Write to me soon.

This time purple asters and autumn leaves,

Sincerely,

Langston

1749 S Street
North West

1. *Hughes got a busboy job at the elite Wardman Park Hotel in northwest Washington.*
2. The Tiger in the House *was published in 1920.*
3. *"Prescription for the Negro Theatre" was published in the October 1925 issue of* Vanity Fair.
4. *Irvin Miller was a producer, playwright, and comedian.*
5. *A 1925 production by Irving Mills.*

CARL VAN VECHTEN TO LANGSTON HUGHES, OCTOBER 13, 1925

Dear Langston,

Of course, I loved the Blues you sent me and particularly the "Po' Boy Blues." I shall be happy and honored to have it dedicated to me.

Covarrubias is just back from Mexico and I have seen the pencil sketch for your jacket. I should think you would love it. Everybody who has seen it does. He will have the finished design in color soon. You ought to have your proofs by now. I have already read proofs on the preface.

The Book of American Negro Spirituals[1] is making a sensation, not only in the press — the World,[2] for instance, awarded the volume an editorial — but also by way of sales. I think they are by far the best arrangements that have yet been made, and you should hear Taylor Gordon[‡] sing them with Rosamond Johnson[‡]! But you will. I've seldom heard anything I like better than their rendering of Done foun' my lost sheep and Roll de ole chariot along.

It's great news that the autobiography is coming along so splendidly. Do finish it up by January, if you can. Of course, you can read over the radio or anywhere else you live. That sort of thing will help the book enormously.

Hotsty-Totsy, I understand, is a success in Paris, under a new name. I have almost decided not to go away. It is too comfortable here. Besides, I think I shall start my Negro novel next week. Have you read The Sailor's Return?[3]

chrysanthemums and moss-roses to you!

Carl Van Vechten

October 13, 1925

Are you a bell-boy now?!!

1. *A songbook compiled and arranged by James Weldon Johnson and his brother Rosamond in 1925.*
2. *The* New York World *was a popular daily in the 1920s.*
3. *David Garnett's 1925 novel about an interracial marriage was published by Knopf.*

LANGSTON HUGHES TO CARL VAN VECHTEN, OCTOBER 29, 1925

Dear Carl,

I've been hoping my proofs would come but they aren't here yet. . . . What do you think of Countee's book?[1] I haven't found it in Washington. . . . Out at the hotel the other day I saw a very smart-looking lady reading your Firecrackers. . . . No, I'm not a bell-boy. I'm a buss-boy, less picturesque, but more nourishing, it happens. I want to save some money to go to college but haven't so far. Who could on fifty-five a month? . . . I'm trying to persuade somebody to lend me three hundred a year for the next three years, said amount to be returned to the lender within the same length of time after my graduation. That would put me through Lincoln, which is where I want to go. I've written James Weldon Johnson‡ of the Garland Fund[2] about it. . . . Do you happen to know some philanthropic soul who might like to take a sporting chance on the development of genius and advance me said loan? . . . How's this for the title of my new book when it's finished:

SCARLET FLOWERS: The Autobiography of a Young Negro Poet because my life, the years like the petals of a bright flower, has been scattered a hundred places by the wind. . . . Clara Smith is singing in Pittsburgh this week. I hope she comes here. . . . If you find Gibson's Revue at the Lincoln in Harlem go see it.[3] They have a little kid of four or five who is a remarkable dancer. And a man who sings the Blues, but not especially good. . . . I hope the Negro novel has been started.

Sincerely,

Langston

1749 S St., N.W.

Washington, D.C.

October 29, 1925

1. *Cullen's 1925 collection,* Color, *included a poem dedicated to Van Vechten, "To John Keats, Poet. At Spring Time."*
2. *Founded in 1922 with Charles Garland's million-dollar inheritance, the Garland Fund was headed by James Weldon Johnson, along with several white liberals and radicals.*
3. *The entrepreneur John T. Gibson owned a movie house in Philadelphia where shows before and after films featured performers like Ethel Waters and Bessie Smith.*

CARL VAN VECHTEN TO LANGSTON HUGHES, AFTER OCTOBER 29, 1925

Dear Langston,

Unfortunately I don't know anybody at present I could ask for what you desire . . . but don't worry about it—if you really want to go to Lincoln, a way will provide itself: somehow they always do, when the desire is behind them.[1]

Scarlet Flowers is a splendid title and I am anxious for you to finish the book. There may be money in <u>that</u> for you. I have written four chapters of my novel and the rest of it is sketched out. It may be good or bad, but it will be different; of that I am sure. Would you mind telling me at what hotel you are employed. There is a chance I may visit Washington when I have finished my first draft. The concert described in the enclosed program will be thrilling. But you will hear them later.

Turkeys and Cranberries to you!

Carl Van Vechten

Sunday

1. *The white philanthropist Amy Spingarn came to Hughes's rescue and lent him the $300 he needed to go to Lincoln in the spring of 1926. Amy was married to Joel Spingarn, a lifetime champion of black rights and an NAACP executive since 1911. Joel established the Spingarn Medal in 1914 to honor the achievements of African Americans. Joel's brother Arthur was also an activist for black rights and would become Hughes's lawyer.*

CARL VAN VECHTEN TO LANGSTON HUGHES, BEFORE DECEMBER 1, 1925

Dear Langston,

Hurray! I'm glad you can come Tuesday night. It will be a late party so please don't make any other engagements. I am getting together people who will help your book and want to meet you. Taylor Gordon and Rosamond Johnson are coming to sing and the Knopfs and Covarrubias will be here, among others, but several of these will not appear until late. I expect you at six, but telephone me when you arrive in town.

with my best wishes,

Carl Van Vechten

I have heard Bessie Smith, Ethel Waters,‡ and Roland Hayes‡ within the last thirty-six hours and now I am immersed in The New Negro.

Saturday

LANGSTON HUGHES TO CARL VAN VECHTEN, DECEMBER 8, 1925

Dear Carl,

Your party was like a dream,¹—not come true but still a dream. I never in life thought I would meet Marie Doro. She's one of the ladies I used to dream about in the days when it would take me more than two weeks to save fifteen pennies to buy a copy of the Green Book. You remember that old theatrical magazine with pictures of Maude Adams and Billie Burke and Anna Held in it, and Gertrude Brooke Hamilton stories about the Great White Way? Well, Marie Doro's name was a flash-back to those days when I would go down to the railroad station in Kansas and touch the side of Pullman cars that had come through from Chicago and say to myself Chicago isn't so far from New York. And a person who had really been to New York was more wonderful to me than angels. When Ruth St. Dennis,² the first real artist I ever saw, came to town to dance I had been about a month saving the fifty cents to go. But then I had a whole

HUGHES AS A BUSBOY AT THE
WARDMAN PARK HOTEL,
WASHINGTON, D.C., NOVEMBER 1925

row to myself. They had reserved the last row for colored folks and no other one but me went!

But back to your party . . . I enjoyed it immensely. Not even my first night ashore in my first foreign port was any more happy. So you understand how much I liked it.

Vachell Lindsay was again at the hotel when I came back. And again he did a very charming thing. When he went away (he must be a very shy person) he didn't say anything but he left at the desk for me a set of Amy Lowell's John Keats with a beautiful letter of advice from one poet to another written on the six fly leaves of the first volume. How shall I thank him for a gift given in such a quiet way?[3] . . . And this afternoon Locke gave me a copy of The New Negro. So I've been lucky about books lately.

Underwood and Underwood took my bus boy picture.[4] They were upstairs taking congressmen and then came downstairs and took me! The Star[5] people say the prints look nice but I haven't seen them yet. There's to be a story in the Sunday Star. And a story in the hotel magazine too if I don't quit too soon. . . . But I think I'll have to quit to write my autobiography,—and if I do I'll starve, so Scarlet Flowers'll probably be my parting gift to the world. But before I pass out I do want to hear somebody sing my Blues.

The lady cashier at my hotel has read all your novels.

Pine needles and snow to you,

Langston

Monday

1. *Van Vechten had a party on December 1 in Hughes's honor. Festivities went on until 5 a.m. the next morning. Among the guests was Marie Doro, the first American performer to give a command performance at Windsor Castle. Miguel Covarrubias, Taylor Gordon, Nora Holt,‡ Rosamond Johnson, and Alfred and Blanche Knopf were also in attendance.*

2. *Ruth St. Denis (1877–1968), cofounder, with Ted Shawn, of Denishawn School of Dancing and Related Arts.*

3. *Hughes first encountered Vachel Lindsay when he came to the Wardman to give a reading at the hotel at the end of November. Hughes managed to slip a few of his poems on Lindsay's table and was amazed to find out that Lindsay read them to his audience that evening. Here, Hughes refers to Lindsay's second visit in early December. Some of Lindsay's advice to Hughes was: "Do not let any lionizers stampede you. Hide and write and study and think." Hughes wrote back: "I will not become conceited. If anything is important, it is my poetry not me . . . I want to keep it for the beautiful thing it is."*

4. *A prominent photographic news agency.*

5. *The* Washington Star.

CARL VAN VECHTEN TO LANGSTON HUGHES, AFTER DECEMBER 8, 1925

Dear Langston,

You gave me permission to do what I liked with your beautiful Blues and I am doing so, but I forgot to warn you to hold off while I am sending them about. You see I am trying a magazine or two first (the music can easily come later). If, by any chance, therefore, you have sent any of them to magazines will you telegraph me at once, as at present they are in the hands of a prominent editor, and, after all, we can't sell them twice.

Soft pedal, too, a little on publicity at present, as it will do little or any good before the book comes out. You see people will forget it and the newspapers won't repeat it at the proper hour. Send everything you have in mind in the way of publicity to the Knopfs and let them spring it on the waiting public at the proper time and it will make twice the effect. I am hoping great things for your book (did I tell you that the binding is the same design as that on Covarrubias' book, but different colors?).

I'm glad you enjoyed the party; I did too, and that is unusual at my own house, where parties are a responsibility. This one wasn't a responsibility: it was a joy.

I had no idea, by the way, that you enjoyed being showered with books: you move so frequently, I thought you mind find them a bother. I really believed that I was encumbering you with too many. Now that I know that you like them, however, I shall presently send you at least one more.

Don't worry over Scarlet Flowers; just do it easily: two lines a day make a book a year or something of that sort. Only Mrs. Knopf is most anxious to see it and indubitably now is the psychological moment when everything chic is Negro. I'm very unsettled about Nigger Heaven. I get too emotional when writing it and what one needs in writing is a calm, cold eye. Perhaps future revisions may be made in that spirit. If not, I am become a Harold Bell Wright.[1]

snowdrops and edelweiss to you!

Carlo V. V.

Friday

*Did I tell you that I have done a paper in between times, called Three Blues Singers? They are Bessie Smith

Clara "

Ethel Waters

I shall send it to Vanity Fair.[2]

1. *An author of popular but syrupy novels.*
2. *"Negro 'Blues' Singers" was published in the March 1926 issue of* Vanity Fair.

Dear Langston,

You should have heard from me before this, but I was suddenly called to Iowa by the death of my father and have been there a week.[1] When I returned I found a letter from Vanity Fair advising me that they would publish a couple of your Blues. There is a possibility that they may be illustrated by Aaron Douglas. I'll ask them to send you a cheque as soon as possible. Did you receive your other cheque from Vanity Fair? I also found the first copies of your book here, and there was a column about you in the New York World last Sunday with a picture. Did you see that? January 23 is now your publication date. Miss Sergeant,[2] by the way, informed me that she liked you enormously. I'm glad it's more or less settled about your going to Lin-

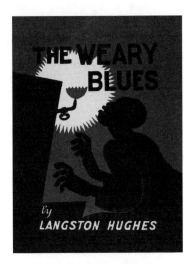

COVER ILLUSTRATION FOR
THE WEARY BLUES, BY MIGUEL
COVARRUBIAS, 1925

coln. I am so far behind in my work—Nigger Heaven is supposed to be finished by March—that for the next few weeks I shall do little but write.

sincerely,

Carl Van Vechten

January 12, 1926

1. *Charles Duane Van Vechten was an early critic of the title of his son's Negro novel: "Your 'Nigger Heaven' is a title I don't like. . . . If you are trying to help the race, as I am assured you are, I think every word you write should be a respectful one towards the black," he wrote in a letter to Carl. The elder Van Vechten died before they could resolve this difference.*
2. *A Knopf employee.*

Dear Carl,

I have been in Baltimore reading at the high school and to the Du Bois Circle and talking up the book. I went back stage to meet Bessie Smith who is playing there and says she has got herself a tent and is going back down in Bam this summer and make a few more thousands. She remembered you and your wife but didn't seem at all concerned as to whether articles were written about her or not. And her only comment on the art of the Blues was that they had put her "in de money."

I have an offer to read in Cleveland next month and also here on the twelfth and at the Civic Club in New York on the 28th. Did I tell you? I made my rent in Baltimore but today I went back to the hotel for a while. I'm tired of being broke and besides my book is going to be sold in the lobby and I need to be on display. However it won't be long.

Thanks for the delightful letter from Dorothy Harvey.[1] . . . and the Herald-Tribune clipping. I hadn't seen it. In order to get my reviews I had better subscribe to a clipping bureau, had I not? Could you recommend one? . . . Locke has done a very nice review for PALMS and Countee for OPPORTUNITY.[2]

I'm glad you're doing the note for the Vanity Fair Blues and I hope they will be illustrated. It will be safe to say that I'm attending Lincoln University.[3] Location: somewhere in the backwoods of Pa. 40 miles from Philly and 60 miles from Baltimore on the Octoraro branch of the Pa. railroad. The station is called Lincoln University, Pa., and there is nothing there but the school so I shall have plenty of country. It's reached only by milk trains — the kind that stop at every house — and one walks a mile up a rocky road from the station. You see, I'm going into seclusion, weary of the world, like Pearl White[4] when she retired to her convent. And I hope nobody there reads poetry. My own poems are about to bore me to death, I've heard them so much in the mouths of others recently. I didn't think free verse was quite so easy to remember. But every young lady I meet seems to know "The calm cool face of the river asked me for a kiss" or else their souls have "grown deep like the rivers."[5] And an appalling number of young gentlemen are sending me jazz poems to be criticized. Have I started a new school or something? Great guns! And the Phyllis Wheatley Readers for Southern schools have asked me to send them something suitable for the children in the grades. If I ever get in the school books then I know I'm ruined.

I like my book immensely and the Knopfs have been lovely in following out all my suggestions about review copies, book shops, etc. . . . Please let me autograph a copy for you when I get in town. And I hope someday the Blues become a book because they are yours. Unless the autobiography gets done and it hasn't gone far. There's been so darn much else to do. And I really want to write it now.

I hope I'll see you. I'll let you know soon just what day I'll be in town. It will perhaps be the 30th. And then I may stay over until Tuesday following. Don't bother about coming to my reading.[6] Readings always bore me sick, just like church, and I am forever amazed at the people who go to them. We had a Blues interlude here that did liven up things a bit and the audience seemed to like my things.[7] But I gave them a short dollar's worth so there was no time to get tired. I asked Block[8] if he wanted a piano-playing Blues boy between halves in New York but he hasn't said anything yet. The music gives a bit of atmosphere for my jazz poems. And gives me a rest. I get tired of talking.

Covarrubias wrote me a nice letter in Spanish the other day. . . . I am going to try the Dial[9] with "A House in Taos," my new inunderstandable poem that Miss Sergeant liked so well.

Please meet Raquel Meller when she comes over.[10]

May your Nigger Heaven wrap you in new clouds of glory. . . . Amen!

Langston Hughes

January 20, 1926

1. *An American writer, formerly Dorothy Dudley. She was one of a trio of sisters Van Vechten had known during his college years in Chicago.*
2. Palms *was a modernist poetry journal whose editor, Idella Purnell, was interested in black writing.* Opportunity: A Journal of Negro Life *was an official publication of the National Urban League and one of the most influential journals of the Harlem Renaissance.*
3. *Hughes shelved his original plans to go to Howard because the school couldn't provide him with any scholarship money.*
4. *A prominent motion-picture actress in the teens.*
5. *These are lines from two of Hughes's best-known poems, "Suicide Note" and "The Negro Speaks of Rivers," respectively.*
6. *Hughes gave a reading on January 31 at the Shipwreck Inn in New York near Columbia University. Two hundred people packed the house, but Van Vechten was not among them.*
7. *Hughes included a blues musician at his January 15 reading at the Playhouse in northwest Washington.*
8. *Harry Block was a senior editor at Knopf and a frequent companion of Van Vechten and his wife, Fania Marinoff.*
9. *From 1920 to 1929* The Dial *was a leader among avant-garde magazines.*
10. *A Spanish vaudeville and cinema star.*

T he Weary Blues *appeared in bookstores in the middle of January of 1926. The book went into a second printing after four months, having sold 1,200 copies. Positive reviews appeared in the* New York Times, The New Republic, *and the* New York Herald-Tribune. *Hughes was surprised by the favorable reaction from Southern white newspapers. He probably wasn't surprised by Countee Cullen's review in* Opportunity, *which criticized Hughes for putting "too much emphasis on strictly Negro themes."*

Dear Langston,

Guy Johnson of the University of North Carolina (co-author of The Negro and His Songs, with Odum[1]) has been here and yesterday he spent the whole day with me, while Rosamond Johnson took down folk Blues. Some of them are delightfully filthy. I like:

> Got a rainbow on ma head,
> So it ain't gwine to rain . . .

I gave him five of your Blues to take back to Paul Green,[2] the editor of the Reviewer. I thought it would amuse you to have them appear in a white Southern magazine.

Also I gave Rosamond The Midwinter Blues and Lament over Love, to see if he could set them. If anyone else has them, flag me off.

I hope you will like what I have written about you for Vanity Fair . . . Do you go to Lincoln next week?

Taylor Gordon gave a theatre party at the Lafayette Friday at midnight.[3] I must say the show was wonderful. Some of the dirtiest lines I've heard around those parts.

tulips and hyacinths to you!
Carlo Van Vechten

February 7, 1926

The second draft of Nigger Heaven finished Friday. I start the third in a couple of days.

1. *Guy Johnson and Howard Odum published* The Negro and His Songs *in 1926.*
2. *A white American Pulitzer Prize–winning playwright.*
3. *The Lafayette put on late-night raunchy musical shows. Giving a "theatre party" meant buying out a whole box for friends.*

February 21, 1926

Lincoln University, Pa.

Dear Carl,

Because I wanted to have time to sit down and write you a decent letter, I haven't written you at all. When I came back from New York I got in just in time to make a dinner engagement and from then on it was something every day and every night until I left.[1] Negro History Week, with the demand for several readings, the public dinner at the "Y" in honor of Locke's book and mine, the before leaving parties given by people who wouldn't have looked at me before the red, yellow, and black cover of <u>The Weary Blues</u> hit them in the eye, teas and telephones, and letters! Golly, I'm glad to get away from Washington.

I read last Saturday night in Baltimore for Calverton and "The Modern Quarterly" group.[2] Had quite a nice time, stayed with them Sunday night, and came on over here. They want to use some Blues, too.

I had a letter from Handy a couple of weeks ago about doing music for them. I have said nothing yet. We can talk it over this week-end when I come up. I think I'm reading for the Civic Club next Sunday.

Hall Johnson tried music for the Midwinter Blues. It's the only one anyone has attempted. So Lament Over Love that you gave Rosamond, or any of the others, are free. . . . I hear the Reviewer is no longer being published, but if it is, I'm glad you've given them five of my Blues. I hope that leaves some for a try at Poetry.

I like the school out here immensely. We're a community in ourselves. Rolling hills and trees and plenty of room. Life is crude, the dorms like barns but comfortable, food plain and solid, first bell at six-thirty, and nobody dresses up,—except Sunday. Other days old clothes and boots. The fellows are mostly strong young chaps from the South. They'll never be "intellectuals,"—probably happier for not being,—but they have a good time. There are some exceptions, though. Several boys from Northern prep schools, two or three who have been in Europe, one who danced at the Club Alabam'.[3] And then there are the ones who are going to be preachers. They're having revival now. But nothing exciting, no shouting. No spirituals. You might find it amusing down here, tho, if you come. I room with the campus bootlegger. The first night I was here there was an all night party for a departing senior. So ribald did it become that the faculty heard about it and sent five Juniors "out into the world." And are trying to find out who else was there. There is perhaps more freedom than at any other Negro school. The students do just about as they choose.[4]

I think I'll be in New York Friday. Of course, I want to come see you some time during the week-end, if you'll let me.[5] Miss Sergeant said something about my meeting Mabel Dodge‡, too, and also this trip I am supposed to meet A'Lelia Walker. Last time she sent two books for me to autograph for her, but I didn't get to see her.

Miguel and Block and Walter made it very pleasant for me last trip, and I enjoyed the dinner and evening with you immensely.[6]

Did Meta[7] get her book? I sent it.

I'm anxious to see "Lula Belle."[8] Some of my poems were in the Herald Tribune last Sunday, I heard, but I didn't see it out here. However a check came so they must a been there.

Sincerely,
Langston

1. *He left Washington for college life at Lincoln.*
2. *Calverton was a pseudonym for George Goetz, who cofounded a radical review,* Modern Quarterly, *with his wife, Helen Goetz.*
3. *A Los Angeles club featuring black entertainment.*
4. *Hughes loved Lincoln, an all-male university. He even pledged a fraternity, Omega Psi Phi. He was well regarded by teachers and students alike, although some of his peers teased him good-naturedly about his celebrity status. In his senior year, Hughes was voted "Most Popular" by the student body.*
5. *Van Vechten had Hughes to his home on February 27, the night before his Civic Club reading. Van Vechten's diary from that day's entry reads: "Dinner alone with Marinoff. Then Langston Hughes comes in & talks till one o'clock."*
6. *Hughes is probably referring to a party Van Vechten had on February 18, which Miguel Covarrubias, Harry Block, and Walter White attended.*
7. *Meda Fry was the Van Vechtens' housekeeper.*
8. *1926 play about a Harlem prostitute by the white playwrights Charles MacArthur and Edward Sheldon.*

LANGSTON HUGHES TO CARL VAN VECHTEN, MARCH 26, 1926

Dear Carl,

Yesterday brought a nice telegram from Lenore Ulric[1] thanking me for The Weary Blues I sent her. This morning one of my classmates committed suicide, or tried to, with a razor. He isn't dead yet. "Negroes are 'posed to cut <u>one another</u> with razors, but when they start to cuttin' themselves, they're gettin' too much like 'fay[2] folks," is the most expressive comment of the student body on the case. I'm hoping the poor boy dies if he wants to, but naturally, they had to tie his neck up and try to save him.

Handy sent me what I believe to be a good contract for setting music to my Blues. I'll let you read it when I come up. . . . Hall Johnson's singers came off well at their recital, he tells me. He said you were there.

Some copies of the second printing of my book came to me this week. . . . I read in the Times where Vachel Lindsay was giving a talk on it Tuesday in New York. Also see where it was put out of the library in Jacksonville, Fla. . . . <u>The Times</u> review last Sunday was interesting. I can't see, though, why they chose "Poëme d'Automne" to illustrate my troubadour-like qualities.

In Trenton, where I read for the colored Teacher's Association a couple of weeks ago I called them "intellectuals" in saying that they might not "get" my cabaret poems, but that night they retaliated by giving a Charleston party to show me how wild they could be. . . . Are you still in New York? I think I'll be in town Thursday for the Easter week-end. I'm due to read at Martin's Book Shop on Friday. Will there be any chance of meeting Rebecca West?[3] I'd like to. I think I'll be staying at Hall Johnson's, but I'll give you a ring soon as I get in.[4] I'm broke but hope to get a ride up on the mushroom trucks that go to market nightly, or else borrow from the school. They are good about lending money out here. Lincoln is more like what home ought to be than any place I've ever seen.

I hope "Nigger Heaven"'s successfully finished. It is, isn't it?

Tulipánes à tu,

Langston

March 26, 1926

Lincoln University, Pa.

1. *The white American actress who played the lead in* Lulu Belle *in blackface.*
2. *Abbreviation for "ofay," or white. Pig latin for "foe," "ofay" is a term sometimes used by blacks to refer to whites.*
3. *English author.*
4. *Van Vechten had a party on April 2. Hughes attended, as did James Weldon Johnson and his wife, Grace Nail; Donald Angus;‡ Marguerite D'Alvarez; and Blanche Knopf, among others. Van Vechten wrote in his diary about the evening: "Langston stayed till 4. I sent him home & went to bed. A wild night."*

Van Vechten was consumed by **Nigger Heaven** *from the late fall of 1925 until he completed a final draft of the novel in February of 1926. His diaries reveal that he took the advice he offered Hughes, writing steadily every day—sometimes for as much as twelve hours—until he went out in the evening. From the start, Van Vechten was wary about the effect his title might have on the public. Several of his confidants shared his concerns. Both James Weldon Johnson and Langston Hughes encouraged Van Vechten to consider alternatives. He had two passionate discussions about the title with Countee Cullen, who "turned white with hurt," Van Vechten wrote in a November 27, 1925, diary entry. Other black friends liked the title. Walter White told him at the beginning of December: "My only regret . . . is that I didn't think of it first so that I could use it." Still, so many reservations from people he trusted worried Van Vechten. He wrote a letter to Alfred Knopf asking him to advertise the book long in advance "so that the kind of life I am writing about will not come as an actual shock." The publisher's announcements assured readers that Van Vechten's approach to his subject would be "direct and serious."*

ADVERTISEMENT FOR *NIGGER HEAVEN*   ADVERTISEMENT WITH
WITH ILLUSTRATION BY MIGUEL   ILLUSTRATION BY AARON DOUGLAS
COVARRUBIAS

CARL VAN VECHTEN TO LANGSTON HUGHES, NOVEMBER 5, 1926
(POSTCARD)

Dear Langston,

Thanks for the copy of the poem—and thanks for The Oracle.¹ Your poems for "Nigger Heaven" have gone to the printer.² As I assured you before, you are at liberty to use these poems in the future in any way you like. You know how grateful I am to you. Everything is settled, & I am very <u>tired</u>. Call me up when you come to town.

Big crowns to you!

Carlo.

<u>Friday</u>, November 5, 1926

1. The Oracle *was the newsletter of Omega Psi Phi, Hughes's fraternity.*
2. *When* Nigger Heaven *hit bookstores in August, it included lyrics from a popular song, "Shake That Thing." Unfortunately, Van Vechten had neglected to get permission to use the lyrics. Panicked by the threat of a lawsuit and possible cessation of the book's distribution, Van Vechten phoned Hughes at Lincoln for help on October 30. Hughes arrived at Van Vechten's house that evening. In one grueling session, he supplied the book with new verses to replace the borrowed ones. These original lyrics went into* Nigger Heaven's *seventh printing. Van Vechten paid Hughes $100 for his work.*

On the train to Columbus

Dear Carl,

Hunter Stagg's party was delightful.[1] He said you wouldn't really call it a party in Richmond but whatever it was, we had a good time,—and just as at "150"[2] the cocktail shaker was never empty. There were eight of us there,—a girl and her brother, four young men, and Hunter and myself. Hunter made a new kind of cocktail of which no one knew the name, so it was christened then and there as the "Hard Daddy" after one of my Blues. The recipe is: to a glass of whiskey add one-half glass of lemon juice and a half glass of maple syrup + ice and shake. It comes out with a sardonic taste like the Blues, and before the evening was over everybody felt like whooping,—and some did! "Hard Daddy Cocktails" have a great effect. If you haven't tried them, do so soon. . . . Everybody was very friendly and we got along famously. I had to read all the poems I had with me,—some of them twice. About midnight Hunter went for more lemon juice and ice and a young man drove home for his Ethel and Clara records and brought back one of Paul Robeson's, too. The girl present had never heard Paul but she went wild over him. Nobody wanted to

FRONT ENTRANCE TO THE VAN VECHTEN
HOME AT 150 WEST FIFTY-FIFTH STREET,
1931

leave but about one o'clock I had to go. I was driven back to Union University in someone's car and the host and several others came along. Everyone still felt like shouting Yee-hoo! when we got there but we thought it wouldn't be wise at that hour of the early morning on the campus of a Christian Baptist Institution.

Like Paul in "The Blind Bow-Boy," Hunter is a beautiful and entertaining person who ought to draw a salary for just being alive. But I don't believe he asked a single Southerner to his party, — not a soul refused to shake hands with me and we all had too good a time! And nobody choked in the traditional Southern manner when the anchovies and crackers went round because they were eating with a Negro. And after three "Hard Daddys" all the glasses got mixed up. Magnolias to you,

Langston

1. *A close friend of Van Vechten's, Hunter Stagg was the literary editor of the Richmond Times-Dispatch. He also served as editor of the Southern literary journal* The Reviewer *with Emily Clark from 1921 to 1924. Hughes had ventured South for the first time to give a reading at Virginia Union, another historically black institution.*

2. *150 West Fifty-fifth Street, Van Vechten's residence and the scene of many memorable evenings.*

1927–1930

S*ince the early years of the Harlem Renaissance, Hughes had become the de facto leader of a clique of young writers who prided themselves on their iconoclasm. Zora Neale Hurston dubbed them the "Niggerati," but they would be known more formally as the "new school" of Harlem Renaissance writers. This submovement's manifesto was Hughes's 1926 essay, "The Negro Artist and the Racial Mountain," published in the June 23 issue of The Nation. "We younger Negro artists who create now intend to express our individual dark-skinned selves without fear or shame," Hughes proclaimed. For his part, Hughes's contributions to this*

COVER ILLUSTRATION OF *FIRE!!*
BY AARON DOUGLAS, NOVEMBER 1926

esprit de corps included poems in the 1926 periodical Fire!! *and his second collection of verse, 1927's* Fine Clothes to the Jew, *sometimes referred to as "F.C.T.T.J." in this correspondence.*

Fire!! *appeared in November of 1926 and featured poetry by Hughes, fiction by Wallace Thurman, a play by Zora Neale Hurston, and drawings by Aaron Douglas and Richard Bruce Nugent. Van Vechten donated money, although Wallace Thurman, who edited the magazine, had originally hoped the journal would burn "without Nordic fuel."* Fire!! *failed to make the splash hoped for by Hughes and his peers. Even though some readers felt like the Baltimore* Afro-American *reviewer, who announced, "I have just tossed the first issue of Fire into the fire," most of the reviews in both the black and white press were lukewarm. Such would not be the case for Hughes's* Fine Clothes to the Jew, *however.*

In early 1927, Van Vechten was still in flight from the chaos caused by Nigger Heaven's *August 1926 release. The reviews were extreme; blacks and whites alike either loved or hated the book, which went through nine printings in its first four months. En route to California, he headed for New Mexico, where he stopped in for a brief visit with his great friend and occasional enemy, Mabel Dodge Luhan.*

CARL VAN VECHTEN TO LANGSTON HUGHES, MARCH 25, 1927
(POSTCARD)

Dear Langston,

Thanks for your paper (thanks a lot for what you say about me) which I think is <u>superb</u>.[1] The situation is <u>easy</u> to explain: You and I are the only colored people who really love <u>niggers</u>.—From Bill Benet's[2] letter you will see that you are in the Saturday Review this week & there is a wonderful review of F.C.T.T.J. in the Brooklyn Citizen for March 20.—I had hoped to hear from you about the Paul Morand[3] party this morning. If you can come, it is after nine o'clock Sunday night & is <u>informal</u>.—You are also invited to Fania's farewell party at Lawrence Langner's[4] on Tuesday evening, march 29 after 9. The address is 14 West 11th Street.

avocados & navajo jewelry to you!

Carlo

March 25, 1927

1. *Van Vechten thanks Hughes for a copy of his two-part essay, "Those Bad New Negroes: A Critique on Critics," which appeared in the April 16, 1927, issue of the* Pittsburgh Courier. *After excoriating Hughes for his "vulgar" volume of poetry,* Fine Clothes to the Jew, *the* Courier *had invited the poet to defend himself in their pages. Hughes wrote decisively, "I have a right to portray any side of Negro life I wish to." Hughes applauded Van Vechten for his "sincere, friendly, and helpful interest in things Negro."*

2. *The poet William Rose Benét was one of the founders of the* Saturday Review of Literature.

3. *Paul Morand was a French writer whose books* New York *and* Magie noire, *both published in 1927, were popular during the Harlem Renaissance.*

4. *Lawrence Langner was the founder and codirector of the Theatre Guild. He and his wife, Armina Marshall, were close friends of both Carl and Fania.*

FANIA MARINOFF AND CARL VAN VECHTEN, BY NICKOLAS MURAY, 1923

LANGSTON HUGHES TO CARL VAN VECHTEN, APRIL 2, 1927

April 2, 1927

Dear Carl,

I've been ill with a severe cold, my first this winter, so I had to miss your parties and everything. I missed a very grand one near here, too. It was given down in Maryland at Port Deposit by the workers on the great Conowingo Dam that is being built. One of our student orchestras played and all the "low-down" folks for miles were there. I understand the very earth shook with the dancing and that there was an average of five fights an hour until the climax came when a little dark lady got mad because nobody would fight with her and stepped out in the middle of the floor and said, "Damn it! Nobody'll mess with me but I'm gonna shoot ma gun, anyhow!" And she emptied the hall. . . . Between dances most of the conversation consisted of the merits of different kinds of pistols and razors and there was great rivalry as to who could show the largest and most beautiful weapons,—just as in a slightly higher society people talk about and compare the kind of automobiles they buy. And those who wanted to fight but had no protection could always borrow. One woman said, "I wish I'd brought ma switch-blade tonight." And her girl friend replied, "I got a German razor here if you need it." All in the calmest and most matter-of-fact way. It must have been grand. . . . Thanks for all that news about the coming Robeson,[1] the new SUGAR CANE,[2] and the reviews. . . . I'm really sorry I couldn't see Fania off or meet Paul Morand, but I'll see you Easter I hope. . . . Porter Grainger‡ tells me that Brunswick has recorded our first Blues. And before I caught cold I read at University of Penn for the anthropologists and a select group. And some of the papers are still calling me names about my new book.[3] . . . The mail bell's ringing so I have to stop. I'm sending you a funny paper I just received headlined NIGGER HEAVEN, also an amusing clipping. You may not have seen either. Please send them back or keep them for me.

Fresh Easter Eggs,
Langston

1. *Paul Robeson had signed on for a year-long concert tour with the Fisk Jubilee Singers.*
2. *A Harlem speakeasy.*
3. *Reviewers at the* Chicago Whip, *the* Pittsburgh Courier, *and the* Philadelphia Tribune *described being positively sickened by the "lecherous, lust-reeking characters that Hughes finds time to poeticize about" in* Fine Clothes to the Jew. *Some cited the book's dedication to Van Vechten as evidence of how low Hughes had sunk.*

CARL VAN VECHTEN TO LANGSTON HUGHES, APRIL 1927

Dear Langston,
I am mailing today the following letter:

Mr. Benjamin Brawley‡
Shaw University
Raleigh, N.C.
My dear Mr. Brawley,

I have read with some interest your paper entitled, The Negro Literary Renaissance, in the Southern Workman.[1] Your opinions are your own, and although I do not share them you are entitled to them. I think, however, that in such a paper, written by a college professor, one might expect a meticulous niceness in regard to matters of fact. You write: "When Mr. Hughes came under the influence of Mr. Carl Van Vechten and The Weary Blues was given to the world, etc." The Weary Blues had won a prize before I had read a poem by Mr. Hughes or knew him personally. The volume, of which this was the title poem, was brought to me complete before Mr. Hughes and I had ever exchanged two sentences. I am unaware even to this day, although we are the warmest friends and see each other frequently, that I have had the slightest influence on Mr. Hughes in any direction. The influence, if one exists, flows from the other side, as any one might see who read my first paper on the Blues, published in Vanity Fair for August 1925, a full year before Nigger Heaven appeared, before, indeed, a line of it had been written. In this paper I have quoted freely Mr. Hughes's opinions on the subject of Negro folksong, opinions which to my knowledge have not changed in the slightest.

I might say a word or two also a propos of the quotableness of the verse of Countee Cullen. Suffice to say that the fact is that he is quoted more frequently, with two or three exceptions, than any other American poet. I myself quoted four lines as a superscription to Nigger Heaven, and two other lines later in the book. I think the concluding lines of his beautiful sonnet, Yet do I marvel, I have seen printed more often (in periodicals in other languages than English, moreover), than any other two lines by any contemporary poet.[2]

I beg to remain yours very sincerely,

signed

And that's that!

Grace Johnson brought Lola Wilson in yesterday to sing and play and dance. She is at Radcliff and she is the daughter of Butler Wilson, head of the N.A.A.C.P. in Boston. It seems that at Radcliff she has danced interpretations of three of your poems (Jazzonia is one, I remember) and she wanted to do them for you, but she is only here this week. First the poem is read, and then, to music, she gives her interpretation (in costume).

I think I already have two jobs for the Allen boy.[3]

I am sending a copy of the Brawley letter to Charles S. Johnson.[‡]

Holly and mistletoe to you!

Carlo

Ethel Waters is coming to dinner tonight!

1. *The African American scholar and critic Benjamin Brawley was vocal about his disapproval of new school Harlem Renaissance writers. In this letter, Van Vechten challenges Brawley's April 1927 essay, "The Negro Literary Renaissance," in which he railed against the "preference for sordid, unpleasant, or forbidden themes" among writers like Hughes. Brawley singled out Hughes in his essay, characterizing him as a "sad case of a young man of ability who has gone off on the wrong track altogether." The "wrong track" was his relationship with Van Vechten.*

2. *In the same essay, Brawley wrote that Countee Cullen's talent was overrated. Brawley claimed that Cullen's 1925 book, Color, lacked even "one quotable passage." The last two lines of "Yet Do I Marvel" are: "Yet do I marvel at this curious thing: / To make a poet black, and bid him sing!"*

3. *James L. Allen was Hughes's favorite Harlem photographer.*

LANGSTON HUGHES TO CARL VAN VECHTEN, BEFORE APRIL 25, 1927

(POSTCARD)

Friday

Lancaster, Pa.

Dear Carl,

Just made a speech asking the Student Y.M.C.A. what they are doing about colleges like this one (Franklin and Marshall) that "doesn't encourage the attendance of Negroes." One of the delegates said that he joined the Ku Klux Klan on account of niggers like me!!

Langston

LANGSTON HUGHES TO CARL VAN VECHTEN, APRIL 25, 1927

25 April 1927

Sunday

Dear Carl,

Just got back from Lancaster and found your letter waiting for me. Your note to Brawley is all that's needful, and I'm glad you took him up on what he said about Countee. . . . Paul's concert was fine, I thought, and he was well pleased with the crowd,—not packed, but certainly quite "select" and all Robeson fans (I gave him your regrets). I met Mrs. Eugene O'Neil there, also her two sisters, and every body went to the "Sugar Cane Club" on the first lap of a party that didn't end until nine the next morning when Mrs. O'Neil invited every body to breakfast at Eddie's. And that afternoon I had to leave for Lancaster to read poetry to the Student's Y.M.C.A. Conference. I seemed to "get away big," even with the ministers, and have invites to Penn State, Eaglemere, and even Union Theological Seminary. Stopped at a white frat house and everybody was fine to me. I heard about a Ku Klux card and some leaving the dining room, but I didn't see it. Three or four colored delegates were there, too,—one from Bordentown. After <u>unending</u> talks on the religion of Christ, I read <u>Blues</u> and spoke on some of the more useful things I thought a student's Y.M.C.A. might do, particularly along interracial lines, both in colleges where there were Negro students and where there were not. . . . Among other curious things I learned that John Hopkins refuses to teach Negroes even through the correspondence courses which they offer by mail! Have you heard from the kid photographer yet?

Dandelions and cherry blossoms,

Langston

Lincoln University

Saturday

Dear Carlo,

I was certainly sorry to hear about your cold still keeping you in. I hope you're all right again now. This weekend is incidentally full of parties (besides the Opportunity Dinner). I wish I could be in town. A'Leila Walker sent a nice note asking me to be her guest at the opening of some new night club. And Crystal Bird[1] writes about the Weldon Johnson's annual literary afternoon on Sunday. And several other people are having dinners and things. Hope you'll tell me about some of them when you write. Or maybe I'll be in town next week. . . . Lots of amusing things have happened out here this week,—with a fraternity initiation and banquet tonight. I've been working hard,—trying to finish my series of short stories for the <u>Messenger</u> and doing an article on Washington for <u>Opportunity</u>. A note from Johnson today says I can never live there again after it is published,—but I don't think it's as bad as that.[2] He's going to let Brenda Moryls[3] answer it, so "society" will have its comeback. . . . The Courier articles are still bringing gangs of letters approving my stand. I had expected to be roasted instead. . . . Allen writes that he has had a note from Walter, he's met A'Lelia Walker,—and several other people to whom I spoke have taken an interest in his work. So that's that. Thanks immensely for what you did. If you meet him, ask him if he knows who Bessie Smith is? He ought to find out. . . . In another envelope I'm returning the letters you enclosed. I see by the papers where Brawley has approved the dismissal of a young professor at Shaw who did not like the policy there of better dining-hall and dormitory conditions for the white teachers than for the colored. So what can you expect from a guy like that? . . . I've been invited to read and be a guest at a Youth Retreat near Boston the end of the month. Miss Emily Green Balch[4] is to be hostess. Is that the lady we know? It comes right in the middle of exams, so I can't go, unfortunately. . . . It is very beautiful out here now.

White dog-wood for you,

Langston

---

1. *Bird was a social and political activist. In 1935, she married Arthur Huff Fauset, half brother of Jessie.*
2. *Hughes refers to "Our Wonderful Society: Washington," his caustic look at the black Washington bourgeoisie. The essay would be published in the August 1927 issue of* Opportunity.
3. *Brenda Ray Moryck won awards for her writing in* Opportunity *during the late twenties.*
4. *Emily Green Balch, whom neither Hughes nor Van Vechten knew, would win the Nobel Peace Prize in 1946 for her leadership in the international women's peace movement.*

CARL VAN VECHTEN TO LANGSTON HUGHES, MAY 11, 1927

Dear Langston,

I know something (a great deal in fact) about all the parties you write of, but I was laid up and didn't go to any of them. I did go to the Opportunity Dinner, however—first to a cocktail party at Dorothy Peterson's.‡ The principal excitement at the Dinner was our late arrival,¹ slightly soused, about which there was much unfavorable comment and the presence of Paul Green who made a speech. Also, as I went out William Pickens² caught my arm to ask me who the "young man in evening clothes" was. It was Bruce Nugent, of course, with his usual open chest and uncovered ankles. I suppose soon he will be going without trousers. Through Walter White a great deal has already happened to Allen. He has taken Taylor Gordon, Rosamond and James Weldon Johnson, Walter, Dr. Du Bois‡ (who is running a piece about him in the Crisis), A'Lelia, Grace Lezama, Paul, Charles S. Johnson, and others are arranged. I think Walter arranged Ethel Waters last night. I shall be photographed as soon as I am handsome enough.* Miss Ovington is writing a book for the Viking Press: character sketches of some Negro celebrities, and it is the present plan to illustrate the book with photographs by Allen. Emily Green Balch is an entirely different person from Emily Clark Balch.³ Jack Stephens of Indianapolis is here and wants to see you. If you are coming over, or if you are not, you might write him at the Hotel Knickerbocker, West 45th Street.

laurel and peach-blossoms to you!

Carlo

May 11

Douglass' drawings for God's Trombones are simply hors de concours.⁴

*if ever again!

1. *Van Vechten's "our" includes Dorothy Peterson, Nella Larsen‡ and her husband, Elmer Imes, Richard Bruce Nugent, and Harry Block, among others.*
2. *An NAACP field secretary, educator, and journalist.*
3. *When she was still Emily Clark, Balch, with Hunter Stagg, edited the semimonthly Southern literary journal* The Reviewer.
4. God's Trombones: Seven Old-Time Negro Sermons in Verse, *James Weldon Johnson's collection of African American folk sermons, was published in 1927 by Viking.*

Memphis

June 11

Dear Carl,

Last night at a revival I heard what was to me a brand new train song with this refrain:

> "We's bound fo' de
>   heavenly depot,
> "Where de angel
>   porters wait."

It's the first time I'd ever heard angels referred to as Red Caps!

Beale Street is not what it used to be according to its present inhabitants. But it's still full of Blues coming out of alleys and doorways. Yesterday I spent the afternoon in a barrel house at 4th and Beale where three musicians, all of whom claimed to have been with Handy, played all kinds of Blues until they were overcome with gin. And the girl who won the amateur contest at the vaudeville show last night sang a Flood Blues something like Bessie's on the record.

"The National Grand United Order of Wise Men and Women of the World" meets nightly just across the street in front of my windows, over the Yellow Pine Cafe. The "P. Wee Saloon" is just down the block.

Tomorrow I'm going to Vicksburg, Miss. and the flood region, then on to New Orleans. My address there for mail will be

3444 Magnolia St.
c/o Mrs. Jackson

> "Ain't gonna sing it no mo," —
>   Langston

Hughes had decided to spend the summer getting to know the South. From Beale Street, he moved on to Vicksburg, Baton Rouge, and then to New Orleans, where he was mesmerized by the voodoo shops and drug stores that "seemed to deal almost exclusively in magic medicaments with strange names," he recalled in The Big Sea.

Havana, Cuba

July 15, 1927

Dear Carl,

Havana is not all it might be at this time of year, yet I've rather enjoyed it so far.[1] There is a marvellous Chinatown here where I went last night with some of the Chinese fellows from our crew. They have cousins there waiting to be smuggled into New Orleans or New York. We had some very good food and a jar of Chinese whiskey (and I'm bringing a jar to you, if it ever gets there. It ought to make grand cocktails.—I hope you haven't stopped drinking again.) Then we went to a house where there are girls in little shuttered rooms built around an open courtyard. There are three floors, and literally hundreds of Chinese walking around and around looking at them. Its right near the Chinese theatre and is always crowded. . . . I am the only "colored" colored person on my ship. The crew is all mixed up,—Spaniards, German, South Americans, Philipinos and Chinese. The confusion of languages is amusing. We are loading sugar here and I think we're going directly back to New Orleans in a few days. . . . Just the day before I sailed I met Walter's brother-in-law and he told me about the little new Carl.[2] Great! . . . I'm glad it was a boy and that it has been so well named. . . . Walter's brother-in-law is a very nice fellow. I'm going to see him when I go back. . . . By the way, I was in New Orleans three weeks without meeting a single "dicty"[3] person,—then someone took me to the <u>Aristocrats Club</u>, I believe the name was, and then invitations began to come in to go places,—and the next day I got this job to Cuba,—so I'm saved. . . . There's a street called Poydras Street where one can hear Blues all night long,—and most of the day, too. A stevedore called Big Mac is particularly good and seems to know a thousand verses. I never heard any of these before:

> Did you ever see peaches
> Growin' on a watermelon vine?
> Did you ever see peaches
> On a watermelon vine?
> Did you ever seen a woman
> I couldn't take for mine?
>
> If you shake that thing I'll
> Buy you a diamond ring.
> If you shake that thing I'll

Buy you a diamond ring, —
But if you don't shake it
I ain't gonna buy you a thing.

Yo' windin' and yo grindin'
Don't have no 'fect on me.
Yo' windin' and grindin'
Don't have no 'fect on me
Cause I can wind and
            grind
Like a monkey climbin' a
      cocanut tree.

Throw yo' arms around me
Like de circle round de sun.
Throw yo' arms around me
Like de' circle round de sun
and tell me, pretty mama,
How you want yo' lovin'
      done.

I lived for a week on Rampart Street which is the Lenox Avenue down there, then I moved into the Vieux Carré just in front of St. Louis Cathedral, in a house with stone floors, wooden blinds, an open court, and balconies, — a very old place and quite charming. . . . To me, New Orleans, seems much like a southern European city. Everything is cheap, and everything is wide open. There is good wine at 30¢ a bottle and even whiskey at 5¢ a drink in some bars. . . . I met the caretakers of the old St. Louis Cemetery, — Creole fellows who do little work and can be found any afternoon behind some cool tomb, with a few bottles of white wine at hand. They took me to meet their families and to several jolly Creole parties and gumbo suppers.

Write to me c/o Mrs. A. C. Johnson, 3444 Magnolia Street, N.O. or else to Tuskegee after July 25. . . . Wish you'd send me Eddie Wasserman's‡ address, too, so I can drop him a card. I'm not sure I remember it correctly. Tell him "hello" for me.

Pañal and Bacardi to you,

Langston

P.S. You can buy all sorts of voodoo stuff in Poydras Street, too, — Follow Me Powder, War and Confusion Dust, Black Cats' Blood, etc. I thought I'd bring you a bottle of Good Luck Water, but I think you'd rather have the Chinese licker.

1. *On a whim, Hughes took a job as a messboy on a ship heading for Havana on July 9. The ship returned to New Orleans on the twentieth.*
2. *Walter and Gladys White named their baby Carl Darrow after Van Vechten and the Scopes trial attorney, Clarence Darrow.*
3. *African American vernacular meaning "self-important" or "snobbish."*

CARL VAN VECHTEN TO LANGSTON HUGHES, JULY 28, 1927

July 28, 1927

Dear Langston,

Your letters have been a joy. I wanted to write you at length but I'm afraid even this won't reach you. Anyway, I'm glad you're headed back. I enclose a clipping which perhaps you haven't seen. Eddie Wasserman's address is 25 Eåst 30 Street. James Allen here takes some marvellous photographs of me—you shall have one—and of Eddie & several others. Miller & Lyles in Rang Tang[1] are on at last but soon will be off, I think. I didn't like it. But Ethel Waters' Africana is marvellous & sure to be running when you come back.[2] Have you ever seen Glenn & Miller?[3] They are with her. Aaron Douglas is now doing new sets for her piece. I've seen a lot of Ethel & taken her around a lot & one night she proudly showed me your book with the inscription. She is very human when you know her—but very shy & on the whole doesn't trust either jigs or ofays. So, quite inconsistently, tells them both what's on her mind.[4] I haven't any news of your songs.

I've been ill for a couple of weeks & my brother died a month ago.[5] & I've stopped drinking—but probably by the time the Chinese whiskey arrives I'll be drinking again.

Hope to see you <u>very</u> soon.

Carlo V.V.

July 28, '27

If you can get me any kind of an autograph—even a cancelled cheque—of Booker T. while at Tuskegee I want it very badly.

1. *Flournoy Miller and Aubrey Lyles starred in this 1927 black musical comedy.*
2. *Produced by Waters's husband, Earl Dancer, the 1927 musical revue* Africana *received crushing reviews from the* New York Times.
3. *Probably Van Vechten meant Glen & Jenkins, a popular singing duo.*
4. *Van Vechten was a great fan and friend of Ethel Waters. He was proud that she was fond of him, too, despite her misanthropic dislike of both "jigs" and "ofays," derogatory terms*

for blacks and whites, respectively. Waters wrote of him in her 1950 memoir His Eye Is on the Sparrow: "Sometimes it seems to me that Carl is the only person in the world who ever has understood the shyness deep down in me."

5. *Ralph Van Vechten, Carl's older brother by eighteen years, died on June 28. Ralph was a successful banker and entrepreneur, and his death made Van Vechten a millionaire.*

LANGSTON HUGHES TO CARL VAN VECHTEN, JULY 28, 1927

(POSTCARD)

Tuskegee Institute

July 28, 1927

Dear Carl,

Have you got my letter from Havana? I had to give it to a customs man to take ashore as we were out in the harbor. . . . Ran into Zora Hurston in Mobile. She has a little car and is driving all around. It was some surprise to see her! This is a great place here. I'm staying two weeks. Langston

JESSIE FAUSET, LANGSTON HUGHES, AND
ZORA NEALE HURSTON, IN FRONT OF THE
STATUE OF BOOKER T. WASHINGTON,
TUSKEGEE INSTITUTE, 1927

Zora Neale Hurston was in Mobile conducting anthropological research for her Barnard mentor, Franz Boas, as well as Carter G. Woodson, Hughes's boss from two years before. Hurston and Hughes were delighted to find each other. "Right off we went to eat some fried fish and water-melon," Hughes remembered in The Big Sea. *They decided to drive back to New York together in "Sassy Susie," Hurston's car.*

LANGSTON HUGHES TO CARL VAN VECHTEN, AUGUST 15, 1927

Fort Valley, Georgia

August 15, 1927

Dear Carl,

Your letter did find me and it was great to hear from you. . . . Zora and I are driving through Georgia in her car. Today we stopped off here for a visit with Mr. and Mrs. Hunt (Dorothy Harris' parents, you know).¹ Their home is marvelous. Tonight we went out in the country to a backwoods church entertainment given by a magician. It closed with his playing on a large harp and singing the Lord's Prayer in a very lively fashion. And his version began like this:

> Our Father who art in heaven,
> <u>Hollywood</u> be Thy name!

Zora has a great collection of songs. . . . We've decided to get some-body conjured while we're down here. There are some great conjur doc-tors in Savannah. . . . We'll be home around the 1st I guess.

Peanuts and poppies,

Langston

P.S.

Carl—

Just heard that Bessie Smith is singing in Macon (her home town) so we're wiring you to come on down. There are so many amusing things to do here and the Hunts are delightful. We're on our way to the old Toomer‡ plantation now where Jean's father was born and where a number of his "poor relations" still live. They say Bessie is a riot. We're 29 miles from Macon but we can hear her echoes down here. . . . Zora says to "hip it on down" this way. . . . Passed a town last night named Tallbottom. Maybe that's where the Blackbottom started. Anyhow the Georgia Grind seems prevalent. L.H.

1. *Dorothy Hunt Harris was the wife of the black artist Jimmy Harris.*

LANGSTON HUGHES AND ZORA NEALE HURSTON
TO CARL VAN VECHTEN, AUGUST 16, 1927
(TELEGRAM FROM FORT VALLEY, GEORGIA)

HERE WITH DOROTHY HARRIS PARENTS BESSIE SMITH
IN MACON COME DOWN JOIN FUN FOR WEEK
ALL RETURN TOGETHER
LANGSTON AND ZARA [*sic*]

an Vechten didn't make it down to Macon for Bessie Smith. Hughes and Hurston were able to get to know her, however, because Smith rehearsed every morning in their hotel.

LANGSTON HUGHES TO CARL VAN VECHTEN, FEBRUARY 27, 1928

Lincoln University,

February 27, 1928

Dear Carlo,

Just a line to warn you that if you haven't seen the <u>Afro</u> and the <u>Courier</u> this week you must do so at once.[1] The former (as maybe you know) announces your entrance into Brooklyn high society, while the latter contains a grand interview which Ethel Waters gave out in Cleveland. Perfectly marvellous! And low-down!

Nothing in the least exciting has happened to me recently and the only thing I have to look forward to is being an usher in the parade at Countee's wedding.[2] I am to wear a swallow-tail coat. Be there! It ought to be good.

I feel very smart these days having passed quite creditably a course in math and another in economics. We are now having a revival out here. I went tonight with the intention of being saved,—but it was such a high-brow meeting that nobody shouted,—so I sat there unmoved and am still a sinner. Have mercy!

Sincerely,
Langston

1. *The Baltimore* Afro-American *and the* Pittsburgh Courier *were prominent black news-papers.*
2. *Countee Cullen married W. E. B. Du Bois's only daughter, Yolande, on April 28 in a lavish ceremony that included three thousand guests. Harlem treated the couple like royalty, but the union didn't last. On June 30 Cullen sailed for Europe with his best man, Harold Jack-man.* Van Vechten ultimately did not attend the wedding.*

CARL VAN VECHTEN TO LANGSTON HUGHES, 1928

Dear Langston:

I am invited to Countee's wedding: so I expect to see you.* I've been in California and New Mexico and what have you?[1] I hope I haven't missed all the colored reviews of Home to Harlem, but the papers will probably praise it because it was written by a shine. If you've seen anything in the Defender, etc., please let me know. Nella's book is out today.[2] Saw a lot of Nora in Chicago.[3] One night Ethel was in with a revolver looking for sweet papa Earl,[4] the dirty mistreater. And the other night at a dance I met Billie Cain and Alma Smith, and Bessie Smith is in town and Porter Grainger has promised to bring that hot mama down.[5]

Woof! Woof!
Carlo

Friday

*as a sheik.

1. *After short trips to Santa Fe and Taos, where he visited Mabel Dodge Luhan, Van Vechten arrived in Los Angeles in late February. By March 6, he was fed up. He wrote in his diary: "My revulsion towards the picture world & all it connotes is complete." Van Vechten had written a quartet of* Vanity Fair *articles about Hollywood during the summer of 1927.*
2. *Nella Larsen's 1928 novel was* Passing. *Larsen and her husband, Elmer Imes, enjoyed life-long friendships with Van Vechten.*

3. *Ralph Van Vechten's widow, Fannie Maynard, died on February 17, and Van Vechten traveled to Chicago for the funeral. During his stay, he spent time with his good friend Nora Holt.*
4. *Earl Dancer was Waters's producer and, at one point, husband.*
5. *Porter Grainger was a composer and an accompanist to Bessie Smith.*

LANGSTON HUGHES TO CARL VAN VECHTEN, MARCH 1, 1928

March 1, 1928

Dear Carl,

I guess you've read <u>Home to Harlem</u> by this time. I hope the colored critics have, too, because if yours was <u>Nigger Heaven</u>, this is <u>Nigger Hell</u>, — and I'm wondering what they can have left to say. I think you'd better start taking the Afro and the Courier all over again.

Spring sap to you,

Langston

J amaica-born Claude McKay's[‡] *first novel,* Home to Harlem, *was published by Harper & Brothers. Two weeks after its March 1928 release it became the first black-authored Harlem best-seller. The novel existed in the shadow of* Nigger Heaven *for years, even though McKay took every opportunity to deny the influence of Van Vechten's novel on his own. Hughes was excited about* Home to Harlem, *as he made clear in a March 5, 1928, letter to Claude McKay: "Lord, I love the whole thing. It's so damned real!" he wrote.*

LANGSTON HUGHES TO CARL VAN VECHTEN, APRIL 4, 1928

Lincoln University, Pa.

April 4, 1928

Dear Carl,

Mighty glad to hear you're back again, but I'm sorry we'll cross one another Saturday. I'll be New York bound. Might even get there Friday. . . . But I hope I'll see you Monday anyhow. . . . All the colored papers but the Tattler have razzed "Home to Harlem" and, of course, you've been mentioned, but the agreement seems to be that Claude has gone much lower-down and betrayed the race to a much greater extent than you ever thought of doing.[1]

The Defender thought it was terrible. . . . I'm anxious to hear about Nora and Santa Fe and Hollywood . . . and the director you said I might meet when he comes East.[2] . . . I'm deeply engaged in getting educated nowadays, — that sort of thing. . . . I hope I get smart sometime.

Sincerely,

Langston

1. *The* Inter-State Tattler*'s review of* Home to Harlem *wasn't glowing, only less contemptuous than most of the others. The reviewer bestowed on McKay the dubious honor of having "out-niggered Mr. Van Vechten."*
2. *Hughes refers to King Vidor, director of* The Big Parade *and* Hallelujah!

*A*llison Davis's article, "Our Negro 'Intellectuals,'" appeared in the August issue of The Crisis. Davis lamented the way black writers had been "making an exhibition of their own unhealthy imagination, in the name of frankness and sincerity." Fine Clothes to the Jew was a prime example of this trend. Davis was very distressed about Hughes's relationship with Van Vechten. "I think that the severest charge one can make against Mr. Van Vechten is that he misdirected a genuine poet, who gave promise of a power and technique exceptional in any poetry, — Mr. Hughes," Davis sighed. In his response, printed in the September issue of The Crisis, Hughes took on Davis's claims one by one. About his relationship with Van Vechten, Hughes wrote:*

I do not know what facts Mr. Davis himself may possess as to how, where, or when I have been misdirected by Mr. Van Vechten, but since I happen to be the person who wrote the material comprising Fine Clothes to the Jew, I would like herewith to state and declare that many of the poems in said book were written before I made the acquaintance of Mr. Van Vechten. . . . Those poems which were written after my acquaintance with Mr. Van Vechten were certainly not about him, not requested by him, not misdirected by him, some of them not liked by him nor, so far as I know, do they in any way bear his poetic influence.

CARL VAN VECHTEN TO LANGSTON HUGHES, AUGUST 2, 1928

Dear Langston,

Allison Davis's article was both assinine and sophomoric. I'm glad you answered it, but what can you think of Du Bois printing such rubbish? King Vidor was here and wanted to find you, but I had no idea where to find you. Nor had Caroline a few weeks ago and she wanted you badly. Perhaps she knows now. I really think she is going to put on a show.¹ She has Paul Robeson, Nora Holt, Ethel Waters, Clara Smith, Taylor Gordon, Glen and Jenkins, and seven or eight others under contract. All Harlem is writing music.

hortensias to you!

Carlo

August 2

I am sailing on the Mauretania on September 5.² You'd better let me see you before then.

My book went to you last week.

1. *The "show" refers to* O Blues!, *which was proposed to Van Vechten in 1926 by Caroline Dudley Reagan as a possible vehicle for Paul Robeson. It foundered when Robeson abandoned the project in December.*

2. *Before sailing on the* Mauretania *for a six-month stay in Europe, Van Vechten gave a going-away party to rival all going-away parties. The only beverage available was champagne, which his guests drank enthusiastically until the late hours. The evening was topped off with Nora Holt's spontaneous rendition of "My Daddy Rocks Me with One Steady Roll."*

NORA HOLT IN HARLEM,
FEBRUARY 27, 1932

8 May 1929

Dear Carl,

It was very good of you to write me before you sailed away again.[1] Of course, I'm sorry you're leaving New York, if it's going to be for a long time, but I'm hoping, and I'm sure, you'll have a delightful sojourn abroad, and that you'll find little Harlems now almost everywhere you go. (I'm enclosing what the Literary Digest copies from a Berlin paper this week.) . . . And you were a mighty big part starting it all. . . . Lately, now that another period in my life is about to come to an end, I've been thinking about the people who've been so very good to me the last four years, and who helped me when I came back from the continent with neither sous nor lires nor pesos, and certainly no dollars. . . . Well, you're person No. 1,—the first human being to whom I received a formal introduction after my hard return to native shores,—the night I landed,—in Happy Rhone's cabaret, the very middle of the dance floor. Don't you remember? The first person, too, to see my poems in any sort of collected form, to send them to a publisher, and to be happy with me (by wire) over their appearance. But you know that, and the rest, too. And I don't want to bore you with thanks. You've been a mighty good friend, Carl, so I want you to have a great time in Europe.

I've been awfully busy the last two months or so making a survey of Lincoln as a sociology class assignment (but mainly for myself). It's finished now, was read here, and has produced some sensational but unintended results,—as we who made it didn't mean for it to get to the papers. I'm enclosing one clipping, but there were several more, besides editorials, etc. Its effect here at Lincoln was upsetting enough to the staid contented Presbyterians who have been easing along in delightful mediocrity for the last 40 years, not caring much if the students improved or not, with the result that Lincoln became a charming winter resort and country club, but not much of a college. (Lovely for me,—but not so good for the serious-minded boys who want and need something else). The survey covered everything,—faculty, curriculum, buildings and grounds, student thought and activities, etc. (2 upper classes) and various complicated looking charts and tabulations were made. (The Afro succeeded in getting only a small part of the material that had been posted in the sociology room).[2] But it would take a whole paper to tell you all about it. Anyway, it was interesting work, and I feel that we've got down some important figures and data concerning some of the grave problems facing Negro education today in schools dominated by white philanthropy, well-meaning but dumb.

This summer I'm going to stay here again and finish my book. (Wish you could read it before I send it in).[3] Six weeks or so more I think will do it. Then I'm free again. Had some offers to teach, Tuskegee among others, but haven't taken them so far,—so I'm liable to meet you in Hong Kong if you keep on round the world.

Tell Fania Hello for me and both you all enjoy yo' selves to de utt'most! Remember me to Paul and Essie, too,—and the kid.[4]

Saluti e bacci,
Langston

Lincoln University
May eighth, 1929

1. *Van Vechten was preparing for another trip to Europe.*
2. *Someone sent the survey anonymously to the Baltimore* Afro-American.
3. *Hughes refers to his first novel,* Not Without Laughter. *He would finish it in the spring of 1930.*
4. *Essie Robeson gave birth to Paul Robeson, Jr., on November 2, 1927.*

CARL VAN VECHTEN TO LANGSTON HUGHES, MAY 16, 1929

Dear Langston,

Thanks for your swell letter—one of the swellest I ever received from anybody. Naturally, it made me very happy. I am sorry to miss your graduation—an appropriate present will celebrate this & everything else in due time—and I am still more sorry to miss reading your novel in manuscript. Well, anyway I am sure it will be good.—I gave you my address, I think, Banque de Paris et des Pays Bas, 3 Rue d'Antin, Paris—but 150 w. 55th or Knopf will always reach me. So please keep me informed as to your address & plans. Mine are uncertain at present. Bless you!

Carlo.

May 16

LANGSTON HUGHES TO CARL VAN VECHTEN, OCTOBER 10, 1929

P.O. Box 94
Westfield, N.J.

October 10, 1929

Dear Carl,

This is the address. And the phone is Westfield 199M. Don't give either of them to any one else for, while I'm working, I want to avoid as many counter-attractions as possible—especially the letters from strange and half-strange people that used to fill my box at Lincoln—where everybody knew [who] I was.[1]

Saw Taylor Gordon yesterday. Also Barthé[‡]. Taylor gave me an absinthe cocktail and said he would take me to meet Miss Draper[‡] so I could get her signature, too. Taylor says he is going to draw his own pictures for her next book,—because he has seen some wonderful things!

Won't be in town this Saturday after all. Couldn't make the appointments I expected until next week, so I'm going to stay out here and work. I feel in the mood again.

Apples and pears to you,
Langston

1. *Hughes had moved to New Jersey for the privacy he needed to work on his novel. He was boarding with an elderly couple.*

CARL VAN VECHTEN TO LANGSTON HUGHES, NOVEMBER 12, 1929

Dear Langston,

Stella Block's exhibition is at the Montross Galleries—Nov. 4 to Nov. 16. 26 E. 56 Street.[1] She lives at 121 Madison Ave (This is the Madison side of the building Eddie Wasserman lives in) & the telephone is Ashland 3988. If you like her things she expects you to call her up. I suggested that sometime you both might do a book of Blues or Cabaret or Street Songs between you. I also suggested NEGRO Xmas cards but it is too late for that this year. I mean "This dancing hot mater[2] wishes you a merry Xmas" etc with a swell picture of the dame opposite! I truly hope you did not hear Gladys sing The Boy in the Boat the other day. I should prefer your ears to be unsullied. I'll swear there were whole minutes in which I felt as happy as if I had been in the Clam House![3]

While you are attending exhibitions go to see Hidalgo's (a Mexican friend of Covarrubius) Wax Figures & Caricatures at the 56 Street Galleries (6 East 56) beginning November 18. Both Marinoff & I are represented in wax. We have not seen them yet!

Yellow tulips & cigar coupons to you!
Carlo.

November 12, 1929
New York

1. *Block was a painter and a dancer.*
2. *I.e., "mama."*

3. *Located uptown at W. 133rd Street, the Clam House featured the vocalist and cabaret performer Gladys Bentley‡ as its prime act.*

LANGSTON HUGHES TO CARL VAN VECHTEN, JUNE 6, 1930

Washington
                                                                June 6, 1930

Dear Carlo,

I hope you'll not be gone by the time I get back on Monday or Tuesday. (Maybe you are sailing on the Bremen Tuesday night. Locke and Marian Anderson‡ sail on it, I understand). I want to tell you about a possible opening I have for next fall—and see what you think of it. Deeter at the Hedgerow Theatre plans a series of plays next fall (opening Labor Day) with part or all Negro casts—Rose, Abbie, etc. On Wednesday I drove up to the Theatre from Lincoln and Deeter and I had a nice talk.[1] I told him I wanted eventually to write for the stage. He showed me all over the place, and said that, if I wished, I might come there sometime in August, perhaps even before the rehearsals on the Negro things begin (to watch the working out of a "white" play as well), and I would be given small parts to play and the opportunity to observe the workings of a repertory theatre and its nightly performances. So in view of that, I think I'll spend my summer working out some ideas for plays—so that I won't go there empty-handed—or rather empty-headed. . . . Do you think the idea a good one—or would there be something dangerous about it?. . . You've been grand to me Carlo. Here's cherry blossoms for you—

                                                                Langston

1. *Hughes spent the summer and fall of 1930 in Rose Valley, Pennsylvania, the location of Jasper Deeter's experimental Hedgerow Theatre Company.*

LANGSTON HUGHES TO CARL VAN VECHTEN, SEPTEMBER 25, 1930
(ON HEDGEROW THEATRE COMPANY STATIONERY)

                                                                September 25, 1930

Dear Carlo,

I said in my letter to you a few weeks ago that it would be a miracle of the Blessed Virgin if it reached you before you sailed for home. Now, seeing that you've arrived home again, I'm sure the letter didn't get to you yet—but I guess it will be re-forwarded to you, so I won't tell you all the same things over. Anyway, here I am at Hedgerow. Have been here almost two weeks, went to work the next day after I got here on a new play, and have been working so hard since that I'm unable to say whether I like the place or not—but I believe I do. Have you seen it? The location is lovely— an old mill in a gentle little Pennsylvania valley. Some of the people sleep in the theatre, some in a house across the road, and the rest (and me) in a cottage a mile or so off, up on top of a hill where the mist and the stars spill over into the valley. We eat on a veranda at the theatre house. Nobody gets paid, but everybody gets fed, laundry is done, and tooth paste, stamps, cigarettes, and all such little things are free for the asking. All the money goes back into the theatre, and everybody works at all the various things to be done besides acting. I'm in the office. The only hired employee is a cook. . . . Deeter says the construction of my play is O.K. and he thinks the situations are very dramatic.[1] I'm hoping it will work up well, but some days the characters will not talk at all—anyhow, I have plenty of excitements besides the conversation: there's a murder, a suicide, and a fight. . . . It turns out that there will probably be no Negro season here. It more or less depended on Deeter's directing THE POTTER'S FIELD, and it seems that he will probably not do it, or not soon, as Paul Green's manager wishes to offer it to Meyerhold[2] for possible new York production by him, since they expect to have him do some American plays here, too. The other things that Jasper intended to put on were a new comedy by Burroughs (colored librarian at the Century Club or the Union Club, I forget which) and some old things like WHITE MAN, the Paul Green one actors, and their regular EMPEROR and OTHELLO which they do right along anyhow. There are three resident colored actors out here for those. . . . Mr. Deeter was kind enough to let me come out and watch rehearsals, etc. of his other plays. Shaw's THE DEVIL'S DISCIPLE opens Saturday. They're also doing Morley's THUNDER ON THE LEFT and a lovely Italian play called FALLING LEAVES soon. . . . I'm mighty glad about the success of your novel, Carlo. I told you how much I like it in my other letter. That last scene in David's bar is a thing to cry over. It stays in my head like Campaspe in her garden, or like the death of the Tattooed Countess, or Byron with the pistol in his hand.[3] . . . How's Fania? And what new, beautiful things did you bring back? I loved your cards. . . . I may stay here some weeks longer. Would like to fairly well finish one play. Don't tell anyone where I am, etc. Maybe nothing will turn out—but here's hoping. . . . Wood asters and brook-music to you,

Comme toujours,

Langston

1. *Hughes refers to his first play,* Mulatto. *It tells the story of a mixed-race main character's rage at his white father, who refuses to acknowledge their relationship.*

2. *The renowned avant-garde director Vsevolod Yemilyevich Meyerhold began his own theater in 1923.*

3. *Hughes remembers the final scenes from many of Van Vechten's novels.* Parties *(1930), Van Vechten's last novel, ends with a scene in David's bar. Campaspe is in her garden at the end of* The Blind Bow-Boy. *The Tattooed Countess dies in* Firecrackers, *and Byron has a pistol in hand at the end of* Nigger Heaven.

1931

In May of 1929, when Hughes was in Westfield, New Jersey, wrestling with his novel, Zora Neale Hurston arrived in town and took a room in a house just doors away. This was no coincidence; both of them were being supported by the same patron, a rich white widow named Charlotte van der Veer Quick Mason, who insisted on being called Godmother. She wanted them near each other so that she could keep watch over both of them. Soon, she sent another one of her "godchildren," a young black teacher named Louise Thompson,‡ to provide secretarial services for Hughes and Hurston.

During her travels in the South, Hurston had gathered material for a play she wanted to write with Hughes. When they heard that Theresa Helburn of the Dramatists Guild was interested in producing some uplifting, lighthearted black theater, Hughes and Hurston set to work on Hurston's material and came up with a folk comedy called The Bone of Contention. The play would eventually become Mule Bone: A Comedy of Negro Life.

Their work was coming along well, until—out of nowhere, it seemed to Hughes—Hurston grew restless. She abandoned the unfinished Mule Bone and abruptly made a trip to the South to do more of her own research. Hughes's disappointment over the play was eclipsed by the subsequent disintegration of his relationship with Mason, who was making Hughes's life unbearable with her relentless need for control over him and his work.

The following letters begin with Hughes back at his mother's house in Cleveland, where he was resigned to stay for a while after Godmother, irreversibly frustrated with Hughes, cut off her financial help. Hughes distracted himself from his troubles by renewing acquaintances with old friends in Cleveland like Rowena and Russell Jelliffe, who ran the Gilpin Players, the nation's most prominent amateur black drama troupe, named for the distinguished black actor Charles Gilpin. Hughes was shocked to discover that Rowena had a copy of Mule Bone. *Hurston had copyrighted the play in her name and then sent it to Van Vechten, who, believing* Mule Bone *to be Hurston's creation alone, sent the play to the Theatre Guild, which then passed it along to Rowena at the Gilpin Players.*

CARL VAN VECHTEN TO LANGSTON HUGHES, JANUARY 19, 1931

Dear Langston,

I read The Singing Dark some days ago, but have not had time to write you about it. I may be wrong, but I am not very enthusiastic about it. It may not subtract anything from your reputation, but it certainly will not add to it. It contains no outstanding poem like The Weary Blues or Mulatto. On the other hand it contains a great many poems based on ideas that have been better expressed by others. I shouldn't wonder if you are pretty nearly through with poetry. However, I found many of the poems admirable and some of them of almost mystic originality—almost all of those in the section entitled Passing Love. And I think the book would gain in force and charm if it were reduced in volume. My choice for rejection (on the grounds of banality, etc.) would be the following: Walls, Old Lincoln Theatre, Barrel House (which I remember I never liked), Bodies, To a New Dancer (if you disagree about this one, look up Karsavina: I do not think she is dead), African Dancer in Paris, For a Woman with Cancer, Burial, To Certain Intellectuals, Brothers, Terminal, Search. Indeed, I find the entire last section (The Singing Dark) weak. Of course, everybody will call the book The Singing Darkey! What shall I do with the mss.?

Zora's performance is not very pretty, but I am not surprised. I have seen some other strange behavior there. I do not know what you can do. Even if she has entirely rewritten the play in a version of her own, she had no moral right to do so without getting your permission. However, perhaps you had better <u>try</u> to do something. I think the play is fresh and amusing and authentic and if properly produced will be a success. Several members of the Guild liked it enormously. So, perhaps you had better put yourself on record by telling a few people what you have just told me so that if the play makes money you can claim part of it. After all, you have standing as a writer and Zora has not and people will believe you. If the Gilpin Players are going to do it, you might threaten suit unless your rights as coauthor are recognized and unless you are financially reimbursed. This is not advice. This is all suggestion. If you have a lawyer friend, you might talk it over with him. Perhaps Chesnutt‡ might be useful right here.[2] I think also the stenographer might be a good witness.[3]

George Schuyler's‡ Black No More[4] is in the house, but I haven't read it. I shall certainly read God Sends Sunday,[5] as soon as possible.

If you want Mule-Bone to succeed: i.e. if you establish your rights, it is my idea that it should be done with a certain stylized exaggeration in costume and gesture (violent colors, with sunflower and watermelon backgrounds, like a Currier and Ives print) and with lots of music. This should be suggested rather than sung. What I mean is a couple o' bars here, a couple there, with some banjo strummings and a mouthorgan or two.

With Nora Holt and Donald[6] I attended a superb drag in Harlem the other night, and then we went <u>everywhere</u>. Harlem is better than ever and wilder, and more English, and more everything, I guess. I love it! . . . I went to a party at Cora La Redd's[7] that is probably the best party I ever went to. It was given for Harold Jackman (whom she had met the night before). So I gave a party for Harold myself, and had Billie Cain and Alma Smith and Al Moore and a few Ofays and this was rather good too . . . Eddie Wassermann went to Cuba and wanted some addresses, but this was before I heard from you and I didn't know where to reach you.

With 17 royal purple dachshunds (housebroken) with polished silver
legs!
Carlo

<u>over</u>
<u>over</u>
!!!

January 19 – 1931
New York

[Handwritten on the back] I have just dug out the letter Zora wrote me when she sent me the play on November 14. In it she says: "Langston and I started out together on the idea of the story I used to tell you about Eatonville, but being so much apart from rush of business I started all over again while in Mobile & this is the result of my work alone." Of course she should have written you to this effect.

ZORA NEALE HURSTON,
PHOTOGRAPH BY CARL VAN VECHTEN, 1934

1. *Van Vechten's teasing had a lot to do with Hughes's decision to change the title of this new collection to* A House in the World. *Knopf declined the manuscript in late January. The poems were never published as a collection.*
2. *The black writer Charles Chesnutt had been a legal stenographer. He also had a law degree.*
3. *The stenographer, Louise Thompson, unwittingly played a central role in this drama. Hurston was jealous of her friendship with Hughes and was convinced that he wanted to incorporate Thompson as a full partner in their writing team. "Now Langston, nobody has in the history of the world given a typist an interest in a work for typing it," she wrote him on January 18, 1931. "Nobody would think of it unless they were in favor of the typist."*
4. *George S. Schuyler's satiric send-up of the mythic underpinnings of racial difference was published in 1931.*
5. *Arna Bontemps‡ published this novel in 1930.*
6. *Donald Angus.*
7. *Cora La Redd was a stage performer.*

LANGSTON HUGHES TO CARL VAN VECHTEN, JANUARY 19, 1931

4800 Carnegie Ave.
Cleveland, Ohio

January 19, 1931

Dear Carlo,

Forgive me for worrying you to death—but once more the MULE-BONE. Last night I talked to Zora by phone. She said she knew nothing about French[1] handling her play, or how it got to Cleveland. I told her how it got here, and that it came in a terribly tangled up version with two first-act endings, and two different third acts—one our collaborated version we did together, another evidently her new version—seemingly leaving it up to the producer to decide which endings and which acts he wanted. I told her the director here, Mrs. Jelliffe, couldn't make head or tail of it (as sent from French) but, liking the version I have here (the one we did together) she [wished] to put it on, and would Zora be willing that she do it, using the script we had originally planned? Zora would not answer yes or no, but kept stalling over the phone and asking what good it would do her to produce it in Cleveland. Then I asked Zora was she attempting to sell the play alone under her name? She replied that at first she hadn't intended to, "but, well—I'm writing you a letter." What she'll say in the letter, I don't know. . . . Anyway, this morning Mrs. Jelliffe phoned Barrett Clark, representative for French and also, I understand, reader for the Guild. She explained the whole matter to him, asking at the same time what he could do so that she could go ahead with her production, as time is getting very short. Barrett Clark said that he had gotten the manuscript through your having first sent it in to the Guild and, feeling that the Guild would refuse it, he had, some weeks ago offered it to the Gilpin Players here; that he didn't know Zora Hurston but that he would get in touch with her at once and see if he could persuade her to allow the Cleveland production to go through, and under our joint names, (since he had not been aware before that I had anything to do with the play).[2] He is to wire Mrs. Jelliffe after he has talked with Zora. . . . Now, Carlo, the situation regarding the production here is this: The Gilpin Players, probably the best Little Theatre Negro group in the country, must open downtown with this play on February 15th, so you see how pushed for time they are. The play came to them through French quite without my knowledge, and bearing only Zora's name, but in such a confused form that I don't see how the Guild or anybody else read it. The Jelliffes are friends of mine and swell people, and realizing the predicament they are in for time, (and also being interested myself in seeing a trial production of the comedy) I am willing to overlook Zora's seeming attempt to get rid of the play without my knowledge, and to do my best to patch up the script from French using the two acts that I have, and the script of the second act which I had worked on with Zora before she went South, and thus enable the Gilpins to put it on out here and to begin rehearsals at once, doing the play under Zora and my names, as she and I had originally intended. This is what I tried to make Zora see over the phone last night but New York to Cleveland calls are expensive and I couldn't talk all night. The Gilpins plan a two-week season for this play, opening under the auspices of the CLEVELAND PLAINDEALER'S Theatre of Nations downtown (which means a great deal of publicity through the PLAINDEALER) and later moving to the <u>Ohio</u> one of the big legitimate downtown houses here, as they have done in past seasons with <u>Roseane</u>, <u>In Abraham's Bosom</u>, and other plays, and with great success.[3] This is their first Negro comedy downtown, and they feel that it would go over big, which would be fine for both Zora and I from the standpoint of both publicity and royalties. . . . The Gilpin Players are in a sense a semi-professional group and have been offered try-outs by the Guild and other New York managers before, and a production here would mean that representatives of the New York people would see it—which is important to us too, since the Guild has turned it down, from all I can discover. . . . So Carlo, would you, please, get in touch with Zora and try to make her see all this. I am not at all angry about her actions, because she always has been strange in lots of ways, but I do hate to see a good Folk-play go to waste, because for some reason I do not know, she no longer wants to work with me. Tell her the Gilpins would be happy to have her come out for rehearsals and the opening, if she wants to. . . . This morning I got some legal advice on the matter and with all the proof I have: a file of notes in my own handwriting, pages of construction and situations, carbons of the first draft, and the testimony of the stenographer who worked with us for three or four weeks, Zora can certainly do nothing at all with MULE-BONE without my permission. Why she should have set out to do so is beyond me. . . . Of course, I know that you knew nothing of all this until I wrote to you, and I hope it won't be putting you to a great deal of trouble, but would you do what you can do to get it untangled, and explain to Lawrence Langner or some of the Guild people how sorry I am that such an unfinished version ever reached them. . . . Since time is so pressing for the Gilpins, if you could send me a night letter or something about Zora's attitude, I'd appreciate it immensely. . . . Snowballs to you,

Langston

1. *Samuel French was a very influential theatrical publisher.*
2. *Rowena Jelliffe told Barrett Clark about Hughes's involvement.*
3. Roseanne *was a 1923 play by Nan Bagby Stephens. Paul Green's* In Abraham's Bosom *won the Pulitzer Prize in 1926.*

CARL VAN VECHTEN TO LANGSTON HUGHES, JANUARY 20, 1931

Dear Langston,

I am sure you'll understand that I cannot mix up in this any more. Zora had one grand emotional scene down here and I can't very well face another. Besides, anything she might promise to do for me would have no effect whatever on her subsequent actions.

Besides all this, on the issue you now bring up I rather agree with her and so do Lawrence and Fania and the others who have read and liked the play. We all feel that a stock production will be very dangerous and might kill the chances of the play completely. I've no doubt the Gilpins, well directed, and with plenty of time might give an excellent performance. I don't know how well they are directed, but it is obvious they have no time at all. Further, it is obvious that the play should be extensively altered, in conference with the director, before it is done at all and music and scenery and costumes are most important of all. But all this, of course, is for your ear. I shall say nothing more to Zora pro or con.

What you say about the stenographer (Madame Wallace Thurman, I believe!¹) is very amusing and I am convinced that this whole situation arises out of some feeling on Zora's part of which you are wholly unconscious. Well, keep me informed. If anything happens here I'll let you know.

Incidentally I have an excellent opportunity to get this play into the hands of Shumlin, the producer of Grand Hotel. So I wish you and Zora would get together sufficiently to agree on an authentic version.*

I am returning The Singing Darkey to you. By the way, did you ever hear that another of your charming books is occasionally referred to as The Weary Blacks.

With 156 yellow warblers bearing pink and blue candy hearts in their
beaks!
Carlo

January 20, 1931

+Perhaps I didn't tell you that Barrett Clark of French & Co., a playreader for the Guild, sent the play on to Cleveland with no authority whatever. And only wrote me after he had done so. I had given the play (with Zora's permission) very privately to Lawrence Langner and he understood it was unfinished work.

*Of course any manager like this would be furious about a stock production unless he had authorized it.

1. *Louise Thompson and Wallace Thurman were married in 1928, but Thompson filed for divorce soon afterward.*

Dear Langston,

Zora came to see me yesterday and cried and carried on no end about how fond she was of you, and how she wouldn't have had this misunderstanding for the world. And said she had written you six typewritten pages and talked to you long distance and said she was going to write to you again. So I hope you are straightened out with her by now.

And she doesn't want the play done in Cleveland, and here I think she is wise. A semi-amateur production of this play will kill it completely. It needs the most careful and sympathetic production and casting and if it gets it, I think it should duplicate the success of The Green Pastures.[1] And sooner or later I think it is quite certain to be produced.

Please keep my name out of any further conferences you may have with Zora about this matter. It wouldn't help any and I'd rather not become involved.

145 red crocodiles with golden tongues to you!

Carlo

1. *Marc Connelly's 1930 Broadway hit.*

4800 Carnegie Ave.
Cleveland, Ohio

January 22, 1931

Dear Carlo,

I hope never to worry you with this MULE-BONE business again. You have been more than kind about it already. A letter from Zora today assures me that she had reversed herself, so I guess the split is over. Some days ago, however, I turned over the whole matter to Arthur Spingarn,‡ but now I shall wire him further that things seem to be coming back to their original point. . . . Zora wired the Jelliffe's some three days ago Okaying the proceedings out here—just a few hours before your first letter came advising against the production. Since then there has been two other wires from her of acceptance, which the Gilpin lawyer considers equivalent to a contract, so they have gone on full blast into production. To try and stop it again now would cause I don't know what other difficulties, and I am just about weary of the whole thing. I am in no way responsible for the beginning of this Cleveland business, and certainly wouldn't have chosen a production here either first—but in the sense that I might not have known what Zora was doing for months, it has been fortunate. Then, too, the Gilpin Players and the Cleveland Plaindealer drama people have been of great aid in untangling the thing for me— a hundred dollars or so burnt up in wires and New York phone calls— so that now I suppose they feel that the play is due [. . .]¹ effort and excitement.

Zora has signified her intention of coming on here in a few days, and all in all, to back out of the thing now would take just a little more effort than I can muster, after this hectic week which ended last night by my being in jail! . . . A not un-exciting experience, by the way. . . . My big- time cousin came by the house about eight with another fellow and a car. I had just finished some New York mail that needed to go off at once, so I asked if they would drop me by the Post Office. They did, and then started up Cedar, one of the big Negro streets here, full of cops all the time. Later I remembered that I had still to get in touch with Mrs. Jelliffe that night. We stopped near a drug store and went in to call, when my cousin and I came out we walked into the arms of two cops. It seems that some [one] dented the back of a taxi cab. The cab driver accused us because our car was parked near-by. He had no witnesses, but evidently wanted to get the money out of somebody to pay for his dent. The cops threatened to beat us into confessing, a whole squad of detectives and policemen arrived in two cars, the wagon was called and off we went to the station. We were not allowed to use the phone there, third degree methods were applied to the boy who owned the car, the police and detectives using their hands and clubs on him before us and the cab dri- ver, the whole bunch of them using oaths and insulting racial remarks, and insisting that we pay this driver for his cab. Finally, getting no satis- faction, they put us all in jail (not the cab driver), kept us there until this morning, made us sign Suspicious Person slips, and turned us loose. The boy must now pay a large bill for towing and storage of his car by the police. I've heard of other innocent Negroes being picked up often here and having to pay bills or fines before they get loose. It seems to be a sort of graft the police are working in the colored districts, where they walk in pairs after dark stopping people and searching them for no rea- son at all. . . . The jail was bitter cold, with a board and no covering to sleep on or under, so if I've caught my death o'cold blame the Cleveland police. The walls were of steel, which made you just that much colder if you leaned against them. So now I know what Bessie Smith really meant by

Thirty days in jail
With ma back turned to de wall.

So with all that, I'm evil in mind, and don't give a damn this Morning whether MULE-BONE is or isn't put on. Brazzle's mule, even in manuscript, has done a mean piece of kicking, and it will probably take all of us several weeks to get unbent again, although Zora writes that she is busy "smoothing out her lovely brow at present." . . . That would be great if Shumlin would consider the play, and when Zora comes here I'll see if we can't get out a script that would be in shape for his attention. . . . In any case, Carlo, you've been grand about the whole matter. Certainly I'm sorry that all this mixup came about, and I trust Zora is, too—but I guess now everything will be the same again. Thank God! So with 7 wish bones, 11 rabbits' feet, and 777 load stones to you, (but no mule bones whatsoever), I am, quand meme,

P.S. I have some music for Paul Robeson. Have you any idea where one might send it to him?

1. *This fragment of the letter was missing.*

CARL VAN VECHTEN TO LANGSTON HUGHES, JANUARY 1931

Dear Langston,
Many congratulations on the Harmon award[1] which you deserve. We dined with the Johnsons last night and they were very much pleased. Indeed, I think he was one of the judges. . . . Your arrest was absolutely fabulous, but I think you might raise an awful stink about it and get some money both from the taxi company and the city. It was obviously a shakedown, because nobody is arrested for a dent in a car, even if [he] has done it. They simply take your address and number. You'd better tell your friends on the Plain Dealer about this and make a lot of trouble. . . . I've thought of another and more important objection to your title: The Singing Dark means exactly the same thing as Caroling Dusk.[2] . . . Your letters are fabulously interesting. Do write me more as soon as you have seen Zora. If the production is good enough, and by that I mean very good indeed, I may come out to see it. Anyway, keep me posted on everything and as soon as you and Zora have reached some agreement whereby the play may be peddled, and put into some kind of shape (and have it done professionally between blue covers, as other plays are done),

let me know and again I'll see what can be done. Of course, this Cleveland production in itself may do the trick. So much depends on the imagination of the producer. This play needs a hell of a lot of producing.

67 Harlem hoofers in red pants doing the Lindy Hop with razors
between their teeth to you!
Carlo

Monday

1. *The Harmon Foundation promoted black participation in the fine arts. Hughes's award consisted of two medals and four hundred dollars, which was at this point the largest amount of money he had ever possessed at one time.*
2. *Cullen's 1927 anthology of verse by Negro poets.*

CARL VAN VECHTEN TO LANGSTON HUGHES, FEBRUARY 2, 1931

Dear Langston, Please thank Zell Ingram for his block prints which are very interesting & particularly for the implied compliment. . . . Have you read H. L. Mencken in the current Opportunity?[1] And "The Fall of a Fair Confederate" (anonymous, but I understand this is Geo. Schuyler's wife) in The Modern Quarterly for January?[2] These two papers will probably cause an earthquake in the regions inhabited by what your papa calls "black monkeys." And have you read <u>Black No More</u> yet? You'd better. Harlem is closed tighter than a drum on account of gang wars. But Nora is singing nightly on East 47 Street & that helps. J. W. Johnson has been invited to preside over a chair of creative writing at Fisk next year & has accepted.[3] Prof. Imes of the same institution will come in to see me today. Please let me know if Mulebone is going to be worth seeing in its present production. I can get Langner to go out & possibly others if it is worth while.

116 green giraffes with bright yellow spots & a couple blue Harlem
gangsters with ruby suspenders & purple socks to you!
Carlo.

February 2

(I sent you some stallions—14, I think, yesterday)

1. *In the February 1931 issue of* Opportunity, *H. L. Mencken argued that blacks were superior to most American whites. He also claimed that Fundamentalist Christian churches were keeping black people down, and urged the younger generation to unburden itself of this last vestige of slavery.*
2. *Josephine Cogdell married the black satirist and author of* Black No More, *George*

Schuyler, on January 6, 1928. Her anonymous essay, "The Fall of a Fair Confederate,"
describes her conversion from a Southern-bred racist to a self-described "Negrophile,"
which happened shortly before she met George in 1927 in the offices of The Messenger,
where he was the editor.
  3. *Historically black Fisk University is located in Nashville, Tennessee.*

CARL VAN VECHTEN TO LANGSTON HUGHES, FEBRUARY 7, 1931
(POSTCARD)

February 7, 1931

Mr. Langston Hughes
4800 Carnegie Ave.
Cleveland, Ohio
Dear Langston:
I never heard of such goings on & I had practically everybody lined up
to go out & see the masterpiece. Of course nothing can be done now
until you & Zora decide who wrote this drama.[1]
  116 Harlem Blackbirds with fallen arches & ivory teeth to you.

C.

  1. *Hurston had gone to Hughes's home in Cleveland intending to make up with him. She*
  became enraged however when she found out that Louise Thompson had also made a visit
  to Cleveland. "She made such a scene as you can not possibly imagine," Hughes wrote to
  Van Vechten. The original letter is quoted in The Life of Langston Hughes *by Arnold*
  Rampersad. "She pushed her hat back, bucked her eyes, ground her teeth, and shook man-
  uscripts in my face particularly the third act which she claims she wrote alone by herself
  while Miss Thompson and I were off doing Spanish together. (And the way she said Spanish *meant something else.)"*

LANGSTON HUGHES TO CARL VAN VECHTEN, FEBRUARY 24, 1931

4800 Carnegie Avenue
Cleveland, Ohio

February 24, 1931

Dear Carlo,
I loved the little booklet about Feathers,[1] the little cat with the rose
nose and the beautiful eyes, who never had any children. Thank you for
sending it to me. . . . The backwash of the recent tempest left me with
something like grippe, and an awful temper. Anyway, I've been more or
less under the weather. The MULE BONE plus the troubles with my dear
patron last spring (and lately the two of them mixed up together) have

had much the same effect on me as that time when I got mad at my papa in Mexico and had to go to the hospital for some weeks.[2] I've got a grand doctor who advises me to take a long trip in the sunshine, which sounds as amusing as anything I can think of by myself; so with Zell Ingram, the artist boy who has a Ford, I'm starting South in a few weeks bound for Florida, Cuba, Haiti, Puerto Rico, Guadeloupe, Martinique, Trinidad and all the black countries of the Carribean. We'll park the Ford in some Florida backyard until we come back, and proceed to the islands, staying in each as long as it proves attractive. I'll have to come back to Jersey to give up my apartment there early in March, so I'll be seeing you. Hope to be there in time for the last Robeson concert. . . .

Well, my Harmon medals came the other day. It turned out to be two, instead of one: a small gold one, and a large one of bronze. You wear the small one, it seems, but I don't know what you do with the big one. They both have ships on them, so I like them very much.[3] . . . The poor number writers are having a hard time here, the way they have to change from one basis to another.[4] A young gangster friend of mine tells me that the Hearst papers have fallen off in sales by three car loads a day here, since the New York clearing house stopped giving out their totals. (He also told me about a recent shooting two days before it came off. He's one of the few colored who sit on the "big council.") They're using the Detroit clearing house now, but nobody believes in it much, so policy seems to be taking its place.

I have BLACK NO MORE but haven't read it yet. Mrs. Schuyler's article was a whang, however! . . . Fisk is to be congratulated on having James Weldon there next year.

The Gilpin Players are doing a manuscript production of Andrew Burris' "You Mus' be Bo'n Agin" this week and he is coming from New York to see it. It's a comedy about preachers, it seems, and is said to be a little like ROSEANE with a church scene for the second act.

I've been making block prints lately for the fun of it. I'll send you one maybe.

THE SINGING DARKIE is now called A HOUSE IN THE WORLD. Considerably cut down and rearranged I've sent it on to Mr. Burton to see what he thinks about it.

With a house full of niggers to you,

Langston

+Is Miguel back?

1. *A limited-edition prose quarto about one of Van Vechten's cats.*
2. *Hughes wrote about his reaction to these events in* The Big Sea: *"Violent anger makes me physically ill." His illness reminded him of an experience he'd had ten years before while*

visiting his father in Mexico: "My stomach kept turning round and round inside me. And when I thought of my father, I got sicker and sicker. I hated my father." His rage landed him in a Mexican hospital for weeks.

3. *He shipped his medals off to Godmother, hoping to soften her anger toward him. She was unmovable.*

4. *Illegal betting was a central — and not unrespectable — feature of Harlem life. A number writer or runner physically took the bets.*

CARL VAN VECHTEN TO LANGSTON HUGHES, FEBRUARY 1931

(POSTCARD)

Mr. Langston Hughes
4800 Carnegie Ave
Cleveland
Ohio

February 1931

Dear Langston:

Your proposed trip sounds marvellous! I'd love to go with you! I hope you bring Z.I. back with you. I want to meet him. The N.A.A.C.P. ball is March 16 (Monday) at the Savoy.[1] Hope you'll be here for that. Miguel is not back but the Knopfs are. I like your new title. Haven't seen Zora at all. There's a Savoy Lindy contest Saturday & the Bentley woman is breaking one down. There's <u>nothing</u> she won't say nowadays.[2]

204 yellow gals to you singing Love for Sale.

Carlo.

1. *Harlem's opulent Savoy Ballroom was also known as "The Home of Happy Feet."*
2. *Hughes wrote admiringly about Gladys Bentley's early years in Harlem in* The Big Sea: *"Miss Bentley was an amazing exhibition of musical energy — a large, dark, masculine lady, whose feet pounded the floor while her fingers pounded the keyboard — a perfect piece of African sculpture, animated by her own rhythm."*

LANGSTON HUGHES TO CARL VAN VECHTEN, MARCH 13, 1931

Friday the 13th!

Dear Carlo,

Thanks for the clipping of Dr. Hirschfeld's on the Lindy.[1] Here is something that may interest you from today's Cleveland News. It seems that Adelaide[2] will be here tomorrow. . . . At the moment I'm speechless — just back home from having my only tonsils out. Rather enjoyed watching the operation — but my Dr. says I can't leave town until next week, thereby forcing me to miss the ball on Monday. Awfully sorry. Walter had asked me to go with them. . . . Spring, I understand, is the hurricane season in the islands. That ought to make Havana even more exciting than when the mid-winter tourists are there. They tie up all the trees along the Malecon and put fences around them to keep them from blowing away!

Did you know that in the days of the Greeks, the doctors let their fingernails grow long and sharp, and used them for operations—in the place of knives? Thus were the first tonsils removed.

Well, I guess my first play is done. (No woman worked with me on this one.) The son has murdered the father, the mother has gone mad—and on Monday I will have it typed. . . . Do you know a good agent? . . . It's called Mulatto. Theme: same as poem.[3]

Well. . . . Here are ten Cuban coons—with bongo's between their
knees—
Langston

1. *The German Dr. Magnus Hirschfeld was known as "the Einstein of sex." With Havelock Ellis, he founded the World League for Sex Reform. He also wrote an article in praise of the lindy hop.*
2. *Adelaide Hall was a popular singer and actress.*
3. *Hughes's poem "Mulatto" roared: "I am your son, white man!" It was first published in the* Saturday Review of Literature *in the fall of 1926. Above, Hughes describes his play that bears the same name.*

CARL VAN VECHTEN TO LANGSTON HUGHES, MARCH 16, 1931
(POSTCARD)

March 16, 1931

Mr. Langston Hughes
4800 Carnegie Ave.
Cleveland, Ohio.
Dear Langston:

Sorry you won't be here for the Ball. Will miss you . . . Why do you get an agent for your play until you have to. Why don't you take it first to Theresa Helburn? She asked for it. Explaining that you wrote it alone. Mr. Chesnutt writes very flatteringly about me in The Colophon, that very expensive print collector's quarterly.[1]

Sunflowers & [. . .][2] to you!
Carlo.

1. *In "Post-Bellum–Pre-Harlem," published in a 1931 issue of* The Colophon: A Book Collector's Quarterly, *Charles Chesnutt wrote: "One of the first of the New York writers to appreciate the possibilities of Harlem for literary purposes was Carl Van Vechten, whose*

novel Nigger Heaven *was rather severely criticized by some of the colored intellectuals as
a libel on the race, while others of them praised it highly. I was prejudiced in its favor for
reasons which those who have read the book will understand. I found it a vivid and interesting story which presented some new and better types of Negroes and treated them
sympathetically."*
2. *Illegible word.*

LANGSTON HUGHES TO CARL VAN VECHTEN, APRIL 1, 1931
(POSTCARD)

Mr. Carl Van Vechten
150 W. 55th Street
New York,
New York

April 1, 1931

Miami
Tuesday
Swell trip down—but can't buy tickets here to Havana. The color-line
business again. Will try our luck in Key West tomorrow. Langston.

H*ughes and Ingram successfully bought
tickets in Key West. They spent two weeks
in Cuba and then headed for Haiti.*

LANGSTON HUGHES AND ZELL INGRAM IN HAITI,
SEPTEMBER 1931

(Air Mail)
Poste Restante,
Cap Haitien, Haiti

May 27, 1931

Dear Carlo,

Have been laying off to write you for weeks, but we've been moving so fast and rough that I haven't had a chance, but at last we come to a stopping place—with the sight of the Citadel 20 miles away on a mountain top.[1] We came across Cuba in old cars that continually broke down, and camions full of peasants and chickens; took deck passage on a French ship at Santiago for Port au Prince and rode in the open for three days with the sugar-cane workers coming home, while the boat went all around Southern Haiti picking up cargo. The last night a storm came up and we slept in the hole with the Haitian crew. Port au Prince struck us as being little more than a collection of wooden huts with tin roofs, gangs of Marines, badly lighted streets, and everything at American prices or higher, so we left for the North. Half way to the Cape the spring floods held us up for nearly two weeks, but we had a swell time. Stayed at St. Marc where there is a splendid beach, mountains all around, and lots of Congoes on week-ends, drums sounding everywhere. (The Congo is a simplified Cuban rumba with a more monotonous rhythm, a more primitive pattern—men and women dancing alone or together as they choose, all circling round and round a sort of Maypole in the middle of a thatched roof, singing and throwing hips.)

We reached the Cape last week, found a grand hotel on the water-front for seamen and Santo Domingan revolutionaries—a place where they play bisque and dominoes all day, and dance to Cuban records, talk revolutions, and drink copoise half the night. The Cape is charming, full of old ruins from the days of the French. Pushed into the sea by the hills, its much cooler, less full of mosquitoes, and not nearly so ugly as Port au Prince. Our windows and balconies look out on the ancient embankments, the bay and the mountains beyond. Room and meals for only $25 each a month! All the native crew from the ship we took at Santiago live here at the Cape, so we have plenty of friends (in fact, they told us of this hotel.) They take us to Congoes, cockfights, dances, and bars; also out on the bay in their fishing boats. (We're hoping for a Voodoo dance this Saturday of which they have told us.) Last week we went to a grand Congo at the foot of the mountains, got tight on sugar-cane rhum, and Zell outdanced the natives. (The snakehips was a new one to them.) The next

morning the musicians came to our hotel and we bought both their
drums, the "Mama" and the "Baby." Need only a "Popa" drum now to have
a full set, but it seems that between the priests and the Marines (both of
whom try to stop the dances and confiscate the drums), "Popa" drums are
pretty scarce, and probably can only be found way back in the hills. . . .
Zell has made some nice heads in Cuban and Haitian woods, and a few
watercolors. Everybody down here takes him for a boxer, and the prettiest
woman I've seen in town, so far, has taken him for her own personal
property. . . . We had a swift and glorious time in Havana. I was surprised
at the amount of publicity our visit got—reporters and flashlights at the
pier, with pictures and a front page story the next morning; later a full
account of my reading at the Cercle Francais; and the front page again
when we were arrested at the beach where we went to meet a professor
from the University and Addison Durland, a most amusing Cuban-
American rich boy who makes swell pictures. (You must meet him when
he comes to New York again.)

They wanted to charge us $10.00 each to come in the beach, refused to
let us wait for our friends at the entrance, and when we stopped outside,
had us arrested charged with "escandolo"—disturbing the peace. They
testified next day that we had bathed inside, put our feet on the beach
chairs and refused to take them down, and generally misbehaved. Of
course, this was absurd as they didn't let us in. The judge, who knew of
the frequent attempts at discrimination there against Cubans of color,
rebuked the beach authorities, cleared us, and made a long oration on
the rights of all people of whatever color under Cuban law to go freely to
all public places. . . . With the rainy season coming on, and boats from
Haiti to the outward islands very difficult to get, we've decided to go no
further South this trip, but to take a sailing vessel from here to the
Bahamas, thence Miami, and home. Zell has a summer job in sight; and I
want to do my novel. The next island of distinctive interest would be Martinique—and its a long ways. . . . I haven't had any mail from the states
for about six weeks, (nor have I seen an American paper in Haiti) so I
don't know what's happening. However, I trust Harlem is still there; and
that you're O.K. I hope you got over the trouble with your leg all
right. . . . I haven't done any work. Been trying to wear my troubles off
my mind. . . . Saw Nigger Heaven & Magic Island[2] (French editions) in
the only bookshop at Port au Prince where I bought my anthologie de
Poesie Haitien. Creole patois is marvellous—like Chinese—full of little
tunes and half-notes. . . . Stars over the black mountains to you,

Langston

1. *The renowned Citadel La Ferrière.*
2. *William Seabrook's 1929 book about Haiti.*

CARL VAN VECHTEN TO LANGSTON HUGHES, NOVEMBER 27, 1931

Dear Langston,

Mark Lutz[1] of Richmond (he is on the News-Leader) has been after the records of the Scottsboro case[2] for some time. He saw Walter White when he was here and Walter promised to send him papers containing the story. What he finally received were copies of the Associated Press dispatches. Now he writes me that in the World-Telegram you advocate the printing of the transcript of the trial. Do you know where he can get this transcript? I think he wants to try to print it, or as much of it as he can. If you do, please let me know or write directly to him: 1123 West Franklin Street, Richmond, Virginia.

I hear you are having triumphs everywhere and selling lots of mothers.[3] Let me hear from you some day. Covarrubias and Rose[4] are back from Bali and were here for dinner last night.

affectionately,
Carlo

November 27, 1931

1. *The journalist Mark Lutz and Van Vechten began an affair during the summer of 1931 that lasted several years and eventually gave way to a lifelong friendship. They exchanged daily letters for thirty-three years. According to Lutz's wishes, Van Vechten's letters to Lutz were destroyed when Lutz died in 1967.*
2. *On March 25 in Scottsboro, Alabama, an armed mob of whites assisted by two police officers dragged nine young black men off a train, accusing them of having raped two white women. Eight of the men were sentenced to die; one was given a life sentence. The Scottsboro case ignited international controversy. In 1976, Alabama's Governor George Wallace pardoned all of the defendants. At that point, only one of them was still alive.*
3. *Van Vechten refers to Hughes's new book,* The Negro Mother and Other Dramatic Recitations. *Van Vechten introduced Hughes to the book's illustrator, Prentiss Taylor,‡ and gave them a two-hundred-dollar loan to start The Golden Stair Press in Taylor's home in Greenwich Village in September. The three men were partners in this venture, a dream come true for Hughes, who was always looking for ways to make his work more accessible to people—particularly Negroes—with low incomes. They launched the press with the publication of* Negro Mother, *Hughes's paean to black motherhood. Hughes sold this small chapbook for a quarter. The distinguished educator Mary McLeod Bethune was one of Hughes's inspirations for the title poem.*
4. *Rose Rolanda was Miguel Covarrubias's wife.*

GLADYS BENTLEY, PRENTISS TAYLOR, AND NORA HOLT,
IN HARLEM, FEBRUARY 27, 1932. PHOTOGRAPH BY CARL VAN VECHTEN

CARL VAN VECHTEN TO LANGSTON HUGHES, DECEMBER 29, 1931

(POSTCARD)

December 29, 1931

Dear Langston:

Many many thanks for Dear Lovely Death, a lovely book of poems.[1]
Did you receive my Christmas card? And did Mrs. Bethune? I haven't
heard from you except through Prentiss since you went away. I suppose
you are much too busy to write.[2] Aaron Copland—just back from
Europe—was here last night. I showed him The Negro Mother & he
wants to set the title poem to music. . . . In every play on B'dway somebody from Harlem is getting lynched! Best to you & my regards to the
very charming Mrs. Bethune. C.

1. Dear Lovely Death *was published by Amy Spingarn's publishing venture, Troutbeck
   Press. It was printed on handmade paper.*
2. *Hughes had met Mary McLeod Bethune during the summer while he was traveling with
   Zell Ingram. She received them in July at Daytona Normal and Industrial School for
   Negro Girls, the college she herself had founded in 1904. It would later become Bethune-
   Cookman College. Hughes was awestruck: "We shared Mrs. Bethune's wit and
   wisdom . . . the wisdom of a jet-black woman who had risen from a barefooted field hand
   in a cotton patch to be head of one of the leading junior colleges in America, and a leader
   of her people," he wrote reverently in* I Wonder As I Wander, *the second volume of his
   autobiography. Bethune renewed his sense of purpose. "You must go all over the South
   with your poetry," she told him. Hughes promptly began a reading tour on November 2
   with his new assistant, Radcliffe Lucas, a former classmate at Lincoln.*

1932–1934

Hughes distanced himself from Mule Bone *and all those involved with it after he found out in the summer of 1931 that Wallace Thurman had agreed to rewrite the play for Hurston—without any input from Hughes.*

For Hughes, the fall reading tour proposed by Bethune was a chance to repair his wounded spirit. The tour took him through every state in the South; he achieved his goal to visit as many predominantly black colleges and universities as possible. Because of the Depression, Hughes persuaded Alfred Knopf to issue a special one-dollar edition of The Weary Blues *for him to sell on tour along with* Negro Mother. *"Few white people bought our book," Hughes said about* Negro Mother *in* I Wonder As I Wander, *"but to Negroes I sold three large printings."*

While on his book tour Hughes made a detour to Scottsboro, Alabama, and visited the Scottsboro defendants at Kilby Prison in Montgomery in late January. There he read some of his poetry to the young men, even though, he reflected in a June 1932 article for Opportunity *called "Brown in America: Kilby," his poems sounded "futile and stupid in the face of death." The visit was sobering: "For a moment the fear came: even for me, a Sunday morning visitor, the doors might never open again. WHITE guards held the keys . . . And I'm only a nig-*

ger poet. Nigger. Niggers. Hundreds of niggers in Kilby Prison. Black, brown, yellow, near-white niggers. The guards, WHITE. Me—a visiting nigger."

The Scottsboro case catapulted Hughes into a more political life. He joined campaigns to protest the trial's outcome and became at one point the president of the League of Struggle for Negro Rights. His poetry of this time reflects his disgust with the Scottsboro case and his dissatisfaction with U.S. race relations in general. He published "At Scottsboro" in the February 15 issue of Contempo: A Review of Books and Personalities, *a radical student newspaper at the University of North Carolina at Chapel Hill.*

LANGSTON HUGHES TO CARL VAN VECHTEN, JANUARY 2, 1932

Carlo—
Would write you a whole letter from here if I dared remain that long. Have lots to tell you—

THE TOWN OF SCOTTSBORO

Scottsboro's just a little place:
No shame is writ across its face—
Its court, too weak to stand against a mob
Its people's heart, too small to hold a sob.

Langston Hughes

At Scottsboro,
January 2, 1932

LANGSTON HUGHES TO CARL VAN VECHTEN, FEBRUARY 10, 1932

[Handwritten] Saw Nella's husband in Alabama the other day.

On tour—
Bethune-Cookman
Daytona Beach

February 10, 1932
Dear Carlo—Of course you know why I have not written you: because this tour has kept me busier than anything I've ever done in my life. The correspondence alone is tremendous, besides travelling six or seven hun-

dred miles a week, and speaking almost every night. If I ever do this again I cannot possibly undertake taking care of the actual bookings myself. My audiences have been swell. S.R.O. in several places. About 1200 people this afternoon (more than half, white, from the big hotels.)[1] Mrs. Bethune is marvellous as a mistress of ceremonies—a sort of black Texas Guinan joyfully clothed in African dignity, presenting myself, with a full orchestra and a chorus of a hundred student voices singing Negro music as a setting for my poems. The aisles and the stage were crowded and lots of people couldn't get in. Next week she's having Oscar Depriest,[2] and later Roland Hayes. She's a power down here. Her campus is lovely now—palms, poinsettas, hanging moss—and cabbages and peas. You'd like it. . . . She sends her greetings to you; and commands that you visit here.

I'd like to tell you all about Chapel Hill;[3] Huntsville;[4] Scottsboro; A. C. L. Adams[5] and Tad; Julia Peterkin's place and the white gentleman on her front porch who didn't introduce himself, and insisted that she was ill;[6] Atlanta; and everything else, but it would take the rest of the night—and it's 2 A.M. now.

Thanks for your lovely card. I'm glad if you liked <u>Dear Lovely Death</u>. Blanche tells me you have a new book, and maybe Prentiss will do the jacket.[7] That's swell! . . . Have you seen Paul? And if you've learned his attitude toward the Gynt musical,[8] please let me know. I haven't done anything on the 2nd act yet—wasn't supposed to until I learned the possibilities for production on the basis on the first—I'm enclosing a list of "mail-stops" so you can see which way the tour leads: through Mississippi in February, then Arkansas, Memphis, possibly St. Louis, and up to the middle West. Back to Texas in April, and then more than likely California in the spring, if sufficient bookings come in. (Is there a Forum in Hollywood that would like to hear all about little yellow bastard boys?[9] If so, let me know.) If I get to the coast, I'll probably stay out there next summer, and write my novel—if I can salvage enough money from this tour to do so. So far, I haven't caught up with my debts yet. (This might amuse you: Of all the colleges I've visited, the only one that failed to pay me the fee agreed on was the white university, Chapel Hill. They said they couldn't collect it all, after "Christ in Alabama" appeared in <u>Contempo</u>—altho they provided me with a packed house—and two parties (Paul Green and Larry Flinn)[10] afterwards. . . . Friends in the North are writing me that I'll surely be lynched. And my mother has wired that I come back at once: prayers are being said at the altar for me in Cleveland! But all the lynchings seem to have moved to the Broadway stage. I haven't seen a one down here. . . . I'd be very happy if Aaron Copland would set The Negro Mother to music. . . . Have you heard of Florence's death?[11] Sterling Brown's first book of poems, Southern Roads, will be out in the spring, he writes me. . . . O, yes, I passed through Zora's home—the actual scene of <u>Mule-Bone</u>. I've just read proofs of Countee's novel.[12] Thought society parts very amusing. . . . Happy New Year. Langston

1. *Hughes had given a benefit reading that afternoon at Mrs. Bethune's college, the Daytona Normal and Industrial School. Bethune was moved when he ended with "The Negro Mother": " 'My son, my son!' cried Mrs. Bethune, rising with tears in her eyes to embrace me on the platform," Hughes reminisced in* I Wonder As I Wander.
2. *De Priest was a black United States congressman from 1928 until 1933, a time when there was very little black representation in the federal government.*
3. *Hughes caused a stir at the University of North Carolina at Chapel Hill—one of the few white schools that booked him on this tour—when he published "Christ in Alabama" in* Contempo, *a student publication at the University. The poem ends with the lines: "Most Holy Bastard / Of the bleeding mouth: / Nigger Christ / On the cross of the South." It enraged white Southern readers as much as it thrilled the magazine's editors.*
4. *Hughes had to be talked out of seeking an interview with Ruby Bates in Huntsville, Alabama. Bates was one of the white girls who had accused the nine Scottsboro defendants of rape. He didn't look for her but he did do some research in Huntsville. "Folks around town said that Ruby Bates had stated that she lied in court; that nobody had raped her. Later under oath she recanted her testimony, declaring the whole story had been a fabrication. . . . But the Negro youths still remained, at Christmas, in the death house," Hughes reflected in* I Wonder As I Wander.
5. *Dr. A. C. L. Adams was a distinguished white physician as well as a renowned collector of Negro folklore who lived in Columbia, South Carolina. The day after Hughes's reading in Columbia, Adams received Hughes at his plantation.*
6. *Prior to this event he and Peterkin had spent considerable time discussing their mutual interest in Negro life and culture at social gatherings in New York.*
7. *Van Vechten's 1932 book,* Sacred and Profane Memories, *was a collection of autobiographical essays. Prentiss Taylor did the jacket cover illustration.*
8. *Hughes worked on the musical* Cock o' the Walk *(later* Cock o' the World*) along with its creator, the Swede Kaj Gynt, who originally conceived of it as a vehicle for Robeson. Robeson would never express more than a casual interest in the musical.*
9. *Hughes's poem "Mulatto" includes the refrain "A little yellow / Bastard boy."*
10. *Larry Flynn was rumored to be Andrew Mellon's nephew.*
11. *Florence Embry Jones was a star at Le Grand Duc in Paris. She quit in 1924 to open her own cabaret. She died a pauper in the United States.*
12. *Cullen's roman à clef about the Harlem Renaissance,* One Way to Heaven, *was published in 1932.*

LANGSTON HUGHES TO CARL VAN VECHTEN, FEBRUARY 17, 1932

(ON RUST COLLEGE STATIONERY)

On tour,
Feb. 17, 1932

Dear Carlo:

If you like the race, you would adore Mississippi, since there's almost nothing but the race down here. . . . Tomorrow we cross the river into

Arkansas. . . . Had an over-flow house in Birmingham last night. Lots couldn't get in. <u>Negro Mother</u> sold like reefers on 131st Street. . . . I sent Fania a cotton bale of dulces from New Orleans.

Sincerely,

Langston

Chez Noel Sullivan
2323 Hyde Street
San Francisco, Cal.

May 16, 1932

Dear Carlo—

Been meaning to write you for weeks, but there's been continual excitement, town after town, people on top of people—and Prentiss Taylor and the Golden Stair Press and the 9 Scottsboro boys. Los Angeles, Hollywood, Hoover Dam, Grand Canyon—and at last a restful haven in the home of Noel Sullivan‡ where nobody can bother you until they've passed three butlers, two secretaries, and my personal assistant![1] . . . This is really a most delightful house (the old Robert Louis Stevenson home) on a high hill overlooking the Pacific where all the boats come in from China. Noel has given me his "Negro Room" with a little jazz band in porcelain and paintings by Block and Justema around. The house has marvellous gardens and flowers everywhere. Ramon Novarro[2] is also a house guest this week—very amusing boy. Last night we went to the opening of <u>The Green Pastures</u>[3] here. Stebbins came out from New York for it.[4] Old man Harrison is still as great as ever, but the cherubims are almost as tall as the angels now. . . . I thought your pictures of me were swell, particularly XXI No. 8, playing the drum, XXI No. 4, XX 28, XXI 1, and XX-30—this latter is grand, looking at the saxophone. I like XXI-1 a lot, too. Prentiss tells me you've gone into the Monastery of Photography, and do nothing but spend all your time in a dark cell.

Tonight I give a reading here; Thursday in Berkeley at the University; and next week in Portland and Seattle; then back down to Fresno, Carmel, and Los Angeles. I've given up the idea of remaining out here for the summer, (as I once thought) and shall be starting back East in early June by way of Santa Fe, Denver, Omaha, etc., having accepted some cross-country engagements via the North. I remember you asked me to let you know if I went to Iowa again. I shall be passing through that state

XXI 8

LANGSTON HUGHES,
PHOTOGRAPHS BY
CARL VAN VECHTEN,
MARCH 27, 1932

XX 28

XXI 1

XXI 4

XX 30

on my way to Minneapolis, and so, if you know of any groups who might care to have me read to them some evening in the June 20's, let me know soon, and I'll probably be back in New York in early July.

<u>Scottsboro Limited</u> was produced quite effectively by the Rebel Players in Los Angeles last week before a big audience at a Counter-Olympics Benefit.[5] I read a mass-chant and every one yelled beautifully at the proper moments.

Saturday I am going to meet Tom Mooney.[6]

You may write me here c/o Mr. Sullivan (to arrive by 28th) if you wish, as I shall stay up North only a few days, and will be passing Frisco again. After 28th mail should be sent to 837 East 24th St. Los Angeles, where I'll be in and out until I leave for the East.

May you have a home in
that rock by and by,
Langston

NOËL SULLIVAN ON THE SUN
PORCH AT HIS HYDE STREET
RESIDENCE, SAN FRANCISCO,
DECEMBER 19, 1933

HOLLOW HILLS FARM, N.D.

1. *While on tour in March, Hughes received an offer of temporary refuge in San Francisco from a wealthy white patron of the arts, Noël Sullivan.*
2. *Ramon Novarro was a popular actor.*
3. The Green Pastures *was the white playwright Marc Connolly's dramatic treatment of the Old Testament from a black Southern point of view. Richard Harrison's performance as "De Lawd" received outstanding notices.*
4. *Robert Stebbins was an American film critic.*
5. *Hughes's interactive one-act play about the Scottsboro case was another Golden Stair Press venture. Until his* Mule Bone *betrayal, Thurman was supposed to collaborate with Hughes on the play.*
6. *Hughes met Mooney, an activist and union organizer, at San Quentin, where he was serving time for a 1916 San Francisco bombing.*

LANGSTON HUGHES TO CARL VAN VECHTEN, NOVEMBER 15, 1932

Ashkhabad, Turkmenia
Soviet Central Asia

November 15, 1932

Dear Carlo:

Probably you thought I never intended to write you, but I believe I did send you cables from Russia.[1] At Moscow, cables were so cheap, I used to send a few almost every time I passed the office, but down here they can't be sent in English, you probably don't read Russian, and Turkmenian is out of the questions. . . . I well remember what you said in prophecy about the picture. Amid great confusion, it was postponed until next year.[2] But, at least nobody walked home. The four months contracts were paid in full, money reimbursed for expenses over, and tickets home supplied via Paris for those who wished. Besides two or three tours over the Soviet Union. Some have staid in Moscow to work: radio, theatres, etc., and one as supervisor of the modernization of the postal service. . . . I'm doing a series of articles for IZVESTIA[3] on the contrast between the darker peoples of the Soviet and the darkies at home, therefore my sojourn in this part of the world. It will be swell material for a book, too, and I've written Blanche that I'll send her the manuscript by March. I'm going practically all over this part of Asia. Have already been in Bukhara and Samarkand, and shall probably go back to Samarkand in January to write up the book, as I liked it there, and have met some nice people. Last week in Bukhara I talked to one of the former Emirs three hundred wives. And got a little of the low-down on palace life. He had forty boys, too, and when he went away he took the boys and left the wives! This one is now cashier of a tea house. . . . Have been out in the desert, with the nomads. . . . And next week, go for a month or so to Tashkent, the admin-

LANGSTON HUGHES (SECOND ROW, THIRD FROM RIGHT) AND
THE MESCHRABPOM FILM GROUP, JUNE 1932

istrative center for these darker Republics. The contrasts here are amazing: camels and airplanes, modern schools for kids who live in yurts,
herd-boys broadcasting nightly on reed pipes from a high-powered radio
station. And brown, yellow, and white mingling from the tea houses to
the highest Soviets. . . . Letters from Prentiss and the printer inform me
in no uncertain terms of the bankruptcy of THE GOLDEN STAIR
PRESS so if I get an advance on this Asiatic book it will have to go to pay
that off.[4] It was too bad the SCOTTSBORO books didn't reach me in
time, as I could have sold out the edition the last month of my tour in
California. I only got them when I had three engagements left. After
FIRE and this, I will hardly venture into the publishing business again in
life. . . . The papers say Nora's gone to Shanghai. I want to come home in
the spring via Siberia, and will go to Shanghai too if it's possible to get
the dollars and the visa. Let me know if Nora will still be there. And
maybe you'll come over. . . . Word from Noel Sullivan says he might visit
New York this month. Have you seen him? . . . And what else is news
back home? Down here I learn nothing of what's going on. My Russian
doesn't penetrate the newspapers. . . . Rose of the desert to Fania, and
happy holidays to you both. . . . Write; c/o Meschrabpom Film, Moscow,
USSR

Sincerely,
Langston

1. *Hughes stayed at Sullivan's until the beginning of June, when he made his way to New
York to join twenty-one other black Americans—actors, writers, students, and artists—*

traveling to the Soviet Union. Louise Thompson had approached Hughes in March about
some Soviet officials who were interested in producing a motion picture about American
race relations. Hughes was slated to be a writer on the film, to be called Black and White.
Participants included Dorothy West‡ and Louise Thompson.
2. *The film was never made.*
3. *A Moscow-based newspaper.*
4. *While he was in Moscow, a bill for $162 arrived from Golden Stair Press's printer.*

CARL VAN VECHTEN TO LANGSTON HUGHES, DECEMBER 31, 1932
(POSTCARD)

[Handwritten description of the image on the front, above]
Carl Van Vechten's apartment—1931
The Venetian seats in the dining-room.

Dear old Langston. Have had hundreds of cards, telegrams, letters, etc.
from you and loved them all! If I haven't written you its because I
thought you would be back before a letter would reach you. But I guess
you are going to live there. So tonight before I got to Rita Romilly's[1] for
drinks & Muriel Draper's[2] New Year's eve party I'll send you a little line.
Also Nora Holt (who is in Shanghai—c/o American Express—do send

her a line)—Noël Sullivan stayed in San Francisco for Christmas. I stay in New York and have become <u>completely</u> a photographer.[3] Do nothing else. When you come back I want to try you again. But I shouldn't wonder if this country would be a Soviet or a Technocracy by the time you arrive. . . . Prentiss is doing sculpture this winter—but he has doubtless written you. I have a page of photographs in the January Vanity Fair but you probably don't see Vanity Fair in the desert with the camels. I hope you'll have a nice book out of all your experiences. I wish you'd made a nice poem in the Road to Life which I adore.

Sprigs of larkspur to you!   Happy New Year!

Carlo.

December 31—1932

1. *Rita Romilly was a dancer, dance instructor, and actress who often had integrated parties with many Harlem Renaissance writers and artists in attendance.*
2. *Muriel Draper was a writer who operated a salon in New York that was frequented by Harlem Renaissance writers and artists.*
3. *Van Vechten began experimenting with box cameras when he was a child. He took pictures intermittently until the late 1920s, when Miguel Covarrubias returned from Europe with a new Leica camera. Van Vechten soon got one of his own. By early 1932, virtually all Van Vechten did was take pictures. As he wrote Fania's brother about his new obsession in January 1932: "It has hit me very hard and I don't do anything else now. I spend most of my days in the darkroom."*

LANGSTON HUGHES TO CARL VAN VECHTEN, MARCH 1, 1933

Meschrabpom Film
Moscow, USSR

March 1, 1933

Dear Carlo, I am sending off to Blanche today a new manuscript of poems called GOOD MORNING REVOLUTION containing the best of the proletarian poems I've been doing the last two years. I hope they're good poems. I've had expert criticism on them over here, and have selected them carefully. Some of them have been talked about quite a lot in the states, and were well received at my readings on the coast last spring. I guess you've seen the furrow GOODBYE CHRIST aroused in the Negro press the last two or three months—but it was defended as much as it was reviled.[1] And the <u>Courier</u> devoted a two-weeks long article to it in favor. I think this book represents pretty well the younger Negro mind today, and will be quite as timely as was my WEARY BLUES six years ago—since everything seems to be moving left at home. Of course, I want you to see the manuscript, and would have brought it to you first had I been at home, as I've done with all my other things. I am anxious to know what you think about it, so please ask Blanche to send it over to you. And then write me. . . . I've decided on DARK PEOPLE OF THE SOVIETS as a title for the Asia book, if the Knopf's approve. And I hope to get it in the post by the end of March. . . . I've lately been writing a number of short stories too, inter-racial tales that I think are amusing, and certainly far and away better than those I once published in the MESSENGER.[2] I have been trying to get Bradley's address in Paris to see if he could place them for me,[3] along with some of the Asian material I have. Or would you suggest another agent in America. I have no experience in selling prose to the magazines myself. . . . I want to get some cash to help Prentiss pay off the Scottsboro man, and to keep me from starving when I get to Shanghai in the spring. One can travel de luxe from here on rubles, but after that—my God! I shall probably join the coolies. Or ask Nora if she needs a handy man. . . . I'm getting spoiled living in the New Moscow Hotel and eating caviar and chicken. Certainly writers and artists fare well in the Soviet Union. . . . The theatres are very interesting this winter. A new art policy has gone into effect, and the poster-propaganda plays (enormously effective in their way) are giving place to a drama less rigidly stylized and of a greater human scope. The new Gorky play, "Egor Bulachev and Others," is very rich and warm and beautifully done at the Vahtango Theatre. It is about the decay of a merchant family on the eve of the revolution. . . . The Gypsy Theatre is delightful. . . . And I've seen just about everything at Tairov's Kamery, where they do O'Neil, and where they tell me they have invited Paul, and that he is interested and is learning Russian in London.[4] It is the most "smart" and "high-brow" of the Russian theatres, brilliant but not as daring as Meyerhold or as solid as some of the others. Rudd,[5] by the way, has a small part in a new Meyerhold play, which he does in Russian. . . . My girl friend at the moment is Sylvia Chen whose papa used to be Foreign Minister of China.[6] She's a modernistic dancer in Moscow now. Her mama was a West Indian colored lady. . . . And so,

Veso Horoshah,

Langston

Several of our movie group who remained here have moved on to Berlin, and I hear that Hitler and the Negroes have taken the town! . . . Dorothy West is still in Moscow acting in the movies. And Mildred Jones[7] (a bobbed girl whom I don't believe you've ever met) is the beauty-sensation of the season. She goes to parties with the local Who's Whos. And knows everybody of importance. She's a nice kid who hasn't learned a word of Russian yet!

1. *Debates in the* Pittsburgh Courier *began on January 14 with a polemic by the Reverend J. Raymond Henderson. "I have read the poem which is not really poetry," he began. "Mr. Hughes simply conceived an idea which he thought would shock the public and remind it that he is still alive and in Russia. Mr. Hughes' sojourn in Russia is evidently responsible for this bit of sacrilege." Melvin B. Tolson countered in the* Courier *on January 28 with an equally impassioned essay. "Nobody who knows Langston Hughes intimately can doubt his sincerity. He has always stood for the man lowest down and has sought to show his essential fineness of soul to those who were too high up — by the accidents of fortune — to understand." He included a dig at the Reverend: "Certain gentlemen of the cloth have a way of becoming self-styled judges on everything. Christ had so much to do that He didn't have time to set himself up as a critic of poetry." Essays for and against the poem appeared in the* Courier *until the end of March. The poem "Goodbye Christ" is reprinted in Appendix II, page 336.*

2. *Hughes published three stories in* The Messenger *in 1927. "Bodies in the Moonlight," "The Young Glory of Him," and "The Little Virgin" were all inspired by his 1923 trip to Africa.*

3. *William Aspenwall Bradley was the most prominent American literary agent in France. He represented Claude McKay, among other well-known writers.*

4. *Paul and Essie Robeson had dinner with the theatre director Alexander Tairov during a visit to Russia in late 1934. The O'Neill production was* All God's Chillun Got Wings.

5. *Wayland Rudd was a black American actor and one of the twenty-two participants in the ill-fated film project.*

6. *Sylvia Chen had grown up in Trinidad and England. She was a dancer whose family had fled from China to Moscow after becoming targeted by the Chiang Kai-shek regime for their leftist political beliefs. She and Hughes became so close while he was in Moscow that they considered marriage. Once he returned to the States, however, Hughes allowed the relationship to fizzle.*

7. *A Hampton University art student. Jones is seated in the deck chair on the left in the photograph on p. 99.*

CARL VAN VECHTEN TO LANGSTON HUGHES, APRIL 3, 1933

Dear Langston, As usual about your work I am going to be frank with you and tell you I don't like Good Morning, Revolution (except in spots) at all. There are a couple swell blues, a poem called Tired, and Christ in Alabama and A House in Taos, both of which have appeared before and are familiar to your readers, on the credit side. The revolutionary poems seem very weak to me: I mean very weak on the lyric side.* I think in ten years, whatever the social outcome, you will be ashamed of these. Why attack the Waldorf? This hotel employs more people than it serves and is at present one of the cheapest places any one can go to who wants to go to a hotel. It even seems a little ironic to me to ask a capitalist publisher to publish a book which is so very revolutionary and so little poetic in tone. This is my opinion: I don't know what his is. You asked me to read the poems and give my opinion to you, and I am sending it right off. I think it is possible (though difficult) to be a good revolutionist and a good artist, too, but I think you'll have to ask yourself more questions (more searchingly) in case you decide to carry on this program. Ask yourself for instance: Have I written a poem? Has it got a new idea? Has it got a new feeling into it? Will it make other people feel? Will it make other people think? Have I written a poem or a revolutionary tract? You see the old contrast between rich and poor, between this one having something the other one wants, needs re-enforcement, a new expression, if it is to say anything to us. It has been done so much. Well, doubtless I'm wrong, but this is the way I feel about things. In other words, I have no quarrel with your linking the American Negro with Communism, if you want to, but I think your expression of this will have to be ever so much more deep, ever so much more sincerely felt before it will touch readers either for its ideas or its poetry. The present book seems to me calculated to appeal only to those who like the sort of things it says already.

I am still taking photographs: Better than ever, and not writing. Alonzo Thayer gave me a marvellous rent party. Run, Little Chillun¹ is almost great and has the town very much excited.° I have not yet read Claude McKay's book. Your letters are swell and you seem to be having a perfect time, but we all miss you.

Best flamingos to you!

C.

April 3

°Your mother is in it. So doubtless you know all about it.
*Why did you leave out A New Song? I like this the <u>best</u> of your revolutionary poems.

  1. *Hall Johnson's 1933 folk drama featured two hundred Harlem residents, including Carrie Clark, Hughes's mother.*

LANGSTON HUGHES TO CARL VAN VECHTEN, MAY 23, 1933

Meschrabpom
Moscow, USSR

May 23, 1933

Dear Carlo,

Swell of you to write me so frankly about my poems. I agree with you, of course, that many of the poems are not as lyrical as they might be—but even at that I like some of them as well as anything I ever did—which is merely my taste against yours, and means nothing, as everyone has a right to his own likings, I guess. . . . About the Waldorf, I don't agree with you.¹ At the time that I wrote the poem it was one of the best American symbols of too much as against too little. I believe that you yourself told me that the dining room was so crowded that first week that folks wouldn't get in to eat $10.00 dinners. And not many blocks away the bread lines I saw were so long that other folks couldn't reach the soup kitchens for a plate of free and watery soup. . . . Blanche bases her note to me on your reactions.[2] Certainly, I am (as usual) willing to make revisions in the book, omitting the least good poems, and perhaps putting in a few new pieces that I have on hand, but I would not like to change the general ensemble of the book. I think it would be amusing to publish a volume of such poems just now, risking the shame of the future (as you predict) for the impulse of the moment. And if Knopf's do not care to do it, they have a perfect right to refuse. One must admit that their clientele hardly consists of workers and peasants, so I could understand how they might feel. . . . I seem to have

BLANCHE KNOPF, PHOTOGRAPH BY
CARL VAN VECHTEN, 1932

a gift for writing unsalable stuff. For years I wrote for the Negro magazines which paid nothing. Now I write for the proletarian journals which pay equally well! Lord have mercy! . . . I wish I could see Run Little Chillun. . . . The Georgian theatre is giving some stunning performances here these days—up from Tiflis for a month's stay. . . . I'm leaving very shortly now, I reckon, for Vladivostok and whatever comes next, so don't write me here any more. . . . I'll see you in the fall. Tell Fania that if she'll just invite me to dinner, I've learned to eat fast by now. The Russians eat like a house afire (when they have anything) and I've been trying to keep up with them for fear of getting left. . . . The May Day Demonstration here was tremendous. Luckily I had a place on the Red Square. That moment when the military parade is over and the Square is cleared, a sea of workers bearing banners and slogans and emblems above their heads pours into the vast space before Stalin and Kalinin and the other leaders—well, there is nothing else like it to be seen in the world. And from then on until darkness they pass. This has even the hundreds of tanks and soldiers and airplanes beat for impressiveness.

Bugles and banners to you,

Langston

1. *Hughes published his sardonic "Advertisement for the Waldorf-Astoria" in the December 1931 issue of* New Masses. *In his April 3 letter to Blanche about the manuscript, Van*

Vechten singled out this poem for criticism: "I particularly dislike this one and this cheap way of thinking—there are, as you know, more people gainfully employed at this hotel than there are guests." In The Big Sea, *Hughes called "Advertisement" the last straw in his disintegrating relationship with his rich white patron, Charlotte Mason, who wanted him to "be and feel the primitive" and give up his political verse. In actuality, Hughes wrote the poem after the split with his patron. "Advertisement for the Waldorf-Astoria" is reprinted in Appendix II, page 333.*

2. *Blanche's April 6 letter to Hughes read: "You have by now heard from Carl regarding the poems so I will write you nothing more other than I think we had better talk about the book as soon as you get back and I would like to hear from you what you think of Carl's suggested changes in it. Much of the stuff I think is grand, but I do agree with him on the necessary revisions and I imagine you will too."*

Hughes *left Russia in June and roamed eastward to Japan. By this time, he had learned enough Russian to make traveling relatively easy. He toured Kyoto, Tokyo, and finally Shanghai, where he dined with Madame Sun Yat-sen. Hughes's tour was cut short by officials suspicious of him and his political alliances; his last few days in Tokyo were spent under police scrutiny. By the time he left, he was persona non grata in Japan. Hughes marveled later, in* I Wonder As I Wander: *"I, a colored man, had lately been all around the world, but only in Japan, a colored country, had I been subjected to police interrogation and told to go home and not return again. . . . I saw quite clearly that color made no difference in the use of race as a technique of hurting and humiliating a group not one's own." He returned to the United States in August.*

LANGSTON HUGHES TO CARL VAN VECHTEN, SEPTEMBER 22, 1933

P.O. Box 1582
Carmel, California

September 22, 1933

Dear Carl,

Fate's against me. Nora Holt came through the other day and I didn't know it until two hours after she had sailed. And you flew out and back while I was still on the high seas—but practically near enough to see your plane. . . . You dog! . . . I've been trying to get settled in life once more. Have the loan of Noel's cottage here at the beach to write my book in.¹ Been down a week and have done another story about white folks and colored folks. I adore writing them. I think they are both so droll, don't you? . . . Did you find my <u>Mercury</u> and <u>Scribner's</u> stories amusing?² . . . Dwight Fiske was at Hyde Street and sang a song that had you in it to a slight extent.³ . . . A fellow named Bill Howe and Jean Sablon, French singer, stopped by here the other day, and said that Max⁴ was doing well in Hollywood and had just signed a contract with an agent. . . . SHOW BOAT is to be done on the stage out here with that swell young colored baritone, Kenneth Spencer, in the Ole Man River role. Which came through Noel Sullivan's recommendation. . . . Billy Justema did a tan, silver, and blue picture of me which I'll probably send on to you to keep until I arrive in New York.⁵ I could never hope to look as decorative in person. Billy has a hollywood studio now. . . . And I'm going for a weekend to one of California's grandest ranches belonging to a lady who has nobody in the world, therefore she plans to spend the winter in China where wars and revolutions will make life worth living. We have a swell John Reed Club here at Carmel with Sunday night lectures in their own barn. . . . I brought you this jolly little Buddist monk from a temple in Japan where the police present their cards before they arrest you. I was coming home anyhow when I got put out. . . . I liked some of your San Francisco pictures. How many dark rooms do you have now? . . . Noel gave a tea for Mrs. Patterson and Lester Carter, one of the Scottsboro mothers and the white boy who travelled with the girls. You would have enjoyed it. I thought it might end in a free-for-all between radicals and conservatives gathered thereat. A colored lady from the best society said the U.S. Constitution was alright for her, and a very rich white lady who follows all the strikes said, "How can you say such a thing?" And the argument went from there. The minister of the A.M.E. church was sitting by the editor of a paper that had just exposed him as a swindler. And Moore, the Communist orator was next to a boy who thought all was hopeless— even Communism. . . . And what is the New York news? I had a nice letter from Prentiss the other day. Was glad to see his cartoon in THE NATION. Write when you have time. Or better still, come out and hear the surf on the Carmel beach. This really is a charming little town.

Sincerely,

Langston

1. *While Hughes was still in Moscow, Noël Sullivan offered him the year-long, expense-free use of a cottage he called "Ennesfree," located in Carmel-by-the-Sea, so that Hughes could*

finish his book of stories. Along with the empty house, Sullivan provided cleaning and cooking staff as well as the company of his German shepherd, Greta. Hughes described what this time meant to him in I Wonder: *"To Noel Sullivan I am indebted for the first long period in my life when I was able, unworried and unhurried, to stay quietly in one place and devote myself to writing."*

2. *In September 1933, "Cora Unashamed" and "Slave on the Block" appeared in* American Mercury *and* Scribner's, *respectively.*

3. *Dwight Fiske was a popular café entertainer. Noël Sullivan lived at 2323 Hyde Street in San Francisco.*

4. *Max Ewing.*‡

5. *The poet and artist Billy Justema published a book of verse,* Private Papers, *in 1944. A close friend of Noël Sullivan's, he was a frequent guest at Hyde Street.*

CARL VAN VECHTEN TO LANGSTON HUGHES, SEPTEMBER 28, 1933

(POSTCARD)

September 28, 1933

Langston Hughes
P.O. Box 1582
Carmel,
California

Terribly glad to hear from you, you old woojums.[1] By all means let me take care of the Billy Justema portrait as long as you like. I'd love to have it around. I did not know about the Scribner story. I'll look that up. But I think Cora Unashamed is one of the very best things you've done . . . as good as "Not Without Laughter" in a different way.[2] I <u>loved</u> it . . . Your letter is full of grand angles. Did I ever tell you that John Reed was a great friend of mine? I was abroad with him once.[3] Thanks for the little carving. I love it. I am still taking photographs all the time & may have an exhibition soon. Ethel Waters is marvellous in the new Irving Berlin show which I saw in Philadelphia. She co-stars with Clifton Webb & Marilyn Miller.[4] Write another long gossipy letter. I love 'em & write more of <u>those stories.</u> God, what a book they will make!

743 blue hummingbirds w/spurs to you!

1. *Van Vechten's nickname for a select few of his close friends. In his correspondence with Gertrude Stein, he is "Papa Woojums," Alice B. Toklas is "Mama Woojums," and Stein is "Baby Woojums."*

2. Not Without Laughter, *Hughes's first novel, was published by Knopf in 1930.*

3. *Van Vechten vacationed with the political radical John Reed and several others at Mabel Dodge's Villa Curonia, near Florence, during the summer of 1913. Reed and Dodge were romantically involved at the time.*

4. *The show,* As Thousands Cheer, *was about life during the Depression.*

LANGSTON HUGHES TO CARL VAN VECHTEN, NOVEMBER 1, 1933

Box 1582
Carmel, Cal.

November 1, 1933

Mon cher Carlo,

I am living so much like white folks these days that I'm washing my hair with Golden Glow. . . . And writing stories that have as many whites in them as colored. . . . Muriel Draper was out here with Mabel Luhan lately and dropped in after luncheon for a liqueur with me. I was interested in her new book and in news of you. . . . I had dinner shortly before that with Claire Spencer and John Evans who've been living together prior to going to Reno to get their respective divorces.[1] Trying it out, as Stephin Fetchit would say, and they make an awfully nice couple. Claire had news of Colin and Jane.[2] . . . And they—that is John—has a peke named Walter that is a legitimate son of Raquel Meller's two favorite lap dogs. . . . And the Jeffer's bull named Haig is the son of President Roosevelt's protecting hound, conceived however before he went into the New Deal. . . . But there are no dogs, even here, as beautiful as Greta, a silver-grey and black police whose lineage goes back to the Black Forest and who barks loud enough to keep strangers from ever interfering with my working hours. Noel lent her to me out of the numerous pack he has at Hyde Street. . . . We were down to Santa Barbara (Noel, Greta, and me) for Roland Hayes concert for the Junior League, and to see if we could get him to sing at Carmel. I guess we forgot to let Greta out. Anyway, she slept on Roland's bed and wet it all up. . . . Night before last I was up to town for the opening of the Coast production of SHOW BOAT where Kenneth Spencer, young Negro basso, did well by Ole Man River. He stopped the show and delayed Estelle Taylor's entrance so long after the curtain went up on the next scene that she came on with the line, "I had a hard time getting here," which I don't know if it belonged in the play or not. Certainly it was appropriate. . . . Our John Reed Club is doing noble work. The day after the fisherman's strike was settled, I went out in the AMAZON for night sardine fishing. . . . We got caught in heavy seas and a fog and were out twenty-four hours. Only got one small haul of three tons. And was I sea-sick, for the first time in my life! Little boats and big boats don't rock the same. . . . I went down to the cotton pickers strike, too. (Noel, also, and all the resident Nat. Com. members.) It was a very thrilling struggle. Caroline Decker, a little 21-year-old blond girl from Georgia, had 8000 Mexicans, Negroes, and whites under her command. The strikers won 15¢ increase on a hundred pounds, which still makes them get less than a dollar a day, as a rule. . . . Last Sunday before last I lectured here on Soviet Asia. Just before the lecture the fire department padlocked our barn, so we had to have it elsewhere. Steffens, in introducing me, said that the fire laws are seldom evoked except when something left is about to come off. (They tried to stop a film of Gorky's MOTHER in the theatre here for the same reason.) And John Reed's mother wrote that he would never have belonged to such a club.* But Steffens and Rys Williams[3] who were in Russia with him contend that he would. So I don't know, and not being psychic, can't call on the dead to speak. . . . Krisnamurti is coming shortly.[4] . . . And a famous movie star who said don't tell nobody he's here is here now resting between pictures, but might come to luncheon Sunday when Noël and some others will be down for the week-end. . . . Well, I had a swell time on the ranch. And in spite of all have done three more stories, one mass song, and two poems. My agent says ESQUIRE has bought a story of mine.[5] And a note from O'Brien asking for my life history.[6] And from Blanche Knopf expressing interest in the stories, so I will send her ten or twelve next week. I think 15 would be enough for a book and will have that many finished shortly, as I must stop writing stories now and get on my Russian book, but still have some interesting ones partly done to finish up. I believe that most of them touch on nuances of Negro-white life in America that haven't been explored before. And when I get around to it, I have a series of pure Negro ones I want to do. I'm glad you liked CORA. . . . I loved your picture of Ethel and have put it behind me on my work room wall. . . . You'll probably be getting an official letter from me and the Scottsboro Committee out here shortly. We're writing all those who've been swell about Negroes in their creative work, and who we hope will help us help those black kids who are living in a state of terror now in their cells in Birmingham. (The lynch temper is growing everywhere. You probably read about those Mexican cotton pickers shot to death out here.)[7] At Carmel we're planning a series of concerts and lectures for Scottsboro Funds to start this month, and a sale of original manuscripts of Negro and white writers, as there are a number of collectors herabouts who buy such things and have expressed interest. . . . Lincoln Steffins[8] has just agreed to head the Nat. Committeee, succeeding Dreiser. And a number of rich young kids who were bored with life till the John Reed Club showed them the excitement, are rallying around to help the oppressed. Now, with deputy sheriffs to aggravate and proletarians to run around with, they are not even mourning the passing of bootleg licker. . . . Meanwhile Tibbett[9] is singing my MOAN on most of his concert programs . . . Wish I could see you, Carlo. . . . Twenty-nine cameras with shutters faster than the Berry Brothers feet,[10] and a dozen dark-rooms darker than Bledsoe to you,

Yeah, man!

Langston

LANGSTON HUGHES, NOËL SULLIVAN (IN THE STRIPED SHIRT), AND
FRIENDS AT HOLLOW HILLS FARM, N.D.

Paul's picture got swell notices, but was a box-office failure out here.[11] I adored the first part, but didn't feel the jungle terror, which should have grown on one, as it did in the play.

P.S.   Had a card from Prentiss today. And prospectus of Nancy Cunard's[‡] book which looking exciting.[12] And a note from Buttita of <u>Contempo</u> saying he's finished a Negro novel of the new South.[13] (But his hero is named Rufus!)

+Is Marinoff back?

*Would he?

1. *Spencer and Evans, whose mother was Mabel Dodge Luhan, were American writers.*
2. *Colin McPhee, a composer, and his wife, the anthropologist Jane Belo, were great friends of Prentiss Taylor's.*
3. *Albert Rhys Williams is most famous as a witness of the storming of the Winter Palace in St. Petersburg in 1917.*
4. *The Indian mystic Jeddu Krishnamurti.*
5. *Hughes's agent at this point was Maxim Lieber, a committed Socialist. He would later be identified as an undercover operative for the Communist party. His other clients included Erskine Caldwell, Carson McCullers, and Nathanael West. The story was probably "A Good Job Gone," published in* Esquire *in 1934.*
6. *For 50 Best American Short Stories, 1915–1939, edited by Edward O'Brien. None of Hughes's stories were ultimately included in the anthology.*
7. *On October 10, 1933, 18,000 Mexican cotton pickers went on strike in Pixley, California. Four strikers were killed before new wages were negotiated.*
8. *Lincoln Steffens was a celebrated prewar muckraker.*

9. *Lawrence Tibbett was a singer and an actor.*
10. *The Berry Brothers dance team consisted of the brothers Ananias, Jimmy, and Warren Berry.*
11. *Paul Robeson made his debut in the "talkies" as the star of* The Emperor Jones, *a 1933 adaptation of the 1920 Eugene O'Neill play. The play is about a black ex-con named Brutus Jones whose craven rise to power leads to his death. Reviewers were generally lukewarm, full of praise for Robeson's star qualities but dismissive of the film itself.*
12. *Nancy Cunard's exhaustive poetry anthology,* Negro, *was published in 1934.*
13. *Anthony Buttita, the editor of* Contempo, *never published this novel.*

CARL VAN VECHTEN TO LANGSTON HUGHES, NOVEMBER 12, 1933

Dear Langston, Your letter asking aid for the Scottsboro Boys got mislaid in the jungle of my desk and I only thought of it when the clipping arrived related Noël's adventures with highwaymen. The name of the chauffeur is new. What's happened to Eddie? Anyway here is a cheque, all I can afford to give you for this cause just now.[1] As for a statement, I have a definite feeling that remarks by Northern writers keep those boys in jail that much longer. If they can be brought to trial without too much talk, maybe they will get out. God knows I hope so.

Your other letter was an enchantment, full of gossip and good writing. I was delighted with it. I have very little news to send you in return. Photography is still my middle name. You are doubtless aware of Miss Waters's triumphs on the stage and on the air. I have always had the feeling that you and Miss Waters were the best artistic bets the race has contemporaneously. I guess I'm right too. Did you read Jim Johnson's autobiography?[2] A swell book. . . . Yes, Marinoff is back. . . . I didnt like Paul's picture much, though I dont see how he personally could have been better.* Did Max write you about Mae West's maid at the opening of her picture?[3]

Hi-de-Ho!

Carlo!

November 12, 1933

*Did you see the original edition in which the word "Nigger" is used & used & used? Or the one in which it is entirely taken out, thanks to the howls of the Negro press?[4]

1. *Van Vechten's check was for twenty-five dollars.*
2. Along This Way, *James Weldon Johnson's autobiography, was published by Viking in 1933.*
3. *Louise Beavers plays the maid in both of West's 1933 pictures,* She Done Him Wrong *and* I'm No Angel.
4. *The* New York Amsterdam News *voiced the opinion of many blacks when its review denounced the use of the word "nigger" in the film as a "disgrace."*

CARL VAN VECHTEN TO LANGSTON HUGHES, NOVEMBER 27, 1933
(POSTCARD)

November 27, 1933

Mr. Langston Hughes,
PO Box 1582,
Carmel, California.

Dear Langston! I <u>loved</u> Poor Little Black Boy.[1] I think you have hit on quite a new vein & I think you could keep it up for a long time if you want to. There must be thousands of stories on this border line. —

Lincoln asked me for photographs of you, J.W.J & P. Robeson for the library. Did I tell you? I am sending 'em. Funny the author of N.H.[2] being thus honored!

4,053 blue dachshunds with gold feet to you!

C.

Monday

1. *The title became "Poor Little Black Fellow." Hughes published it in* American Mercury *in 1933.*
2. Nigger Heaven.

LANGSTON HUGHES TO CARL VAN VECHTEN, DECEMBER 6, 1933

P. O. Box 1582
Carmel, California

December 6, 1933

Mon cher Carlo,

Swell of you to send that check for Scottsboro. Please accept through me the Committee's official thanks for your generous support. Several checks and excellent statements have come in from my letters, particularly from the Southerners, DuBose Heyward, Paul Green, and Blair Niles. You probably saw Fannie Hurst's fine letter in the New York papers. . . . Haven't been able to get any sort of response from Julia Peterkin, though. Or Roark Bradford. . . . Guess you heard about President Roosevelt denouncing lynching over the radio the other night. Well, we certainly stormed up a barrage of wires to him from out here, so maybe that helped some. Noel and some other members of our Committee were just about to go to Scottsboro when the trials were again put off.

At least, they were making plans about going. We're holding a big Scottsboro meeting in San Francisco next Wednesday with Micklejohn and me speaking, and Noel and the Southernaires singing, and God knows what all. . . . Did I tell you they did my play out here and had built the electric chair so strong it took them nearly ten minutes to break it up, all with immense excitement from the audience like an old time melodrama?

I've sent off a dozen short stories to Knopf to consider for a book.[1] Hope they let you look at them, too. Only four out of the lot are not yet accepted for magazine publication. I expect to have two or three more to add to the collection before the month is up. One, REJUVENATION THROUGH JOY, will concern a group of Park Avenue mystics restoring their souls with a Negro jazz band, bringing the primitive to their country colony. And another will be about a Negro charity school in the South, and the compromising road its principal must travel.[2]

Thanksgiving I went up to the city to see Tibbett in EMPEROR JONES, some parts of which I liked and others not at all.[3] It was quite a deal more niggerless than the picture and much more expensive to see. I don't believe so many of the race were there anyhow to witness the classic doings. Did I tell you Jimmy Cagney and his wife have a cottage here? And that they were in for dinner with me one night and did all their old dance steps afterwards. . . . No, Max didn't let us know about Mae West's maid at the opening. . . . Eddie is still here. But Glenn is the other chauffeur who does most of the out of town driving. And makes marvellous speed. . . . Since the bandit incident Noel has been in one auto smashup, unhurt, and has had one car stolen, and has given a grand dinner for the stariest opera stars, and has lost a dog by death that lived with him in Paris; besides passing through San Jose just before and shortly after the lynching. . . . Did you see Ethel's life described in the Jan. RADIO STARS magazine?

Reindeers and sleighbells to you,
Langston

Awfully good portrait of you on that postcard. Did you make it yourself? Lincoln should also have that! What's wrong with them?

1. *Hughes called the collection,* The Ways of White Folks, *a title probably inspired by Du Bois's groundbreaking 1903 book* The Souls of Black Folks.
2. *This story, "The Professor," did not make it into* The Ways of White Folks. *Instead, Hughes published it in the May–June issue of the literary journal* The Anvil, *where it appeared as "Dr. Brown's Decision."*
3. *The white performer Lawrence Tibbett played the lead role, in blackface, in the 1933 opera of* Emperor Jones.

Dear old Langston: Blanche sent me The Ways of White Folks yesterday morning and last night after dinner I tackled it with a great deal of hope, as I have enjoyed the three stories I read in the magazine. Well, all my hopes were realized. I read the book through at a sitting and was THRILLED. I think it is superb from beginning to end (including the magnificent title). In fact I think it is the best thing you have done and I am PROUD of you . . . I have been shouting for you and Miss Waters* ever since the day you came along and it gives me great pleasure to be snooty to those unfortunate people who believed more in Florence Mills¹ and Countee Cullen. In fact, I was RIGHT.

Now, as to your book. I would put in the two stories you are writing. (Some day you should write about the girl—Fredi Washington for example—who with all white Paris at her feet or what not sighs for brownskin. Harlem tale in a rich setting on the Riviera or Paris). I would suggest that you delete the last sentence of Little Dog. The story would be stronger without it. In fact always your tendency is to say too much rather than too little and you might think about this in going over your text. Reticence is more powerful in literature than shouting. However, in no instance do I want to destroy your personality and this is the only specific case I would mention. I am not writing this paragraph to Blanche. I am just sending her my hosannahs!² You are pretty cute.

I have not seen Tibbett in The Emperor Jones. I did not like the picture <u>at all</u>. . . . If you see Cagney again please tell him to let me photograph him.

Your picture has gone to Lincoln.

Laurel wreathes to you, brown Genius!

Carlo

December 15, 1933

*Get Miss Waters' new record of 'I just couldn't take it, baby"

1. *Florence Mills was a spectacular and much-loved singer and dancer. When she died at the age of thirty of appendicitis, Harlem gave her a funeral befitting royalty.*
2. *Van Vechten raved to Blanche Knopf about the manuscript in a letter also written on December 15: "All of it is good and some of it, I should think, is great. . . . I am glad to feel this way after my reaction to that communist book of poetry." He added: "Something has happened to the lad; he has grown up, I guess." The Ways of White Folks was published in 1934. Hughes dedicated it to Noël Sullivan.*

Mr. Langston Hughes
P.O. Box 1582
Carmel, California
Dear Langston:
I hope you got a letter from me telling you how crazy I am about The
Ways of White Folks. But I sent it airmail & the weather is so bad perhaps
it blew down! — Blanche is crazy about it too. Who won't be? — Everybody
is sure to love it!

Carlo

Monday

Day after Christmas, 1933

Carmel, California
Dear Carlo,
Had been in the city for ten days and came back and found your letter
and your card. Terribly glad you liked my stories, and Blanche also. Was
most interested in your comments on them. I had a lot of fun writing
them. Noel said the same thing about the last sentence of LITTLE DOG
some time ago, so it comes off the end. Maybe I will do one about Fredi or
somebody such, some time. . . . At the moment I'm all excited about a
play I'm about to write with someone out here. But remembering the last
collaboration, I must be crazy. At least I shall hire two lawyers and buy a
gun at once. And will tell you <u>nothing</u>, so that you will not have to prove
and fend when the controversy starts.[1] . . . Noel had a big party (did I tell
you) for Shan Khar.[2] Iturbi[3] was there also, but for a long time folks
thought he was an Italian bootlegger. Emily Whitfield and her new husband there. It seems I met her once before at your house. She is lots of
fun and will be down here at Carmel tomorrow. . . . And the Race had a
big surprise party for Noel in advance of his birthday at which Etta
Moten,[4] up from Hollywood, sang and danced divinely among other
things that almost shook the house down with Ethiopian vigor. . . . John
Evans and Claire Spencer back from Reno married, were here for dinner
with me before going off to Taos for Christmas. It seems that they left sort
of high and forgot to take Mable's[5] Christmas present, so had to wire back

for somebody to find it and send it on. . . . I had one Christmas dinner with Steffens (who is better) and Ella Winter and little Pete,[6] and another with Noel, and some hot egg-nog with a Race family who have a garage here, and some champagne at night, so I passed the Yuletide full and tight. Hope you had a happy time, too. . . . Weston has taken some swell pictures of Cagney.[7] I'll tell him about you when he comes back. Been meaning to go over to Jeffers for some days,[8] but haven't got around to it. He's promised us a manuscript for our Scottsboro benefit and auction to be held in Frisco next month. All the folks who didn't give money, we asked to give first draft original manuscripts or paintings, etc. Got some swell stuff: Dreiser, Powys, Dos Passos, Cullen, Dell, John Evans, Steffens, (Claire Spencer promises a signed unpublished D. H. Lawrence poem) Strachey, Steig, Aaron Douglas, Edward Weston, John Howard, Max Ernst, O'Shea; signed hand written scores from Still, Hall Johnson, old man Handy, etc. It's to be a swell Junior League tea-pouring affair at the Beaux Arts. . . . I told you Roland Hayes was singing for Carmel Music Society Jan. 6th, and giving a percentage to Scottsboro, didn't I? And we have several other concerts coming off next year, Noel's among them. . . . Can't get a peep of any sort out of Julia Peterkin. She won't even answer our letters. But several of the other Southern writers have been swell. . . . Since our activities out here the California papers have at least begun to report news of the Scottsboro trials, and one of the big columnists has written about it twice. They didn't seem to have heard about it before, this far West. . . . Did you see the big ad in ESQUIRE this month about my story I told you they bought but were a bit backward about publishing? It's being put to a vote, with nice illustrations.[9] . . . Loved your photo of Ethel you sent me, also the one of Prentiss and the Zulu. You must get Etta Moten if she comes back East. . . . Ed Best and his wife, a most likable couple flew East just before Christmas and will probably call you up while they're in town. Ed is Noel's secretary. They left by the night plane and had sent a wire from Omaha before I woke up in the morning. Ain't that sumethun? Did you go that fast, too?

Ten abalones to you, and one star fish.

Langston

Terribly glad of Ethel's latest successes! There's a lot about her in the press these days. Do you suppose she'd sign a photo of herself (preferably one of yours) for Scottsboro? It would look swell at our exhibit.

1. *Hughes set to work with Ella Winter on* Blood in the Fields, *a play about Caroline Decker and the San Joaquin Valley cotton strike.*
2. *Ravi Shankar led India's Shankari Musicians.*
3. *Jose Iturbi was a concert pianist who acted in several movies during the forties.*

4. *A black singer and actress. Moten's career was enhanced by her fluency in French, German, and Italian.*
5. *Mabel Dodge Luhan.*
6. *Lincoln Steffens still lived with his ex-wife, Ella Winter, a radical writer. Winter, Steffens, and their young son, Pete, were Hughes's constant companions in Carmel.*
7. *Edward Weston was a noted photographer.*
8. *The poet Robinson Jeffers was one of Carmel's most revered residents.*
9. *"A Good Job Gone" is about a white man whose life is ruined when his young black mistress discards him. In January, the editors at* Esquire *titillated readers with a summary of the story and asked them to write and make arguments for or against the story's publication. Controversy raged on in letters to the editor for months, until a positive reader's vote convinced the editors to publish the story in the April 1934 issue of the magazine.*

LANGSTON HUGHES TO CARL VAN VECHTEN, FEBRUARY 21, 1934

Dear Carlo,

Did I tell you thanks for sending me that swell record of Ethel Water's which half of Carmel village has fallen in love with? . . . And did I tell you about my birthday, or have I written you this month, I have been so busy, what with books and Scottsboro and all? Well, I went down to the Big Sur with Una and Robin Jeffers, and later Noel came along, too. Way up on the cliffs above the Pacific on the only really wild coast left, we drank wine and ate salami and I told Jeffers you wanted to take his picture the next time you came out here. (I will send you some snap shots I took that day.) Then in the evening they came in for a party with Marie Welch[1] and Ella Winter and some others. And Noel had brought some champagne from the city. We had a swell time. . . . And I have had luncheon with your cousin[2] again and played Ethel's STORMY WEATHER for her, and she sent us a check for Scottsboro and says she might go up to the city for our Sale next week.[3] . . . She was awaiting my books which she said you were sending her. I had given her the DREAM KEEPER but had none of the others here. It seems the WEARY BLUES is out of print now, anyhow. . . . Some swell manuscripts from England have arrived for our Sale—Huxley, Swinnerton, Russell, Huddleston; and from New York, a marvellous Steichen print, four Lynn Wards and two Julius Blocks. . . . Guess you saw the ESQUIRE controversy, but they have bought HOME besides and are publishing it in the May number following A Good Job Gone. And maybe I told you all this before. . . . The ocean sounds like thunder today even with all the windows closed.

A thousand sea gulls to you,
Langston

Carmel
February 21, 1934

1. *Marie de Lisle Welch was a poet.*
2. *Mary Van Vechten Blanchard was Van Vechten's cousin, the adopted daughter of his father's brother, Giles Fonda Van Vechten. She lived in Carmel, California.*
3. *Hughes engineered an auction in San Francisco of manuscripts, books, visual art, and other gifts from writers and artists to help the Scottsboro defense effort. James Cagney was the auctioneer.*

CARL VAN VECHTEN TO LANGSTON HUGHES, AFTER FEBRUARY 21, 1934

Dear Langston: Your letters are works of art and pleasing to the mind and eye. Your birthday party sounds marvellous. And Im so glad you and Mary Blanchard are getting on so well together.¹ Please write me about the Sale. I was very disappointed in They Shall Not Die.² The courtroom scene is good, but it is a bad play and it is laid on so thick that you just dont believe it; at least I didnt. But the Negroes are good and quite beautiful. I wish they had been a little more human. They are just very sweet boys while ALL the white characters, including Walter White (not of course the Labor Defence) are made out to be fiends. There is a very spurious love interest between Lucy Wells (Ruby Bates) and a travelling salesman that made me sick to my stomick. Emma Goldman* attended the same performance I did and agreed with me that it was very bad propaganda. But Four Saints in Three Acts, by Gertrude Stein and Virgil Thomson is another thing.³ This Spanish opera interpreted by a Negro cast as Spanish saints is too divine, both gay and devout and altogether lovely. I have seen it three times. The performance is superb. Everybody is agreed about this. And certainly historical; because white characters on the downtown stage have not been assumed before by Negroes. Certainly not on the opera stage. And your friend Zora has just written a very swell novel (Jonah's Gourd Vine) which Lippincott's will publish presently. This is so good that I think you and Zora had better kiss and make up.⁴ She is at present working with Mrs. Bethune at Daytona Beach.⁵ I am still photographing madly and was very disappointed that Noel didn't fix it up for Ramon to come around while he was here making personal appearances. He sang Señor Platero charmingly. Miss Waters is off the air but she is now the star of a downtown nightclub in addition to her other duties in As Thousands Cheer. I saw Adelaide Hall at a very amusing cocktail party yesterday and she is opening next Sunday at the Cotton Club. Harold Arlen's new number is called ILL WIND.⁶ Watch out for this.

    tons of Carlifornia poppies and four chow dogs to you!
       Carlo!

                Monday

PS.   Have you see Nora Holt? She had thought to be in New York
by now.

*I am photographing her next week.

1. *On February 5, 1934, Van Vechten wrote to Mary: "You and Langston seem to have fallen in
   love with each other. . . . He is a sweet boy and I knew you would like him. So today I am
   sending you two of his books,* Not Without Laughter, *his fine novel &* The Weary Blues, *his
   first book of poems."*
2. *John Wexley's 1934 play about the Scottsboro case.*
3. *The Virgil Thomson–Gertrude Stein collaboration* Four Saints in Three Acts *impressed
   Van Vechten enough for him to feature it in his last novel,* Parties *(1932), in which a character speculates that the production would "end all opera." Van Vechten wrote the introduction to the published text, including a quotation from Thomson about his decision to use an
   all-black cast: "They alone possess the dignity and the poise, the lack of self-consciousness
   that proper interpretation of the opera demands."*
4. *Hurston got a $200 advance from J. B. Lippincott for* Jonah's Gourd Vine *(1934), her
   autobiographical novel. She explained the title to Van Vechten in a February 28, 1934 letter: "Oh yes, the title you didn't understand. (Jonah 4:6–10). You see the prophet of God sat
   up under a gourd vine that had grown up in one night. But a cut worm came along and cut
   it down. Great and sudden growth. One act of malice and it is withered and gone."*
5. *Hurston's $200 advance for* Jonah's Gourd Vine *went quickly. So she eagerly accepted
   an invitation from Mary McLeod Bethune in December 1933 to establish a school of dramatic arts at Bethune-Cookman College in Daytona Beach. Hurston arrived in mid-
   January 1934, but she stayed only until April, finding the situation unproductive.*
6. *The white songwriter Harold Arlen wrote show stoppers for the Cotton Club, most
   famously "Stormy Weather," which he and his partner, Ted Koehler, wrote for Ethel Waters
   in 1933. Arlen wrote "Ill Wind" for* The Cotton Club Parade *in 1933.*

LANGSTON HUGHES TO CARL VAN VECHTEN, MARCH 5, 1934

Dear Carlo,

Mighty happy to have your letter. Just got back from the city. Our auction was a great success, took in some $1400 and still have a great deal of
material left over as we had to close at midnight. Cagney was due back in
Hollywood the following noon. There will probably be a Los Angeles
sale, too, now. Two of your Ethel pictures went for $4.00 each. The others
were not offered and will be put up at the Southern sale. The Jeffers went
for $67.00. A Cullen for $25.00. A Shaw letter for $20.00. Julia Peterkin
and Roark Bradford both sent things at the last minute.

Thanks for telling me about <u>Four Saints</u> and <u>They Shall Not Die</u>. I'm
nearly dying from not being able to see either of them!!

Re-submitted (revised and renamed) my book of proletarian poems to
Blanche.¹ I know you <u>don't</u> like them, but I <u>do</u> like them, and have been
reading them with loud acclaim, even before the conservative Y. M. &

Y. W. C. A. groups out here. At least, they would be timely if published
soon, I believe.

You know, I gave up to Zora all rights on <u>The Mule Bone</u>. Awfully glad
about her novel! Is she still mad at me?

All I'm worried about now is paying off $158.00 Prentiss & I still owe
on <u>Scottsboro Limited</u> and for which the man has got the law after me.

Noël probably didn't know Ramon was in New York.

Steel-heads and spring salmon to you-

Lang

1. *Originally titled* Good Morning, Revolution, *this collection was renamed* A New Song.

CARL VAN VECHTEN TO LANGSTON HUGHES, MARCH 20, 1934

Dear Langston, In looking over your volume of poems again I find I
like them even less than I did last year. In fact, I find them lacking in any
of the elementary requisites of a work of art.* This opinion has nothing
to do with the opinions expressed therein. I find myself violently at vari-
ance with the opinions expressed by Diego Rivera's flaming frescos in
the Workers' School on Fourteenth Street, but I am drawn back to them
repeatedly by his vital and superbly imaginative painting. I think A Good
Job Gone is 100% better propaganda for the Negro (here an artist is working who exhibits a Negro character arrogant with a white character) than
the whole book of poems, which I find, as art, as propaganda, as anything
you may care to mention, Very Very Weak. Doubtless I am wrong. At least
you can rely on my being frank with you. If you are interested at all, I
could say a lot more (would that you were here so we could talk), but
doubtless you are fed up with the subject already.

I am delighted that the auction was such a success and am sure you
will have another big one in Los Angeles. Your activity and vitality delight
me and I think it is pretty swell the way you fit into all situations and cli-
mates. . . . I took some pictures of Four Saints and will probably send
them to you later, together with some of Miss Etta Moten, sweet lady who
arrived with a letter from Noël and your name on her lips. Thank you for
sending her. I dont see how Zora or anybody else can be mad with you.

I wrote you, I think that I am sending to Noël and you Emma Goldman
and Marc Chadourne, who is going around the world with a photographer, for Paris-Soir. He wrote Chine, which Miguel illustrated, and a
number of other books including one called "L'U R S S sans Passion."

You will like him, I think. He speaks English well. I took him to a cocktail party in Harlem and he sent everybody (and broke 'em down).

I do hope sometime some of you persuade Ramón and Cagney to pose for my camera. Im doing Miriam Hopkins' today.

768 white penguin feathers for 76 black swans to you!

(and an owl)

March 20, 1934

[Handwritten in the margin] *This is a little too sweeping. I am speaking "generally." There are certain poems in the book that are very good indeed. Only less good than your best work in this form. — But nothing sufficiently novel or strong to rate as "first class." I think your public has a right to demand only the "first class" of you after "Not Without Laughter" & "The Ways of White Folks."

[At the end of the letter] Emma Goldman is a charmer. I so hope you can arrange for Mary Blanchard to meet her.

Ethel is going back to Brunswick . . . Fannie Hurst[2] (who has just been visiting Bethune-Cookman College) tells me Zora sent her novel to 3 publishers simultaneously & they <u>all accepted</u> it! Only Lippincott got there first. You will love this Opus! I am reading Erskine Caldwell for the first time. Have you tackled him? I am a good deal more than enthusiastic about Tobacco Road & God's Little Acre. He is making Poor Whites glamorous to me!

1. *A popular stage actress who went on to have a successful career in the movies in the thirties and early forties.*
2. *Fannie Hurst was a white novelist who was a great fan of Hurston's, and employed her for a time as a live-in secretary.*

Hughes *wrangled mainly with Blanche about* A New Song. *She agreed with Van Vechten and wrote Hughes to that effect in a March 12 letter: "I don't think this is the moment for you to publish a book of poems — I think that you have become much too important than this poetry is and that the publication of such a book now would tend to hurt your name*

rather than help it." Hughes wrote back stonily on May 15. "Dear Mrs. Knopf,"
he began (he had heretofore referred to her as "Blanche"), "In regard to my
manuscript of verse, 'A NEW SONG' which is now in your office, and concern-
ing which you wrote me before you went away: I would not like to have you pub-
lish it merely to please me, since you do not like it. I do feel that it is important
however that the proletarian poems therein be published soon, and that they be
published in a form available to a working class audience, that is, in a cheap
edition. Therefore, I would appreciate very much you releasing the book so that
I might turn it over to the International Publishers or some others who cater to a
workers public and who will distribute it through workers' bookshops, unions,
etc. throughout the country." The International Workers Order sponsored a
printing of 15,000 at fifteen cents a copy in April 1938.

CARL VAN VECHTEN TO LANGSTON HUGHES, SEPTEMBER 22, 1934
(POSTCARD)

Mr. Langston Hughes
c/o Noël Sullivan
2323 Hyde Street
San Francisco
California
Dear Langston,

I have some photographs of Louis Cole & Bricktop but do not know
where to send them.[1] You do not tell me where you are & I get cards from
Reno, etc . . . and you never answered my question about that book of
verse. If it ever gets published anywhere—I mean the one I don't like—
please see that I have it for my collection. . . . Roy Atkins of the Cotton
Club[2] is my latest "color" print!

Best to you & Noël & Eddie—and Elsie[3] if she is still there!
C.

Sept. 22

1. *The black performer and nightclub hostess Ada Beatrice Queen Victoria Louisa Virginia*
   Smith was called Bricktop because of her bright-red hair. Hughes met her when she was
   singing at Le Grand Duc in Paris in 1924. Within a year, Bricktop was managing Le
   Grand Duc. She opened several of her own clubs over the years. Louis Cole was a stage
   manager and entertainer at Bricktop's club in Paris in the thirties.
2. *Roy Atkins was a member of the Cotton Club floor show team.*
3. *Elsie Arden was an actress and a singer.*

Box 1582
Carmel, Cal.

October 3, 1934

Dear Carlo,

I would love to have the photos of Bricktop and Louis. You may send them here, for here I still am, and probably shall be. At least, until I sell some more short stories. I went to the bank the other day and my account was overdrawn, so I found myself in debt, and quite back to normal. . . . I have however just written a story that is both mystic and Marxian, as well as four dimensional, so it ought to find a market.[1] . . . Did I tell you that I met William Saroyan last time I was in the city. He gave me his new book all bound in gold bands and beautifully printed. He is a very Armenian looking young man, Americanly nervous at the same time something like Jimmy Cagney, and says he used to work for an undertaker whose slogan was, We Give You Lots For Your Money. He wants to edit an anthology of the worst short stories written in America. He says they would be just as moving and just as revealing as the best. He and Tillie Lerner[2] and I had supper together after my lecture. Tillie Lerner is a little Communist girl writer who came out of jail recently to find that while in jail, she had become famous. Harry Hansen[3] had a syndicated column about her, and as a result several publishers had representatives trying to find out which jail she was in. She now has a marvellous contract with Random House which she had just signed the day I met her, so she showed it to me. 15% of the royalties, 75% of the movie rights, and a lot of other things most writers never get until they're Hemmingways. Besides a big cash advance. I told her it was better to be discovered than to be established. She needs the money, though, because her husband lost his job when the boss happened to look in the paper and see that she was in jail. . . . I lectured at Paul Elder's Bookshop, and there were so many people they had to put a rope across the steps. So I had to repeat my talk again at 3:30 for the other crowd. Quite a few books were sold, for which I am duely thankful. . . . Roy Atkins is the real tall boy, isn't he? Did you take all of him? . . . Constance Kanaga, a well known lady photographer in S.F., took me last Sunday. I haven't seen the results yet. . . . Tell Fannia I was delighted to read of her success in the new Elmer Rice play.[4] Hope I get to New York in time to see it this season. . . . My proletarian poems will not come out in a book after all. My agent thought it best not to try to place them now, so they rest in peace. . . . Elsie was down last weekend, delighting the Carmelites with the new stories she brought from New

LANGSTON HUGHES AND
WALLACE THURMAN, N.D.

York. We hadn't even heard that they were calling Mei Lang Fang,[5] Mae East, after our own Diamond Lil. . . . I guess you know Wallace Thurman is in Welfare Hospital, with T.B.[6] If you have any new books or magazines that you don't want and have any way of sending them over to him, I know he'd like them. He says he doesn't get enough to read. (No wonder,—he can read eleven lines at a time. That's the way he kept his job at Macauley's as a reader.) . . . Noel sends his best to you. He has just bought a new piano. . . . I have an article in Asia this month.[7] And if you see my piece in Theatre Arts, let me know.[8] I can't buy it out here.

10 little colored hound dogs to you,

Langston

1. *Hughes refers to "On the Road," a story in which Jesus Christ himself makes an appearance. It first appeared as "Two on the Road" in the January 1935 issue of* Esquire.
2. *The writer and activist Tillie Lerner became Tillie Olsen in 1943.*
3. *Harry Hansen was the author of a column that was syndicated nationwide.*
4. *The play was* Judgment Day. *Brooks Atkinson wrote of Fania's performance in* The New York Times Theater Review *on September 13, 1934: "As a pyrotechnical opera singer Fania Marinoff introduces a flourish of good comedy in the second act."*
5. *This Chinese opera star and female impersonator extraordinaire conducted his first American tour in 1930.*
6. *Thurman was admitted into the Welfare Island Charity Hospital in July and never left. He died there on December 22, 1934.*
7. *"Soviet Theater in Central Asia," was published in the October 1934 issue of* Asia.
8. *"Tamara Khanum, Soviet Asia's Greatest Dancer," appeared in the November 1934 issue of* Theatre Arts.

1935–1940

A friend of Noël Sullivan's had invited a group of people to spend a weekend at her cabin on Lake Tahoe in the High Sierras. Hughes was so near the California-Nevada border that he decided to investigate Reno, a city about which he had long been curious. He had been staying in Reno for a month, when he got disturbing news that called him to Mexico.

Van Vechten was encouraged by the success of Four Saints in Three Acts to suggest an American lecture tour for Gertrude Stein, which began in October 1934 and ended in May 1935. Van Vechten acted as a tour guide and host for Stein and her companion, Alice B. Toklas, on part of this very successful tour. At the beginning of 1935, he was in Virginia on the Southern leg of the tour with his "dames Woojums," as he sometimes called them.

San Ildefonso 73
Mexico City, D.F.

February 2, 1935

Dear Carlo,

I've been down here a little more than a month now. My father died
while I was in Nevada, and the three old ladies with whom he lived
refused to do anything about the estate until I arrived. It turned out that
there was a will and he had left everything to them, but they want to
divide it four ways with me, so after the lawyers' fees and the 20% government tax is taken out, I think maybe there will be just about enough to
cover my trip—so I've decided to stay here awhile and have a good trip
while I'm at it. . . . The old ladies, three sisters, all devout Catholics and
unmarried, are perfect darlings. They knew me when I was first here as a
baby, and they are spoiling me outrageously, waiting on me hand and
food, bringing me little presents every time they go to market, and having
their servant prepare the whole gamut of Mexican dishes for my benefit.
They are all in heavy mourning for my father. One of the remaining
twenty-five churches allowed a priest in the Federal District is just across
the street from us, so I go frequently to mass and vespers, and they pray
daily that I will embrace the faith. Every night at nine, they lock and bolt
the courtyard door, and after that hour no one but a Saint could come in,
so I have been getting plenty of sleep lately. Yesterday was my birthday
and for breakfast they made two huge earthen ware bowls full of <u>buñue-
los,</u> a kind of gigantic pancake like a small wagon wheel, fried to a crisp
in a big skillet, and especially for <u>dias de fiesta.</u> And for dinner we had all
sorts of swell Mexican dishes: a steaming soup of beans and herbs into
which one squeezes lots of lime juice; a dry soup of macaroni and toma-
toes; several kinds of fish, because it was Friday; a big bowl full of hot
mixed vegetables; squash candied with strips of sugar cane; and at the
end a divine mixture of wine, orange juice, and <u>zapote,</u> a very black tropi-
cal fruit that looks like crude oil when it is mashed and mixed, but tastes
like ambrosia. And with all that a bottle of old Rioja wine that they have
had for years. But the dear old ladies assure me that yesterday's dinner is
as nothing compared to the one I shall have on my Saint's Day—because
down here a birthday does not compare with a Saint's Day. Mine is Saint
James, but I don't know on what date it falls. . . . Every Sunday I go to the
bull fights. But only last week did I discover that the <u>novilleros</u> are much
more exciting than the fights in the big ring. In the little suburban plazas
where the young and unknown youths are out to make a name for them-

selves, most amazing and dangerous stunts are performed such as one almost never sees at El Toreo where the already famous and highly paid matadors perform. Last Sunday I saw a boy whose nick name is The Godson of the Killer, get his silken trousers ripped wide open by his first bull, only to have them sewn up behind the barrera—and again ripped wide open on the opposite leg by his second bull. This seemed to make him angry, and in placing <u>banderillas</u> he got too close and was thrown for a row, landing flat on his back like a ton of bricks. But he got up, shook his head violently, and went on with the fight. At the end he was carried around the ring, ragged and bloody as he could be, on the shoulders of the crowd. They get 5o pesos a week from which they must pay their helpers—but what they want is 20,000 and seasons in Madrid and South America. In the <u>novilleros</u> you can see what it takes for a torero to get where he wants to go—if he lives long enough. . . . Your perfectly charming pictures of Bricktop, Louis Cole and Roy Atkins were waiting for me in Frisco when I came through from Reno. I brought them with me down here and have enjoyed having them a great deal. I think they're the best of all your work I've yet seen. Brick is as darling as ever. Wish I could see her again. . . . I have been awfully broke lately, with having to send money home and all, so I went over to Nevada to work without being bothered with anything else—left all my mail and everything in California—and while I was there wrote ten stories and four articles. Two of the stories are out: ON THE ROAD in the January ESQUIRE and OYSTER'S SON in THE NEW YORKER on January 12. But I was so tired when I got down here, that I haven't done much of anything lately—except read DON QUIXOTE in Spanish, which is awfully amusing. I haven't even looked up my friends here—Walter White's sister-in-law and Fernandez de Castro the Cuban writer who is now in the Embassy. It has been so pleasant not being known for awhile, not having to make speeches or go to teas or read anybody's manuscripts or be interviewed, that I am loath to break the spell. So for that reason, haven't met any Mexican writers or artists yet, or anybody, except very simple people who just think I'm an extraordinarily dark American who has lost his father— so they give me plenty of sympathy! . . . I have been thinking of you often and meaning to write. I hope you and Fannia received my Christmas card. I guess you know of Nora's father's death. . . . Have you any news of how Muriel is making out in Moscow? And are you going to Arthur Spingarn's dinner on the 12th? Is Fannia's play still on? And have you ever taken any pictures of Father Divine?¹ . . . Are Miguel and Rose coming down here this winter? I thought his things in Vanity Fair (the Dali paintings) were swell. . . . I live only a block from the Diego Rivera frescoes in the Ministry of Education, and see them almost every day. . . . The next time you write a note for one of my books, you can say that my alliances with the white race are getting closer and closer: I now have a German step-mother whom my father married five or six years ago, but they were lately separated, so he also left her nothing! She is a nice fat lady who makes grand soups.

Mangoes and sugar cane to you, also six jarros of pulque and ten
Mexican hats,
Langston

1. *Father Divine was born George Baker in 1880. He was a charismatic religious leader whom his followers likened to God. His Peace Mission was one of the most successful religious organizations of the twentieth century.*

LANGSTON HUGHES TO CARL VAN VECHTEN, FEBRUARY 26, 1935

San Ildefonso 73
Mexico City, D.F.

February 26, 1935

Dear Carlo,

Rose and Miguel tell me that you are thinking about coming to Mexico. Hurry up and come on, will you, while I'm here. We are having some swell times, and I am meeting almost everybody, including Diego and all his wives. My friend, Jose Antonio Fernandez de Castro, the Cuban writer, is here connected with the embassy. I went to a dancing party there Sunday night with Havana rumba music.

Miguel told me about your party for Gertrude Stein. . . . He and Rose have a charming house in Tizapan, a nearby village. . . . And I think you'd find some grand people to photograph here.

Write soon and don't wait months like I did. I guess you received my letter of a few weeks ago. . . . There is a French boy here, Henri Cartier,[1] who is a great friend of Bricktop's. He loved your pictures of her.

Best regards to Fannia. Also Elsie Arden if you see her.
Sincerely,
Langston

1. *Hughes and the young photographer Henri Cartier-Bresson were roommates temporarily and friends for the rest of their lives.*

CARL VAN VECHTEN AND FANIA MARINOFF
TO LANGSTON HUGHES, OCTOBER 24, 1935
(TELEGRAM)

LANGSTON HUGHES=
VANDERBILT THEATRE 48 ST EAST OF BROADWAY=
LOVE TO YOU AND YOUR FIRST PLAY=
CARLO FANIA

[Handwritten note]
(Opening of "Mulatto" Oct. 24, 1935
New York
L.H.)

•

The morning after the opening of Hughes's play Mulatto, *the reviews were devastating, particularly in their treatment of Hughes. Brooks Atkinson of the* New York Times *expressed the opinions of most reviewers when he concluded that Hughes lacked the necessary "dramatic strength of mind . . .*

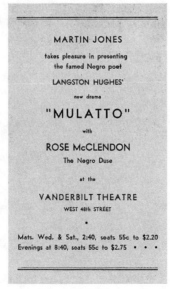

MARTIN JONES

takes pleasure in presenting
the famed Negro poet

LANGSTON HUGHES'

new drama

"MULATTO"

with

ROSE McCLENDON
The Negro Duse

at the

VANDERBILT THEATRE
WEST 48th STREET

•

Mats. Wed. & Sat., 2:40, seats 55c to $2.20
Evenings at 8:40, seats 55c to $2.75 • • •

driving story in
the reviewers didn't
play bore little resem-
original creation.
tin Jones, had taken
Hughes out of roy-
him with the same
toward all the black
ordeal and the final
Hughes went back to
had moved there in
his mother, who had
her breast.

to tell a coherent,
the theatre." What
know was that the
blance to Hughes's
The producer, Mar-
over the play, cheated
alties, and treated
contempt he directed
actors. Shaken by the
insult of the reviews,
Oberlin, Ohio. He
September to care for
discovered a lump in

ANNOUNCEMENT FOR *MULATTO*

212 S. Pleasant St.

November 29, 1935

Dear Carlo,

I enjoyed your card, and thanks for reminding me through Miss Rubin of the Knopf office that I should be looking out after my MULATTO. Strange to say, I've received no sort of communication from Mr. Rumsey of the American Play Company since I left New York, although I've written him asking him why and wherefore; and I've never seen a box office statement since the play opened. I'm sure they've taken in Five Thousand Dollars by now, or else they wouldn't be running. (That's the amount of which I get 5%; over the first Seven Thousand, 10%, minus, of course, the advance.) They probably don't owe me any money yet, but shouldn't they be sending a weekly statement anyhow?

I've got a whole act done of a new play, among other things. And a long poem called LET AMERICA BE AMERICA AGAIN.[1] If I just had more time, and less to do, I'd get more done.

Sorry about our pictures, but when I come back (which probably won't be until after Christmas, broke as I am) you can take some more. I'll probably go on to Chicago while I'm out this way and get the material I need for my novel.

I hope you and Fania had a grand Thanksgiving.

Sincerely,

Langston

1. *Hughes published this poem in the July 1936 issue of* Esquire.

Dear Langston, I should think it would be your personal agent and not the American Play Co. who should get boxoffice statements of Mulatto. In any case, Ben Washer was here the other day and said he didnt think your agent was watching it at all and this is not the custom in the theatre where the hawks congregate to collect all they can. Personally I know nothing more about it than this. Of course if you do anything, dont use Washer's name. Ben said, however, that from NOW ON (and maybe sooner) you should be collecting from $100 to $150 per week, so if you are POOR, it is because you want to be. Your agent or you should get a statement from the beginning of the run <u>every Saturday</u>. YOU CANNOT BE LAX OR TOO GRACIOUS IN THE THEATRE.

If you want America to be America again we'd all move out and leave it to the Indians, and I wouldnt mind doing that, except Id hate to move back to Holland, and you to Africa. Besides probably The Hollanders took Holland away from the Trogladytes or such. Maybe your poem isnt about giving American back to the Indians!*

I hope your mother is better or being cared for in some way.

I cant wait till I take some more pictures of you. Im in a big show at Radio City and here is my first notice! By none other than Henry McBride who is the leading art critic of America. . . . Bricktop, Taylor Gordon, and Ethel Waters, are among my subjects. So is your friend Emma Goldman.

      1009 ripe porgies swimming in a cutglass bowl full of gin to you!

Carlo

Monday

*That would be <u>their</u> poem, however! You must remember that!

V an Vechten's exhibition at Rockefeller Center's Radio City Music Hall ran from late November until late December. Other participating photographers included Rockwell Kent, Frank Crowninshield, Manuel Komroff, Richard L. Simon, Joseph Wood Krutch, Harry Bull, and Willard D. Morgan. After seeing Van Vechten's work, Henry McBride proclaimed in the New York Sun that "literature's loss is photography's gain." He goes on: "The studies of Gertrude Stein, Theodore Dreiser, Fania Marinof [sic] and Lynn Fontanne are not only vital but packed with fourth-dimensional insinuations." Thrilled with this review, Van Vechten pasted it in his scrapbook and wrote underneath: "This is my first photographer's notice!"

Chicago, Illinois

December 19, 1935

Dear Carlo,

I haven't written because I've been terribly busy. I've finished up one play, a Harlem farce about the numbers called LITTLE HAM which my agent is now having typed, and which I'll let you read, if you'd like to, shortly. And for the last two weeks I've been here in Chicago completing a Southern Negro folk play with Arna Bontemps, a play that we began in California and which I think is quite as good as Zora and I's unfortunate venture.¹ (I hope better from the standpoint of amusing theatre.) It's based on a saying in some parts of the South that when a jackass hollers a woman's love comes down! A jack being a sexual animal!

That was a swell clipping you sent me about your photographs. But I don't see how critics (and people) could help but like them. I want you to take some in Mexico.

Arthur Spingarn secured for me statements of MULATTO up to the end of November, the first six weeks of the run, which left me short $26 of beginning to be due some money. No doubt, they must owe me something now, and I've been waiting for later statements, but they haven't come yet, so I've written Mr. Spingarn again. My agents apparently are not very much concerned about collecting for me, Mr. Rumsey of the American Play Company—so I'm letting Maxim Lieber, who has been handling my stories (and who is agent for TOBACCO ROAD) take charge of my new plays. He at least answers letters and reports promptly on even the smallest sale. And apparently likes LITTLE HAM, who was a shoe-shiner, but becomes a number writer.

I am going back home to Oberlin tomorrow for Christmas, but I hate very much to be broke and unable to buy my mother a few presents and make it pleasant for her, as it's been a long time since I've spent a Christmas at home. I was hoping something would come in from MULATTO, but seemingly it isn't, at least not promptly—so I am wondering, Carlo, if you could perhaps lend me $25 which I will repay you from my very first check from any source. If MULATTO continues to run, I hope to be able to repay you also the $200 which I already owe you, dating from my Park Avenue crash. If you can, airmail it to my Oberlin address below, and I'll be plenty grateful, in time for Christmas shopping.

I'm awfully sorry about Rose's illness.² It seems that there's almost an entirely new cast in the play. I keep getting clippings about changes. I'd like to see the new boy that they have, and also how Mercedes Gilbert gets along with Rose's part.

My best to Fannia, and twenty little ole jacks with red ribbons around their necks to you,

Sincerely,
Langston

212 S. Pleasant St.
Oberlin, Ohio

1. *The play was* When the Jack Hollers.
2. *Rose McClendon became ill with pneumonia while starring in* Mulatto. *She died soon afterward.*

CARL VAN VECHTEN TO LANGSTON HUGHES, JANUARY 4, 1936

Dear Langston, I must say I am rather fond of Little Ham.[1] The piece lacks plot and could have more incident and intensity; the last act is fairly weak, and YET, I think, PLAYED, say by Bessie Smith and Bill Robinson,[2] the comedy would keep an audience in roars. It is real Harlem folkstuff and gathered none too soon. I am convinced, after hearing Marian Anderson, that the folk Negro will be done for in another generation. I think this little play has a chance, if it is properly produced. Whom are you sending it to? I might suggest Norman-Bel Geddes who says he is on the lookout for plays and if you send it to him, by all means mention my name. Brock Pemberton might just be interested in this and so might Delos Chappell.[3] Dont send it to any one without any money as it needs an expensive production with almost a real Savoy at the close. I am sorry you are having such a time with Mulatto. The play is running away. And maybe you'll get your money all in a bunch. You <u>are</u>

BLACK VIRGIN OF MONTSERRAT

being industrious. Think of turning out this play over night! I am proud of you. Do you know about Juanita Harrison? She appeared in the Oct and Nov numbers of the Atlantic and I LOVE her.[4] Please find some library and look her up. You wont be sorry! To revert to MA,[5] she is a Sensation.

789 sensations to you too!

Carlo

Friday

I enclose the celebrated Black Virgin of Montserrat.[6]

1. *Hughes's play* Little Ham *is a comedy set in a shoe-shine parlor and a beauty shop in 1920s Harlem. The story revolves around the highs and lows in the life of Little Ham, Hamlet Hitchcock Jones, a shoe shiner and numbers runner.*

2. *Fifty-year-old Bill "Bojangles" Robinson's performance in Lew Leslie's* Blackbirds of 1928 *brought audiences to their feet. He headlined at prominent black nightclubs in New York throughout the 1930s.*

3. *Geddes, Pemberton, and Chappell were all prominent theatre producers.*

4. *The* Atlantic Monthly *introduced Juanita Harrison as "an American colored woman who at the age of thirty-six undertook to work her way around the world. Born in Mississippi, she had a few months of schooling before she was ten. Then began an endless round of cooking, washing, and ironing in an overburdened household." The magazine published excerpts of the letters she wrote during her travels.*

5. *Marian Anderson.*

6. *The statue of the Black Madonna is called "Our Lady of Montserrat," or "La Moreneta." It sits on Montserrat mountain, in the Catalonia region of Spain, and is said to work miracles.*

LANGSTON HUGHES TO CARL VAN VECHTEN, MARCH 25, 1936

2245 East 80th St.
c/o McNaughton
Cleveland, Ohio

March 25, 1936

Dear Carlo,

"Little Ham" opened last night with great success seemingly.[1] I couldn't go, having been ordered to bed. You know, I had grippe in New York, and was ten days in Edgecombe Sanitarium, and no sooner got up from that than I got word that my mother was worse, and I had to come out here. Now, I seem to have had a relapse myself, temperature and all, but not so bad-off as I was, so I'll probably be out in a few days. We took mama to a hospital. She is at the stage where severe pain is beginning, so has to have opiates most of the time.

I saw one rehearsal of the play, and it looked quite amusing. The Gilpins are doing a swell job with it, considering their limitations and the size of their stage. Tiny is very well cast, also Madam Bell.[2] Little Ham himself not so much so, the difficulty being to find a small enough fellow with the proper sparkling personality. His size is O.K. and he's one of their best actors, but not so much verve or lightness as we wished. Anyway, it seems to make an entertaining show. I wish you could come out and see it.

"Mulatto" was due up for arbitration last week. I haven't heard what happened.[3]

How did the pictures come out? I hope all right. I am not in jail, but I am in bed—and in Cleveland—so God knows when you'll get to take any more. Besides, I have a stiff neck now, and couldn't turn my head. Even if I had been at the opening last night, I wouldn't have been able to bow.

Sincerely,
Langston

Advance sale was so heavy, they're playing another week.

1. Little Ham *premiered at Karamu House in Cleveland on March 24. On March 25, the* Cleveland News *called it "a hilarious comedy." The* Cleveland Call and Post *complimented its "hilarious lines and good clean humor."*
2. *Tiny Lee is a hairdresser in the play. Madam Lucille Bell is the "proprietress of Paradise Shoe Shining Parlors," where much of the action takes place.*
3. *Hughes sued for back royalties on* Mulatto. *Even though Martin Jones bragged that he planned to make it difficult for Hughes to collect his money, the arbitration was settled in Hughes's favor.*

CARL VAN VECHTEN TO LANGSTON HUGHES, MAY 13, 1936

Dear Langston, Im delighted with all your news. I was afraid something had happened to you because it was so long since I had heard from you and here you bob up bright and shining and even send a cheque, for which, thank you! Im so glad your mother is improved, that you are better, that you have a nice place to live, and that Mulatto is at least paying royalties. It is announced in this morning's paper that Ernest Truex's son is supplanting Leon Janney.[1] So I guess its going on and on. We are going to move in the fall and we are getting ready for that now (some job with all my books) and tomorrow we're going down to the Eugene O'Neils to stay for a few days (Ill be back before the 21st).[2] I saw Macbeth last night for the third time. Again crowds, again cheers, again all sorts of excitement! Ive found out at last what Harlem really likes. Have you ever heard of any other playwright who could create standing room at every performance at the Lafayette for five weeks?[3]

Best dolphins to you and do come back to NY some day; Id like to talk
with you,*
Carlo

Wednesday

*AGAIN!

1. *The black actor Leon Janny played one of the leads in* Mulatto. *Phillip Truex replaced
   him.*
2. *Carlo and Fania moved to 101 Central Park West. They visited Eugene O'Neill and his
   wife, Carlotta Monterey, on Sea Island, off the coast of Georgia.*
3. *The Harlem Negro Theatre's production of* MacBeth *had "thousands of people milling
   around the Lafayette Theatre hoping for seats," according to the* Amsterdam News. *The
   Harlem Negro Theatre was a WPA (Works Progress Administration) initiative.*

LANGSTON HUGHES TO CARL VAN VECHTEN, JUNE 1, 1936

Dear Carlo,

I've been expecting almost every day to be in New York and to thank
you in person for the photographs which were really swell this time. And
it was most kind of you to send me so many. I've mailed some out to Noel
and other friends on the coast. My mother and brother¹ were crazy about
them and wanted almost all of them for themselves. Those of Bessie were
marvellous, especially the one with the Grecian head, and the other with
that and the Negro head over her shoulder together. But they're all too
good! . . . I'm trying to finish up the Gynt musical before leaving.² . . .
WHEN THE JACK HOLLERS is done and has gone off to the agent to
be copied. I've asked him to send a copy to you (my copy) so just keep it
until I come. I think it might amuse you. As a play, it seemed to me better
than LITTLE HAM, although not so funny. It wasn't meant to be. It's a
DRAMA. . . . I'll take the Justema picture, too, when I come, so don't
pack it up. . . . Where are you going to move anyhow?

99 penthouses and a balloon to you, if that's what you want.
Langston

2256 East 86th St.
Cleveland, Ohio
June 1, 1936

I've had a card from Nora saying that she is coming East this month.

1. *In 1915, Hughes's mother, having previously divorced James Hughes, married Homer
   Clark, a cook by trade. Gwyn Shannon Clark, Homer's then two-year-old son by a previ-*

ous marriage, became Hughes's stepbrother. Hughes always considered Gwyn (called Kit)
kin, and looked after him financially at different points in his life.

2. *Hughes returned to* Cock o' the World *at the behest of Kaj Gynt, who had a renewed*
determination to secure Paul Robeson's interest in the project.

LANGSTON HUGHES TO CARL VAN VECHTEN, FEBRUARY 19, 1937

2256 East 86th Street
Cleveland, Ohio

February 19, 1937

Dear Carlo,

Ever since the holidays I've been meaning to write you, but various things from plays to a bad cold in bed have kept me from my letters. It seems that there is nothing like the theatre to keep one's life in an uproar. But wonder of wonders (such a wonder that I may be repeating myself and telling you again) MULATTO, at the insistence of the Dramatists Guild, finally came through with several weeks' back royalties just before Christmas with the result that I paid the rent three months ahead, bought a new suit, and a new typewriter, and hired a stenographer to help me get my literary life in shape. . . . I loved the Harriet Beecher Stowe house pictures you sent me. By the way, the Gilpin Players are giving as their next production a new version of UNCLE TOM'S CABIN called FRESH OUT OF HEAVEN by a young white playwright, Gerald Davidson, whose first play it is. It seems to be very modern in form so far as staging goes, showing interiors and exteriors at the same time, etc. . . . They will probably do a comedy of mine next if I can get it finished in time: all about what goes on in the lobby of a cullud hotel. . . . At the moment I'm trying to finish the libretto for Grant Still, based on the play TROUBLED ISLAND, which I've recently sent you in case you'd like to read it.[1] Still writes from Hollywood that he has already put down a number of musical ideas for it, and is anxious to get to work. I think I may go out there for a few weeks in the spring. . . . What do you think of it as a play? Cleveland critics did not like it a great deal, (other than McDermott) but the audiences seemed to enjoy it. It needed, of course, a much larger cast and stage than the Gilpins were able to give it. . . . This summer I have a job for the first time in many years: conducting a tour to the Soviet Union for Edutravel, with the accent on the study of National Minorities, leaving New York July 3rd and returning August 31st. London, Scandanavia, Lenningrad, Moscow, the Caucasus, the Black Sea Riviera, Kharkov, Kiev, and out probably via Vienna and Paris. I'm glad about London as I've never been there. Nor to Vienna. The more people that go,

BESSIE SMITH, PHOTOGRAPHS BY CARL VAN VECHTEN, FEBRUARY 3, 1936

the more I get paid, so I hope there'll be a mob, providing they're not all people who wake up at seven o'clock in the morning.[2] . . . It seems that MGM is making movie shorts especially for Negro consumption, filming just now in Chicago, and are going to use two of my songs, according to Margaret Bonds, the girl who did the music for them. (She's a very talented young lady who's been piano soloist with the Chicago Symphony, and who has made beautiful settings for a number of my poems.) Did I ever tell you that I spoke to Elsie Roxborough about the possibility of your photographing Joe Louis, and she said she thought she could arrange it?[3] Or maybe you've photographed him by now.[4] Elsie is the girl who dramatized Walter White's FLIGHT and is on the student staff of the Little Theatre at the University of Michigan. . . . Did I tell you that I spoke to the Cleveland Writers League a few weeks ago, and a young man there told me that of all the writers in the world the two he'd most like to meet are yourself and Gertrude Stein, you being his chief admiration! . . . Tonight Marian Anderson sings here. I am going—my first time out of the house for a week due to the cold I caught, I believe, at a Spanish meeting where Ralph Bates, the English novelist of THE OLIVE FIELD, made a thrilling talk about what he'd recently seen in Madrid and Barcelona. He gave me news of several people I know there. Pablo de la Torriente-Brau, a leader of the Cuban students and a friend of mine in Havana, has been killed on the Madrid front, I was sorry to hear. . . . Next month I'll be East and hope to see you. Thanks so much to you and Fania for your birthday and Christmas wires. And with very best regards to her,

Sincerely, as ever,

Langston

1. Troubled Island *was an ambitious meditation on the life of Jean-Jacques Dessalines, the early nineteenth-century liberator and ruler of Haiti. It was Hughes's third production at Karamu House, the Gilpin Players' theater. The play opened on November 18, 1936, in Cleveland.*
2. *Hughes's Edutravel job was sponsored by the Inter-Racial Study Group. The tour was called "National Minorities in Europe and the Soviet Union."*
3. *Hughes met the beautiful Elsie Roxborough when she came to the premiere of* Troubled Island. *He describes her in* I Wonder As I Wander *as "the girl I was in love with then," referring to the fall of 1936. Hughes quickly became embarrassed by Elsie's behavior—she fed stories to the black press that they were to be married—and distanced himself from her. Elsie was very light-skinned and before long she began passing for white. After 1938, none of her black friends ever heard from her again. For several years, however, Hughes received every Christmas "a carefully chosen little present—with no return address on the packet." Before Hughes, Roxborough had been linked publicly with Joe Louis, who was managed in part by her uncle.*
4. *Van Vechten photographed Joe Louis in 1941.*

LANGSTON HUGHES TO CARL VAN VECHTEN, JUNE 15, 1938

66 St. Nicholas Pl.
Apt. B-53, New York City

June 15, 1938

Dear Carlo,

Your very kind loan has been of more help than I can tell you, since those last weeks of my mother's illness with the large hospital and doctor's bills had exhausted all my resources. And yours and Fania's lilies were so beautiful that they were used as a garland of flowers within the casket itself by the ones who prepared the burial.[1]

There has been so much to do this week that I haven't had a chance to come down and see you. Among other things, I am trying to get the apartment ready to (in typical Harlem fashion) rent out a room, since I have one too many. And my brother has gone to Mass. to see about a summer camp job there.

I was so sorry to learn from Rita last night that one of the young women who works for you was unable to get in one night recently to see DON'T YOU WANT TO BE FREE.[2] We had left her name at the box office, but sometimes the person there is changed, which may account for it. So to make sure this time, I am enclosing two tickets for any Thursday

DON'T YOU WANT
TO BE FREE ?

A NEW PLAY BY
LANGSTON HUGHES DIR.
APRIL 24, ~ ~ ~ 8:30 P.M.
HARLEM I.W.O. COM. CENTER
317 WEST 125 ST ~ ADM. 35¢

ANNOUNCEMENT FOR
DON'T YOU WANT TO BE FREE?

or Sunday from now until the end of June, the 30th being the last performance this season. I hope she will want to come again, and please extend to her my regrets about the last time. It must have been the evening of my broadcast and I wasn't there.

Rita is casting the LOWER DEPTHS as a studio play for us.[3]

Earl Jones,[4] our leading man, has two offers to go on the sure enough stage: or rather one definite one in the new Max Gordon social revue for the fall, and the other as proposed understudy for Rex Ingram in HAITI. And two others of our cast have been approached professionally also as a result of our downtown appearance, which seemed to have gone rather well, but not so good as uptown.

Let me know when you want to take Earl's picture. Richard Wright is in seclusion in Brooklyn and is hard to get at. Working on a new novel already contracted for, I believe.[5]

Best to you, Langston

1. *Carrie Hughes suffered with cancer until she died on June 3. Fania and Carl's flowers were the first to arrive. Van Vechten helped Hughes financially with the burial expenses.*
2. Don't You Want to Be Free?: A Poetry Play: From Slavery Through the Blues to Now—and Then Some!—with Singing, Music and Dancing *was the first effort of the Harlem Suitcase Theatre, a cultural organ of the International Workers Order and the realization of Hughes's personal vision.* Don't You Want to Be Free? *was Harlem's longest-running play to date, captivating audiences for 135 performances.*
3. *Rita Romilly was never able to get an adaptation of this Maxim Gorky play off the ground.*
4. *Robert Earle Jones, father of James Earl Jones, starred in* Don't You Want to Be Free? *He was one of the most successful actors of his generation.*
5. *Van Vechten photographed the writer Richard Wright on June 23, 1939.*

CARL VAN VECHTEN TO LANGSTON HUGHES, OCTOBER 25, 1938

Dear Langston, Here are a few pennies for your theatre. Thanks for letting me see these skits.[1] They would make clever blackouts in a revue.

Drop in when you get time and if you havent ask Dorothy to drop off the records sometime when she is driving downtown.

best of everything to you!

Carlo

Tuesday

1. *Hughes apparently asked Van Vechten to take a look at some skits he was getting ready to stage for the Harlem Suitcase Theatre.*

LANGSTON HUGHES TO CARL VAN VECHTEN, OCTOBER 28, 1938

Dear Carlo,

You can't imagine how handy your contribution of Ten Dollars comes in to The Harlem Suitcase Theatre, just when we are struggling to get props and costumes together for our opening Sunday. Even to run a suitcase theatre without sets takes an unbelievable amount of money, what with printing, lights, wigs, chairs, piano tuned, pianist to pay, typing of promp books, telephone calls, whips and bullets, to pay for! It is a costly art.

This week has been a killer with the Cleveland Gilpins wiring every-day for a new play I've promised them, the WPA musical wanting a Negro skit at once, PINS AND NEEDLES[1] seeming to suddenly have the same requirement, and our own dress-rehearsals and opening to prepare.

The Blues Opera is coming along swell. And the Grand Opera is done, so Still writes me from California. So shortly I expect to leap from aria to aria, The Suitcase to the Metropolitan!

I want to bring your records down myself. How about Monday or Tues-day? I'll telephone.

Sincerely,

Langston

October 28, 1938

New York

P.S. Enclosed two tickets for Sunday. (Or any Sunday). November 9, Mrs. Goode lectures for us on the education of little Paul.[2] On November 17, an all-blues evening: Blues in dance, music, art, poetry, and the drama! Better come!

1. Pins and Needles *was a musical revue by Harold Rome. It opened on November 27, 1939.*
2. *Mrs. Goode was Essie Robeson's mother.*

1379 E. Washington Blvd.
Los Angeles, California

February 25, 1939

Dear Carlo,

The other night I came across a charming essay of yours about your first night in Paris that I have never read before. In somebody's anthology of modern prose.[1] I liked it very much. Your article on MAMBA'S DAUGHTERS in the recent OPPORTUNITY is excellent, too.[2] And I guess you know that just about every paper in the country, white and colored, carried the news of that unusual and grand ad in the TIMES in which you-all paid tribute to Miss Waters.[3] I'm mighty proud of her success and trust the play will be running when I get back to town in April. I would hate to miss it. . . . Just now, and for the first time in years, I have a job! (And not only a job, but two, both at once). Clarence Muse and I are writing a picture for Sol Lesser's company (an RKO subsiduary, it seems) to star the kid singer, Bobby Breen.[4] It's to feature Negro slave songs and Stephen Foster tunes, is laid in 1847 in Louisiana, has a showboat in it, as well as Stephen Foster, Abraham Lincoln, and John Wilkes Booth—a dead end kid of the period. Almost every day they hand us something else to put into the story. And since Marian Anderson's three concerts here have been sell-outs, the studio is now considering writing a part in for her—if they can get her! . . . Hall Johnson's Choir is to do the music behind Bobby. And Leonore Ulrich is to be the Creole hussy who almost succeeds in her schemes to have the guardian fleece the boy of his plantation and his fortune and his faithful old Negro slaves who would rather face death than leave little Massa. . . . I find it amusing and not unprofitable working for Hollywood. Except that they want things in such a hurry they can't really want it good—which, however, is their own affair—since they have been in the business a long while and ought to know. Anyhow, I've been paying off a debt a week, and with four weeks to go, I'll just about clear up all my worries of last spring. Then, if the Lord ever blesses me with another Hollywood job, I'll start picking up the old debts of the springs before that. Thanks so much! . . . I hope I can do something for you sometime. . . . My other job is revising ST. LOUIS WOMAN for the Federal Theatre.[5] It's exciting material to work with, the 1890s in St. Louis. I'm inserting the music and popular songs of the period, and I think it will make a swell show, a kind of Negro Diamond Lil, to follow RUN LITTLE CHILLUN now in its 32nd week out here, but still packing them in. . . . Outside those two jobs, the only other things I'm doing is directing DON'T YOU WANT TO BE FREE for an amateur group, to open about the middle of March. . . . I've heard that Miguel is on the coast. Do you know where? . . . How is Fania? My best to her. . . . Please keep the pictures of Earle for me that I never had a chance to call for. I'll be back in the spring.

Here's wishing you everything that you wish yourself,

Sincerely,

Langston

1. *What Hughes discovered was the first chapter of Van Vechten's first novel,* Peter Whiffle, *which was anthologized in* Modern American Prose, *edited by Carl Van Doren, in 1934.*

2. *In a February 1939 review of* Mamba's Daughters *for* Opportunity *Van Vechten gushed about Waters: "Whatever may be said for or against the play, the performance of Ethel Waters in the role of Hagar calls only for the highest superlatives and has received them from all the critics. Rarely have I encountered such unanimity of opinion, such consistent enthusiasm. Seldom have I seen a first night audience so excited, so moved, so carried away by 'make-believe.' The fact is that the audience and the critics were enjoying what is known as 'great' acting, a phenomenon so rare that any generation is granted only a few examples of it, a phenomenon almost unheard of on our contemporary stage."*

3. *The January 6, 1939,* New York Times *ad read: "The undersigned feel that ETHEL WATERS' superb performance in Mamba's Daughters at the Empire Theatre is a profound emotional experience which any playgoer would be the poorer for missing. It seems indeed to be such a magnificent example of great acting . . . that we are glad to pay for the privilege of saying so." The "undersigned" included Van Vechten, Judith Anderson, Tallulah Bankhead, and Dorothy Gish. Van Vechten was responsible for the ad.*

4. *Hughes had come to Los Angeles on December 4 as part of a lecture tour, but stayed on to work with the black actor and musician Clarence Muse on a vehicle for the white child star Bobby Breen. Muse had impressed a young white Hollywood producer, Sol Lesser, with his staging of Hall Johnson's* Run Little Chillun. *Muse, who headed the Negro unit of the Federal Theatre Project in Los Angeles, had always wanted to collaborate with Hughes on a movie; this was their chance. They finished the first draft of "Pirates Unawares" in early December.*

5. St. Louis Woman *was an adaptation of Arna Bontemps's 1931 novel* God Sends Sunday. *The original adaptation was created by Bontemps and Countee Cullen, but Clarence Muse agreed to be a part of this production only if Hughes agreed to revise the play completely.*

CARL VAN VECHTEN TO LANGSTON HUGHES, MARCH 1, 1939

Dear Langston, To get a cheque for $100 just before the income tax is due is something that doesnt happen to this baby often.¹ Thank you very much. I was even more pleased to hear about all your good luck. The piece of prose you read about my first night in Paris is an early chapter of Peter Whiffle which I certainly thought you had read. A Negro Diamond Lil sounds swell and I hope it comes off that way. A'Lelia Walker could

have played that part! I think the greatest break the Negro Race has had
in a long time is this BAD PUBLICITY for the DAR and isnt Mrs. Roosevelt a honey?[2] Edward Robinson in Hollywood has a painting by Grant
Wood called Daughters of American Revolution depicting four hatchet-
faced old crones looking mean over their tea-cups. There are postcards of
this (I used to have some) but I dont know where they could be found.
Why dont you write E. G. Robinson? ANYWAY I think it would be
delightful if all the Negroes in the USA, including CVV, would begin to
use this postcard extensively. By the way I wrote Who's Who I was surprised NOT to find the names of Marian Anderson and Ethel Waters and
it seems (the editor wrote me back at once) they have been bombarding
Miss A with questionnaires since 1936 and never had ONE reply. They
asked me if I could help. So I am using the influence of the NAACP and
Hubert Delany[3] to see if I can get her to send in the required information. The editor also told me they had just sent a questionnaire to Miss
Waters. So I asked about that and she had already thrown it away. So I got
her another one and I am working on that myself! Miguel is doing a
mural for the Mexican Building in the San Francisco Fair. It is probably
finished but I think he is still out there. His address in SF is the Plaza
Hotel. Do you see Nora Holt? If you do please give her my love. I miss her
very much and please tell William Grant Still to call me when he comes
East as I MUST photograph him. Earle Jones at last accounts was doing
Joe Louis in the movies.[4] Tonight the Negro Actors Guild Ball. I have a
box and Morris Ernst[5] and his wife and Eddie Wassermann, among
others, are going with me. Fania is well and sends love and so do I,

with 131 silver (housebroken) dachshunds to you!

Carlo

March 1, 1939

1. *Hughes used his salary from his Hollywood projects to pay off a lingering debt to Van
   Vechten.*
2. *In 1939, the Daughters of the American Revolution (DAR) refused Marian Anderson the
   opportunity to perform at Constitution Hall in Washington, D.C., because she was black.
   Outraged, Eleanor Roosevelt resigned from the DAR in protest. On Easter Sunday,
   Anderson performed in an open-air concert at the Lincoln Memorial before an audience of
   75,000.*
3. *Hubert Delany was a lawyer and one of the most important political figures in Harlem.*
4. *In the 1940 movie* The Notorious Elinor Lee, *written, produced, and directed by Oscar
   Micheaux and Hubert Julien, Robert Earle Jones plays a prize-fighter, a character based
   on Joe Louis.*
5. *Morris Ernst was a theatrical director.*

Hotel Grand
51st & South Parkway
Chicago, Illinois

May 3, 1939

Dear Carlo,

I have, of course, been meaning to write you for weeks, but my last days in Hollywood were such hectic ones! The scenario, as usual, did not get finished in time.[1] But after a dozen people had torn it apart, putting Page 87 before Page 3, and Scene 42 in front of 6, the studio hired me beyond the time of our contract and right up to the hour of leaving to help put it together again. Or rather, talk it together, since 99% of their time was spent in story-conference. And since I'm not much of a talker, I'm afraid I didn't help any. They would do the most amazing things, like somebody in the top office putting the leading man on a white horse between story-conferences: the budget man saying next morning that he didn't know there was supposed to be a white horse and he saw no sense in it because we had exceeded the budget for animals already: we, <u>who wrote the picture</u>, said we hadn't put in a white horse, and didn't know it was there; whereupon the Director spoke up and said he thought it was a good idea to have a white horse because it lent dignity to the leading character. Yes, said the budget man, but you already have all other kinds of horses, besides mules, pigs, cows, and pheasants, and now you want a white horse! But I don't want the horse, said the director. I didn't put it there, but since it is there, I said I think it lends dignity to the leading character. Who gave you the horse, the business manager demands of the secretaries. None of the secretaries know who dictated the horse into the script. But about that time the Producer himself arrives and says he put in the horse, but is willing to take out the horse, if there is no need for another horse. Whereupon the Story Analyst says if they are going to pay him, they might as well listen to him once in awhile. And he speaks upon the subject of the horse. By this time, it has become a point of honor with the budget man <u>not</u> to have the horse. And finally after more than an hour's discussion, the horse comes out, and the plantation owner walks from the smoke house to the sugar mill. Thirty seconds of film, $25.00 for the rental of a horse to make the shot. Eight people and three secretaries engaged a full hour in an executive story conference on the point of the horse—when three horses could have been bought, fed, and ridden throughout three pictures on the salary expenditures used up by talking about the horse! And that is Hollywood! . . . The other day they sent me the final shooting script, and I see the horse is back again! . . . The picture is now before the cameras, they say, and Clarence Muse and I are to get full writers credits on the screen for both the original story and the screen play, as well as two songs contained therein, GOOD GROUND and LOUISIANA, the former for the Hall Johnson Choir, and the latter for Bobby Breen, the theme song, since it all happens "down yonder where the bayous are flowing, where the warm gulf winds are blowing, and where in lovely glory the wild rose leans over the highroad that leads to New Orleans!" . . . They think it might be a hit song and sell 200,000 copies! God preserve it and the horse until they both reach the screen.

Well, now I am in Chicago writing a book, on the movie money—that autobiography you told me I should write a long time ago. And I have about a hundred pages done. If you see Blanche or are telephoning her soon, will you tell her about it? I think I shall stay here for about three weeks more and get a first draft done, because I know if I come to New York there would be too many other things to do. And writing it from memory without any notes, letters, clippings or anythings, is probably the best way of doing it anyhow.

Thanks so much for the picture of Ethel. Remember, you still have my promised pictures of Earle Jones. His film, LYING LIPS, opens here next week and I shall surely see it.[2] What you must see if you come out to Chicago is the Amateur Fights at the Savoy on Tuesday nights. They are knock down and drag out, with Tiny Parham[3] playing SEA FOOD, MAMA between the rounds on a pipe organ! Imagine swing on a pipe organ at a colored prize fight!

I never saw Nora, but spoke to her by phone. Missed everybody. Studio kept me too busy. . . . Hold tight!

Langston

1. *Sol Lesser rejected* Pirates Unawares, *so Hughes offered him another script, eventually called* Way Down South, *which Lesser accepted.*
2. Lying Lips, *another product of the Micheaux-Julien team, opened just a few weeks after* The Notorious Elinor Lee. *A cautionary tale for black men too casual in their relations with black women, its cast was almost identical to the cast of* Elinor Lee.
3. *Hartzell "Tiny" Parham played the organ and piano. He got his start as a vaudeville performer.*

CARL VAN VECHTEN TO LANGSTON HUGHES, AUGUST 18, 1939

Dear Langston, Very glad to hear from you. When you get lost, you get lost. Everybody asks where you are and I say, Maybe in China! It happened that I was printing the pictures I took of you in Washington

Square yesterday afternoon just before your letter came. So Ill send these to you soon. Arna Bontemps was here today and posed for pictures.[1] I liked him so much. Ive never had much chance to talk to him before. I think the pictures will be good too. Have you read about the recent discovery of Bland's (the man who wrote "Carry me back to ole Virginny" and who is often called the Black Stephen Foster) grave in a little cemetary outside Philadelphia?[2] I wish youd write a poem about this and him some time? He deserves greater fame . . . Have you read about Dorothy Maynor (Norfolk, Virginia, black, short and stout) who made a sensation singing at a Boston Symphony party at Stockbridge. The Times gave her a column and a half. She sang Mozart. and spirituals and is booked for a fall concert in New York.[3] Or do you know the song, Mene Mene Tekel (about Mussolini and Hitler: the handwriting on the wall) sung by Dorothy Harrison, a colored lady garment worker in Pins and Needles?[4] Or the next THREE CENT Booker T. Washington stamp promised for next year?[5] Sometimes I think we should keep a diary of these events from year to year. Im sure you know that Joel Spingarn is dead and that there is to be a big production of A Midsummer Night's Dream, with Benny Goodman conducting the orchestra and with Maxine Sullivan and Butterfly McQueen in the cast.[6] Sidney Peterson is going back to Puerto Rico (with Vera) next week.[7] He has a swell job. So he and his wife and Dorothy and her father are dining here Friday. Im sure you know the Actors and the stagehands are having a row (both AFoL). Fm[8] went to Atlantic City for THAT. Luc[c]ioni has bought a farm in Vermont to work in during the summers and I imagine his family will live there. His Ethel hangs over the mantel till she goes to Pittsburgh in the fall when I shall miss her frightfully.[9] Have you heard Ella Fitzgerald's records of Have Mercy and I want the waiter with the Water? Both superb . . . I just had a letter from Nora: so she must be in L.A. Do you know a Fay Jackson from there who is here now? Are you breathless? I am.

happy days, siestas, and four Viva Chiles* to you!

Also my affection!

Carlo.

August 18

*a new drink I discovered at the Fair.

Dorothy tells me DYWTBF is to be done in Mexico.[10] Congratulations! And what are you writing? Is your autobiography finished?

1. *Van Vechten photographed Hughes's dear friend Arna Bontemps on August 15, 1939. Van Vechten and Bontemps would also become friendly.*

2. *James Bland was a composer and minstrel performer. "Carry Me Back to Old Virginny" is the state song of Virginia.*

3. *The soprano Dorothy Maynor (born Mainor) made her solo singing debut in early August 1939 at the Berkshire Musical Festival in Lenox, Massachusetts. The* New York Times *called her performance "extraordinary" in an August 13 article. She followed up with a much-anticipated concert at Town Hall in New York, where reviewers concluded that she had "one of the most remarkable soprano voices of her generation."*

4. *The antiwar song "Mene Mene Tekel" was written by Harold Rome, the librettist of the musical* Pins and Needles.

5. *"All Post Office Department records for first-day sales of a 10-cent stamp were broken when the Booker T. Washington item in the 'Famous Americans' series was released at Tuskegee Institute, Ala., on April 7," the* New York Times *announced on April 14, 1940. The first-day sale of more than $28,000 exceeded the record made by the Mark Twain 10-cent stamp, released in February of that year.*

6. *Swingin' the Dream was a musical adaptation of* A Midsummer Night's Dream. *The black actresses Maxine Sullivan and Butterfly McQueen played Titania and Puck, respectively.*

7. *Sidney was Dorothy Peterson's brother. The siblings were very close.*

8. *Fania Marinoff.*

9. *The artist Luccioni was at one time known as Vermont's painter laureate. He did a much-admired bronze head of Ethel Waters.*

10. Don't You Want to Be Free?

LANGSTON HUGHES TO CARL VAN VECHTEN, SEPTEMBER 6, 1939

Dear Carlo,

Thanks so much for the pictures. Also the card of Dick Wright, which I think is excellent. . . . I thought you might like these two little puppies, Nordica and Africa.¹ Very slowly, on a smooth surface, put Nordica's nose to Africa's tail and see what happens! . . . The book is going along swell. I've written Blanche requesting an advance—my Harlem landlord seemingly having very little faith in the possibilities of Art, having sent me a threatened eviction notice for being half a month behind in the rent, apparently not remembering that I paid three months ahead in my good Hollywood days. . . . Friends of your cousin's tell me she is still in Michigan, but I hope to see her on her return. And shall. . . . I've just finished a 2nd revision of Arna and Countee's "St. Louis Woman" and think it is a swell play with lots of color and music. I hope someone will do it. Thinking the new version might amuse you, I'm asking my New York typist to post you a copy when she's done. Please send it on to me here when you've looked at it.

Noël returns his best to you. He's distressed about the world nowadays, and the general inhumanity of human beings. He has nine dogs, lots of little goats, sheep, and calves, and finds their attitude the soundest of all. I reckon I do, too. . . . Gas masks and gardenias to you,

Langston

1. *This card was missing from the letter.*

November 2, 1939

Dear Carlo,

I have been so deep in THE BIG SEA that I couldn't come up for air, let alone for letters. But this is to let you know that waves of manuscript are about to descend upon you in the form of the completed book. And I would be most grateful to you if you would read it, cut out the names of those people who were NOT at your parties, and otherwise advise me as to what you believe I should take into consideration in the final polishing up which I will do after the Knopf's have read it, also.

The manuscript went off to you Monday, by express, so you should have it by now, or certainly today, or tomorrow. When you have read it, kindly send it directly to Blanche Knopf for me, as I have written her it is coming.

I would, of course, immensely appreciate, as usual, your frank opinion of it. Since I am still working on it, I cannot see it very clearly—as I am now cutting and preparing some chapters for possible magazine publication—but will not do PARTIES or NIGGER HEAVEN until I hear from you.

The missing chapters concern the writing of a novel and my last days at Lincoln. Also there are one or two inserts still to go in—particularly a TATTLER write-up concerning one of A'Lelia's parties. I have someone attempting to locate such a write-up for me in New York. Would you by any chance have kept any of those old TATTLER clippings?

With the chapters to be inserted, the book will run to 450 pages, which seems to me enough for one volume. Besides, the end of the Negro Renaissance seems to me a good place to stop, although I shall continue with the writing of it on through to the end—up to now. But the South, Russia, Soviet Asia, Japan, China, MULATTO, Madrid, and Hollywood as now outlined are quite enough material for another book of the same size—and certainly too much for a single volume. Besides being quite another phase of my life. Do you not agree?

About Luccioni, I will write to him soon, and would love to have him

BIRTHDAY CELEBRATION AT THE KNOPF HOME IN PURCHASE,
NEW YORK. STANDING FROM LEFT TO RIGHT: ETTIE
STETTHEIMER, CARL VAN VECHTEN, JAMES WELDON JOHNSON
WITH HIS ARMS AROUND FANIA MARINOFF, WITTER BYNNER,
GRACE NAIL JOHNSON. KNEELING: BLANCHE KNOPF AND
ALFRED A. KNOPF, JR. PHOTOGRAPH TAKEN BY ALFRED A.
KNOPF, JUNE 17, 1931

do my picture, but as things stand now, I won't be coming East before late
January or February — as I want to go straight ahead with my writing. And
this is an ideal place to work. Besides, having paid my New York rent well
ahead, I am broke again.

Thanks so much for the James Weldon Johnson booklet which is
BEAUTIFUL.[1] (Noel also sends thanks and will write soon.)

And thanks, too, to you and Fania for inviting me to the anniversary of
your wedding. It came three days after the date, or I'd have sent a wire. Or
maybe even flown there! Because I would have liked so much to have
been with you. CONGRATULATIONS and my love to you and Fania!
Swellest of swell couples!

Muriel Draper and the Chester Arthurs[2] were here for luncheon not so
long ago — or rather the week-end — but it went so fast it seemed like luncheon. . . . And after them came the young Douglas Fairbanks. His wife is
from Virginia where my various grandpa's came from. . . . And I didn't
know until Ester Arthur told me that I was descended from the Eliza-
bethan poet, Francis Quarles. But his poetry was so moral I am afraid he
wouldn't like the blues! (Or maybe he might if he were here today.)

Jimmy Johnson tells me that our little blues opera DE ORGANIZER
is in rehearsal at Labor Stage.[3] Have you heard tell of it? I haven't.

I wish my big opera was in rehearsal somewhere.[4] I heard TRISTAN with Flagstadt the other day in San Francisco,[5] in the middle of the most dressed-up audience I ever saw, with diamonds by the ton, and orchids like rose bushes.

An orchid tree to you and an equator of diamonds,

Comme toujour,

Langston

Rita! Dorothy! How are they?

1. *Published by Fisk University in 1938, the booklet was a commemorative pamphlet about the late James Weldon Johnson featuring articles by Arthur Spingarn, Sterling Brown, and Van Vechten. Before he died tragically in a car accident on June 26, 1938, Johnson named Van Vechten executor of his estate.*
2. *Chester Arthur was the son of the twenty-first president.*
3. *Hughes collaborated with the renowned pianist and composer James P. Johnson on* The Organizer, *a leftist one-act musical play.*
4. *He's referring to* Troubled Island, *for which he wrote the libretto.*
5. *At San Francisco's opera house, Hughes enjoyed soprano Kirsten Flagstad's performance in* Tristan und Isolde.

CARL VAN VECHTEN TO LANGSTON HUGHES, BEFORE NOVEMBER 12, 1939

Dear Langston, I am completely enchanted by The Big Sea and certainly it is the best thing you have done. Not feeling very well I stayed in night before last and started reading it with the intention of going to bed after reading a few of the opening pages, but I couldnt lay it down and I read on until 12.15 by which hour I had finished it. I would have written you at once but I have been sick on my back ever since until this minute. I had the mss. sent on to Blanche at once of course, but, however she reacts, my enthusiasm remains at white heat. I think you have done something.

My criticisms and suggestions are on minor points.

In the first place, I think you are quite correct to divide this book into two parts.[1] Only I think you should give the reader an indication of this, on the title page perhaps the two dates (of your birth and of the happenings at the end of Volume I) and then I think you should write a short foreword explaining why you hadnt told the whole story in the first volume.

Had you thought of illustrations? They might add. Again they might not.

About the Tattler. I once tried to get a number and was not successful. I havent the copy you want. We should certainly have saved a file and perhaps somebody has. Write Geraldyn Dismond,[2] 434 Lafayette Street, Apartment D-2.

P. 227 (the page numbers refer to your mss.) The Medicis didnt live in Venice.

Gurdjief[3] is misspelled throughout and youd better have your french gone over pretty carefully. You write Café, for instance, in Café de la Pais, without an accent and when you mean strawberries, you write fraise, which is ONE strawberry. I noted ever so many slips of this kind. Personally when I use foreign languages, I always make it a point to see that a NATIVE examines my copy. I think it would be a good idea in your case.

The Wallace Thurman chapter is excellent. He comes to life. But the Stettheimers NEVER lived on Park Avenue* (if you can tell me more about the occasion when you went there, perhaps I can help you out as to where they did live. Florine of course has always had a studio and I think I recall taking you <u>there</u> once). And dont you mean the Wertheims when you mention Wertheimers at the James Weldon Johnson. Dont you even mean Alma Wertheim? She was divorced from Maurice when she started going there.[4] Grace Johnson is living with the Nails at 2801 Seventh Avenue and you can ask her anything like this youd like to be sure of. You see you CANT be that careless about facts and spellings and dates in an autobiography without convincing the reader the whole thing is phoney. So please verify everything.

Bessie Smith's exact and baleful words (p 363) after d'Alvarez had finished singing were, "Dont let nobody tell you you cant sing."[5] Bessie arrived dead drunk at that party and had a FULL pint glass of straight gin when she got there. She sang with a cigarette in the corner of her mouth and she didnt hold it there with her fingers. Nor did she drop it. But she was in magnificent form and sang the Blues like a low-down Black Angel. I LOVED Bessie.

On Page 304 you misspell Olivia Wyndham's name and give her a title. She is <u>not</u> Lady, but Miss.[6]

Please take out the reference to a fat friend party (p. 305) given for Mamie Smith[7] and d'Alvarez. This may be true (I dont recall it) but Marguerite has fallen on evil days, is most melancholy, and this would hurt her very much.

P.306. It was MY bon voyage party, NOT Nora's (she came to say goodbye) and it was NOT in the lounge but in the Prince of Wales Suite on A Deck which I had on occasion (because the boat was empty and I knew somebody in the Cunard Line offices). There was no piano. Nora sang My Daddy Rocks Me unaccompanied. The remark about the Spirituals is exact but it was made by <u>Alice</u> Foote McDougall.[8] Jack Colton,[9] who came to see me off, brought her to the boat with him. She was NOT sailing. About 30 people from Harlem were there. We had champagne; it was very gay, I remember.

I see nothing to change in the chapter on Nigger Heaven. Congratulations!

Bricktop is arrived and has called up. She is coming to lunch as soon as I can have her. Paul and Essie and Grace Johnson were here for the anniversary. So were the Lin Yutangs.[10] I hope you will look into Zora's new book. It is very good indeed. Dorothy Mayner makes her debut at Town Hall on the 19. And Earle Jones is to play Oberon in the Swing Midsummer Night's Dream. Fania has been helping him.

my affection and admiration to you!

Carlo

Friday

*p. 301

And please remember me <u>always</u> to that sweet Noël!

1. *Hughes eventually completed two biographies:* The Big Sea *(1940) and* I Wonder As I Wander *(1956).*
2. *The journalist Geraldyn Dismond wrote society columns for black newspapers like the* Amsterdam News, *the* Pittsburgh Courier, *and the* Inter-State Tattler. *From 1928 until 1931 she was the* Inter-State Tattler's *managing editor.*
3. *The mystic Gurdjieff comes up in Hughes's section about Jean Toomer, who was at one time a disciple of the religious leader.*
4. *Alma and Maurice Wertheim were weathy white patrons of the arts.*
5. *In a section called "Downtown," Hughes recalls the impression opera diva Marguerite D'Alvarez made upon Bessie Smith, who had never heard of her before that night.*
6. *Hughes may have listed Wyndham in an earlier draft as one of the guests at a typical Van Vechten cocktail party, but she does not appear in the book.*
7. *Mamie Smith was a talented and versatile black singer and performer.*
8. *In this "Downtown" episode, Hughes describes Holt as "the scintillating Negro blonde entertainer." Holt sang "My Daddy Rocks Me with One Steady Roll," which led McDougall, identified as "a well-known New York matron" to exclaim "ecstatically, with tears in her eyes: 'My dear! Oh, my dear! How beautifully you sing Negro spirituals!' "*
9. *Jack Colton, known professionally as John, was a playwright.*
10. *Lin Yutang was a celebrated Chinese philosopher and writer, most famous for his 1937 book,* The Importance of Living. *Van Vechten wrote the introduction to a cookbook written by Yutang and his daughter.*

CARL VAN VECHTEN TO LANGSTON HUGHES, NOVEMBER 27, 1939

(POSTCARD)

Langston Hughes
Hollow Hills Farm
Monterey, Cal.

Dear Langston, Blanche just called me and says she is writing you she likes the book etc. And she told me some of the changes she is suggesting. Dont take all this too literally, as I dont entirely agree with her. I think by making VERY MODERATE alterations in what you already have you will be doing enough to please her. But, as always follow your own bent! oyster crackers to you!

Carlo

I n a November 28 letter to Hughes, Blanche Knopf told him that The Big Sea was "too full of 'I met so and so . . .'" She suggested he cut out nearly one hundred pages of this and compress it into "a sentence or two." The next day, probably swayed by her conversation with Van Vechten, she revised her position in another letter to Hughes, specifically regarding his sections about Wallace Thurman and Van Vechten. "Carl had so much to do with both you and the whole development and I realize that Thurman had a great deal to do with you too. Therefore in this section I think wherever these two things apply . . . it should remain."

CARL VAN VECHTEN TO LANGSTON HUGHES, NOVEMBER 29, 1939

Dear Langston, I talked with Blanche this morning and discovered that she meant the chapters about me and Wallace Thurman were not sufficiently clear, (i.e. to the uninformed reader). Far from being too long, they may be too short. I was distressed to have them removed as they are, to my mind, an essential part of the book's integrity: so Im glad this point is cleared up. When you look at these chapters then look at them from this angle: have you explained everything sufficiently to the uninitiated. I dont recall a chapter about the Dark Tower.[1] There certainly should be something about this. In fact A'Lelia was such an unusual and picturesque character I think you could let yourself go a little more on her. If I dont hear from you pretty soon, after my enthusiastic (and otherwise) letters and the number of telephone conversations I have had in your behalf with Blanche, Ill think you dont like me!

Brick[2] was here for dinner last night in her most reserved and ladylike mood. But she was grand. Jimmie Daniels has opened a new and chic club on 116th Street.[3]

four frolicsome spiders to you!
Carlo!!

November 29, 1939

To Marian Anderson tonight with Essie.

1. *The Dark Tower was A'Lelia Walker's literary salon. She established it in 1928 at her 136th Street Harlem townhouse. She borrowed the name from Countee Cullen's column in* Opportunity.
2. *Ada "Bricktop" Smith.*
3. *Jimmie Daniels was a well-known black entertainer. His New York club was called Bon Soir.*

LANGSTON HUGHES TO CARL VAN VECHTEN, DECEMBER 3, 1939

Sunday

Dear Carlo,

Am rushing off to Montaloo where Noel is singing a Forsyth setting of my "Negro Speaks of Rivers" today. Reason I haven't written you is I've been down with cold, too; in Frisco getting a platinum and gold tooth that's mortgaged my future to debt; been deep in arranging (belatedly) a spring lecture tour to pay for the tooth; been answering a mountain of mail piled up while writing book; a whole avalanche of things all at once. But I'll be writing you tomorrow soon as I get back. Loved your letters, cards, ELKS PICTURES!! and all. Adore that △ of you, Blanche, and the "Big Sea."

Sincerely,
Langston

CARL VAN VECHTEN TO LANGSTON HUGHES, AFTER DECEMBER 3, 1939

Glad, dear Langston, to hear from you at last. Enclosed is news from Philadelphia. Dorothy Maynor called up for your address. And Luigi's Ethel got the popular vote at the Carnegie Show at Pittsburgh, as the favorite picture in the SHOW!' Sorry you arent here to see Swingin' the Dream, altho' it doesnt quite come off. Nevertheless much of it is swell.

Please assure me you arent taking any of ME out of The Big Sea. Noël writes he'd rather have you there than any one! The James Weldon Johnson Memorial Meetings begin again next week.[2] Have you heard that Zora is married again.[3] The Robesons have loaned us their (Jacob Epstein) head of Pauli.[4]

Pies and tarts to you!

Carlo!

Wednesday

Better send me a Nice Long Letter.

1. *At the Carnegie International Exhibition in 1939, Luigi Luccioni's bronze head of Ethel Waters won first prize by popular vote.*
2. *Van Vechten originally wanted to have a statue erected in Johnson's honor on the corner of Seventh and Lenox Avenues. Walter White agreed to help raise money and Richmond Barthé soon began drafting possibilities.*
3. *On June 27, 1939, Hurston married Albert Price III, a recreation worker with the WPA in Jacksonville, Florida. She was 48; he was 23.*
4. *The English sculptor Jacob Epstein sculpted the heads of both Paul Robeson and his son (Pauli) in bronze. Van Vechten eventually purchased the sculpture of Paul senior.*

LANGSTON HUGHES TO CARL VAN VECHTEN, DECEMBER 9, 1939

Hollow Hills Farm
Monterey, California

December 9, 1939

Dear Carlo,

The last two or three weeks I've been writing so many letters and doing so much copying that for the first time in my life, my eyes hurt, so I guess I must be tired. But things piled up so during the writing of the book, and the letter drawer got so full of mail that I was afraid to open it—quite enough for a Hollywood celebrity it looks like—without my having the secretarial assistance available that I imagine a Hollywood celebrity must have if they ever keep up with correspondence at all. . . . One interesting thing anyhow is that I discover that I've had two songs published within the last couple of months and both of them, as played over by Noel's accompanist, sound pretty swell. Particularly AFRICAN DANCE by Connie Bemis that Exclusive (Mills) has brought out and are having (or hoping to have) Cab Calloway play. It's a semi-popular kind of number with a grand tom-tom beat rhythm underneath. And the other one is SHARECROPPERS by Joseph Rubel and published by Transcontinental in Steinway Hall. Noel says he is going to sing the latter. Meanwhile, I've still got to write the composer notes. . . . Erskine Caldwell is about to show up

on a folk lore survey of America.[1] And I've just answered a three months
old letter from Alan Lomax saying that my version of the DUPREE
BLUES I sent him is the best one he or his father have come across,[2] and
asking for more of the various blues verses I've collected, so I just got
around to copy out for him those things I happen to have among my
notes here. I thought you might be amused at some of them, too, (maybe
there're one or two among the lot you haven't heard, you ole blues-lover,
you) so I'm enclosing a copy for you. . . . I have a lot more in New York
somewhere. . . . Then in the midst of the letter writing (in fact last Monday after I got back from Noel's concert—and the very day I meant to
write you a long letter) I sat down at the typewriter and wrote eleven
poems instead! Including the SEVEN MOMENTS OF LOVE I sent you.[3]
Don't know what struck me, but something, so that I didn't get anything
else done that day. . . . And the next day I wrote a song that, of course, so
far has no music to it except the music in my own head—and I don't
know how to put that down, and can't carry a tune—not even my own
tune so anybody else knows what it is. . . . I loved and appreciated your
letters and you would have heard from me last Tuesday had not all these
poems come into my head. I am sure you know I haven't any intention of
cutting you out of the book (because you have been my main literary
help—not influence, mind you, as some critics claimed[4]—because I see
no reason why you should take the blame for WALDORF ASTORIA
since it isn't even in your style. But I doubt if Mr. Brawley—God rest his
soul[5]—knew the difference. Do you suppose? Like all those gentlemen
from the Philadelphia Police and Firemen's Social Club who protested
before the judge against MULATTO and it turned out had never even
read it. (much less seen it.) In fact, I doubt if some of the left white and
right cullud have ever read either you or I.) So that is why it seems to me
important to leave YOU and ME in the book, so that at least, if they want
to read about themselves, they'll have to read about us, too. Don't you
think so? . . . I read both your and Blanche's various suggestions and
shall shortly go to work polishing up on the basis of them. Certainly, I
greatly appreciated the corrections which you gave me. And I shall cut
out the D'Alvarez bit that doesn't need to be there, anyway. Also I'll have
all the French checked carefully, and various other little details that
hadn't been taken care of when I sent the script to you. . . . Now that I
haven't looked at it for a month, no doubt I'll see various dull spots
throughout that I couldn't spot while still fresh from working on it. And I
can cut about 15–18 pages by taking out the story, SPANISH BLOOD and
some of the other inserts in the Harlem section that Blanche thinks is, as
a section, too long and too full of extraneous people and material. But I
don't think it wise to cut practically the entire section as she and Mr.
Straus advise because that phase of Harlem's rise to culture and neo-

culture seems to me to be of historical importance and interest to quite a few people, both white and colored, who weren't there but would have liked to have been. Only probably I haven't (as you suggest) made it quite clear enough in terms of myself and me moving and developing against and in and through that background, so I shall see what I can do about that. . . . Neither you nor Blanche commented on the title: THE BIG SEA. Does that seem a good one to you? . . . Personally I don't care much for pictures in autobiographies because you imagine one thing as you read, and then look at the pictures and all your illusions of swell and romantic reality are almost always immediately grounded by the awful looking folks in the pictures. Most people read much better than they look, don't you think? Even the divine Isadora.[6] Even the handsome (so many think) Vincent Sheen.[7] . . . Unless all the pictures were taken by you or somebody equally as good who made them something worth look-ing at for themselves as photos and not necessarily as people. . . . If pic-tures were used, I have about a million from various parts of the world of various people and animals I have known from Topeka to Tashkent, but selecting them would be almost as much of a job as writing the book was, so unless you and Blanche really wanted them, we could just as well, I think, leave them out. Maybe, if folks feel that they need to know what the author looks like NOW (and you permitted) that photo of me with the hat on taken in the village might be good on the back of the dust cover, or on the inner flap. Or Noel has a very good one with his dogs taken on the lawn here with the whole Carmel Valley for a background beside me. . . . Gee, I have such amusing things to put in the second volume about the picture in Russia, the folks in Haiti, and Mrs. Bethune bawling out the young white gas station boys all the way up from Florida everytime she got out of the car to go to the washroom and came across those familiar southern signs staring her in the face when she wanted to pee with dig-nity: WHITE LADIES/COLORED WOMEN. . . . "Young man, is such a thing democratic?" she would say. . . . Also Martin Jones on MULATTO: "Why there's no problem in this play. It's all about sex—and everybody has that!" . . . Or Sol Lessor requesting me to, "Make a MAN out of Bobby Breen. Nothing sissy because he's already that. And nothing aggressive—because he's already Jewish." . . . And about that Moscow lady who said, "I've told my husband all. I love you! And am going with you to Siberia." And I said, "No m'am!" But there she was on the Trans-Siberian![8]

I was simply delighted to have the Elks Parade pictures. Some of them are just as interesting as the ones you last sent me of a former year. The tenement fronts with the people on the fire-escapes are particularly fine, I think. And I love the marching ladies and the fellows on horseback, and the two drummers. . . . I sent Dorothy Maynor a wire but perhaps too late for the concert as I thought it was in the evening, but I guess she got it just the same. . . . No, I hadn't heard about Zora being married again, but Arna just saw her teaching down in North Carolina and wrote me a glowing report of her charm, general mellowness, and the fact that she hadn't had but one quarrel since she'd been there, and she came out on top in that one, putting a professor in his place that everybody wanted to see put in his place.[9] . . . How is JOHN HENRY coming along?[10] Too bad SWINGIN' THE DREAM isn't a smash it. . . . Lew Lesie has been looking for an angel to back ST. LOUIS WOMAN but seemingly hasn't found one.[11] So Michael Todd is now said to be interested. . . . Wish I'd been at dinner with you-all when Brick came. I hope she will like what I've put in the book about her. . . . Excellent picture of Arna you sent me. . . . Did you hear that Richard Wright's book is to be the Book-Of-The-Month for January?[12] I hope it is true. Those who have read it say it is like Zola. . . . Noel has given nine performances as Dr. Rank in the DOLL'S HOUSE and was very good. One of his black caracule sheep has just had a little black lamb that must have been born walking because only a few hours old it is already out in the field. It is about as big as a foot high toy lamb and so thin—just an inch or so of chest . . . that it looks like a silhouette with only the legs splayed out. I have never seen so cute a little animal. . . . We have caught one tarantula and two black widows on the farm of late. So I have just been spraying my shutters to run everything out that may have been sleeping there.

Ten little lizards with jeweled tails to you, sir.

Sincerely,

Langston

1. *Caldwell and Hughes may have met in 1933 when Hughes became a client of the literary agent Maxim Lieber, who also represented Caldwell.*

2. *John Lomax was a noted folklorist. His son, Alan, is the author of several major works on folk music.*

3. *The poem, subtitled "An un-sonnet sequence in Blues," consists of seven stanzas. Hughes was paid one hundred dollars when the poem was published in the May 1940 issue of* Esquire.

4. *Hughes refers to the controversy surrounding their relationship, particularly after the appearance in 1927 of his volume of poetry,* Fine Clothes to the Jew. *Critics who disliked the book feared Hughes had come under the pernicious influence of Van Vechten, whose novel* Nigger Heaven *continued to haunt him in the black press.*

5. *Benjamin Brawley, perhaps the most vocal critic of Van Vechten, Hughes, and other Harlem Renaissance writers, died on February 1, 1939.*

6. *The modern dancer Isadora Duncan.*

7. *The popular writer and journalist James Vincent Sheen.*

8. *Hughes's story about Natasha, the "Moscow lady," appeared, like many of his tales about his travels, in the second volume of his autobiography,* I Wonder As I Wander. *Hughes met Natasha at a rehearsal at the Meyerhold theatre. "She had a buxom body, a round Slavic face—not beautiful, not ugly—and was very healthy-looking," he wrote. She also had "a one track mind." The two shared a bed at least once at the end of Hughes's Moscow stay. Even though Hughes found her "fun and wholesome in body as an apple," he soon tired of her enthusiastic attention and dramatic public scenes. Finally, when Hughes was on his way out*

of Moscow in the spring of 1933, Natasha appeared on the Trans-Siberian Express, express-
ing her desire to return to the States with him. Hughes gently but firmly turned her away.

9. *Hurston was hired by the North Carolina College for Negroes in Durham to organize a*
drama program in July 1939. Bontemps wrote to Hughes about his encounter with her in a
November 24 letter: "To top it all, Zora was there. She lectured there a year ago and got
her hooks in so good she is now on the faculty, teaching dramatics. She gave me a wonder-
ful time. Zora is really a changed woman, still her old humorous self, but more level and
poised. She told me that the cross of her life is the fact that there has been a gulf between
you and her. She said she wakes up at night crying about it even yet." The professor in ques-
tion was probably Dr. James Shepard, president of the school, with whom Hurston crossed
swords throughout her year-long tenure there.

10. *In late November, Robeson went into rehearsals for Roark Bradford's play about the leg-*
endary black cultural hero John Henry.

11. *Lew Leslie had a successful career producing black musicals and revues in the 1920s.*

12. *From Bontemps's November 24 letter Hughes learned that* Native Son *had been chosen as*
the January Book-of-the-Month Club selection.

CARL VAN VECHTEN TO LANGSTON HUGHES, AFTER DECEMBER 9, 1939

Langston, my lad! Seven Moments of Love is a wonderful title for your
next book of verse, which please begin to get ready (Big Sea is a marvellous title: Blanche and I and everybody who has heard it admires it pas-
sionately. I dont see how I escaped mentioning it.) I like these VERY
MUCH, especially No III which happens for no good reason (I LOVE 'em
all) to be my favorite. I like the snatches of blues too. By the way Seven
Moments cry for music and will be set like the rest of your verses. Tell
Noël that Dorothy Maynor's first record is out (Victor): Ave Maria and
Gretchen am Spinnrad, both Schubert. Her concert WAS at night and
she got your telegram. See current issue of Life (Dec 11) for her bowing
with me in the foreground![1] In the new Theatre Handbook edited by
Bernard Sobel, just sent me, I read under Negro Theatre: "Laudable and
generously helpful to the cause of all art have been Carl Van Vechten's
confirmations, recognitions, and appraisals of Negro talent and growing
culture."[2] Here is another clip on Mulatto. When you DO write a letter
you certainly write one. I thought the old farm had been foreclosed when
I got all those papers from you today. I LOVE it. Did you hear a song Paul
Robeson sang on the radio one Sunday afternoon recently, a wonderful
number, but I dont know the name of it. John LaTouche wrote the
words.[3] I hope some day to have the privilege of seeing Noël act or of seeing him in concert. How does he ever manage to get to the theatre on
time!? In the meantime I am glad he is going in for these activities. I agree
with you FULLY about the Harlem section of The Big Sea and if you
keep it in and even enlarge it Ill stand back of you. You are the last historian of that period who knows anything about it and its got to be down

and people will love it. I agree with you, it could be made more personal, and dont forget the Dark Tower. In fact whenever you can bring A'Lelia in Ill love it. Characters like that are endeared to me even when they are unpleasant and A'Leila was never exactly that, altho' we used to fight like anything OFTEN. Then she would bring me to open a bottle of champagne in her bedroom and Id fight with her again because she was giving me better than her other guests. I even liked Dr Du Bois once in her house when the matter of Madame Walker's hair restorer came up and W E B said, quick as a flash, "I always use it." You are probably right about pictures too. I was not advising them. I merely asked you to consider the question. I think a frontispiece of YOU wouldnt be a bad idea and you have lots of good ones by Weston and everybody and maybe I can take the best one yet next time you come east. Anyway you havent yet been done in color.* Swingin' the Dream was wonderful in spots. They made the mistake of making it too expensive. Benny Goodman, who wasnt needed at all, set them back $2500 a week. Of course he played divinely and had several Negroes in his band including the old Small's drummer and Fletcher Henderson at the piano, but it interrupted the action.[4] My adored Ella Fitzgerald is to be in Young Man with a Horn with Burgess Meredith.[5] You'd find Lew Leslie not so hot (in lines like your Green non-producer of cash). I hadnt heard about Wright's book, but it is probably true as publication has been postponed. Aren't you afraid of Black widows and tarantulas?

    1001 thises and thats to you and always, luck, and pleasure, and lots to
eat and drink!
Carlo

Monday

Definition of a Horse Show:
A place where horses show their asses to horses' asses who show their horses!

Barthé has a new full length African statue. I took the Baroness D'Erlanger to see it today.[6] It goes to the new Whitney Museum show as does Lucioni's Ethel!

+Owen Dodson has sent me two plays to read. Ever heard of him?[7]

*I mean I'm going to!

1. *The picture's caption reads: "An ovation greeted Maynor as she came out to bow at the end of the concert. In the boxes sat star singers. Standees lined the walls. Everybody wanted more encores." Van Vechten is visible in the front row.*
2. The Theatre Handbook and Digest of Plays, *edited by Bernard Sobel, was published by Crown in 1940.*

3. *On November 5, Paul Robeson sang "Ballad for Americans" as part of his friend Norman Corwin's half-hour CBS series on democracy,* The Pursuit of Happiness. *As a result of the thunderous public response, Robeson repeated the performance on New Year's Day, and eventually made a recording of it that became an instant hit. "Ballad for Americans" was written by the poet John La Touche as "The Ballad of Uncle Sam."*

4. *The pianist and band leader Fletcher Henderson joined Benny Goodman's band in 1939 as an arranger and pianist.*

5. *Neither Ella Fitzgerald nor Burgess Meredith appeared in this 1950 film.*

6. *Edwina d'Erlanger was the wife of the Baron Leo d'Erlanger, whose title was German but whose family had lived in England since the nineteenth century. The baroness was a model, dancer, and actress, as well as a well-known hostess in London.*

7. *Owen Dodson was a black poet and playwright. At the time he wrote to Hughes, he was juggling appointments in the drama departments of both Spelman College and Atlanta University. Dodson had an enormous impact on black theater. Perhaps Dodson sent Van Vechten his best-known play,* Divine Comedy, *written in 1938 and produced at New York's Federal Theatre in January 1977. Hughes probably met Dodson not long after he sent a letter of praise for Hughes's* Don't You Want to Be Free? *in June 1938.*

LANGSTON HUGHES TO CARL VAN VECHTEN, DECEMBER 15, 1939

Carlo,

You took the words right out of my mouth! I mean about a new book of poems. Lately, I've been going through my old poetry, throwing away, revising, and having copied, and I've come across more than two dozen blues, a dozen or so dialect poems in the blues mood, and a projected blues playlet. Those with SEVEN MOMENTS OF LOVE and DEATH IN HARLEM (which I think is one of the best poems I ever wrote) plus the Blues Sequence from DON'T YOU WANT TO BE FREE would, it seems to be, make a light and amusing book, all in the same manner and mood, good for both reading and recitation, and of interest to blues and jazz fans as well. Prefacing it all, I might put a short introduction on Blues. And if, added to all that, Knopf wanted to throw in illustrations in the Harlem manner by E. Simms Campbell,[1] let us say, or Covarrubius in his early and so swell style, it would make a marvellous and grand HEY HEY cullud and colorful book. That I think would be lots of fun. And ought to sell, too!

DEATH IN HARLEM, you know, is that long poem in jazz tempo about Arabella Johnson and the Texas Kid that appeared some years ago in an obscure little magazine that promptly went bankrupt after one issue—so practically nobody knows the poem—as it was too long for the regular magazine.[2]

In any case I shall put them all together and send them off to you or

Blanche to see how you-all like them. I am glad you liked SEVEN MOMENTS OF LOVE and I hope somebody will put music to them — but good old blues kind of music. Then if Paul would only sing them!!! . . . Come to think of it, Porter Grainger might be a good fellow to set them to music. So many of the old blues records were his — and I have just recently been playing them over. One of the best cooks in all Carmel is an enormously stout colored lady named Willa Black Whit who has stacks of old blues records under her house — since she broke her victrola some years ago. But now with the loan of one of Noel's, she has gotten them all out — and you can hear Bessie anytime singing in the Carmel Woods.

Now that you mention it, I can see you-all clearly sitting right there at Dorothy Maynor's concert. She was a sweet little girl (and intelligent) if she's still the same as she used to be.

Your cousin is back and as soon as I get off the farm at all I am going to see her. I have never been so snowed under with undone things in my life. But when I write a book I let everything else go. Now I got to get out from under.

Just in your last letter I learn that Zora is married. And in this week's paper I see that she is getting a divorce.[3] What goes on here? Huh? Such expenses as such things involve one in!

I also see by the papers where Nora Holt is opening a swanky beauty shop in Los Angeles.[4] Therein, no doubt, she'll turn colored brunettes by the scores into blonds. Maybe all of 'em.

Thanks so much for keeping me in touch with MULATTO. Otherwise, I might not know. However, from my agent I did learn that all the agitation is largely political — a colored alderman wishes the play to be housed in a theatre where he would get a rack-off as well as a remembrance for getting it by the Mayor. It seems he got fixed up for his influence with the Mayor, but the producers refused to agree to the use of the rival theatre, they having picked out one of their own. So he just got the Mayor to crack down. And from that all the rest followed — with most of those whose jobs depend on the city joining in the opposition to the play. For a minute, from the looks of some of the clippings, I thought they were offering the Negro Philadelphians a combination production of both NIGGER HEAVEN and MULATTO. That, I imagine, would really wow 'em.

A horse show must be truly wonderful! But did you hear the one about the old man whose three sons were triplets and who all got married on the same day to three sisters? Well, that night the old man gave a little wedding supper just for them. And when they were seated at the table, he said, "Children, before I say grace, I have an announcement to make. I am an old man and I know I will not live long enough to enjoy all the money

I have. So I have decided to give the first one of you couples that bears me an heir, <u>Five Millions</u> cold cash! Now let us bow our heads and thank the Lord." The old man bowed his head to say grace and when he lifted it—they were gone.

Would you like to have 100 little very light green with jeweled backs and speckled paws very green little baby frogs gamboling beside a fresh fish fountain? Well, here they are!

Sincerely,
Langston

Holow Hills Farm
Monterey, California
December, 1939

P.S. I loved the thises and thats, but I also want some thems and those!

1. *E. Simms Campbell was an artist, illustrator, and cartoonist whose work appeared regularly in* Esquire *in the 1930s. Campbell, who rarely used black figures in his works, did the illustrations for* Popo and Fifina, *a 1932 children's novel written by Hughes and Bontemps.*
2. *"Death in Harlem" is a long narrative ballad in the style of "Frankie and Johnnie." It was published in* Literary American *in June 1935, having survived rejections by seven major magazines.*
3. *Hurston officially filed for divorce in February 1940, claiming Price had problems with drinking and violence. They reconciled briefly but never lived together for more than two weeks at a time during their relationship. The divorce was finally granted on November 9, 1943.*
4. *The* Tattler *announced on October 4: "Not unlike the glamorous Nora, the salon is streamlined in every detail. . . . Miss Holt promises to bring Hollywood service to West Side business and society matrons." The Nora Holt Beauty Salon was the first black-owned business in the historic Vermont–West Jefferson district of Los Angeles.*

CARL VAN VECHTEN TO LANGSTON HUGHES, DECEMBER 25, 1939

Dear Langston, Your letter and the book came. What do you want me to do with this? I dont think it is a very good idea mixing the Knopfs up with TWO books at the moment. I mean one book is enough at a time for public, author, or publisher, to say nothing of the reviewers. However, I'll follow your instructions as soon as I have them. Maybe The Big Sea is sufficiently far away in the future, so that something else could be done in the meantime. If NOT, I advise patience. I mean if The Big Sea is to be published in 1940, why that is enough for 1940 and no use confusing the issue now. If, however, The Big Sea is going over to the spring of 1941, no harm at all in publishing a book of poems in the fall of 1940. So you let me know, please. The Blues, in fact the whole book, is swell! And a popular idea at the moment. But has Simms Campbell a Harlem manner? Every poem in the book will be set to music: you have great luck that way. TAC gave a won-

derful jam session at Carnegie last night and dug Ida Cox out of obscurity to appear. She has a big voice but she is no Bessie or Clara, not by a long shot. The youngsters, of course, think she is, but she lacks the intensity of temperament and never "laughs to keep from crying" or breaks your heart at all. Sister Tharpe I dote on and there was a Golden Gate Quartet that I doted on, very sophisticated spirituals, but such tone! Benny Goodman and Count Basie performed with their respective players and Sonny Terry (blind) on his Harmonica had the house in an uproar. I always dote on the Boogie Woogie players who must have been astonished to find themselves seated before three very grand Steinways.¹ Here is a thought for today: A lady I know says there are TWO Races and ONLY TWO: Blonde and Brunette! I dont seem to get over laryngitis and may have to go somewhere where it is WARM. Is it warm in California, please? Merry Christmas to Noël and yourself and a thousand baubles of every color to you from
Carlo!

Christmas Day

You will soon receive notification about the James Weldon Johnson Memorial (the idea from beginning to end, is <u>mine</u>, by the way) and I hope you will stir some contributions, even if small ones, out of some of the California friends of the Race, of Jim, and of the Negro Sculptor Barthé. If you do not hear soon about this from the proper sources, Ill write you myself.

1. *The Theatre Arts Committee put on* From Spirituals to Swing, *a musical jamboree at Carnegie Hall on December 24. The blues singer Ida Cox sang, and Sister Rosetta Tharpe "left the house ecstatic" with her "inspired guitar" and vocals, according to the December 25* New York Times. *The Golden Gate Jubilee Male Quartet put on "a real sermon in a hot jazz tempo." The self-taught harmonica player Sonny Terry was the "high spot" of the evening when he "made his little tin toy express a human feeling that reached the hardened hearts of 3,000 New York sophisticates." The Boogie Woogie players — Albert Ammons, Meade Lux Lewis, and Pete Johnson — played piano regularly at Café Society. The blues singer Joe Turner joined them for the December 24 show. The African American poet and literary scholar Sterling A. Brown‡ was the commentator for the evening.*

LANGSTON HUGHES TO CARL VAN VECHTEN, JANUARY 4, 1940

Dear Carlo,

Just a quick note to tell you that <u>it is warm</u> out here. This is, of course, the "rainey" season, but so far pretty day, not much rain at all. And in Los Angeles, from all I hear, it is positively hot. Here today, for instance, I'm working in my shirt sleeves with all the windows open.

About the Blues book, of course I would leave the time of its publication (and that of "The Big Sea") up to those who <u>know</u> about such things—the Knopfs.¹ But while I'm here at Noel's, I'm trying to get as much <u>put</u> down and as many things put together as I can. Once away (and especially on lecture tour) I have so little chance to write, or assemble material. There's no argument between us about the time of publication. Nichevo! . . . But I'm awfully glad you liked the poems. Robin and Una Jeffers seem to be crazy about them and ask to hear them read almost every day!!! . . . Tomorrow Noel, Lee,² and I are off for a visit with the Arthur's at Oceano. . . . The holidays were gay. Rajni Patel (young Indian youth leader) arrived for New Years with greetings from Paul and several London friends. I'm invited to go to India someday. Might.

6 boxes with sliding panels and hidden keys to you.

Langston

+Hope you get quite well soon. How's "John Henry"? Have you seen it?

1. *Knopf would publish a revised version of this manuscript, titled* Shakespeare in Harlem, *in 1942, at Van Vechten's urgings.*
2. *Leander Crowe was a Canadian by birth who spent a great deal of time at Hollow Hills in the company of his close friend Noël Sullivan. His short stories and poems were sometimes published in Carmel newspapers.*

CARL VAN VECHTEN TO LANGSTON HUGHES, JANUARY 9, 1940

(POSTCARD)

Langston Hughes
Hollow Hills Farm
Monterey, Cal.
% Sullivan.

Dear Langston, My cold is leaving me and maybe I dont have to go to a hot place. No I havent seen John Henry yet. It opens tomorrow night and we are going with Essie. Ill let you know. I <u>dote</u> on the poems. In fact (in print) I always like you best when you <u>sing</u> and least when you <u>complain</u>. But I suppose you feel like doing both. Ill send you data on the James Weldon Johnson Memorial soon. You were slated for the SMALL committee¹ but we couldnt use you because you werent here.

orange blossoms and [. . .]² to you,

Carlo

+Love to Esther & Chester!

1. *The James Weldon Johnson Memorial Committee included Theodore Roosevelt (chairman), Walter White (secretary), Gene Buck (treasurer), and the Hon. Fiorello H. La Guardia (honorary chairman).*
2. *Illegible word.*

LANGSTON HUGHES TO CARL VAN VECHTEN, JANUARY 18, 1940

Dear Carlo:

You must be psychic sending me a postcard of Jimmie Daniels just after I'd been talking a lot about him to (can't remember the guy's name) Bronson Cutting's[1] best friend from New Mexico that we met at Chester and Ester's. He was also telling me about Al Thayer[2] who's been having a hard time in Hollywood but has started to come out on top again.

I'm dying to know about John Henry . . . And I'm glad your cold is better . . . And ESQUIRE bought SEVEN MOMENTS OF LOVE dropping a dollar a line in my most empty lap and thus temporarily saving my good name and my life.[3]

Russell Jelliffe has written me about his talk with you regarding the Gilpin Players and their urgent need for a modern workshop to replace the burned out buildings.[4] You know, of course, my feeling regarding the Gilpin Players. I think they can become the Negro Abbey Theatre, and certainly they are the ONLY permanent Negro theatre in America, and the ONLY place I or any other fairly good Negro playwright can be assured of a chance to see try-outs of our plays. And now that the Federal Theatre is gone,[5] we need the Gilpins more than ever. And the enlarged plans that they are hoping to carry through, including as they do the training of Negroes in every branch of the theatre, and the establishment of Fellowships for playwrights, etc., seems to me most important. The Jelliffes themselves have a fine free attitude about the scripts used, ranging from the religious to the radical, comedy to tragedy, and for 16 years they have fought against both the intolerance of many whites and the bigotry and ignorance of many Negroes composing the Cleveland community who wanted in one way or another to limit the scope of the players and their plays—but in spite

JIMMIE DANIELS, PHOTOGRAPH
BY CARL VAN VECHTEN, N.D.

of all, and a bank crash that robbed them of a laboriously built up fund, and in spite of the present fire, they've kept on producing. And I hope that they will now find help to grow and enlarge because I think they've proven their worth and their potential (and actual power) as a force in American theatre.

Noel was greatly interested in hearing about the proposed Weldon Johnson Memorial. I shall speak of it whenever I go on my lecture tour this spring.[6]

Dudley Field Malone was here the other day and Noel invited various Irish in for dinner but they all talked so loud that nobody could hear each other let alone Mr. Malone.[7] The Irish are sometimes like colored, I reckon.

A wood tick buried its head in my arm and I had to go have it cut out.

I wish Rita could see all the new baby goats.

A black caracule kid to you,

Langston

1. *Cutting was a New Mexico senator from 1927 to 1928 and then a United States Senator from 1928 to 1935.*
2. *Al Thayer was a fixture at parties during the Harlem Renaissance. He was a model and an aspiring actor.*
3. Esquire *bought "Seven Moments of Love: An Un-Sonnet Sequence in Blues" for $100, which was the most Hughes ever received for one of his poems. The poem would appear in the May issue.*
4. *The Karamu House, which showcased the work of the Gilpin Players, was destroyed by a fire after the envious author of an editorial in a local black newspaper suggested the place be torched. Van Vechten was one among several wealthy white friends Hughes contacted on behalf of Karamu.*
5. *The House Committee on Un-American Activities launched an investigation in 1938 that led to the abolition of the Federal Theatre Project in 1939.*
6. *On February 10, Hughes began a lecture tour in Pennsylvania that would take him all over the South until the late spring.*
7. *Dudley Field Malone, a New York attorney, was assistant secretary of State under President Wilson.*

CARL VAN VECHTEN TO LANGSTON HUGHES, FEBRUARY 3, 1940

Dear Langston, Im sorry I couldnt do anything for the Gilpin Players, which I am very much in sympathy with, but my givings are budgeted to such a degree that if I overstep the bounds by an inch I am in debt to myself* for months. I hope he found what he wanted in New York . . . John Henry was very dull and even bad.[1] Some of the music was good but it was over-orchestrated and over-sophisticated and hardly anything came right but Handy's Careless Love which sounded like heaven in the middle of everything. Dudley Malone is a honey and I love to hear him talk loud but I havent seen him for ages. . . . Ive photographed Marian

Anderson at last and ELLA FITZGERALD. What a lamb Miss Anderson is! An angel! Herewith is my Opportunity article about the Memorial.[2] They have bitched this considerably by printing a photograph of Augusta Savage's UNFINISHED head of Jim and calling it Barthé's, but even Time and Life make errors and why not Opportunity? Luigi expects you to come in and pose for him in March and Ethel's portrait is at present adorning the Whitney Gallery*° on West Eighth Street. When you come back you'll be photographed in color.

strings of pearls to you!

Feb. 3

*and the grocer!
*°I attended this with Ethel & was that fun! She was surrounded by autograph hunters & admirers.

1. *The play opened on Broadway on January 11, 1940, and closed after only seven performances. Most reviewers praised Robeson's performance.*
2. *"The Proposed James Weldon Johnson Memorial" was published in the February 1940 issue of* Opportunity. *In the article, Van Vechten described the proposed memorial as it had been conceived and sketched by Richmond Barthé. It was a "monument in bronze, not of James Weldon Johnson, but to his Black and Unknown Bards, the creators of the Spirituals," he wrote. On one side of the marble base of the memorial would appear a bas-relief of Johnson's head. On the other side would be carved a stanza from one of Johnson's poems.*

LANGSTON HUGHES TO CARL VAN VECHTEN, APRIL 23, 1940

c/o Arna Bontemps
703 East 50th Place
Chicago, Illinois

April 23, 1940

Dear Carlo,

Just in from the South and find your wire waiting for me here.[1] This is my first breathing space between lectures, so I'll do my best to write the Weldon Johnson appeal article this week. I have to speak in Cleveland next Monday and may come from there to New York as Blanche wants to discuss the book with me, and urges me to come.

FROM LEFT TO RIGHT: LANGSTON HUGHES, ARNA BONTEMPS, AND HAROLD JACKMAN, JUNE 11, 1942

The South Side is a solid sender.[2] I keep looking for Bigger running over the roof tops. See plenty of his brothers in the streets.

I want to make this night air mail, so hastily but

Sincerely,

Langston

+Simply couldn't write anything on tour. Folks don't give you time. Now I got to sleep 3 days to catch up and get my mind composed.

L.H.

1. *Hughes didn't actually end his tour until the middle of May, when he returned to Chicago to seek comfort in the Bontemps's home.*

2. *Richard Wright's novel,* Native Son, *was an immediate success when it was released in 1940. Book-of-the-Month Club had selected the novel as its January offering. Hughes wrote Wright enthusiastically on February 29, 1940: "It is a tremendous performance!" Still, Hughes had reservations about the nihilistic tenor of the book, particularly as it pertained to black lives. On April 28, he spoke about the book to a gathering at the Chicago Public Library and cautioned listeners not to take Bigger Thomas as a representative of all blacks. Knopf decided to link* The Big Sea *to* Native Son *in their ads, "to get some benefit out of all that publicity," Blanche explained to Langston in an April 19, 1940, letter.*

CARL VAN VECHTEN TO LANGSTON HUGHES, JULY 30, 1940

Dear Langston, You were very sweet to send me an early copy of The Big Sea, so marvellously inscribed. You know already how much I like this book, apart from page 321, et seq!, but Ill be writing you more about it from time to time. I read the parts that were printed in Town and Country[1] and Ive been fishing about in the Big Sea itself and I love all your big splashes. Also Im very proud to have Un Chant Noveau and will report on this, later.[2] Why DIDNT you inscribe this one? Maybe you dont mean for me to keep it.

Barthé reports he has a new version done of the Johnson Memorial, but Walter White, whose mother died in Atlanta, is not in town, so nothing can be done about this yet. I havent yet received the blurb on the JWJ Memorial that you promised me in six weeks when you went away. In fact I havent heard from you at all till now. So please sit down and write me the news. How did the Negro fiesta in Chicago go? I think you must know that that sweet gentlewoman, Mrs. Chesnutt, died.[3]

There are two new Negro singers: Louis Burge and Virginia Lewis.

Ethel Waters (Grand!) is at the Paramount this week. Dorothy Peterson has a new car. Where and how are YOU?

>   my affection to you always,
>   Carlo!

July 30

If YOU are not sending The Big Sea to Mrs. Blanchard, I want to, please. So let me know.

I wrote you that the Negro poet you wanted me to photograph never answered my letter.

1. *The July 1940 issue of* Town & Country *printed an excerpt from* The Big Sea *entitled,* "When Harlem Was in Vogue."
2. Langston Hughes: Un Chant Nouveau, *by the Haitian physician and scholar René Piquion, was the first book-length study of Hughes and his work. It was published in Haiti in 1941 and included an introduction by Arna Bontemps.*
3. *Susan Perry had been married to Charles Chesnutt since 1878.*
4. *This is Carl Van Vechten's interpretation of a cat viewed from the rear. He signed off this way from time to time in letters to Hughes and other correspondents. Van Vechten had a lifelong fascination with cats, and published two books devoted to them.* The Tiger in the House *(1920) concerns the role of cats in cultural history.* Lord of the Housetops *is a collection of cat stories Van Vechten edited in 1921. Both were published by Knopf.*

CARL VAN VECHTEN TO LANGSTON HUGHES, NOVEMBER 22, 1940

Dear Langston, Blanche let me see Shakespeare in Harlem. I love the title and most of the book. I have suggested some omissions including ALL of the section labelled Lenox Avenue. Seven Moments of Love is all superb Hughes and the whole book sings that kind of wistful loneliness you have made peculiarly your own. You have been set to music more often than any other Negro poet, save Dunbar and Pushkin and probably James Weldon, who wrote so many songs for Rosamond to set. AND BY THE WAY WHERE IS THAT PAPER ON JAMES WELDON YOU PROMISED ME YEARS AGO?*

Blanche says you suggest Simms Campbell as illustrator.¹ I am only familiar with his work about sleek blondes, but doubtless he has more sepian talents concealed somewhere about him. Could Zell Ingram do this? Or one of the students at Karamu? I met Mrs. Jellife recently.

I wrote to tell you I had completely lost the letter in which you gave me Zell's address but have heard nothing from you since except by way of De Organizer. I have never seen this on the stage but it might be effective there with the music. Reading it I would say it stopped too soon, before the Organizer became the boss and turned the sharecroppers into a racket, before the Government became the Boss and exploited 'em unmercifully. At least, now, through some talent or other (Joe Louis) or through a kind boss there is some small chance of escape. In the instances I name there could be none. I'll reserve the matter of Great White Fog[2] until I see you, but I might add that I could write a more bitter play about the Negro (with more poignant reasons for his despair) between now and breakfast time. If I did doubtless Id be jumped on by every body of every race east of the mississippi. I <u>won't</u>!

Have you seen Mrs Blanchard yet?

I was shocked and amused to read of your run-in with Mrs McPherson, an old friend of mine.[3] I gave a dinner for her once!

Last week I had a swell party with many from Harlem down to see Harlem in Color.[4] Jimmie Daniels is giving a housewarming Sunday. December 8 the Negro Theatre Guild is eating a lot to honor Bill Robinson.[5] Ethel's show is a smash and Gosh, how good it is![6]

Give my love to Noël and keep some for yourself!

November 22

Carlo

Photographed Ethel as Petunia in CITS, but they are <u>not</u> ready!

*Did you see the statue Chez Barthé? You've never told me.

1. *Blanche vetoed both E. Simms Campbell and Zell Ingram as possible illustrators for* Shakespeare in Harlem.
2. Big White Fog *was a 1938 play by the black playwright Theodore Ward.*
3. *Hughes was in the middle of a promotional luncheon for* The Big Sea *at the upscale Vista de Arroyo Hotel in Los Angeles when the evangelist Aimee Semple McPherson and her entourage appeared to picket him. She was enraged by Hughes's "Goodbye Christ," which referred to her "in a manner most uncomplimentary," reported the* Los Angeles Examiner *on November 16. McPherson handed out leaflets of the poem and accused Hughes of having communist affiliations. Hughes was embarrassed when the hotel's manager canceled his talk.*
4. *In 1939 Van Vechten began making Kodachrome slides of a variety of subjects, and "Harlem in Color" was probably a slide show of his latest efforts. Van Vechten's friend and biographer, Bruce Kellner, described these shows in a letter to me: "Remember what a NOVELTY color photography was at the time! He set up little matching chairs in small rows, usually in the foyer because it was big but sometimes for a few people only in his studio. By the 1950s, these events could be rather uncomfortable because if you didn't Ooh and Aah enough over each one as if it was some masterpiece out of the Uffizi, he'd get miffed and call a sudden halt. On the other hand, they could go on at deadly length sometimes and the only way to curb his enthusiasm was to deliberately stop oohing and aahing."*

5. *At the dinner, sponsored by the Negro Actors Guild, an ex-mayor of New York City called Bill Robinson "an American gentleman." Other attendees included Ethel Waters, Noble Sissle, Katherine Dunham, Olivia Wyndham, and Walter White.*

6. *Ethel Waters starred in the 1940 Broadway play* Cabin in the Sky *as Petunia Jackson. Directed by George Balanchine and Albert Lewis,* Cabin in the Sky *(CITS) opened on October 25.*

LANGSTON HUGHES TO CARL VAN VECHTEN, DECEMBER 6, 1940

AMERICA'S YOUNG BLACK JOE
WORDS AND MUSIC BY
LANGSTON HUGHES
&
ELLIOTT CARPENTER

One tenth of the population
Of this mighty nation
Was sun-tanned by nature long ago.
We're Americans by birth and training
So our country will be gaining
When every citizen learns to know:

I'm America's Young Black Joe!
Manly, good natured, smiling and gay,
My sky is sometimes cloudy
But it won't stay that way.
I'm comin', I'm comin' —
But my head AIN'T bending low!
I'm walking proud! I'm speaking out loud!
I'm America's Young Black Joe!
This is my own, my native land,
And I'm mighty glad that's true:
Land where my fathers worked
The same as yours worked, too.
So from every mountain side
Let freedom's bright torch glow —
Standing hand in hand with democracy,
I'm America's Young Black Joe!

Dear Carlo, This is one of the songs I've done for the new revue.[1] Do you like it? It ends up with a series of bugle calls in the music!!! . . . And here are some further clippings about Aimee from the local cullud paper.²

Sincerely,

Langston

1. *"Young Black Joe" was the climactic song in a skit about Joe Louis that was staged at an NAACP event. Hughes wrote the song with the composer Elliot Carpenter.*
2. *The November 21 black-interest newspaper* California Eagle *chortled,* AIMEE MUZZLES POET HUGHES. *Other black papers followed the story. The November 30* Pittsburgh Courier *announced:* AIMEE MCPHERSON IS SAID TO HAVE STAGED "DEVILKRIEG" AGAINST HUGHES. *The November 30* Toledo Voice *ran the headline:* EVANGELIST INCITES RIOT AGAINST LANGSTON HUGHES.

CARL VAN VECHTEN TO LANGSTON HUGHES, DECEMBER 20, 1940

(POSTCARD)

Dec. 20, 1940

Langston Hughes
Hollow Hills Farm
Monterey
California

Dear Langston, I LOVED America's Young Black Joe. Here is Ethel as Petunia in Cabin in the Sky right back at you in return. You would have doted on the Bill Robinson dinner. Dont let Aimée get you down. Did you see your name in the list of eligible bachelors in the Amsterdam News?¹ I wrote you Id lost your letter with Zell Ingram's address, but you've never supplied it and are we to give up hope that you will write a blurb for the JWJ Memorial? Four pounds of tiger teeth to you! C

ETHEL WATERS AS PETUNIA IN
CABIN IN THE SKY. PHOTOGRAPH
BY CARL VAN VECHTEN

1. *In his* Amsterdam News *column, "All Ears," Bill Chase wrote on December 14: "With dear old 1940 having just 17 days to go, we thought it wouldn't be a bad idea (tho not entirely new) to list for the last time New York's eligible (and perhaps . . . desirable) bachelors." Langston Hughes was "likable, conscientious but somehow enveloped in a thin cloud of mystery." Richmond Barthé, James Allen, Romare Bearden, and Count Basie also made the list.*

1941–1944

A imee Semple McPherson's campaign against Hughes and the poem "Goodbye Christ" gathered strength when the Saturday Evening Post reprinted her handbill alongside Hughes's poem in their December 21 issue. Like McPherson, the Saturday Evening Post was smarting from having been named in the poem. Hughes suggested to Blanche Knopf that they consider suing the Post for reprinting the poem without permission, but she thought such a move would be unwise.

Hughes's distress over the negative press brought on by McPherson's campaign led him to draft a statement, "Concerning 'Goodbye Christ,'" on January 1, 1941, which he sent to every person and institution whose opinion he valued, including the Knopfs, the Rosenwald Fund, and the Associated Negro Press. It reads as follows:

Almost ten years ago now, I wrote a poem in the form of a dramatic monologue entitled GOODBYE CHRIST with the intention in mind of shocking into being in religious people a consciousness of the admitted shortcomings of the church in regard to the conditions of the poor and oppressed of the world, particularly the Negro people.

Just previous to the writing of the poem, in 1931 I had made a tour through the heart of our American Southland. For the first time I saw *peonage, million dollar high schools for white children and shacks for Negro children (both of whose parents work and pay taxes and are Americans). I saw vast areas in which Negro citizens were not permitted to vote. I saw the Scottsboro boys in prison in Alabama and colored citizens of the state afraid to utter a word in their defense. I crossed rivers by ferry where the Negro drivers of cars had to wait until the white cars behind them had been accomodated before boarding the ferry even if it meant missing the boat. I motored as far North as Seattle and back across America to New York through towns and cities where neither bed nor board was to be had if you were colored, cafes, hotels, and tourist camps being closed to all non-whites. I saw the horrors of hunger and unemployment among my people in the segregated ghettos of our great cities. I saw lecture halls and public cultural institutions closed to them. I saw Hollywood caricatures of what pass for Negroes on the screens that condition the attitudes of a nation. I visited state and religious colleges to which no Negroes were admitted. To me these things appeared unbelievable in a Christian country. Had not Christ said, "Such as ye do unto the least of these, ye do it unto Me."? But almost nobody seemed to care. Sincere Christians seeking to combat this condition were greatly in the minority.*

Directly from this extensive tour of America, I went to the Soviet Union. There it seemed to me that Marxism had put into practical being many of the precepts which our own Christian America had not yet been able to bring to life for, in the Soviet Union, meagre as the resources of the country were, white and black, Asiatic and European, Jew and Gentile stood alike as citizens on an equal footing protected from racial inequalities by the law. There were no pogroms, no lynchings, no Jim Crow cars as there had once been in Tzarist Asia, nor were the newspapers or movies permitted to ridicule or malign any people because of race. I was deeply impressed by these things.

It was then that I wrote GOODBYE CHRIST. In the poem I contrasted what seemed to me the declared and forthright position of those who, on the religious side in America (in apparent actions toward my people) had said to Christ and the Christian principles, "Goodbye, beat it on away from here now, you're done for." I gave to such religionists what seemed to me to be their own words merged with the words of the orthodox Marxist who declared he had no further use nor need for religion.

I couched the poem in the language of the first person. I, as many poets have done in the past in writing of various characters other than themselves. The I *which I pictured was the newly liberated peasant of the state collectives I had seen in Russia merged with those American Negro workers of the depression period who believed in racial and economic difficulties. (Just as the* I *pictured in many of my blues poems is the poor and uneducated Negro of the South—and not myself who grew up in Kansas). At the time that GOODBYE CHRIST first appeared, many persons seemed to think I was the characterized* I *of the poem. Then, as now, they failed to see the poem in connection with my other work, including many verses most sympathetic to the true Christian spirit for which I have always had great respect—such as that section of poems,* Feet of Jesus, *in my book, THE DREAM KEEPER, or the chapters on religion in my novel, NOT WITHOUT LAUGHTER which received the Harmon Gold Award from the Federated Council of Churches. They failed to consider GOODBYE CHRIST in the light of various of my other poems in the ironic or satirical vein, such as RED SILK STOCKINGS—which some of my critics once took to be literal advice.*

Today, accompanied by a sound truck playing GOD BLESS AMERICA and bearing pickets from the Aimee Semple McPherson Temple of the Four Square Gospel in Los Angeles, my poem of ten years ago is resurrected without my permission and distributed on handbills before a Pasadena Hotel where I was to speak on Negro folk songs. Some weeks later it was reprinted in THE SATURDAY EVENING POST, a magazine whose columns, like the doors of many of our churches, has been until recently entirely closed to Negroes, and whose chief contribution in the past to a better understanding of Negro life in America has been the Octavious Roy Cohen stories with which most colored people have been utterly disgusted.

Now, in the year 1941, having left the terrain of "the radical at twenty" to approach the "conservative of forty," I would not and could not write GOODBYE CHRIST, desiring no longer to épater le bourgeois. *However, since those at present engaged in distributing my poem do not date it, nor say how long ago it was written, I feel impelled for the benefit of persons reading the poem for the first time, to make the following statement:*

GOODBYE CHRIST does not represent my personal viewpoint. It was long ago withdrawn from circulation and has been reprinted recently without my knowledge or consent. I would not now use such a technique of approach since I feel that a mere poem is quite unable to compete in power to shock with the current horrors of war and oppression abroad in the greater part of the world. I have never been a member of the Communist Party. Furthermore, I have come to believe that no system of ethics, religion, morals, or government is of permanent value which does not first start with and change the human heart. Mortal frailty, greed, and error know no boundary lines. The explosives of war do not care whose hands fashion them. Certainly, both Marxists and Christians can be cruel. Would that Christ came back to save us all. We do not know how to save ourselves.

LANGSTON HUGHES TO CARL VAN VECHTEN, JANUARY 3, 1941

Dear Carlo,
    The flu has got me down, not Aimee. . . . Rain, rain, rain, out here. . . . I saw Mrs. Blanchard at a distance a few days before Christmas on the street evidently doing her shopping. She looked well as I passed in a car. . . . Lots of people liked your lovely card. . . . Will write soon.
                        Sincerely,
                        Langston

CARL VAN VECHTEN TO LANGSTON HUGHES, JANUARY 12, 1941

    Dear Langston, Perhaps you shouldn't have apologized for your Goodbye Christ. Perhaps it was okay! Anyway, your apology reads very well. Ive written the Rosenwald Fund glowingly about you, but I cant get a word out of you about the JWJ piece. You dont even say you WONT do it.
                    hands across the states to you!
                        Carlo

                                            Jan 12

Community Hospital
Carmel, Jan. 26, 1941
Dear Carlo,

I am much better and the doctor says I'll get up tomorrow.[1] The sciatica-arthritis-like pain is almost gone. I was groggy with pills last time I wrote you so I don't know what I said. I have seen plenty visions lying here, but opened my eyes, they weren't there. Almost the only time in my life I've lost my appetite. I eat so slow now the waiters are amazed . . . I'm hoping to be out this coming week, doctor says. The bills here are like the Ritz. But everybody is so kind and good. I have made up in my mind wonderful things to write while I convalesce — starting with Jim Johnson.

Saroyan is in town today. I like him, but can't see him now. Only a few people a day, mostly from the farm. . . . Joseph Auslander says they have Grace Nail Johnson helping them on the Library of Congress Collection.[2] He is delighted. . . . I sent you a paper about Robin's birthday. Noël's dinner was delightful. Just before I took to my bed. . . . Lying here I think often of you and Fania and you brighten my day. There is nothing like illness to make you remember what good times were like. . . . I will write more when I am better. Lots of good news about "Am. Young Black Joe" catching on all over South, kids singing it. Hail, Hey!

Affectionately,
Langston

Wish I could see you.

1. *On January 14, Hughes was diagnosed with an advanced case of gonorrhea at the Peninsula Community Hospital in Monterey. He had been infected during the first week of December, while he was in Los Angeles.*
2. *The Library of Congress had approached Grace Nail Johnson for her husband's papers to serve as the anchor of a poetry room in James Weldon Johnson's name.*

February 1, 1941
(My Birthday!)

Dear Carlo,

Looks like ill-fate dogs even an explanation about the James Weldon Johnson article (which is truly coming soon now, soon as I get on my feet.) My first letter to you from the hospital, just after I got here, has just been returned today. Fell down in an airplane and your address on the envelope and the whole middle got eaten out. Strange! Anyhow, here it is. The middle part I guess was where I told you how I came to be here: flu—worry about Hollywood shows, Aimee, N.Y. eviction (tenants behind on rent my apt.), coming lectures, broke, doctor's bill—relapse—laid flat with post-flu acute arthritis. Wow!!! Dopey with pain pills for two weeks. But much better now-third week here. And going home—back to the farm today. My birthday. Soon as Noël comes from mass.

Dear Mrs. Blanchard called. She is so good and kind. She said she'd just had a note from you recently. Expressed regret at not being able to write you as often as she would like, but says she is well, and loves you in her heart.

(That after all is the main thing, isn't it? Even when people fail otherwise.)

Wrote Dorothy about same time I did you. Hope her letter didn't go down by plane also. None other has come back yet. . . . Had a nice note from Harold Jackman today. . . . I'll be at the farm all spring. Why don't you come out here for a week? You'd like this Carmel Valley in the spring. . . . My love to Fania.

I'm sending this by train.

Best to you,
Langston

P.S. Did you see (or have I mentioned this) the swell send-off Schuyler gave you and "Nigger Heaven" in The Pittsburg Courier of a couple of weeks ago?[1]

How come you are not in New York Post Office directory? The letter came back here.

1. *In the January 18, 1941, issue of the* Pittsburgh Courier, *George Schuyler wrote about Van Vechten in his column, "Views and Reviews": "Of the novels about Harlem life, Carl Van Vechten's 'Nigger Heaven' is still tops, and I am familiar with all the others."*

CARL VAN VECHTEN TO LANGSTON HUGHES, FEBRUARY 3, 1941
(POSTCARD)

Dear Langston, Your letter and the enclosure from St. Louis just arrived. You HAVE been having a time. I hope things are better NOW. The Committee has practically (a few more have to see it) approved of

Barthé's new Memorial. I'll ask him to send you a photograph as soon as it is settled. I asked Mrs. B to send you some flowers for us. Did she? And did you get the telegram that went to you on your birthday. I havent seen Schuyler's piece about me and BURN to. Have you got it and can you loan it to me or do you have the exact date?

love Carlo

LANGSTON HUGHES TO CARL VAN VECHTEN, FEBRUARY 5, 1941

Feb. 5, 1941

Dear Carlo,

Home and much better!¹ Yours and Fania's lovely wire on my birthday helped me no end. And the most beautiful flowering plant from you two I've ever seen waiting for me when I got home—a kind of glowing little tree growing out of white pebbles in a white pot. It's very charming in this all blue room and makes me no end happy. Tell Fania I adore it—and loved your card "Pour la vie."

Did you see what George Jean Nathan said about the Negro theatre in the February "Esquire"?² Very amusing, and fairly true—except that he missed one point or under stressed it. The avenues for escape from Negro poverty are so much fewer than for poor whites. Current case in point—the defense contracts. Urban League surveys show for instance: plant with government contract of hundreds of thousands of dollars hires thousands extra men in Kansas City—all white except for <u>two</u> Negro jan-itors. Reason: not accustomed to Negro workers in other capacities. That's the twist to <u>our</u> drama. But he sure is right about the lights not working—if the producers are amateur cullud! (I recall <u>Don't You Want to Be Free</u>. Only 3 spots and no two ever worked at once!!!!)

Just had a swell letter from Prentiss. . . . By the way, "The Big Sea" has discovered for me one of my white relatives from Virginia—a lady, wife of former head of Eng. Dept. of University of Chicago. She had bor-

"POUR LA VIE" CARD, FROM THE
VAN VECHTENS TO HUGHES

rowed the book from her maid. Was startled to see therein the name of Quarrles, of Louisa County, one of her own grandparents—and mine! . . . (Forgive pencil. Am in bed and ink ran out). . . . Noel had a little birthday party for me. Much excitement of late. Never a dull moment at the Farm. Many guests, dog-fights, car overturned, lambs born, secretary dissappeared, returns, new butler from New York (145th & St. Nicholas), Roland Hayes passed by, a snake captured at the gate, spring, plowing, coyotes howling, mimosa in bloom. . . . I began my new book last night— off to a good start. But being still mostly in bed, can't type as yet. . . . A mountain of mail about Aimee awaited me. Letters from Bishops and sinners, left, right, colored, white, pro and con. Radio offers even on church programs!

Affectionately, Langston

Did you get your airmail letter out of the wreck I sent on?

1. *Hughes was released from the Peninsula Community Hospital on February 1, after a three-week stay. He would recuperate in the main house at Noël Sullivan's estate, Hollow Hills Farm, until he was well enough to return to "Ennesfree," the private cottage loaned to him by Sullivan.*
2. *In "First Nights & Passing Judgments," the critic George Jean Nathan began a discussion about Negro theatre with a couple of points: "Two things are more or less inevitable in the Negro drama. First, the drama is pretty certain to deal with the awful time a Negro has in this white man's world. And second, the scene, if laid indoors, is pretty sure to show a room papered in violent cerise (Also, if the play is presented by Negroes, the lights don't work)." All of these things were true of* Big White Fog, *he wrote. Hughes took issue with his argument about black employment opportunities: "With more than eight million white men unable to get jobs and many of them homeless and starving in this country, the Negro wail of arbitrarily imposed poverty loses much of its timbre," Nathan wrote. He cited Hughes among many Negroes whose success contradicted myths about the hopelessness of Negro life. "So why all this yowling?" he asked in his conclusion.*

CARL VAN VECHTEN TO LANGSTON HUGHES, FEBRUARY 10, 1941

Dear Langston, We are delighted you are improving so rapidly and that you have gone back to Noël's. Your illness has been a bit of luck for me in that you have sent me quite a pile of swell letters. Your letters are always very full of your personality and are always very welcome. By the way, I see Shakespeare in Harlem is in the new Knopf catalogue, announced for April! I can't wait!

I missed Cousin Lolly comes North,' to' I had that number of the New Yorker for the Clare Boothe profile. So I sent out for another copy and it really is terrific. I havent had as much of the real old south blown in my face for days.

Blanche is just back from Texas and reports she saw Henry Miller in New Orleans; so I guess he'll be with you some day. You give me the address of William Artis and Zell Ingram but in the same letter you say they are evicted. Anyway the Baroness is in Beverly Hills.

Some of us went to see Barthé's new conception of the Memorial last Saturday and were crazy about it, BUT we cannot pass on it till the whole committee and Grace Johnson report.

Harold Jackman found the Courier for me, so dont bother. I was immensely pleased with what Schuyler said because he is a critic I respect very much, as much as any, in fact. I also agree heartily with what he has to say about Native Son.[2]

I had a very nice letter from Noël telling me you were sick. He also said he might get to New York soon. If he does surely tell him to look me up and get photographed, PLEASE.

Those "pour" la vie cards were made for us one night by a man with a pen in a café in Harlem Montmartre,* the name of which escapes me but you would know it. Im sorry I didnt know Noël needed a butler. Joseph Spell, just freed of a charge of rape, is in need of a job.[3] He is basking in publicity in the Amsterdam News office and has a tremendous fan mail! He certainly woulda pepped things up out your way.

Yes, I got the torn-up airmail letter. Did I tell you I got my african model a job with Katherine Dunham?[4]

       love,
       Carlo

                        February 10, 1941

*une fontaine!

1. *Written by Marion Sturges-Jones, the short story "Cousin Lolly Comes North," was pub-lished in the January 11, 1941,* New Yorker.
2. *In his January 18 column Schuyler also wrote about* Native Son: *"There is excellent writ-ing in 'Native Son,' but there is also a lot of aimless indignation, Communistic meandering and pointless psychologising. It fails to ring true because the characters are so many Char-lie McCarthy's. 'Native Son' is either a psychological study or a plea for a squarer deal for the young Negro caught in the web of Uncle Spider. As the former it has no racial signifi-cance. As the latter it defeats its purpose by turning the reader against young Negro Amer-ica as acted by 'Bigger Thomas.' "*
3. *On February 7, the butler Joseph Spell was acquitted of the charge of raping his former employer, Eleanor Strubing. That Spell was black and Strubing white made this a signifi-cant case for black New Yorkers. As a Harlem resident, May Chinn, told the* Amsterdam News: *"To my mind the verdict is a proof that there is still some justice left in the world."*
4. *Allen Meadows was the "african model." Van Vechten called him "Juante."*

LANGSTON HUGHES TO CARL VAN VECHTEN, APRIL 5, 1941

Dear Carlo,

Enclosed is my article about James Weldon.[1] I do hope that even at this late date it will be of some use. Please feel free to revise or correct it as need may dictate. Or if there is something more you might wish me to do to it or about it, please let me know. . . . If it would be of any aid to the Committee, I would be happy to make an appearance or two for them in a reading of my poems and an appeal for funds at any time or place they might arrange—without charge on my own part—other than transportation involved. . . . Any blanks or other material the Committee might wish distributed in these parts, I'd be delighted to give out to persons I know here.

Noel had 14 to luncheon today in honor of Mann.[2] He and his wife, youngest son and the daughter whose husband was lost at sea were here and we found the two charming. Mr. Mann is building a house in Brentwood hear Los Angeles and, since his son lives at Carmel, expects to be hereabouts often.

Moe Gale is trying to get me to do a series of radio sketches based on LITTLE HAM.[3] I reckon I should try, but the air never intrigued me much. And the hours I have wasted writing for the theatre and getting nowhere have caused me to more than ever prefer LITERATURE between book covers.

Wish I could see NATIVE SON[4] and PAL JOEY.[5] If I just had a plane and a pilot! How I would get about.

Two pale emerald frogs with onyx eyes and a pearly snail to you,

Sincerely,

Langston

Hollow Hills Farm

Monterey, California

April 5, 1941

---

1. *Hughes finally produced a blurb about the statue that Van Vechten could use for publicity purposes.*
2. *Noël Sullivan was friendly with the German expatriate writer Thomas Mann.*
3. *Moses Gale was the son of Sigmund Gale, the mastermind behind Harlem's Savoy Ballroom. Hughes's outline for a radio series he called* Hamlet Jones *made Gale "rhapsodic," Maxim Lieber, Hughes's agent, reported. Two sample scripts requested by NBC earned Hughes the most lucrative contract he'd ever had: $75 per week escalating to as much as $400 per week if Gale found a major sponsor for the series.*
4. *Orson Welles directed the Broadway version of Richard Wright's novel; it was cowritten by Wright and Paul Green. The show opened on Broadway on March 24, 1941, to very strong reviews. Canada Lee starred as Bigger Thomas.*
5. *A two-act musical based on John O'Hara's novel of the same title. It opened at the Ethel Barrymore Theatre on December 25, 1940.*

Dear Langston, I am enchanted with the piece about JWJ and you are an angel to do it so well and it isnt late at all, but just on time. Im glad it didn't come before as it might have got used up. Walter White is busy in Detroit with the strikers.[1] Arthur Spingarn has had a bad case of blood poisoning and sees nobody. Theodore Roosevelt and Gene Buck havent yet seen Barthé's figure to pass on it and I wont let it go through till everybody passes on it. Then it goes to the Mayor and the Art Commission and if they will give us the location we'll begin working intensively again and your article will be the first thing we'll use. Its sweet of you and like you to offer to lecture for the cause too and probably we'll ask you to later. Too, I have in mind the exhibition of the model in some public place with a girl standing beside to catch pennies, dollars, and nickels. I cant think of anything more exciting than doing a Harlem book with you.[2] I think a wonderful way to do it would be for you to look at a pile of photographs and write whatever came into your mind about each of them, about a page to a photograph. But we'll talk about that later. Did I tell you I am getting rid of my collections to Museums and Libraries as fast as possible? All my own manuscripts and books to the manuscript room of the NY Public Library. I am thinking of giving my Negro collection, including records, letters (including yours, not to be opened until we die) books, photographs etc to Yale, principally because they have nothing along this line. The collection would do much more good there than in a Negro University where much of it would indeed be meaningless. Tell Noël his pictures will probably be done next week.[3] I am WAY WAY behind. Meanwhile here is a sample for YOU. I love it and hope you and Noël will too. Ill write you all about Native Son later. I photographed Canada Lee the other night, but these wont be printed for months. As for Pal Joey Id love to do it with a Negro cast headed by Bobby Evans and Ethel Waters. Did you hear the Defense Broadcast the other night? Did you hear about the tea of the Negro Actors' Guild when Bill R danced with his wife? I think Henry Miller is on his way to you, but gosh, you are having enough celebrities. I dote on the Manns. . . . Love to you, and Ill write again soon when I get time.

Carlo!

Wednesday

1. *Walter White, secretary of the James Weldon Johnson Memorial Committee, was involved with the strike against Ford Motors' River Rouge plant. He was instrumental in forcing the United Auto Workers to endorse equal pay for black and white workers.*
2. *Van Vechten and Hughes had discussed collaborating on a book that would combine Van Vechten's photographs and Hughes's prose. Unfortunately, this book, which Hughes*

dreamed would be "gay, funny, sad, glamourous, and high-hat all at the same time," never came to pass.
3. *Van Vechten photographed Noël Sullivan in 1941.*

CARL VAN VECHTEN TO LANGSTON HUGHES, JUNE 8, 1941

Dear Langston, The Need for Heroes¹ is terrific and somebody should have said it loud years ago and I guess you had the idea when you started to write ballads for Harlemites to sing and W C Handy had it too, but nothing much has come of it yet. As Somerset Maugham recently told me, "It is very hard to get a story out of a good woman or a happy marriage." Listen Langston, Ethel Waters is a hero. She's a Cinderella in real life. She used to scrub floors and look what she's doing now. And today in the papers you can read she was elected to the Actor's Equity Council and with a great big vote, more votes than those with which Lillian Gish was elected. For the first time a Negro has been elected to the Council of this big Union and there was no publicity, nothing even in the Negro papers, and nobody electioneering for her. She was just put on the ballot and voted in!* Congratulations too on your 20 anniversary as a poet. We loved your card announcing this,² but I wrote you about that. The current Crisis seems pretty much devoted to YOU.³

I must tell you what I am doing. I am giving all my Negro collection: books, manuscripts, letters, music, phonograph records of Bessie Smith etc to Yale University (principally because they have one of the best kept libraries Ive ever been in and will accept ALL my conditions). I have named the gift: "The James Weldon Johnson Collection of Negro Arts and Letters, founded by Carl Van Vechten."° They are going to give a big Negro show when they have the collection in hand and I hope you will be here to go to New Haven for this . . .

As for Barthé's statue, we are at last down to the Art Commission of the city of New York and until they have seen this and passed on it we can do nothing more. This is more or less Walter White's job. When that is settled your paper will come in most handy. I had hoped it would be settled weeks and months ago. BUT . . .

I Love The Need for Heroes . . . and I salute you!

When are you coming East?

> Fania and I send our love to you,
> Carlo

June 8, 1941

*Nobody complained or said BOO or Jim Crow or whatever either!
°The name is to <u>encourage</u> others to add to the Collection.

1. *Hughes's essay "The Need for Heroes" was published in the July 1940 issue of* The Crisis. *It begins: "If the best of our writers continue to pour their talent into the tragedies of frustration and weakness, tomorrow will probably say, on the basis of available literary evidence, 'No wonder the Negroes never amounted to anything. There were no heroes among them.' " The situation was urgent: "We have a need for heroes. We have a need for books and plays that will encourage and inspire our youth, set for them examples and patterns of conduct, move and stir them to be forthright, strong, clear-thinking, and unafraid."*

2. *Hughes personally sent out two hundred fifty postcards with a reprint of "The Negro Speaks of Rivers" accompanied by the announcement: "MY FIRST PUBLISHED POEM" to commemorate his twenty years of writing and publishing.*

3. *The* Crisis *celebrated its resident genius in its June issue with a full-page notice about Hughes's "Twentieth Anniversary."*

LANGSTON HUGHES TO CARL VAN VECHTEN, OCTOBER 8, 1941

Hollow Hills Farm
Monterey, California

October 8, 1941

Dear Carlo,

I had meant to write you long ere this but the vicissitudes of life and travel have been such. I'm just back from a month in Los Angeles consulting movie folks about stories for Paul to no final end, either artistically or financially—except that I spent my own good time and money. (Witness Verse 1 & 2 of enclosed blues.) Also the Dramatists Guild finally succeeded in collecting a check for me from the Ellington show, so when they wrote me to that effect, I immediately went and bought a suit. But by the time the check reached me, the show had closed their account and it was no good. As usual, I am now swearing off the entertainment field FOREVER.

Barthé arrived this morning about seven and was sitting out by the pool when I woke up. He brings lots of news of New York and were glad to see him. Also before breakfast, Sonny, a year old pure bred dachshund cohabited with Jitters, a ten year old Scotty, by accident when nobody was around or thought such a thing would happen. And the morning mail brings word of the near arrival of Katharine Dunham, husband, secretary, and various dancers who are to stay here at the farm, recital in Carmel Friday. In the night I completed enclosed blues and my fifth short story of the month.

Thanks for that swell picture of Joe Louis. . . . Dorothy sent me some wonderful books of Puerto Rican poetry today. . . . And the Pan-American Union sent a nice clipping about me and translations of my poems from a Rio paper, all in Brazilian. . . . And Senorita Petit,[1] a Chilean writer was just here, who has written a play showing that Communism is just like Fascism. . . . And Noel has just decided after luncheon to take the Scotty to the vets to have a douche—as he already has twelve dogs on the place. . . . Did you see Nora's picture in last week's AMSTERDAM looking younger than ever?[2] Also did you see the marvellous article in Dan Burley's column (September 13) about Ethel moving her furniture out while Eddie was playing in Joe's golf tournament in Detroit?[3] The rumor in Los Angeles was that he was flying out to cut Archie's head.[4] But he hadn't arrived up to last week. . . . You know I will be DELIGHTED to sign all those things for you as soon as I get home—which is imminent. And am also dying to get on our Harlem book with you. . . . I adore your pictures and think the world ought to have a chance to see them, too, before it goes entirely to rack and ruin. . . . How awful it would be if Communism, Fascism, and Democracy all became one and the same! The Chilean lady seemed most pessimistic about the entire human race. And the management of the Dunham concert here just called up in the midst of this letter to say she was having an awful time housing the other 18 or so of the group, so Noel has offered to take three more in one of his outer houses. But at least under Democracy—even if they can't sleep in Carmel, they can still dance—and under Hitler they couldn't even do that. So I am all-out for ousting him and all his works—even though some of his works have beat him here—so we have to do a little ousting at home, too.

Mrs. Blanchard is back, Noel tells me, and looks splendidly well.

Rosamond Johnson, Clarence Muse, and I worked on the outline of what ought to make an amusing musical while I was in L.A. But all the money the theatre owes me now, I don't know why I should start on anything else.

I did four librettos for Katherine Dunham, though, while I was down there—one to be danced to the ST. LOUIS BLUES. . . . Also did a song called SUGAR HILL with the Brown Sisters of which this enclosed poem is a spoken interlude.

Man, I thought I told you about Lil Green months ago! KNOCKING MYSELF OUT is my favorite of hers.

ME AND MY CHAUFFEUR by Memphis Minnie isn't bad, either.[5]

I know William Attaway but haven't had a chance to read his books. He is Ruth's brother, the girl who played the maid in the New York company of YOU CAN'T TAKE IT WITH YOU, you know.

Zora is living in Los Angeles proper now and is said to be finishing a novel, and planning to do an opera with William Grant Still, and not meeting anybody until her work is done—although everybody seemed to have already met her.

Still had finished a specially commissioned song, PLAIN CHANT FOR AMERICANS, for the Centennial of the Philharmonic, and hopes to come East for its playing.

Thanks for the Yale Bookplate. I am saving all my manuscripts to bring for the collection when I come.

I hope to get a couple of lectures to pay my way across in November.

I wish I knew about SHAKESPEARE IN HARLEM. I have a number of poems now I could add to it.

Arna's children's anthology, GOLDEN SLIPPERS, is due out.[6] Also the big Sterling Brown CARAVAN OF NEGRO LITERATURE.[7]

I met some wonderful cotton pickers in Arizona and heard some good blues. . . . Did I ever send you this one:

When I take you back the streets will be paved with gold.
Baby, when I take you back, streets will be paved with gold.
You'll do no mo' messin' around 'cause you'll be too goddamned old.

Also I heard a pistol fired off in a crowded bar just for fun—and the poor guy was put in jail! But just look at Europe!

Ten Scotch Dachshunds to you,
Sincerely,
Langston

1. *Magdalena Petit was the author of* La Quintrala, *a novel about seventeenth-century Chile, published in 1942.*

2. *The October 4 issue of the* Amsterdam News *carried a photo of Nora Holt and Ada "Bricktop" Smith, "two of the most famous Negro hostesses of history."*

3. *"Dan Burley's Back Door Stuff" in the* Amsterdam News *reported that Eddie Mallory was "knocked out with surprise at seeing his clothes hanging up in an empty apartment" when he returned to the 114th street apartment he shared with Waters after the Joe Louis golf tournament in Detroit.*

4. *Archie Savage was "the bounding dance ace of the Kay Dunham mob," according to Dan Burley, referring to the Katherine Dunham Dance Company. If a romantic triangle existed between Waters, Savage, and Mallory, it doesn't come up in Waters's 1950 autobiography* His Eye Is on the Sparrow.

5. *Born Lizzie Douglas, Memphis Minnie was one of the most influential female blues artists of her day.*

6. *Arna Bontemps's* Golden Slippers: An Anthology of Negro Poetry for Young Readers *was published by Harper & Row in 1941.*

7. *The* Negro Caravan: Writings by American Negroes *was edited by Sterling Brown, Arthur Davis, and Ulysses Lee. It was published in 1941 by the Dryden Press.*

CARL VAN VECHTEN TO LANGSTON HUGHES, OCTOBER 27, 1941

Langston, my lad, But Yale will be Crazy for the manuscripts and when they get them you will receive a special receipt from them. I think also later I can get you a short job in connection with the collection. At any rate you are the one I'll recommend! It will amuse you too! The reason I am temporarily withholding the manuscripts is this: I have other manuscripts of yours and I am having a handsome box with a leather label made by my binder to include all these. When that arrives the whole will be presented to the JWJ collection at Yale. DON'T LET THIS KEEP YOU FROM SENDING OTHER MANUSCRIPTS IN THE FUTURE. WE CAN FIND ROOM FOR AND WOULD LOVE HAVING ALL THE MANUSCRIPTS YOU CAN GIVE US. If the Schomburg collection¹ is famous for Dunbar manuscripts, let this one be famous for HUGHES!* Arthur Spingarn has already given the collection a tremendous lot of books . . . He has so many that now he has lots of duplicates, expecially of old and rare books and he asked me down on Friday to take my pick of these and I picked out everything we hadnt already. He promises more and this morning in the mail he sends another. In the meantime Ive photographed Maxine Sullivan and Edna Thomas² and William Attaway is promised but seems to be a little Coy. I approve highly the new poems you have sent Knopf for Shakespeare in Harlem and you will be most enthusiastic about the illustrations, of that I am sure. They are really magnificent. I have seen Arna Bontemps book but Sterling Brown's isnt out yet. Two new books by Ofays: At George's Joint and Royal Road (a modern Negro's story told in terms of the Christ: Noël might be interested in this one).³ Do you know C L R James?⁴

Well, hearts and flowers and affection for you (in which Fania joins me)
Carlo!

October 27

*All your letters will go there, <u>sealed</u> till after your death if they contain any personal matters about others. I'll go over them carefully & add notes! If you have any letters of mine, I'd like them to go there eventually too. I have <u>all your</u> letters.

Hasn't Noël any significant Negro material he can give us?

I <u>love Domestic Happenings</u>.⁵

1. *The renowned bibliophile Arthur Alphonso Schomburg sold his collection of material on the history of blacks in the United States, Spain, and Latin America to the Carnegie Corporation in 1926. The collection was deposited in the 135th Street branch of the New York Public Library and grew quickly under Schomburg's continued guidance. Today, the*

Schomburg library has one of the world's leading collections relating to black culture, including the manuscripts of Paul Laurence Dunbar.
2. *Edna Thomas was a black actress.*
3. *Mr. George's Joint was published in 1941 by E. A. Wheaton. Royal Road was published the same year by Sheed & Ward.*
4. *Cyril Lionel Richard James, born in Trinidad, was a historian, writer, and activist. James was a deeply influential Caribbean intellectual of the twentieth century.*
5. *Hughes may have published this poem under a different title.*

LANGSTON HUGHES TO CARL VAN VECHTEN, OCTOBER 30, 1941

Hollow Hills Farm
Monterey, California

October 30, 1941

Dear Carl,

You really should not tell me you are going to give all my letters to Yale because I will now become self-conscious and no doubt verge toward the grandiloquent. Besides I was just about to tell you about a wonderful fight that took place in Togo's Pool Room in Monterey the other day in which various were cut from here to yonder and the lady who used to be the second wife of Noel's valet who came to New York with him that time succeeded in slicing several herself—but you know the Race would come out here and cut <u>me</u> if they knew I was relaying such news to posterity via the Yale Library. So now how can I tell you?

Meanwhile I have come across Miss Etta Moten's home address which is: 3548 Vernon, Chicago, Illinois. She recently gave two concerts here on the coast, but did not pass by Carmel so I didn't get a chance to ask her about her father.[1]

I will be delighted to have my manuscripts in a handsome box with a leather label. But if I were to send you all of them, you would need a trunk, so I will only send certain ones from time to time. The other day I sent another one called PASSING about some Negroes who wanted to jive some white folks but got double jived themselves.[2]

You know, I have all your letters, too! And most of your books—even if they are well worn from being lent out. I have a whole series of letters from Ezra Pound, too, about getting Frobenius translated in entirety into English that might also be good for Yale. And some from Zora that would be excellent for some Ph.D. to get his degree on in 2042.

Sure, I would love to have a little short job at Yale. Out of my next job I promise to pay off all the rest of my debts.

C. L. R. James I met in Paris. Also I believe again in Los Angeles. He was the leading colored Troskyite of the English speaking world. Said to be very brilliant. But he did not seem to have much of a sense of humor. And I do not believe he would go near Togo's Pool Room in Monterey—which is where Fannie cut Virgil in the phone booth the other day. And somebody else cut a soldier (among others). And Argyle was cut on the arm and they put it in a sling. But when he got home he found he had also been cut in the <u>side</u>! But the very thought of Yale prevents me from going further!

Thanks so much for reading the new poems for SHAKESPEARE IN HARLEM. I hope they go into it. And I am dying to see the drawings. I did not think the ones in GOLDEN SLIPPERS very good . . . I haven't seen GEORGE'S JOINT nor ROYAL ROAD yet . . . But I've read reviews of them . . . And publicity blurbs . . . And I hope (even beg and entreat via letters to the entire Knopf staff) that nobody will, in publicizing my book or writing the blurb, use the words:

childlike

primitive

un-moral

amoral

or

simple

which, aside from being untrue when applied to the American scene, have been quite out-worn in describing Negroes and books by and about Negroes.

As Ruth Chatterton's[3] mother said when she tripped over the rug in the foyer on West 55th Street, "<u>Merde, alors!</u>" Only I, too, would say it in English, were it not that Yale has now got me cornered.

Besides the NAACP has just asked me to write a credo for them to open all their meetings with from Boston to San Diego. And people who write credos would hardly cuss in English, would they?

They say when Virgie came out of the phone booth her <u>cou</u> was in ribbons.

Which reminds me of why Mamie Smith never made any more records.

My love to Fania,

Sincerely,

Langston

P.S. I saw Mrs. Blanchard yesterday in the drug store. . . . Lotte Lehmann[4] will be a guest of Noel's shortly. . . . Poor Barthé has had a slight stomach upset and wasn't feeling at all well when he left. Is in

L.A. . . . The Dunham Dancers are giving FOUR dance recitals at the Biltmore this week. . . . I told you, did I not, that I did four librettos for them. They said they were terrific—but as usual in the theatre, now want them all changed around!

1. *Van Vechten wanted to know who Etta Moten's father was. Perhaps he wondered if he was Benjamin "Bennie" Moten, a famous jazz bandleader. In actuality, Moten's father was a San Antonio minister.*
2. *Hughes published this story under the title "Who's Passing for Who?" in the 1945–46 issue of* Negro Story *magazine.*
3. *Chatterton was a celebrated actress of the 1920s.*
4. *Lotte Lehmann was a well-known soprano of the twentieth century.*

CARL VAN VECHTEN TO LANGSTON HUGHES, NOVEMBER 4, 1941

Caro Langstonia, I am delighted with you and your work and your letters! I think you have completely grown up and represent the Negro* at his BEST. As a spokesman for the Negro you are unique because you know all kinds and classes WELL and like all kinds and classes. To some extent this is also true of your relationship with ofays. I see your name everywhere and I guess you are Garvey, Father Divine, James Weldon Johnson, and James L Ford[1] all rolled into ONE. Your paper in Common Ground, for instance, is restrained and eloquent.[2] Frederick Douglass could not do better. And Passing which you have just sent me, is redolent with a frothy irony which is not too bitter and when the tale is read white and black BOTH have been hit. Pardon the applause, please, but that is the way I feel and, having watched you grow up, it is a pleasure to report progress . . .

Incidentally the history of the race in America can pretty well be read in autobiographies: (1) William Wells Brown[3] (2) Frederick Douglass (3) Booker T Washington (4) W E B Du Bois (5) James Weldon Johnson (6) The Big Sea and its successor. As a matter of fact the second volume of your life will have to be more weighty than the first. It should, I think, seriously discuss the plight of the Negro (and the hopes) in modern American, and Im afraid you'll have to tell at last whether or no you think Communism is the way out . . . Of course, you can avoid all this, but at the expense (somewhat) of your reputation. It will be EXPECTED.

Pardon the sermon, please.

By the way, your letter reads even BETTER now that you know it will be deposited at Yale. I havent started on letters yet, And this is a job. Everything has to be arranged chronologically and carefully read (1) for notes of explanation, which I add, when necessary, (2) to discover if there is anything about the letter which demands temporary suppression. Those letters which might offend somebody just now will be put in a sealed package waiting your death and mine (though either of us could remove this seal on the death of the other, if found advisable, or both of us could do so in concert if we decided some day they could be read without harm). I hope you will give my letters to Yale too under more or less the same conditions. If you dont find time to edit them, let me do it!

I am more grateful than I can say for the new manuscript. You CAN send a trunkful, if you desire. They will be more than welcome at Yale. You will get a formal acknowledgment from the Library later, of course. But at present, these are waiting a box. Ezra Pound and Zora would be wonderful for Yale!

Curiously, your report of the cuttings in the Monterey Poolroom follow a recent evening I spent, and loved to spend, with William Attaway, who was describing similar goings-on in a Harlem poolroom! He even sees cuttings at the Savoy, which I never did . . .

Dont be selfconscious about Yale. Henry Miller puts more shits and fucks and cunts in than ever when I assure him his letters are destined for college halls . . . I guess HIS should go to Bryn Mawr or Vassar . . . The gals could read 'em and masturbate.

Most of the new poems for Shakespeare, I liked, some of them I was enthusiastic about . . . I must say Harlem Sweeties[4] hit me hard. I read it aloud one night to a group. One I was quite fainthearted about, Deceased;[5] they seemed to have a similar feeling about it in the Knopf office and so decided to leave it out. I hope you wont mind this excision of two lines. . . . The Golden Slippers illustrations are stinko. Is Henrietta Bruce Sharon ofay?*[6] I question the taste of the selection in many respects. WHY should young readers be invited to read Countée's Incident: Baltimore, for instance?[7] If you like dont like YOUR illustrations, I wouldnt know what you would like. Whatever else they are, they are works of art and extremely novel in conception . . . My feeling about illustrations corresponds entirely with that of Diaghileff who before he was a ballet impresario was an art critic. He wrote in an article that illustration should be "subjective." If we demand that an illustrator's art be mainly descriptive, we limit his scope, and set insuperable difficulties in his path. It is sheer madness to demand of illustration that it render the soul of the poet or his most secret thoughts: for what it amounts to is asking that the painter shall become a poet, too, which is neither possible nor helpful. The whole significance of the illustrator's art lies in its utter subjectivity; all that we ask of him is his own interpretation of a poem, story, or novel. An illustration should never be expected to complement some piece of writing, nor merge into it; far otherwise. It should light up the creation of the poet with the strictly personal illumination that emanates from the painter. The more startling that vision is, the more completely it expresses the personality of the painter, the greater will be its importance. In a word it is a matter of complete indifference that the poet shall be able to say, "Yes, that indeed is how I see it." What really matters is his saying, "Ah, so that's how you see it."

I hope this letter is not too long for you. . . . You've said so little about Barthé that perhaps he didnt enjoy himself, or you didnt enjoy him. . . . Did Mamie Smith get HER throat cut? Rosamond Johnson was here yesterday, inscribing music (with historical significance) and getting photographed in color. He recommended highly a record from the Duke Ellington show,[8] I Got it Bad, and that aint Good. Are these your words . . . More and more material is piling up for you to inscribe. I am working like mad and photographing and printing in between.

Fania and I send out love to you,
Carlo!

November 4

*or anybody!
*°This isn't rhetorical. I want to know <u>for Yale!</u>

1. *Van Vechten meant James W. Ford, a leading black American Communist of the 1930s.*
2. *Hughes published "What the Negro Wants" in the Autumn 1941 issue of* Common Ground. *His essay detailed seven needs for African Americans: employment and educational opportunities; decent housing; full participation in government; legal fairness; public courtesy, "the same courtesy that is normally accorded other citizens"; and social equality in public services— "We want the right when traveling to dine in any restaurant or seek lodgings in any hotel or auto camp open to the public which our purse affords. (Any Nazi may do so.)"*
3. *William Wells Brown was the first African American to publish in several genres. He was also a political activist.*
4. *This poem begins: "Have you dug the spill / Of Sugar Hill? / Cast your gims / On this sepia thrill: / Brown sugar lassie, / Caramel treat, / Honey-gold baby / Sweet enough to eat."*
5. *The poem "Deceased" eventually appeared in the collection* One-Way Ticket *(Knopf, 1949): "Harlem / Sent him home / In a long box- / Too dead / To know why: / The licker / Was lye."*
6. *The illustrator of Bontemps's* Golden Slippers, *Henrietta Bruce Sharon, was an "ofay," or white.*
7. *Countee Cullen's "Incident" reads: "Once riding in old Baltimore, / Heart-filled, head-filled with glee, / I saw a Baltimorean / Keep looking straight at me. / Now I was eight and very small, / And he was no white bigger, / And so I smiled, but he poked out / His tongue, and called me, 'Nigger.' / I saw the whole of Baltimore / From May until December; / Of all the things that happened there / That's all that I remember."*
8. *Duke Ellington composed the music for his revue,* Jump for Joy, *which opened on July 10, 1941.*

Dear Carlo,

Thanks for your delightfully long letter and all the nice compliments and advice. I agree with you about the second part of The Big Sea. Only I don't want it to get so weighty that it weighs me down, too.

Barthé left Los Angeles Thursday for Chicago. We enjoyed his visit greatly here. But I didn't report it in more detail because nobody got cut, and it was just a pleasant quiet time, with some dinner parties, and teas, and cocktails. And Ethel Waters came by one Sunday morning for breakfast with Archie and a car full and Noel took them all to call on Mrs. Blanchard.

It was too bad Eulah and I didn't get around to having our colored party while Barthé was here. (Eulah Pharr is Noel's housekeeper, and a very charming person who's been with him for twelve years or more.) But we had it Thursday, cocktails 3–6, except that it lasted from 3 to 3 in the morning—and nobody made a move to go home before midnight, and then didn't go. The joint jumped. We had about 5o. And played plenty Lil Green. Everybody was dressed down, and most proper in a gay manner, and nobody got too high or anything, except one girl got mad when she heard her soldier boy intended to take another girl home, so she simply pulled all the wires out his car so it wouldn't budge—which left him and six other members of Uncle Sam's citizen army stranded out here in the country, and they had to be taken back to Fort Ord in our station wagon just in time to hear "reverie" blow in the morning.

Your paragraph on the art illustration was most interesting. And I am sure the Kauffer drawings are charming. But still, if they come out with NO hair on their heads—after all the millions that have been spent with Madame Walker and Mr. Murray[1]—my Negro public—whom I respect and like—will not be appreciative. I wrote as much to Blanche when I first saw the samples. Harlem just isn't nappy headed any more—except for the first ten minutes after the hair is washed. Following that the sheen equals Valentino's and the page boy bobs are as long as Lana Turner's. And colored folks don't want no stuff out of an illustrator on that score. Even Lil Green has finger waves. And if some of the ladies in SHAKE-SPEARE IN HARLEM don't have them, too, <u>I will catch hell</u>—in spite of whatever "strictly personal illumination emanates from the painter." Do you get me?

I'm sure Henrietta Bruce Sharon is white. But since I couldn't swear it, I've asked Arna to let you know. (But she draws heads and feet as if she were.)

Duke's I GOT IT BAD is good. But unfortunately the words aren't mine. They're by Paul Webster, the white chap who wrote most of the show.

No, Mamie Smith didn't get her throat cut. She just lost her contract. Why, I will tell you when I see you. (Leaving space at the bottom of this here letter for annotation.)

I am now on my way to hear Lotte Lehman sing.

Ere I lay me down in questa tomba obscura I shall try to find all your letters for Yale, but they are in so many various files, boxes, suitcases, and trunks stored from here to yonder that I shall start here to finding recent ones tomorrow.

To whom are you giving your Mary Bell's?[2]

The blues seem to be coming back in a big way. Every club out here now has a blues singer as a part of the floor show. And Joe Turner was the hit of the recent Duke show, pulling it out of polite prettiness.[3]

Did I tell you I did a libretto of THE ST. LOUIS BLUES for Katherine Dunham, a danceable story woven around the song?[4] Hope she uses it. But she rather thinks she ought to do Latin American things—Cuba, Brazil, etc. Easier to sell to concert managers and Hollywood.

So,

Sincerely,

Langston

November 8, 1941

1. *Hughes is referring to Murray's Pomade, a common hair-care product used by black men during this period. Madame C. J. Walker became a millionaire when she developed and marketed a line of black hair-care products in the early twentieth century.*
2. *Mary Bell was the housekeeper for the sculptor Gaston La Chaise as well as an unknown artist in Boston when Carl Van Vechten met her in 1937. He subsequently engineered several public exhibitions of her work, and gave his correspondence with Bell to the James Weldon Johnson Memorial Collection.*
3. *The blues singer Joe Turner appeared in Ellington's 1941 revue,* Jump for Joy.
4. *Hughes had been composing various ballet scenarios for the black American dancer and choreographer Katherine Dunham.*

John Macrae, Jr., *vice president of the publishing house E. P. Dutton, sent Hughes a copy of* Mr. George's Joint, *by the white writer Elizabeth Lee Wheaton, and asked for his reaction to it. In his response, Hughes took issue with the way the company was promoting the book. He referred to an ad in the October 26* New York Times Book Review *when he wrote: "I personally fail to see where the tale is either* magnificent *or true to the 'Negro as he really is.' " Hughes considered both the ads and the novel insulting to blacks. "Most Negroes are quite hard working, honest, early-to-bed people, as are other Americans. . . . Books like MR. GEORGE'S JOINT just simply do not represent the American 'Negro as he is.' "*

CARL VAN VECHTEN TO LANGSTON HUGHES, NOVEMBER 17, 1941

Dear Langston, I LOVED your letter to the Dutton's. And I sent you a postcard last week re: At George's Joint. To me the book is entirely devoid of feeling. Nobody in the book has any feelings at all: SO, it becomes monotonous and uninteresting and untrue. After awhile you stop believing it. I have no objections to people drinking and screwing in books. In fact Ive written books like that myself, but to make them entirely bereft of mother love, romantic passion, of any regard for property, or any inhibitions whatever, is to make them so inhuman that they don't stand up as characters. So I applaud everything you say. . . . I am sending this letter* WITH the book to Yale, as it hasnt gone yet. . . . Well, I heard Lil Green at the Apollo Saturday. She is the nearest thing to Bessie Smith that this effete age can offer, tho Bessie never needed a microphone to put herself or her voice over. She is very sweet and good looking to boot. I sat in a box with Ella Fitzgerald who didnt like her much which is a good sign. Alfred sends me an announcement of a new edition of Not Without Laughter! Is Eulah Pharr any relation to Kelsey Pharr? . . . I cant recall about the hair in the Kauffer drawings as I didnt look at them from that angle. But THEY ARE ART. Maybe Blanche got 'em fixed according to your desires, but in any case your criticism is not an art criticism but an economic or social one. It is highly probable indeed that in a few years EVERYBODY will be having nappy hair again and loving it. Some few sensible persons go in for it now . . . BUT I GET YOUR POINT, and next time you want to put over something like this, write me about it <u>too</u> as I will raise any kind of stink you want me too and I will understand what you are talking about, which sometimes they wont in the office. . . . For instance it would be quite legitimate, if he wanted to, for Kauffer to illustrate a modern white novel in hair done in the style of Louis XV. Beardsley did this sort of thing all the time . . . Velazquez and Veronese on the other hand painted biblical scenes in renaissance costumes. . . . With these things in mind, it is hard for editors and painters to understand the ways in which Negroes are touchy, but I UNDERSTAND. Well, I hope the hairs will be okay. The pictures, in any case, are beautiful. Arna hasnt let me know whether Sharon is white. . . . My Mary Bells go eventually to Yale, I dare say, but not quite yet. . . . As a matter of fact what books and letters and phonograph records and photographs Ive got will take me months more of intensive labor, but its going to be a good collection when it gets there and pretty fully explained, which it isnt anywhere else. . . . No, you didnt tell me about your libretto for the St. Louis Blues, an excellent idea, and KD should jump for it. We shall all miss you and your distinguished presence very much at the Library today.¹ I got a preview on Saturday and felt as if I were dead. It was very impressive. You'll know when you get laid out at Yale!

Affection to you and hope to see you in NYC soon,

Carlo!

November 17, 1941

*I mean your letter to McCrae. And some day Ill find your letter about Lanterns on the Levee to put with that book!

1. *The New York Public Library had arranged an exhibition of the books and manuscripts that Van Vechten had donated to the Manuscripts and Archives Division as the Carl Van Vechten Collection. He wrote to the writer Hutchins Hapgood in 1941 about his commitment to preserving his materials: "I am preparing for death, bombs, destruction, and disasters, ie, getting my manuscripts and books and letters into collections, libraries, museums, etc, where they stand more chance of being preserved and protected. . . . I have enough to do to occupy me at least till the next war or revolution. And in the meantime if I am bombed I die busy!"*

In April 1941, Hughes received a $1,500 fellowship from the Julius Rosenwald Fund to write a series of one-act plays about black heroes for high schools, colleges, and amateur theatre groups. The Rosenwald Fund was established in 1913 by Julius Rosenwald, president of Sears Roebuck and a champion of black education. Hughes's fellowship included the use of an office at the Rosenwald Fund headquarters in Chicago. On November 20, Hughes arrived to begin researching his project. He took a room at the Good Shepherd Community Center, a black settlement house that was quickly becoming known as a center of black intellectual life in Chicago. He slept there, but spent a good deal of time with his close friend Arna Bontemps and Bontemps's family.

Dear Carlo,

You will soon have a trunk full of drafts. . . . Your letter and card both delightful. Comment on MR. GEORGE'S JOINT most interesting. . . . Please look and see if the Kauffer drawings have any hair on their heads next time you see them. . . . Arna says the GOLDEN

LANGSTON HUGHES, PHOTOGRAPH BY
CARL VAN VECHTEN, 1938

SLIPPERS artist is white. . . . Yesterday afternoon Dorothy Maynor sang before a capacity SRO—three hundred extra seats in orchestra pit— audience of 3,900 at Chicago Civic Opera House. Gave four encores at the end of program. Then came out to dinner with me and ate turkey which she carved herself with an expert touch. . . . Carlo, you remember that picture you took of me with hat on in front of the house in Greenwich Village? I think it is one of the best ones I've ever had. Good Shepherd Community Center here where I'm staying wants one for its walls. Also Dorothy Maynor wants one. And the Rosenwald's office. Would it be possible for you perhaps to send me copies of it for them? Don't if it is too much work or trouble. . . . Eulah Pharr is no relation to Kelsey Pharr. . . . NATIVE SON is a hit here selling six weeks ahead, they say. I shall go shortly. . . . Snowflakes and snowbirds to you,

Langston

c/o Arna Bontemps
703 East 5oth Place
Chicago, Illinois

Chicago, Illinois

December 13, 1941

Dear Carlo,

I've been intending to write you for some days now to thank [you] for your cards and letter, and most especially for the photographs which I am delighted to have, as have been those to whom I presented one. It's the full face one that I like best of the two. I think it's swell. . . . Gordon Parks,[1] young Negro photographer here, just took some interesting pictures of me which he is permitting me to send Knopf in case they'd like them for publicity. He's just had a successful one man show downtown here. . . . I liked Kauffer's pictures very much. And the hair is there, Jack! . . . I persuaded Arna to dig out some manuscripts for you which he says you have received and acknowledged. . . . I've been working every day at the Rosenwald Fund's offices trying to finish one of the Fellowship plays before I leave—a long one that will probably be put on here in February or March. And Arna and I have done a radio bit for Canada Lee to do on CBS BILL OF RIGHTS program along with the Governor of Illinois tomorrow[2] . . . I'll be seeing you soon.

Best to you,
Sincerely,
Langston

1. *Gordon Parks, Sr., is still known for his portrait photography.*
2. *Bontemps and Hughes called their show "Bill of Rights Salute to Freedom." The actor Canada Lee read a script on black achievement before an audience that included the governor of Illinois.*

Dear Langston, Thanks for sending me Shakespeare in Harlem so promptly. It is an incredibly handsome book and I have already read it twice through with growing enthusiasm for the contents. I loved these in mss. but I love them more printed. You have such an innocent charming way of saying things that BURN DEEP and your lines are so easy-going that it takes some time to realize that they are memorable. They sink into the mind like the folklore of the nation. This is now one of my favorite books of yours. Southern Mammy Sings, Harlem Sweeties, Ku Klux, and Ballad of the Sinner are some I like the best, but I LIKE THEM ALL. . . .

This will be a great addition to the Yale Collection when it gets there. . . . By the way I dont find the lines you wrote on the fingers of the jacket of my copy of the book.¹ Did you make these up or borrow 'em from somewhere else? DONT FORGET TO ANSWER THIS QUESTION . . . And if its any of my business is Louise, Miss Thompson?

Have you seen the honors that have been heaped on my head? If you have, you havent congratulated me. Any way The Schomburg Collection takes a national poll every year to determine the six whites who have done the most for inter-racial relations and Im one of the six. O Boy, this pleases me! Ethel is here, with Archie, who is "Sonny" to her. They dined here last week, have gone to Boston for picture house appearances, and return next week when Im giving them a party. If you will be here February 25, you can COME, please.

Grace Johnson's father died yesterday. He was 89. You can write her at the Hotel Theresa. I sent all the loose material on to Yale and you should get an official receipt. Im having boxes made for the manuscripts and the things you signed. These should be ready before you get back. I still find there are questions you have to answer in regard to some of the material.

Affection to you and Hi-De-Ho in the Midwest!

Carlo!

February 15, 1942

And Im looking forward to another trunkful of materials please!

1. *The cover of* Shakespeare in Harlem *features a wishbone and a die sitting on top of a brown hand. On Van Vechten's copy, Hughes wrote on the fingers: "The wishbone is broken. The dice have thrown a deuce. The song's an old familiar tune—What's the use?"*

LANGSTON HUGHES TO CARL VAN VECHTEN, MARCH 18, 1942

Good Shepherd Community Center
5120 South Parkway
Chicago, Illinois

March 18, 1942

Dear Carlo,

Just about a year ago, you remember, your letter to me in California got burned up in an airplane crash. Now, look what happened to your last card! It arrived during the hurricane downpour a few mornings ago, dripping wet. The mailman's bag must have been flooded, as I couldn't make out more than a couple of words. So would you kindly write it all over again?

Maybe that was just my just deserts for not having written you for so long. First I was finishing my play,[1] then I went down to Virginia for lectures, then I started rehearsals, producing and directing the play myself, so I have been no end busy, without a breathing space from morning to night.

I am delighted that you continue to like SHAKESPEARE IN HARLEM as it now appears between covers. Thanks for your kind blurb on the jacket. What I wrote on the cover I made up to go with the design. It is not nor will be elsewhere published. Louise is Louise Thompson.

I like the appearance of the book very much. But am a bit sorry some colored people are not liking the dice on the jacket, so I am taking it off for readings before Negro audiences.[2] Also I was a little puzzled at the arrangement of some of the excellent Kauffer drawings. For instance, the pretty little boy who appears in front of the BLUES FOR MEN section— when the rough-looking guy on Page 92 would more nearly suit the mood of the blues, which are tough songs. And the snob on Page 48 ought to face the poem, SNOB, instead of what everybody takes to be a picture of Joe Louis there, page 26. Everybody in the office agreed with me on this and Mr. Jacobs[3] said it might be possible to shift the arrangement in the next edition, if one there be. Hope so.

Do give my best to Ethel. And I'm writing Grace Johnson.

Did you get the chronology sheet of NOT WITHOUT LAUGHTER I posted you just before I left—and did it help straighten out the various drafts?

I am sending shortly for Yale the drafts of the new play and a final copy[4]—as it now stands. Please read it if you have a chance and let me know what you think of it. It seems to be working out pretty effectively in rehearsals and will be better when the chorus and the music are added in a week or so. Do you remember that marvellous fat lady in the Chicago Federal Theatre <u>Swing Mikado</u>? She is doing Mammy for me. Wish I had Earl Jones for the lead, so far not very satisfactory filled here. All the husky young men seem to have departed for the army. Two big consignments of Negroes left the South Side since I've been here.

Would love to see the Stage Door Canteen, and you therein.[5] So glad the colored boys are welcome.[6]

Did you hear my song, THE NEGRO SPEAKS OF RIVERS (Margaret Bonds setting) on FREEDOM'S PEOPLE program last Sunday?

Enclosed a clipping for you—or Yale—that you might or might not have seen. Look who was with you at the Karamu Art Show! . . . So, quand meme, et tourjours,

Langston

1. *The play was* The Sun Do Move, *named after one of the most celebrated African American sermons. It told the story of a slave named Rock, who tries to reunite with his wife and*

son. It was performed by the Skyloft Players, organized by Hughes at the Good Shepherd Community Center, on April 24.

2. *Hughes complained to Arna Bontemps in a January 27, 1942, letter: "Knopf, added to my other troubles, have put a wishbone and a dice on my book jacket! They think it's charming." Later in the year, he asked Blanche either to put out a new edition in a plain cover, or in "anything but dice and wishbones."*

3. *Sidney Jacobs was in charge of production at Knopf.*

4. The Sun Do Move.

5. *The Stage Door Canteen opened on March 2, 1942, under the auspices of the American Theatre Wing War Service. Its purpose was to serve and entertain military personnel. Vogue magazine reported in its May 15, 1942, issue: "At the Stage Door Canteen, for Service Men only, actresses sweep floors, artists clean the refrigerator, playwrights mop tables, producers stack chairs. The Service Men do nothing but have a good time." When the Theatre Guild officially lent its support to the Canteen project, Fania Marinoff was one of the first to volunteer. Van Vechten quickly followed, never missing his regular Monday and Tuesday busboy shifts for three years.*

6. *Van Vechten was determined that the Stage Door Canteen would be an interracial environment.*

H ughes was surprised in July when he received an invitation from Newton Arvin, a director of the Yaddo writers and artists colony in Saratoga Springs, New York, to spend a few weeks there. The promise of free room and board on top of such a prestigious offer was irresistible. When Hughes arrived on August 4, he became Yaddo's first black resident fellow. Other resident fellows that summer included Katherine Anne Porter, Carson McCullers, and Kenneth Fearing.

CARL VAN VECHTEN TO LANGSTON HUGHES, AUGUST 12, 1942

Dear Langston, You were BAD to go away without saying goodbye, but Id rather you say Hello when you return. Anyway here are some pix of Jimmy Davis[1] and he gets some by the same post. Ive seen Yaddo, even photographed it, so no need to describe it. If you get on with Miss McCullers, tell her I'd like to photograph her some time. I dote on her books. I also correspond with Brick and know her street address. Please help her to get Vodery started on the way to Yale![2] Kenneth Fearing, I think you told me, is Genevieve Taggard's husband.[3] Some of the others I dont know. Ask Mr. Malbandian if a GOOD Armenian restaurant persists

in NY. I saw Paul as Othello in London
twice, but I am missing this one, at least
for the moment. I am reading JWJ letters before they go to Yale, arranging Max
Ewing material,[4] photographing This is
the Army,[5] printing pictures of Eugene
O'Neill for Yale, and canteening madly.
Did the three Negroes from TITA yesterday. . . . Exactly when do you plan to
return?

Hands across the state!
Carlo
August 12, 1942

JIMMY DAVIS, PHOTOGRAPH BY
CARL VAN VECHTEN

I may go to the Eddie Mallorys
tonight. A housewarming for their love
nest in the BRONX.

1. *The pianist and singer Jimmy Davis, a friend of Hughes's, had recently been drafted. He would eventually take advantage of an offer by the French government for GIs to study in France; in 1948, he settled permanently in Paris. He was best known for the song "Lover Man," which he cowrote with Roger "Ram" Ramirez and Jimmy Sherman in 1941. Billie Holiday recorded it in 1944.*
2. *Will Vodery was a black composer and bandleader. Van Vechten wanted his material for the James Weldon Johnson Memorial Collection.*
3. *Fearing and Taggard were well-known poets.*
4. *A writer and musician, Max Ewing killed himself in 1934 at the age of 31, not long after Hughes reported good news about him to Van Vechten in the September 22, 1933, letter on page 106. Van Vechten wanted to preserve Ewing's letters because, among other reasons, they chronicle New York social life in the 1920s.*
5. *This Is the Army was a musical comedy written by Irving Berlin featuring an all-military cast.*

Van Vechten was devoted to the Stage Door Canteen, the recreation center for servicemen. He described what it meant to him in an April 1943
article for Theatre Arts, "An Ode to the Stage Door Canteen." The
center was absolutely democratic, "perhaps one of the few democratic institutions in existence anywhere," he wrote. It changed people's lives: "The place has
brought people together who never knew each other before and given their lives

a new social direction. Is it any wonder that almost every one who sees the Stage
Door Canteen for the first time bursts into tears from sheer happiness that such
things can be?"

Yaddo
Saratoga Springs, N.Y.

August 12, 1942

Dear Carlo,

I see in the TIMES this morning where William Jourdan Rapp died.[1]
He it was who, according to Wallie's friends, took charge of all his effects
and manuscripts after his death—except the few that Miss Grant[2] had in
Harlem. It might be wise to write his widow and see if she could retrieve
any for Yale.

Thanks immensely for your note and the photos of Jimmy[3] which just
came. I think they are most successful pictures—in that they look "just
like him," capturing his personality as well as his appearance. He is a
most likable and amusing fellow, as I think you will agree if you get to
know him better. Certainly one of the compensations of writing poetry is
that people like you and Jimmy come walking into one's life on the carpet
of a poem. THE WEARY BLUES brought you along, via the OPPORTU-
NITY dinner, didn't it? And that poem of mine about, "This is no time for
compromise or fear," caused him to come to see me—just at the moment
when I needed somebody to make piano copies of THE NEGRO
SPEAKS OF RIVERS and FREEDOM ROAD!

I have breakfast every morning with Mrs. McCullers, at which time we
unite in damning Georgia. I shall ask her if she would like to have her
picture taken.

Carlo, did you have any copies of the Negro THEATRE ARTS left?[4]
You offered me one once and I didn't take it, thinking I could buy some
more. But after I had given my copy away, I found I couldn't find any
place downtown the day before I left, and it isn't on the stands at all up
here. If you have an extra one, I'd appreciate it enormously if you would
save it for me.

Kenneth Fearing, it turns out, is not Genevieve Taggard's husband.
Her husband is Kenneth Durant.

Mr. Malbandian lives in Providence, not New York, but anyhow I will
ask him about restaurants.

Have you heard Jack Meredith sing at the FAT MAN IN THE BRONX?[5]
They say he is good.

And who are the three Negroes from (and what is) TITA? I never heard of it.

Saturday is the big race (horse) day up here. To the track I hope to go.

The Race has one advantage during blackouts — they are wonderfully invisible in the dark. But quite audible. I was on the Race street in Saratoga the other night when a blackout occurred.

Juan Minorance, Spanish painter, is here, also Katherine Anne Porter. We had good old ham and sweet potatoes for dinner last night. Everybody ate so fast I couldn't keep up with them, and so didn't get a 2nd helping.

This is the only house I know of that has a fountain in the living room. According to the zodiac, I believe, I was born under the water sign. Anyhow, I am impressed.

Sincerely,

Langston

1. *Rapp, a white playwright, was a feature writer for the* New York Times. *In 1928 he collaborated with Wallace Thurman on the play* Harlem, *which opened at the Apollo Theatre on February 2, 1929.*
2. *Helene Grant had been a member of Wallace Thurman's social and intellectual circle in the 1920s.*
3. *Jimmy Davis.*
4. *The August 1942 issue of* Theatre Arts *was devoted to "the Negro in American theatre."*
5. *Jack Meredith was the featured singer at this club in the Bronx, New York.*

CARL VAN VECHTEN TO LANGSTON HUGHES, AUGUST 17, 1942
(ON JAMES WELDON JOHNSON MEMORIAL COMMITTEE LETTERHEAD)

Dear Langston, Ive been away for a few days and when I come back, I find your letter. . . . While away I have read a book called Sabbath Has No End,¹ by John Weld (ofay) a story of slave days on a plantation where the slaves were "well treated." Without much trouble, Mr Weld shows you that it was impossible to treat slaves well and gives many many intricate reasons in the course of his story. In many ways a vivid and extraordinary story. . . . Ive also been reading many Negro letters for Yale, including the correspondence re Mulebone which includes letters from YOU and Zora and Barrett H Clark and Lawrence Langner and Theresa Helburn. It's a pretty complete tale and your letter regarding Zora's tantrum in your mother's room in Cleveland is wonderful. She had a tantrum in my library at 150 West 55 Street too and threw herself on the floor and screamed and yelled! Bit the dust in fact. You woulda loved it, had it not concerned you. Something very important has happened, perhaps for the first time. Life in the August 17 issue has a couple of pages concerning the fire that destroyed part of the managery of Ringling Brothers and it gives the name of the incendiary, but it does not say he is a Negro or print his picture! On my return I find a bundle (for Yale) a mile high from Walter White, another full of music from William Dawson,[2] another smaller package from Verna Arvey[3] and many letters promising help. Arna writes that he has already seen Georgette's manuscript and talked it over with her about a year ago.[4] WHY will people behave in this fashion? She has said she had never heard of him. Obviously I cant trust Miss Harvey on the next go-round. Mr Knollenberg has just given the Yale Collection some terrific letters, including items of Lincoln, Frederick Douglass, and Harriet Beecher Stowe. . . . and Ray Stannard Baker[5] has given us a tremendous amount of important material. I had already planned to write Mrs Rapp but thought I would wait till Mr Rapp had been dead a minute. I guess people would walk into your life even if you didnt write poems, but perhaps the poems makes 'em walk in quicker. . . . MY LAST copy of Theatre Arts went to Noel, as you requested. Somebody told me the magazine was out of print, but I'll see what I can do. You shall have a copy if there is one.* My reserved copy, of course, went to Yale. . . . Im afraid Kenneth F is somewhere in the catalogue as Miss Taggard's spouse. If so, this info came from You, you rascal! I havent been to Fat Man in the Bronx though Eddie and his blonde wife asked me to the housewarming at their Love Nest.[6] It was too hot and too late a party, so I didn't go. Tita, Gate,[7] is This Is The Army! And I have photographed the three leading Negroes. . . . In the Pennsylvania station last night there wasnt a single porter. I lugged a 90 pound bag (full of letters and books) about a mile in pitch blackness (the roof is glass and they keep the lights out). Your slow eating habits will be a distinct disadvantage to you in a boarding house where you are expected to talk. Better take vitamines. The Everleigh Club[8] in Chicago also had a fountain in the living room. Some of the best families used to fall in. affection to you and FM even sends a kiss, after your "Tell Fania I love her!"

Carlo!

Monday (Im off to the Canteen SOON)

*It is out of print and at a premium, but I got a copy for you!

Dorothy writes only today that she has the copy of The Red Decade[9] you borrowed & will return it. You never did tell me if there are more Negro References.

1. *Published by Scribner's Sons in 1942.*
2. *A composer and conductor.*

3. *A talented pianist, Verna Arvey was the wife of composer William Grant Still.*
4. *Georgette Harvey was an actress and singer. She was writing an autobiography about her years in the theatre that Van Vechten thought was interesting but needed editorial help. He suggested she send the manuscript to Bontemps.*
5. *A journalist and author.*
6. *Fat Man in the Bronx was Eddie Mallory's club.*
7. *"Gate" was a common salutation during World War II. It probably derived from "Gate-mouth," a popular nickname for Louis Armstrong.*
8. *A high-toned Chicago brothel where Van Vechten sometimes played the piano in his youth.*
9. The Red Decade: The Stalinist Penetration of America, *by Eugene Lyons, was published by the Bobbs-Merrill Company in 1941.*

CARL VAN VECHTEN TO LANGSTON HUGHES, OCTOBER 8, 1942

Langston, my Hearty! I am terrifically obliged to you for The Negro Speaks of Rivers, and Madame Alberta K Johnson,¹ including the piece that came today. I am in Love with Madam Johnson already and I think you should do a whole book of her! I got a questionnaire too, occupational, but altho' there were hundreds of occupations listed, author and photographer were not among them. So I wrote them in. Today I get a notice to come see my draft board so maybe Ill get sent to Hawaii. . . . I got lots of Canteen stories to tell you. In the first place Fania was in Washington for the opening (I mean the very first opening minute). So she was taking food checks and when the first boy came in she stood up and shook hands with him and said You are the very first BOY. So when the first Cullud boy came in she got up and shook hands with him and said Im glad to see you. You are the first cullud boy to come in. She said five or six more came in before she left at 7 for NYC . . . A couple of Tuesdays ago when I [was] captain of our canteen, there were a dozen cullud hostesses. So one tall very black sailor (he couldnta been blacker) just tapped soldiers on the shoulder, cut in and danced with white girls. This went on for an hour and a half, me watching every minute for an incident, if any. It is another proof of my theory, often expounded to you in regard to white restaurants, that Negroes are kept down because they lack NERVE and initiative. This sailor was not fresh, but he knew how to talk and dance and he behaved naturally as if he were used to dancing with white gals every night . . . Nothing whatever of an unpleasant nature occurred. Between dances he stood and chatted with white service men on the floor. . . . Monday a nice looking colored boy came up to me and asked where the colored hostesses were . . . I said Id love to know. "Does the canteen keep em out?" he inquired. "God forbid. We get down on our knees to try to get them here." "Well, I guess it doesnt matter anyway," he said. "When they DO come they always jump with the white boys." Make what you will of these incidents, all interesting. . . . Listen, Kid, lots of things are happening to me. My photograph show (Theatre) opens at the Museum of the City of NY on November 17 for SIX weeks.[2] On November 20 Roberta Bosley and her group are giving this ole cullud man a dinner at Port Arthur.*[3] Dance Index is devoting the next number to my old studies of the Ballet.[4] Ive had quite a lotta fan letters lately. Wanta read a few?° The one that pleases me the most (altho' Im ticked pink by the lot) is the one that came this morning from Catherine Freeland. Be a good sport, please and return all these letters by return mail. I send God's Blessing to you and much affection,

Carlo!

Thursday
101 Central Park West
New York City

Knollenberg[5] wrote today asking for info regarding Carter Woodson.[6] So I referred him to you.

*You gotta come to this!
°Four enclosed![7]

1. At Yaddo, Hughes invented his savvy heroine, Madame Alberta K. Johnson. He wrote a suite of poems called "Madam to You" about this character.
2. The show was called "Special Exhibition: The Theatre Through the Camera of Carl Van Vechten." It ran from November 18 until January 11 and included photos of Marian Anderson, Cab Calloway, Salvador Dali, Lillian Gish, James Weldon Johnson, Vincent Price, and Ethel Waters.
3. The November 28, 1942, New York Age reported: "Friday night at the Port Arthur Restaurant, in Chinatown, when the James Weldon Johnson Literary Guild tendered a dinner in honor of Carl Van Vechten, a galaxy of socialites were in attendance. This event offered fashion writers, social scribblers, and all those connected with the women's page, enough material to give them writer's cramps." Walter White was the master of ceremonies for a program that included a reading by Margaret Walker, a recent winner of the Yale Younger Poets Award, and music by Marian Anderson. Among the two hundred people present were Stephen Vincent Benet, W. C. Handy (who performed), Zora Neale Hurston, and the Knopfs.
4. Lincoln Kirstein's monthly magazine, Dance Index, put out a September–October–November issue devoted to Van Vechten's dance criticism. On November 29, the New York Times called it "virtually a source book for anybody's dance library."
5. Bernhard Knollenberg was head librarian at Yale University from 1938 to 1945.
6. Hughes was working on Woodson's landmark study, Free Heads of Negro Families, when he first met Van Vechten in 1924.
7. On the envelope, Van Vechten noted that the letters—from Lincoln Kirstein, Verna Arvey Still, Georgia Douglass Johnson, and Catherine Freeland—were returned.

CARL VAN VECHTEN TO LANGSTON HUGHES, OCTOBER 13, 1942

Dear Langston, Pardon the slight push I gave you yesterday, as the letters all came back today. Thank You. I am awful mad I missed Zell Ingram, but I dare say he will be back some day. I hope manuscript and everything of Freedom Road will soon reach me.[1] Did you hear about the speech I made at the launching of the Negro Dance Theatre on Sunday, the very first public speech I ever made?[2] I liked doing it so much that I probably am going to be a great bore talking publicly at great length and leaping from public dinner to public dinner! It is my next career. Harold, too, is being drafted.[3] I hope you both will be spared the horror of a second front. I havent seen Dust on the Road[4] yet, but I am almost as curious as you about it. Did I tell you that I have deposited all the correspondence re Mulebone at Yale? What a place that will be for finding out what happened to us Racians! And did I tell you that Mrs Rapp wrote me [she would] give me all the Thurman material as soon as she gets around to it?

    forty nights of pleasure to you and days of sin and leisure!

                                    Carlo

                                              October 13, 1942
                                              101 CPW

    Roberta LeNoir, singing That Eagle, got developed at long last hier soir.[5]

1. *Hughes thought the song "Freedom Road"—written with Langston's friends Emerson Harper and his wife, Toy—would achieve the success of the World War I anthem "Over There." "Hitler, he may rant. / Mussolini, he may rave. / My boy's protecting freedom / With the bravest of the brave . . . ," the song proclaimed. Hughes's friend Kenneth Spencer introduced the song at Café Society, where it earned a permanent place in the program. Hughes mailed his song to black colleges and high schools and sent out news releases to step up publicity.*
2. *Like those of the other speakers, Van Vechten's remarks were about "the history of the Negro's association with dancing as a fine art and the contribution that will be made to it by the newly organized Negro Dance Company," reported the* Amsterdam News *on October 17. Alain Locke also gave a speech.*
3. *This was an unfounded rumor. Harold Jackman was not drafted.*
4. *Hurston's autobiography,* Dust Tracks on a Road, *was published by J. B. Lippincott in 1942.*
5. *Rosetta—not Roberta—LeNoir performed "That Eagle of the U.S.A.," a song Hughes composed with Emerson and Toy Harper, at the Stage Door Canteen and again at the dinner given in honor of Van Vechten at the Port Arthur Restaurant in Chinatown on November 20.*

Hughes began a lecture tour on November 18 and was unable to make the November 20 dinner tribute to Van Vechten. He sent his regards by way of a piece of comic verse that is reprinted in the appendix.

CARL VAN VECHTEN TO LANGSTON HUGHES, NOVEMBER 25, 1942

Dear Langston, It was like a Christmas tree with everything on it coming to me and when Canada Lee read your poem it was like all Christmases everywhere from the beginning of time come to me at once. You MUST know how very sweet your poem is and how much I loved it but you can never know the sensational way Canada read it! As a speaker (FIRST TIME, please) I followed him and fortunately for all I wasn't nervous and I got a big hand too. Mr Knollenberg was detained in Washington, but Mrs Knollenberg came down and was enchanting and picturesque and gracious, which exactly describes her. Essie Robeson came in from Enfield (Paul was in Chicago and wrote me a wonderful letter) and I never heard from Miss Waters at all! This all happened after the opening of my photograph show (of which I enclose the catalogue and the publication of Dance Index with my ballet material (of which I am preserving a copy for you), so Saturday found me pretty much of a wreck. Thanks for your TWO telegrams (one to Roberta). Somebody took down all the speeches and Im having a box made for Yale of the whole affair with the letters and telegrams etc. so you can go into this sometime. I had such a good time I am determined to have at least one a year. Please dont miss the next one!

My love to you,
Carlo!

November 25, 1942
101 Central Park West
New York City
EN 2, 8748

Margaret Walker is A honey.[1] I am photographing her.

1. *Margaret Walker made her public debut the night of the November 20 tribute. She was introduced by Stephen Vincent Benét, who described her work as "being written about her people and for her people with humor, character, and with directness." Van Vechten photographed Walker on November 27, 1942.*

Dear Langston, Everybody else seems to hear from you but me: Tom Rutherford tells me you are definitely set to go into the army, having passed your physicals, etc., directly you are through with your lecture tour.[1] However, I see by this morning's paper that the age limit is NOW 38, and I believe you were born February 1, 1900, so I guess we can all breath freely again.[2] I hope so. Listen Private Hughes, if you ARE going into the army, or anyway on general principles, leave a note somewhere that your letters, manuscripts etc. are to go to me for Yale. I havent got The Sun Do Move yet, or my letters to you, or the Jimmy Davis stuff, or lots of other material. If you DONT go to war, may be you'll have time to dive

LANGSTON HUGHES WITH
ETHEL "TOY" HARPER, WINTER 1946

into some of this before McNutt[3] asks you to be a welder or something. But if NOT, please make a NOTE and SIGN it and have it witnessed, and tell Mrs. Harper besides! There is lots more to talk about, but I hope you will be home soon!

> Apples and oranges to you, and whatever you want!
> Carlo

> December 6.
> 101 CPW: NYC

Please give a thought to that shawl, too.[4] That shouldnt be left floating!

1. *When Hughes received his questionnaire from the Selective Service in October, he answered: "I wish to register herewith, as a citizen of the United States, my complete disapproval of the segregating of the armed forces of the United States into White and Negro units, thus making the colored citizens the only American group so singled out for Jim Crow treatment, which seems to me contrary to the letter and spirit of the Constitution and damaging to the morale and well-being of not only the colored citizens of this country but millions of our darker allies as well." The board responded by classifying him 1-A, or imminently draftable.*

2. *Roosevelt didn't sign the order deferring the draft for men over 38 until 1943. Hughes was born in 1902, so he would still have been eligible.*

3. *Paul McNutt was chairman of the War Manpower Commission.*

4. *Van Vechten hoped Hughes would donate one of his most precious possessions to the collection at Yale: a shawl worn by Sheridan Leary, his grandmother's first husband, when he accompanied John Brown on his historic raid on Harper's Ferry. The shawl was riddled with bullet holes. Hughes would eventually donate it to the Ohio Historical Society.*

Mrs. Harper was Ethel Dudley Brown Harper, a friend of Hughes's mother's, whom he usually referred to as "Aunt Toy." She and her husband, Emerson, became like family to Hughes when he moved in with them in 1942. Emerson was a musician and Aunt Toy, a dressmaker. Their two-room flat at 634 St. Nicholas Avenue served as Toy's sewing room and Emerson's studio, as well as the eating and sleeping quarters of all three residents. Hughes would live in Harlem with the Harpers for the rest of his life.

LANGSTON HUGHES TO CARL VAN VECHTEN, JUNE 6, 1943

634 St. Nicholas Avenue
New York, 30, New York

June 6, 1943

Dear Carlo,

I have been trying to write you for a month of Sundays to thank you for sending me so many of the Canteen photographs, and to tell you and Fania how pleasant and friendly it was to find your greetings at Lincoln on the day I received the white and gold hood and became a Dr!¹ . . . Also I wanted to tell you (for benefit of Yale) that Richard B. Moore has opened a bookshop, the Douglass Book Center, at 141 West 125th Street, where he has many old Negro books on display and for sale—you know, he has quite a collection of slave biographies, etc. He also has two charming sets of Negro LIBERTE ET EGALITE postcards published in Paris during the Exposition celebrating the anniversary of freedom in the French West Indies. Certainly the Collection ought to have them, if it hasn't. They're a dollar a set—some in colors . . . Of course, I've saved all the manuscripts of FOR THIS WE FIGHT for Yale.² Been writing on it right up to today. Lots of changes, comme toujours au theatre. Earl Jones is in it, big as life. Also Rosetta Lenoire, and the head colored hostess lady at the Canteen. . . . Also Charlie Swing, who was amazed to see himself on a postcard. (I asked him if he was the boy on the one you sent me. He was.)

And wants you to send him one (or some) too. His address is 182 St. Nicholas Avenue. . . . Been so busy since I got through lecturing that I haven't seen anyone. But hope to see you soon. Have gangs of stuff for Yale. . . . You must go to the Golden Gate to one of those Battle of Song sometime.[3] Standing room only today, and Georgia Peach had them shouting in the aisles. They had six uniformed nurses present to bring the shouters to! Dozens of quartettes (of five, six, and seven members) sing for hours. Langston

1. *Hughes received an honorary degree, a doctorate of letters, from Lincoln University on May 18, 1943. On May 23, 1943, Hughes wrote proudly to Arna Bontemps: "You should see my degree, which is all in Latin. The University also gave me a hood of velvet and satin and silk and what-not. . . . Carl Sandburg gave the commencement address, which was good, but like almost all other addresses, including my own, too long. I was sitting on the platform for more than three hours and got both hungry and sleepy." Hughes had once considered Sandburg his "guiding star."*
2. *Hughes wrote the performance piece* For This We Fight *for the Negro Freedom Rally on June 7, 1943, in Madison Square Garden. The show sold out. It had a cast of two hundred.*
3. *The Golden Gate Ballroom rivaled the Savoy in popularity when it opened in 1940.*

CARL VAN VECHTEN TO LANGSTON HUGHES, JULY 19, 1943
(POSTCARD)

Dear Langston, Jim Crow's Last Stand* is here at <u>last</u>![1] I'll try Ivan Black on Miss Primus.[2] Thanks for writing Ottley.[3] And thanks for the Yale material to come. I hope you can help us out on Powell Lindsay.[4] Kiss Brick on the right ear for me, please.[5]

> Your affectionate
> Carlo

Monday

Edward III is drafted.

*I love it & have ordered <u>more</u> to give away.

1. *Hughes's collection* Jim Crow's Last Stand *was published by the leftist Negro Publication Society of America in 1943.*
2. *Pearl Primus was a dancer Van Vechten wanted to photograph.*
3. *Van Vechten wanted the black journalist Roi Ottley to contribute the manuscript of his 1943 book, "New World A-Coming": Inside Black America, to the James Weldon Johnson Collection.*
4. *Powell Lindsay was a director who was the head of the Negro Playwrights' Company and the Negro Drama Group.*
5. *Bricktop was performing in Saratoga Springs.*

Dear Carlo,

I do not yet know who Edward III is, nor what PTO is, and such lack of knowledge worries me no end. . . . Kappo Phelan, a cousin of Noel's who writes New Yorker style stories is here . . . Morton Zwabel[1] arrives today . . . SOCIAL NOTE: Miss Carson McCullers and I were entertained at dinner Sunday at the home of Mr. Jimmy Elliott, leading colored barman here. He had chickens and champagne for us. And was it good! . . . Sugar Hill[2] is very mad at Harlem about the riots.[3] The letters I have received from the better colored people practically froth at the mouth. It seems their peace was disturbed even more than the white folks' . . . Several glamour girls of the Hill's Cafe Society–La Mar Cherie set lost their fur coats that were in storage for the summer (nee pawn shop), so I don't blame them for being mad . . . I reckon I lost my watch which was in Herbert's being cleaned — and Herbert's was cleaned out! Well, time was when I had no time-piece before, so I guess I can get along. . . . The MUSICAL COURIER, I understand, contains my picture. And THE NEW WORLD, a Canadian magazine, contains an article of mine on THE FUTURE OF THE NEGRO with a big picture spread of the colored artists. Perhaps Yale should also know that THE PROTESTANT has an article by Claude Williams on Detroit. . . . The Princess Dulaney[4] is also known as Princess Wahoo.

Sincerely,
Langston

Yaddo
Saratoga
8/5/43

P.S. According to the TIMES the man who owns the Braddock where the first shot was fired lives on Central Park West right down by you.

1. *Morton Zabel was the editor of* Poetry *in the mid-1930s.*
2. *Sugar Hill, bordered by Bradford Park and Washington Heights, was home to Harlem's aristocracy.*
3. *In early August, a riot erupted in Harlem when a white policeman shot a black soldier after the soldier intervened in an argument between a black woman, Margie Polite, and the policeman. The soldier was wounded, but Polite shouted up and down the Harlem streets that the soldier had been killed. The New York State Guard had to be called in to establish peace, but not before five civilians were killed and five hundred arrested.*
4. *A fortune-teller Hughes visited in July.*

Langston!

> Edward I: Edward Waterman[1]
> Edward II: Edward Donahoe[2]
> Edward III: Edward Atkinson, now a buck

private at Camp Upton. They go on to VI and Edward IV is McKnight Kauffer! The other two are unknown to YOU. I have already explained PTO,[3] but your lack of education appalls me! I wish to God I mighta joined you at Jimmy Elliott's dinner. . . . I know <u>why</u> the riots and so I can understand and they MAY have done some good locally, but the effect on the general public is extremely bad and has given the other side unexpected comfort and ammunition. If such riots are organized the people who organize them should do so publicly and then others would know what they are doing and WHY they are doing it. Ferinstance, the suffragettes broke windows, then waited till they were arrested, then went on a food strike till they were released, then broke more windows and went through the whole program again. Eventually they got the vote. The trouble is in the present case too many people are saying, "Negroes are hoodlums and DANGEROUS. Keep them DOWN." If they had a good reason to break these windows they should have announced it.* Propaganda, as you know, is often more effective than action. Thank you for the use of the hall! Anyway, if the riots were organized° and intended as a lesson to extortionists and exploiters, WHY did they attack pawnshops which hit hard at Harlem! Pearl and Mildred[4] tell me many of their friends lost their dearest possessions. Ive got The Protestant and will order the New World if you'll tell me the date. Ive asked for this before. Any luck with Ottley about his manuscript? He is sailing soon, I hear. Did I send you Sergeant Daniel's (James) address? Here t'is:

H and S Company 847th.Eng.Avn.Bn.
A P O No 644
%Postmaster, New York, N Y

No, you never sent me a set of Los Angeles colored postcards. I have written for information regarding them. Arna has written the most beautiful paper about me for the Yale Gazette.⊞ And Mr. K is writing a piece thanking the principal donors (to date). All this for the October number. Mildred Thornton (nee Perkins) being in very bad health is leaving us which leaves a hole in our lives which nothing or nobody else can quite fill. Fortunately Pearl Showers is still here. The boxes for your manuscripts (seven or eight of them) are here and will probably be here till you get back as I still need a couple of signatures. They are very handsome and imposing. I found I hadnt enough Defender pieces for a box yet. The Sun do Move is not yet boxed because you said I hadnt the final draft yet. But gradually you are piling up in grand style in this collection and may be studied at leisure by some future historian of American writers in general and the Race in particular. Excuse me for being long winded and allow me to remain affectionately yours,

August 12, 1943

Carlo!

*and of course the effect would have been doubled without the looting.
°I have been told just this by people who should know.
✠It is like a very <u>warm</u> obituary!!

1. *Eddie Wasserman had changed his name to Waterman.*
2. *An editor at Knopf during the 1920s.*
3. *Van Vechten used "PTO" as an abbreviation for "photograph."*
4. *Pearl Showers and Mildred Thornton; they worked as domestics in the Van Vechten–Marinoff household.*

LANGSTON HUGHES TO CARL VAN VECHTEN, AUGUST 13, 1943

Yaddo
Saratoga Springs
New York

August 13, 1943

My dear Carlo,
I am delighted to know what PTO is, and who the various Edward's are. How do you know the other two are unknown to me? I am acquainted with a great many people! . . . Among other things, the address of Mr. Theodore Ward's shoe shine parlor turned up. It is: Mr. Theodore Ward, 621 East 63rd Street. Chicago, Illinois. (If that was the address you-all used for the Yale letter, then I have no other, nor as yet have received any from Chicago where I wrote.). . . From Mr. Roy Ottley I have had no answer. He probably has the WORLD on his mind, not Yale[1] . . . Who said the riots did any good? And how are all those people going to announce in advance that they are suddenly going collectively mad? . . . The VERY BEST column on the riots is Dan Burley's BACK DOOR in this week's AMSTERDAM NEWS.[2] Be SURE to read it! It's wonderfully funny! . . . All the best cullud people declare they have been

set back Fifty Years. I don't exactly know from what. . . . Thanks for Jimmie Daniel's address. I've sent him some songs. . . . Harold Shapiro, a
Boston composer here in residence, has made an amusing jazz setting of
one of my MADAM TO YOU poems, the one about the Number Writer.
He thinks Duke should set them all. If so, I think Jackie Mabley[3] should
sing them. . . . If you get no cullud colored post cards from Los Angeles,
I have two or three left I will give the collection, so let me know. . . . I am
so sorry Mildred Thornton is leaving you. I shall miss her. Please tell her I
hope she gets well soon. . . . I have several sacks full of letters and manuscripts sorted out here and ready for those Yale boxes. I believe you were
informed that the last draft, mimeographed, of THE SUN DO MOVE,
could be gotten for One Dollar from the IWO[4] Educational Department,
80 Fifth Avenue, New York. And I thought you told me once that you had
gotten it. That is all there is of it, as I think you have the rest. At least, I
thought I gave you all of it . . . I am delighted that Arna's piece is
good. . . . The song to which Bill Robinson dances on the drums in
STORMY WEATHER is mine.[5] . . . I reckon you saw the article about
Duke Ellington with colored pictures in the current, August 7, (last
week's, rather) SATURDAY EVENING POST.[6] THE NEW WORLD for
August (Toronto, Canada) contains my article. I have been meaning to
order some. But deadlines and things have prevented me from doing so.
One more to meet on a radio script Monday, then maybe I can write a few
letters. I have hundreds to answer. My public sends me a great deal of
affection, my publishers so few checks. . . . Mrs. McCullers has gone
home to Georgia as her father is not well. . . . Mr. Morton Zabel has
arrived . . . Miss Margaret Walker departs early next week for New York.
She has given up her teaching position and will lecture all over this fall
and winter, being booked by one of the big agencies. . . . She doesn't
make carbons of her stuff, so apparently has to keep the drafts. . . . Miss
Blanche Calloway[7] is in town and will visit Yaddo Sunday at three. . . .
This Sunday Rev. Lawson is holding a celebration at the Golden Gate
with ALL the Quartettes, and the Three Big Sisters, including Georgia
Peach. I should have told you before as maybe you might have gone and
reported to me. I know there will be great shouting all over the place, and
many nurses reviving folks! I wish I could be present. . . . Carson thought
the Lillian Smith[8] phamplet swell, and took it to Georgia with her. One of
the leading characters in her now being-written book is a Negro boy
looking for God but doesn't find him—not even in New York.

Sincerely, with leapfrogs,

Langston

1. *Hughes was skeptical about Ottley's new book,* "New World A-Coming": Inside Black
America. *He remembered the title incorrectly in an August 5, 1943, letter to Bontemps:*

"NEW DAY A-COMIN' says Mr. Roi Ottley. NEW NIGHT would probably be better. (How sweetly optimistic is the cullud race!)"

2. *Dan Burley's August 14 "Back Door Stuff" column included anecdotes about the looting, but he ended on a serious note: "The outburst was in reality a revolt of the common people against the symbols of white supremacy they contend with every day."*

3. *A vaudeville performer, Jackie "Moms" Mabley was the first successful female African American stand-up comedian.*

4. *International Workers Order.*

5. *The song was a musical version of Hughes's 1923 poem "Danse Africaine."*

6. *"The Duke of Hot" was the title of a lengthy profile of Duke Ellington in the August 7, 1943,* Saturday Evening Post.

7. *Blanche Calloway was Cab's sister, and an entertainer in her own right.*

8. *The writer Lillian Smith was the author of the 1944 antilynching novel* Strange Fruit.

CARL VAN VECHTEN TO LANGSTON HUGHES, AUGUST 16, 1943

Dear Langston, What letters you write! Maybe I do too. Sometimes I wonder if OUR letters wont be the pride of the Collection . . . I havent got around to sending yours to me yet, but will this winter! My remarks on the riot were based on sworn statements of certain harlemites that they had been organized for weeks (everybody had his orders). Yours are based on the belief that it was a casual turnout. I have an idea that both of these theories were true. A FEW had planned something, probably, and the mob trailed after. You are right that Harlem is much more indignant about (and much more aware of) these riots than downtown and I dont know any one more indignant than Pearl Showers and Mildred Thornton. So it isnt all Sugar Hill indignation. Roi Ottley came to be photographed Saturday and definitely we are getting the manuscript. When he saw your beautiful boxes, he almost swooned and exclaimed, "The Schomburg Collection doesnt keep things like this." Of course, nobody else does and even Yale wouldnt, if I didn't do it myself. The material turned into this Collection is in a condition thanks to my energy and foresight which not many other Collections can boast. It is hard work and endless, but I think it is worth it. I have a DEFINITE FEELING that in LESS than five years Yale will have a chair of Negro life and culture[1] and whoever sits in that chair will have the best source material in the country to guide him . . . Anyway Ottley promises all letters, manuscripts, what not, in the future. Of course I have the IWO Educational Alliance edition of The Sun Do Move, but I had noted something on the other mss. about waiting for the "final draft" and got confused. I'll have a box made for TSDM soon.[2] Florence B Price[3] of Chicago sends me her Symphony in C Minor (manuscript of the full score) . . . This is Harold's work.[4]

ALL RIGHT: Edward IV is Edward James
                    Edward VI is Edward Nelson Barclift who dances in
                    TiTa (Ive already explained TiTa to you, so dont ask
                    about that.)

The address you send for Theodore Ward is indeed not the one we gave to Yale, so I will try this with pleasure. Jackie Mabley, while good, is not important enough to sing YOUR songs, but I'll be glad to get Shapiro's mss if you can get it for me, and I hope the Duke sets the others. I expect to be deluged with manuscripts and letters when you return. The boxes will still be here, as certain things have to be signed. Besides, I have to catalogue the contents of these boxes before they go and am up to my ears in other matters for the moment. TOM says they are investing in 5oo Lillian Smith pamphlets to give to Junior Hostesses at the Canteen. I didnt see Duke Ellington in the Post but have sent for this. I note you have ordered a copy of the New World for the Collection and I have sent for the Musical Courier. Even if you dont reply to other letters, answer MINE. Our correspondence will be historical. Tell Mrs. McCullers that "God Cant Be Found in New York" would make an excellent title. Bricktop had a birthday last Saturday. Was she up your way? Dorothy P is moving again. So is Dr Sidney. Have you read a book called Race, by Ruth Benedict?⁵ When are you coming back?

                                  fondly,
                                  Carlo

                                                     August 16, 1943

*The enclosed p.c. is obscene but the cullud gal is just as attractive (or even more attractive) as or than the ofay girl. A copy goes to Yale!

1. *Yale didn't begin a program in Afro-American studies until 1968.*
2. The Sun Do Move.
3. *Florence Price was a black composer.*
4. *Harold Jackman played an important role in the early stages of the James Weldon Johnson Collection.*
5. Race: Science and Politics, *by the anthropologist Ruth Benedict, was published by the* Viking Press *in 1943.*

LANGSTON HUGHES TO CARL VAN VECHTEN, AUGUST 20, 1943

Yaddo
Saratoga Springs
New York

                                                     August 20, 1943

Dear Carlo,
Where can I get some more of those BLACK AND WHITE cards? I want a whole gang of them! . . . And thanks enormously for all those

handsome pictures of myself you keep digging up from somewhere! When did I ever look like that? You must have known I needed some pictures for the Harlem Branch Library and various other folks who have written me for likenesses. . . . I just wrote a good column for the DEFENDER on THE DETROIT RIOT BLUES based on the old Clara Smith record with the refrain, <u>This Morning</u>.[1] Remember? Something about, "I even hate to call your name this morning." Drafts, naturally, for Yale. . . . Where did Miss Peterson move this time? I believe she is cullud, moving so much! . . . Writers War Board declares my script, IN THE SERVICE OF MY COUNTRY, best ever written on the subject of the cullud soldier.[2] That I do not believe, being modest, but anyhow I will give the drafts to Yale. . . . They have not yet reported to me on PVT. JIM CROW. . . . Margaret Walker says her parents used to whip her all the time when she was little, and regretted she was so frail they could not whip her more. Her mama used to say, "My poor child's back is too weak to stand all it ought to have on it." . . . Jackie Mabley could too sing anybody's songs!!!!! . . . Enclosed is a new MADAM TO YOU.*

Sincerely,
Langston Litt.D!

*Three in next issue of POETRY with "Crowing Hen Blues." Also have poem in FANTASY (950 Herberton Ave., Pittsburgh, Pa) this month so I hear tell.

1. *In October 1942 the* Chicago Defender *offered Hughes a weekly column, which he called "Here to Yonder." A thousand words per column earned him fifteen dollars. He began his column on November 21. On September 11, 1943, the "Here to Yonder" column was titled "The Detroit Blues." It began: "An old colored man in Detroit was sitting on the front stoop of a ramshackle rooming house around the corner from Hastings street a few days after the riots. The tune of an ancient Clara Smith record kept running through his head as he hunched over in the warm sunshine." The song included lines about the riots and the war, like: "My only child is Over There, / Don't know why, don't know where. / My only child is Over There / This morning." Hughes connected domestic and international problems in his final lines: "Maybe if the President himself would just explain . . . to the old man on that ramshackle porch in Detroit and to the rest of the confused colored people in America—to the whites, as well, for that matter—all of us would understand better that it is the Facist-minded here in THIS country as well as abroad we must fight in order to win this war in any real sense."*

2. *The Writers' War Board and the mayor of New York asked Hughes to contribute to their efforts to contain mounting racial tensions in the city. Hughes responded with a few songs and two short plays, "In the Service of My Country," about racial cooperation among the workers who built the Alaska–Canada highway, and "Private Jim Crow," about segregation in the armed forces.*

CARL VAN VECHTEN TO LANGSTON HUGHES, AFTER AUGUST 20, 1943

Cher ami, The Clara Smith Blues you refer to (NOW in Yale) is Nobody Knows the way I feel this morning.

  "   "   "   "   "   "   "   "

I feel like I could scream and cry
But Im so downhearted I'd rather die
Nobody knows the way I feel this morning.

It is MY favorite of Clara's songs and I used to cry when I heard her sing it on or off a record. Miss Peterson hasnt moved YET. I found those black and white cards on Broadway, three for a nickle. I'll try to find the place again and send you the address. Your new Madam poetry is beautiful. Here are some more pictures. We are painting and things have to be moved and things turn up. So leopard skins and Coty perfumes and blue-berry pancakes to YOU!

Carlo!

Monday

LANGSTON HUGHES TO CARL VAN VECHTEN, AUGUST 31, 1943

Dear Carlo,

Jay Jackson, you know, who did the Black and White card, is cartoonist for THE CHICAGO DEFENDER, so I wrote him about where to get them. He says they may be ordered from Mr. Samuel Tichnor, Colour-Picture Publishers, 292 Main Street, Cambridge, Mass., and that he has sold them some two or three designs. He does not know how many have been printed yet, and had not even seen the one we know. . . . My brother's wife's baby is a girl. It makes three he has. . . . Mr. Arna Bon-temps has removed himself to Fisk.[1] . . . Miss Blanche Calloway is still summering in Saratoga, but Miss Bricktop at last reports had returned to New York. . . . The NEW REPUBLIC is shortly due to carry an article of mine which they bought before the riots but asked me to bring up to date, so I put in there about how the Negro has been set back fifty years in the opinion of the better folks.[2] . . . Miss Carson McCullers has a wonder-

ful story in the August HARPER'S BAZAAR. (Or did I mention it to
you?) About a hunchback, a criminal, and a woman.[3]

Sincerely,

Langston

Yaddo
Saratoga
August 31, 1943

1. *Bontemps became a Fisk University librarian in September 1943. He had a master's degree
in library science from the University of Chicago.*
2. *Hughes published "Down Under in Harlem" in the March 20, 1944, issue of* The New
Republic.
3. *"The Ballad of the Sad Café."*

CARL VAN VECHTEN TO LANGSTON HUGHES, SEPTEMBER 9, 1943

Dear Langston, I have just got off eight of those big boxes of theatre
photographs (By CVV) for the NY Public Library. YOU occur twice in this
series. I have also written about you in a paper about the theatre aspects
of the JWJ Collection for the Theatre Annual. Would you be good
enough to notify me when the paper about the Better folks of Harlem

CARL VAN VECHTEN AT THE STAGE
DOOR CANTEEN. PHOTOGRAPH
BY SAUL MAURIBER, C. 1943

appears in the New Republic. I cant tell
you how much I thank you for telling
me about Carson McCullers' ballad of
the Sad Café. We have Harper's Bazaar
in the house, but I never look at magazines unless somebody (it is usually
You) tells me to. This one is out of this
world and terrific and wonderful. I have
the Tom Boggs Anthology for Yale and
your letter will be laid in it when it goes
there.[1] The Collection is full of such
association items. With the original
title, the poem is beautiful, but with the
changed title it will cause many people
to wonder, coming from you . . . Are
there any other Negroes represented in
this book (which you will write in when
you return: WHEN DO you return?)?
Fania had just about become an A1 cook
when she took to her bed. Food in

restaurants now is about a dollar an ounce. I come home hungry and nib-
ble on biscuit or candy. But the best antidote for a good appetite, I find, is
the Stage Door Canteen: The sight of so much food always drives my
appetite away and I can work there contentedly for hours with no hunger
pains. The Italian news is not bad, is it?

fondly,

Carlo!

September 9, 1943

I have just photographed an extremely beautiful merchant seaman
(cullud) age 21 who used to be an undertaker and is devoted to the arts.
He is from Cleveland, Marcus Jackson by name!

1. *Tom Boggs's 1942 anthology was called* An American Decade. *He included Hughes's
poem "There Are Words like Freedom." Hughes wrote to Boggs from Yaddo on September
1: "Thank you for sending me your beautifully printed AMERICAN DECADE. I am
delighted to be included therein. But listen, wsn't that poem when I sent it to you called
REFUGEE IN AMERICA? At any rate, that is the title under which it appeared in THE
SATURDAY EVENING POST, and it is about refugees in America, not Negroes who certainly don't have any where near the freedom that refugees in America have. So those
noble words I speak of do not make us quite so sentimental. We still have to ride in Jim
Crow cars." Boggs wrote back that he was unaware of the title change.*

*I*n February 1944, Hughes began a nearly-four-month-long tour that took
him through Chicago, Cleveland, Kansas, West Virginia, Arizona, and
Utah. His tour was sponsored by Feakins, Inc., perhaps the most prestigious speaking bureau in the country. Hughes was the agency's first black client.

LANGSTON HUGHES TO CARL VAN VECHTEN, APRIL 23, 1944

Odgen, Utah

April 23, 1944

Dear Carlo,
The Yale Collection ought to be receiving JAZZ, a wonderful little
magazine published in England, all mostly about Negroes and our music.
Some of the articles in the recent numbers they've sent me are by cullud.
Others are by Nancy Cunard. The March (1944) issue is devoted entirely to

the late Jelly Roll Morton. Another issue has a tribute of Ma Rainey—
mentions the greatness of Bessie. (I am doing a Defender column on it—
as to why the Race has no such magazines itself.

It is published at:

Jazz Sociological Society
140 Neasden Lane
Neasden, N.W. 10.

Noël now has 15 dogs! Also a goat dairy that would delight Rita.

April 21 is historical. After my reading at Berkeley Interracial Community Church, I had made my first thousand $'s—the most I have ever had
at once in life! Shortly I shall begin to pay my debts.

(I may also give a party!)
> Two Thousand to You!
> Sincerely,
> Langston

<u>CARL VAN VECHTEN TO LANGSTON HUGHES, APRIL 28, 1944</u>

Dear Langston, Thanks for all the thises and that's you have sent me
for Yale and for myself . . . I recently sent a lot by express and yesterday
the Library truck came down from New Haven and took away five big
packages which were too valuable to send any way but personally conducted. Thanks also for your letters and cards and all the information
therein contained. Col Bousfield of Huachuca¹ has sent me no colored
posters as yet, but I have written Lt Davis² to ask him if he will help me
find the postcards and I have contacted all and sundry about Jazz. Are
you sending your copies of this? I am very excited about your having
$1,000. I wish I had. My taxes always surprise me with my pants down
and not a cent to pay them. But I pull through some way. Can you let me
know a little more definitely about what number of the New Republic
contains your paper.* The opening of my show in Harlem was most successful, but I wish you had been there. It is marvellously displayed which
is an unexpected pleasure: I wasn't quite expecting THAT of a High
School³ . . . So come back soon and we'll all be glad to see you.

In the meantime four red roses and MORE MONEY to you!

April 28

Last night I attended the "Best Built Man" contest at the Y in Harlem.
This was fun and inconceivably grotesque in spots . . . The Adonises
(white and cullud) are obliged to POSE to display their muscles and

some of the attitudes were honeys. I still havent heard the story of your MUGGING.[4] . . . Fisk is going along grandly and Arna has begun the display of certain items.

*Its very difficult to get back numbers of anything now.

1. *Fort Huachuca, in southeastern Arizona, was the largest black army post in the country.*
2. *Jimmy Davis.*
3. *Van Vechten donated a collection of his prints, called the James Bowers Peterson Memorial Collection, to the Wadleigh High School for Girls in Harlem. Peterson was the founder of the New York* Age *and the father of Van Vechten's dear friend Dorothy Peterson, who was a teacher at the school.*
4. *In January 1944 in Harlem a man attempted to mug Hughes, threatening him with a razor. After a brief struggle, Hughes emerged "triumphant with the weapon!" he told Margaret Anderson of* Common Ground. *He wanted to donate the razor to the James Weldon Johnson Collection at Yale but the police kept it as evidence.*

V*an Vechten was in the process of establishing the George Gershwin Memorial Collection of Music and Musical Literature at Fisk University. The collection was named after Gershwin because of his use of black musical forms and also because he was white. As Van Vechten explained in 1960 in an interview for the Columbia University Oral History Project: "I said at the time that I thought this would interest people of other races to go and look up things in their respective places." Time magazine found Van Vechten's formula intriguing: "One way to get Negroes to visit white schools and vice versa is to tempt them. Novelist Carl Van Vechten* (The Tattooed Countess, Nigger Heaven, Peter Whiffle) *has done just that with a scheme involving Yale and Fisk Universities," the magazine reported in its March 6, 1944, issue. The collection didn't open officially until 1947.*

CARL VAN VECHTEN TO LANGSTON HUGHES, AUGUST 25, 1944

Dear Langston, Here are a few questions I want you to answer about the new batch. The are two novels in Portugeuse by Castro Soromenho. One of them at least has a Negro subject, but is <u>he</u> a Negro? There is a program of George Oppenheimer's Here Today, offered by the Little Theatre Company of St. Louis. Is this a Negro company? . . . There is a manuscript of The Negro Speaks of Rivers. Is this manuscript in the hand of Margaret Bonds? Who drew the picture of you in chalk. Is it Aristides Gatos* and who is HE? I like the picture, by the way. And who is Geraldine Prillerman (?) who drew the picture of the naked blonde with a cache-sexe on the drum? These are all the questions I will ask you tonight. I have read the second installment of Richard Wright's I Tried to be a Communist and like it much better than the first.¹ It is obviously a part of the autobiography he is writing and if it is all like this it will be interesting to read.°

hand and glove,

Friday August 25

*I cant read the signature.
°Further I have been reading Howard Fast's Freedom Road.² It is an amazing account of the Reconstruction era. Rich in incident & argument. but the characters are not rendered credible.

1. *Wright's explosive indictment of his former allies appeared in two parts in the August and September 1944 issues of the* Atlantic Monthly.
2. *A novel published in 1944 by Duell, Sloan, and Pearce in New York.*

LANGSTON HUGHES TO CARL VAN VECHTEN, AFTER AUGUST 24, 1944

Dear Carlo,

I do not know if Soromenho is colored or not? In Portugal a colored person would have to be black to be Negro, anyhow. The letter accompanying the books is in that box, from someone at the Modern Museum here in New York who might be able to answer your question. They were just sent to me out of the clear sky. . . . I do not recall anything about the HERE TODAY program, nor even that it was in that box. . . . The NEGRO SPEAKS OF RIVERS manuscript is in the hand of the composer, Margaret Bonds. . . . The crayon picture of me was made by a grade school kid at P.S. 113 where all those kid letters are from in the two packets. . . . Geraldine Prillerman is a colored girl who studied "art." Virginia State, I believe, but is now in New York. . . . Tolson's book of poems, RENDEZVOUS WITH AMERICA is out.¹ . . . Mr. Ralph Ellison, 306 West 141st Street, New York, 30, is going to be a good writer, I believe, so why don't you ask him to give all his drafts to Yale, as he is writing all the time, and likes to write so well he won't do any other kind of work if he can help it, and will probably in due time pile up a great big lot of stuff, which you-all might as well have. . . . My stenographer has just arrived so I will have to go to work. Since she has brought me a piece of cake, I will eat it first.

Sincerely,

Lang

P.S. You need a new typewriter ribbon!!
I saw Howard Fast the other day and he told me his book was good.

1. *Dodd, Mead published the poet Melvin B. Tolson's first collection,* Rendezvous with America, *in 1944.*

CARL VAN VECHTEN TO LANGSTON HUGHES, AUGUST 29, 1944

Hello Langston, I have followed your suggestion and asked Ellison for his manuscripts. Thanks for your letter of information. I have also written Arna asking him for dinner and you will be invited if he accepts. Is Tolson a Negro and who publishes his Rendezvous with America? (I mean is this published by a downtown firm or do I write to a Negro house for it?) Is PS 113 largely Negro or not at all? You dont send me a dollar, gate!

anyway powerful ideas to you!

Carlo

August 29, 1944

Ive spruced up my ribbon a LITTLE, you see.

LANGSTON HUGHES TO CARL VAN VECHTEN, AUGUST 31, 1944

Dear Carlo,
Tolson is cullud. Dodd Mead published his book. (Downtown.) PS 113 is largely cullud, too.
"Anna Lucasta" is an amusing old time comedy dramer.[1] Audience seemed to love it last night—as did Aunt Toy.
Thanks for the new ribbon. Also Miss Maynor.

Langston

1. *Philip Yordan originally wrote this drama about the trials of a Polish American family but no producer would option it. Harry Wagstaff Gribble and Abram Hill, the founder of the American Negro Theatre, rewrote the play as a comedy about a black family and it became one of the biggest hits of Broadway's 1944 season.*

1945–1949

Van Vechten continued to solicit and arrange contributions to the James Weldon Johnson Memorial Collection while Hughes began a four-month national lecture tour on January 29, organized once again by Feakins, Inc. He opened his tour at the State Teachers College in Eau Claire, Wisconsin. After a few engagements in Michigan, Wisconsin, and Massachusetts, he headed for the South. "I do not wish under any circumstances, to travel by bus in the South," he told his booking agent. Despite his careful planning, Hughes could not have anticipated the degree and variety of Jim Crowism he would encounter all over the United States during his tour, particularly on the Southern leg. He wrote Arna Bontemps about an infuriating incident in a March 2, 1945, letter: "One steward in Alabama asked me if I was Puerto-Rican. I said, 'No, hungry!' and he handed me a menu. The waiters recognized me, and were most courteous. A Navy man who sat in front of me asked if I was Cuban. I said, 'No, American. Are you Cuban?' " Hughes ended his tour with a June 7 appearance at a high school in Summit, New Jersey.

June 26, 1945

Dear Carlo,

This was a good lecture season and at long last I can pay off all my lit-tle debts—which I am devoting this here evening to doing! You remem-ber you lent me a couple of hundred right after the Park Avenue crash.[1] It was a great help to me at the time, and certainly a mere check can't begin to repay you for your kindness but, anyhow, here a check is! The interest will have to be my gratitude for your friendship all these years, and your kindnesses not only to me, but to many artists and writers, and to the Negro people. . . . Happy Birthday to you, although a bit belatedly! . . . Cool breezes and watermelons to you all summer long,

Sincerely,
Langston

1. *When Hughes's patron, Charlotte Mason, dismissed him on May 26, 1930, a loan of two hundred dollars from Van Vechten helped see him through the difficult time that followed.*

Dear Langston, Your very sweet letter and the cheque arrived this minute and touched me very deeply. I kept no record of any transaction like this and it was a complete surprise to learn that you owed me money. However, I know some one at the moment who needs help very badly and I will apply part of it to that cause; the rest of it will go towards buying more expensive books for the George Gershwin Memorial Collection at Fisk University.

I have been thinking about you all day anyway because I have been working on your material for Yale. . . . You asked me if your records' had arrived: they never have. FURTHER: I havent yet seen the pocket ver-sions of your books presumably to appear in the ARMY series.[2] Are those out yet? When they are out I think Bill Raney[3] can get me the set.

Hearts and Flowers to you and after the war maybe I'll be coming to
YOU for crutches,
Carlo

June 27, 1945

Of course, I am very happy you are making money.

1. *Early in the summer, Hughes mailed to his close friends a set of four ten-inch records called* The Poems of Langston Hughes. *The selection of thirty poems covered the range of his poetic style. The collection was issued by the Asch Record Company.*
2. *"The Army series" refers to cheap paper editions of popular books produced for overseas military personnel.*
3. *Eventually, William Rainey became an editor at Rhinehart, but Van Vechten knew him first as a soldier.*

CARL VAN VECHTEN TO LANGSTON HUGHES, JULY 9, 1945

Dear Langston, I went out of town on Friday and didnt have a chance to listen to your records until last night when I ran them over several times with glowing enthusiasm. You record, of course, like a thousand dollars; your charms gets over and your enunciation is as clear as a bell. Moreover you are straightforward; there is nothing phoney or arty about your delivery. You give us the substance of your poems undiluted. And what a substance! I more and more appreciate your genius; you have a special aptitude for speaking for the "people" and more and more you become their official spokesman and more and more you tell the world what the more miserable members of your race are seeking. Your career has been a consistent one: you have never let your Negro friends down and I am sure they will never let you down. On the contrary you are being built up into a most imposing figure. Thank you for the use of the hall and keep up the good work.

My warmest affection and admiration to you always,

Carlo

July 9, 1945

LANGSTON HUGHES TO CARL VAN VECHTEN, JULY 11, 1945

July 11, 1945

Thanks for the nice note about the records, Carlo. I am glad you like them. . . . I will be down soon and bring you some more Yale stuff, and check up on whatever you have there for me to sign, etc. . . . GLAMOUR magazine for July has a couple of articles you-all should have—one by Walter White, and various Negro pictures. You also must get the BOOK OF AMERICAN NEGRO HUMOR just published by THE NEGRO DIGEST COMPANY in Chicago with an introduction by me, and a couple of columns of mine in it. . . . HARPER'S, too, has an article by Earl

Brown on DETROIT.[1] . . . And Arna tells me that TIME, June 18, Page 51, had a piece about his cousin, Leslie Collins,[2] but I didn't see it. . . . I have one million unsorted letters for Yale, but I probably will need an Endowment in Research to get around to reading them. I can't hardly read the ones I get every day, and do the rest of my work.

Sincerely,

Langston

1. *Earl Brown, a correspondent for* Time *and* Life *magazines, published "Detroit's Armed Camps: The Collapse of Industrial Discipline" in the July 1945 issue of* Harper's *magazine.*
2. Time *magazine reported that Leslie Collins was the recipient of the nation's first Ph.D. in American culture. Today, he is a professor emeritus at Fisk University.*

CARL VAN VECHTEN TO LANGSTON HUGHES, OCTOBER 2, 1945

Dear Langston, The material I have on hand from you is nearly ready to go to Yale; so don't be amazed if you get a receipt almost any minute. I have been reading a lot of the Here to Yonder columns and am more and more impressed by them. I feel certain that a volume of Simple[1] and another volume of assorted columns would sell, particularly if they were offered bound in paper at say a price of $1 so that our people could buy them freely and read them on the subway as they went back and forth from work. Of course this wouldnt keep ofays from buying them too! I am quite mad about Deep are the Roots.[2] The afternoon we saw it, you could feel that the audience was deeply disappointed the boy and girl didnt get married. After this I think there is nothing connected with race discussion or action that wouldnt be tolerated on the NY Stage. The acting is as good as any I can remember, except for Gordon Heath who doesnt even begin to touch his part. If he were good in it he would be the sensation of the ages.

Why doesnt somebody write a play in which Negroes and whites talk and eat and walk together but in which no mention is made of color? The plot would concern something else and their friendship would be taken for granted and not explained. And I still think the idea of Beecher's All Brave Soldiers[3] would make a magnificent stage show. The papers seem to have stopped yelping about St Louis woman.[4] . . .

Hands and gloves to you,

Carlo

Tuesday

1. *Hughes introduced his wildly popular everyman character Jesse B. Semple, or "Simple" for short, to readers of his* Chicago Defender *column in February 1943. At first Hughes used this character as a way to cultivate black interest in the war, but it wasn't long before Simple was spouting opinions about everything from politics to Shakespeare. Hughes would eventually publish five collections of his Simple columns, beginning with* Simple Speaks His Mind *in 1950.*

2. *A 1945 play by Arnaud d'Usseau and James Gow,* Deep Are the Roots, *was about an interracial love affair in the deep South during World War II.*

3. All Brave Soldiers: The Story of the SS Booker T. Washington, *by John Beecher, is an account of life aboard the SS* Booker T. Washington, *a racially integrated ship. It was published in 1945 by L. B. Fischer Publishing Co.*

4. St. Louis Woman, *a Countee Cullen–Arna Bontemps collaboration, was a musical comedy about black high life at the race track in the 1890s. Many black critics were disturbed by its celebration of seedy lifestyles. The show opened on Broadway in 1946.*

LANGSTON HUGHES TO CARL VAN VECHTEN, NOVEMBER 9, 1945
(ON HOWARD DAYTON HOTELS "FRIENDLY SOUTHERN HOSTS" STATIONERY)

Hotel Anderson
Anderson, Indiana

Nov. 9, 1945

Here sleep I—in the best hotel—in this former Klan territory! The sun do move!

Langston

O n October 29, 1945, Hughes began a brief reading tour in the Midwest. Moments of triumph like the one he describes above were rare. Generally the tour was a disappointment. "I never was so glad to get back to New York before in my life!" he wrote Arna Bontemps in a November 14, 1945, letter. "The Middle West raw, cold, and prejudiced, trains crowded and smoky and travel the worst I've seen it so far, soldiers going home and mad, and air like pre-cyclone weather in Kansas used to feel, with open and under-cover gust of fascism blowing through forlorn streets in towns where desperate little groups of interracial Negroes and whites are struggling to keep things halfway decent."

CARL VAN VECHTEN TO LANGSTON HUGHES, JANUARY 22, 1946

Dear Langston, I was glad to hear from you, particularly that you are going to see Mary Blanchard. We didnt hear from her at all at Christmas which is so unusual I telegraphed her and got a belated reply that she had been ill but was recovering. Please report on her condition to me. Of course, she is old, but hitherto she has never SEEMED old. Her eyes, too, may be bothering her more. I have at least three unopened bundles from you, maybe more, but I do not think three have come since you went away, tho I cannot be sure, as, indeed, you have been gone some time. It would be SAFER to notify me every time you send a box. At least I have acknowledged receipt of each box as it came. I am sending three terrific cartons off to Yale today with more theatre material. This is beginning to look like the authoritative Collection of Negro Theatre Material and believe me we have a lot. As you cross the country, pick up more for me, please. . . . Every donor's name is mentioned on the material he sends for these theatre boxes and also on the table of contents inside each box. There are FOUR boxes of Theatre material from the James Weldon Johnson private Collection alone. . . . By the way the boxes for his manu-scripts, pamphlets etc are here and they are a pretty sight. I think you have about as many at Yale (you will have more!) but nobody else sizes up to these. You can see them when you return as they will not be gone until I have read the letters in the letter files. Countee died actually of uremic poisoning of the kidneys, but he had terrifically high blood pressure. I was one of the pallbearers at the Funeral which was somewhat stuffy and much too long. Several people spoke up and prayed and sang and the whole business lasted over two hours. There were no Spirituals, surpris-ingly. You seem to miss all the EVENTS, like deaths and weddings and dinners, but I've taken in most of the Harlem ones for the past twenty years. WHEN ARE YOU GOING TO DO THAT ARTICLE FOR THE DEFENDER PLEASE?[1] Are you going to get back in time for St Louis Woman? Arna is enchanted with the way rehearsals are going, but that is a bad sign in the theatre, at least that is the superstition. Cant you get Mrs Showers the Spingarn medal for wrapping some 800 cartons for Yale and Fisk?[2]

four brightcolored roosters to you and a hen to make them happy!

Carlo

January 22, 1946

I think it is wonderful you are flying. Me, I <u>love</u> to fly!

1. *Hughes had promised to write about the James Weldon Johnson Memorial Collection in his* Defender *column. He would finally do it in 1949.*
2. *Van Vechten wrote in his catalogue notes: "Pearl Showers has been our second maid since 1931. It is she who does all the bundle wrapping for Yale."*

Countee Cullen was only forty-two when he died. The funeral was held at his father's church, Salem Methodist Episcopal Church in Harlem, the same church in which he had married Yolande Du Bois in 1928. He was survived by his widow, Ida Cullen, whom he had married in 1940.

Before he died, Cullen was enraged and troubled by the criticism St. Louis Woman *had received from blacks, many of whom took their cue from the play's most vociferous critic, Walter White of the NAACP. With its risqué story line,* St. Louis Woman *was an easy target. Cullen died before the play went into rehearsal.*

CARL VAN VECHTEN TO LANGSTON HUGHES, JULY 4, 1946

Dear Langston, I read through Fields of Wonder last night with great pleasure.[1] Of course I am already familiar with a great many of these poems but I like them all the better for knowing them better. The poem called "END" has always been a great favorite of mine, since I encountered it in the Yale manuscripts, and I never read the last line, "There is no door" without a shudder. I like the title enormously too and it suits the book, but you havent been quite true to your avowed intention of making this book purely lyrical without social or political significance. The last group, of course, is almost entirely composed of songs of this character. You have never written anything more political than "When the Armies Passed," "Indonesia," or "Today." This may or may not be a mistake; certainly it would be a mistake to announce your intention of writing a "purely lyrical book."

I told you I heard St Louis Woman was doing badly. And now it is closing. I feel very sad about this and very sympathetic with Arna and Ida Cullen. But I have managed to photograph Ruby Hill this week and expect to photograph Pearl Bailey tomorrow![2]

Happy Fourth of July to you, sir,
Carlo

July 4, 1946

Do you want "Fields of Wonder" back or what?

Remembrance seems to be misspelled both in the Table of Contents & on page 30.

1. *Hughes sent his new poetry manuscript to Van Vechten for his reactions, a tradition since his first book,* The Weary Blues *(1925).*
2. *Ruby Hill and Pearl Bailey had leading roles in* St. Louis Woman, *which closed on July 6, 1946.*

LANGSTON HUGHES TO CARL VAN VECHTEN, AUGUST 8, 1946

August 8, 1946

Dear Carlo,

Thanks immensely for your letter about FIELDS OF WONDER. I have just revised the manuscript and returned it to Knopf's, taking the word "lyric" off the title page so nobody will get confused.[1] Our plan is to follow this with another book of mostly Negro poems, then in a couple of years or so, a COLLECTED POEMS.

I don't believe I sent you a copy of PERO CON RISAS, the Argentine edition of NOT WITHOUT LAUGHTER, after all, as I find two here, so I am sending one along in the next batch of Yale material. Also here is a card about a booklet you may want to order, if you haven't it already.

Did I, by any chance that you recall, ever give Yale my big gray sort of ledger-like looking scrap book of clippings from the WEARY BLUES, etc. days? Is it listed on your catalogue? I've been looking all over for it lately, not remembering having given it to you.

My Auntie Reed died in Lawrence the other day. She was about the age of Mrs. Blanchard.

And Emerson departed today for New Mexico to take a job with a band out there.

STREET SCENE's lyrics are almost done. I'll let you see them soon, and there are piles of drafts you'll have after the opening. (Scheduled for Christmas week in New York.)

Henri Cartier-Bresson and his wife, a very charming Javanese dancer,[2] just had luncheon with us. She is preparing for winter appearances here. In case you might want to photograph her, their address is: 315 East 58th Street, New York. (You took pictures of him once, remember?)

Please give FIELDS OF WONDER back to the fellow when he brings the Yale material. And I'll see you soon as I get through with this SS SHOW—which I trust will be in a week or so now. I have to go up to Elmer's again tomorrow to work.

Sincerely,
Langston

1. *Hughes took Van Vechten's advice temporarily, but his determination that this book would be his "first more or less lyric book," as he told Blanche Knopf, won out, and the word appeared on the dust jacket when the book was published in April 1947.*
2. *Bresson's wife was Retna Moerindiah. She was known as Elee.*

*I*n late August 1946, Elmer Rice asked Hughes to join him and the composer Kurt Weill as a lyricist on their new project, an opera based on Rice's play Street Scene, for which he won the 1929 Pulitzer Prize. In his August 8 letter to Van Vechten, Hughes refers to their venture as the "SS show." Having admired both the play and its movie version, Hughes was thrilled for two reasons. Not only did he long to work with Rice, but also he was aware of the precedent-setting move the playwright had made by inviting a black writer to participate in a project about white people. Hughes remembered ten years later: "That I, an American Negro, should be chosen to write the lyrics of Street Scene did not seem odd or strange to Kurt Weill and Elmer Rice. They wanted someone who understood the problems of the common people. . . . I did not need to ask them why they thought of me for the task. I knew."

LANGSTON HUGHES TO CARL VAN VECHTEN, AUGUST 15, 1946
(POSTCARD)

There's a poem of mine in the July 30 New Masses' so I see. . . . Street Scene is at the doing over and over stage. Shows, I do believe, were designed to bring authors to an early grave!
                                        Langston

1. *"Labor Storm."*

CARL VAN VECHTEN TO LANGSTON HUGHES, AUGUST 16, 1946
(POSTCARD)

Dear Langston, I know all about the theatre, and nothing can surprise me. But you wont mind the work if it is a success. Thanks for the tip about

the masses. You will never believe it but Josh White¹ kept an engagement
with me and is photographed.

Ever,
Carlo

August 16

1. *A black blues and folk singer and guitarist.*

Street Scene *was scheduled to open in New York on January 9 at Broadway's Adelphi Theatre. Hughes, Rice, and Weill were trepidatious; their
Philadelphia opening on December 16 had gone so badly that the three
men were forced to rework the play before the New York debut.* Billboard *magazine summed up the complaints of most reviewers with its advice: "A gargan-
tuan task of scissoring is needed." A team of show veterans including Oscar
Hammerstein helped trim the production by thirty minutes. Still, by the end of
their three-week-long Philadelphia run, the show had lost over $50,000. Carl
and Fania attended the night of* Street Scene's *New York opening.*

'STREET SCENE': Three who collaborated on the musical version of the famous play due Thursday at the Adelphi—l. to r.
composer Kurt Weill, author Elmer Rice and lyricist Langston
Hughes.   *Photo by Graphic House*

FROM *PM,* JANUARY 6, 1947

CARL VAN VECHTEN TO LANGSTON HUGHES, JANUARY 19, 1947

Dear Langston, We LOVED Street Scene and so did everybody else in the very crowded theatre. In fact it is terrific. You have done a very tight job; the music is beautiful; the cast perfect . . . and as for Stoska:[1] I kiss my hand to the sky! . . . The applause was genuine and very big; ALL the papers have long enthusiastic articles again today[2] (I'd send them to you but they go to Yale, of course!) and I guess you will be a very rich man. . . . I dont want to appear too grandfatherly, but I HOPE you will invest all the money you can afford to so that you will have an income come rain come shine. Success of this kind in the theatre does not come every day. . . . Fania loved it just as much as I did and wants me to tell you so (she couldn't have loved it MORE than I did!)

Although I work about 14 hours a day, material for Yale has piled up on me to such an extent that I am very very far behind, but I HOPE to get it cleared up some day. Two large packages came from you this week.

I congratulate you and Hearts and Flowers to you!

Carlo

January 19, 1947

1. *Polyna Stoska of the Civic Opera was a leading member of the sixty-person* Street Scene *cast.*
2. *New York reviewers loved the tighter version of* Street Scene. *In the* New York Times, *Brooks Atkinson called the score "fresh and eloquent" and the cast "superb." As for Hughes's lyrics, they "communicate in simple and honest rhymes the homely familiarities of New York people and the warmth and beauty of humanity." The New York* Daily Mirror *declared the play a "solid hit." The New York* Daily News *called it "a work of great individuality which makes no compromise with Broadway formula."*

L*angston, Carl, and Fania met in Nashville at the opening of the George Gershwin Memorial Collection of Music and Musical Literature at Fisk University on April 25, 1947. Hughes stayed on to participate in a seminar on contemporary writing with Arna Bontemps and the poet Robert Hayden, who had recently joined the faculty.*

Hughes and Bontemps decided to collaborate on an anthology of black American poetry. When Hughes approached Blanche Knopf with the idea, she was skeptical. A senior editor at Doubleday immediately offered him $1,000 for

the book, a much larger advance than he had ever received from Knopf. Hughes
presented the new contract to Blanche as if Arna had arranged it, but Blanche
saw through his ruse. In July, Hughes confessed to Bontemps: "Blanche was
apparently kinder mad because Knopf did not get the Anthology, but I DO
NOT CARE about that." As usual, Van Vechten was privy to the back and forth
between Blanche Knopf and Hughes.

CARL VAN VECHTEN TO LANGSTON HUGHES, MAY 9, 1947

Langston, my fine lad, Blanche absolutely repudiates your statement
that she turned down your poetry anthology. I thought it was strange
because I have had many talks with her about it and in none of them did
she indicate Knopf was not publishing the book. As a matter of fact a
salesman became so enthusiastic about the idea that the chances of publication increased rather that diminished. For the sake of the record,
Blanche wrote you in November 1946 that it was impossible to discuss
this matter by mail, and suggested you come in to talk it over next time
you visited New York. This she says you have never done.

AT THE OPENING OF THE GERSHWIN MEMORIAL ROOM
AT FISK UNIVERSITY ON APRIL 24, 1947. LEFT TO
RIGHT: CARL VAN VECHTEN, HELEN CHANNING
POLLOCK, LANGSTON HUGHES, FANIA MARINOFF,
AND CHARLES S. JOHNSON

The Knopfs are very interested in my idea of a Charles S Johnson autobiography and Alfred has written him to this effect.

Chester Himes,‡ whose next book is coming out in the fall, wants a place to live this summer while writing a new one. He called me today to ask about Yaddo. I dont know how you go about this but I told him you would know. PLEASE answer this by return mail and tell me to whom he should write and whether Yaddo is free or you pay something. You know: give us the answers!*

I am so deluged in Yale, Fisk, Gertrude Stein, and NOW Mary Garden,¹ that developing or printing pictures is out of the question for the time being, but you know that you will get pictures as soon as they are available.

A couple of weeks ago I wrote Wallace Van Jackson asking him to send me five copies of the catalogue of the current show of the Countee Cullen Collection at Atlanta. Could you get these for me . . . ?°

Philippa Schuyler and her mother will be entertained by Mr Babb² at Yale tomorrow . . . and the money from the James Weldon Johnson Memorial Fund (for a statue) is being transferred to Yale to start an endowment fund for the James Weldon Johnson Memorial Collection of Negro Arts and Letters.

I thank you,

Carlo

May 9, 1947

*<u>Important</u>
°They came in the mail just as this was written.

1. *Van Vechten had offered to help the opera singer Mary Garden write her memoirs, and she had sent a draft to Van Vechten for his opinion. The nature and amount of his criticisms enraged her, and a heated correspondence between them went on from January until June 1947.*
2. *James T. Babb was the assistant librarian at Yale.*

V an Vechten asked Hughes for the Atlanta material because Hughes had temporarily taken up residence in the city, having accepted an invitation to spend the spring semester of 1947 as a visiting professor of creative writing at Atlanta University, a historically black institution. He offered a course in creative writing, as well as one called "The Negro in American Poetry." In mid-May, he went to New Orleans for a vacation.

May 13, 1947

Mr. Carl Van Vechten
101 Central Park West
New York 23, New York
Dear Carl:

I am just back from New Orleans and find your letters and cards awaiting me. Since I have a lot of work to read for my Creative Writing class today, I am dictating this note to you quickly in order to answer your questions.

I expect by now that Yaddo has perhaps filled its quota for the coming summer. I know that Arna Bontemps and Horace Cayton[1] have already been invited there. However, the person to whom Chester should write is: Mrs. Elizabeth Ames, Yaddo, Saratoga Springs, New York. The only charges at Yaddo were for laundry which had to be done outside, but all other living expenses are taken care of by the estate.

The period of time for which one is invited seems to vary greatly, running from three weeks to three months, I suppose depending upon the number of guests expected during the season.

Shirley Graham[2] might be a possibility to write a book about Karamu House; she is a former Clevelander and is very familiar with the work there. Certainly Arna would be a good person if he had the time for it.

I suppose you were so long in receiving the Cullen Collection catalog because Mr. Van Jackson left for Washington and Liberia about a month ago.

You must go to New Orleans sometime as it is a <u>de</u>lightful town.

Sincerely yours,
Langston Hughes

LH:wmb

---

1. *A black sociologist and educator.*
2. *The writer Shirley Graham was the second wife of W. E. B. Du Bois.*

CARL VAN VECHTEN TO LANGSTON HUGHES, AUGUST 17, 1947

As Professor of English at Atlanta, dear Langston, and as lecturer to the People, don't you think you owe it to yourself to find out something about Chancellor Williams (colored) whose The Raven[1] (a novel about 200,000 words long with many important Negro characters) was published several years ago and whose pamphlet "What I would do if I were white" was reviewed by Eleanor Roosevelt.

ALSO what about W Adolphe Roberts?[2] (See Who's Who in America). Wenzell Brown says on page 80 of "Angry Men—Laughing Men"[3] that Roberts is colored. He was born in Jamaica (or the Barbadoes).

Chester Himes's new book will be out in a minute.[4] It is utterly magnificent, but the subject on ALL counts is extremely controversial. Certainly Chester is more sensitive to the shades of race neurosis (on BOTH sides) than any one who has yet written on the subject.

I've found a WONDERFUL Negro pianist, genre classical, age 22.

Hearts and Flowers to you,

Carlo!

August 14, 1947

Love to that wonderful Toy!

Thanks for telling me about Nellie.[5] I hear about her since from all and sundry!

1. The Raven *was published by Dorrance in 1943.*
2. *Hughes would meet the journalist and novelist Walter Adolfe Roberts in October 1947 when Hughes was invited to Jamaica to lecture at the University College of the West Indies.*
3. Angry Men, Laughing Men: The Caribbean Caldron, *a sociocultural study of the Caribbean, was published in New York by Greenberg Press in 1947.*
4. Lonely Crusade *was published by Knopf in 1947.*
5. *Hughes admired the singer Nellie Lutcher, who would record Hughes's song "Baby, What's Your Alibi" in the spring of 1950.*

LANGSTON HUGHES TO CARL VAN VECHTEN, SEPTEMBER 9, 1947

September 9, 1947

Dear Carlo,

In the package which I sent you by messenger today were several DEFENDER columns. With these enclosed, it makes all up to date of the new ones.

Did you ever find the missing ones? Perhaps they were mixed up with the STREET SCENE stuff. But some must have been in the packages which I sent you by express from Atlanta just before leaving there. What I could do is send you carbons of the missing ones from my files—except

that I don't know which ones you have or haven't. And also, of course, the
first drafts would not be attached, since they were with the ones that are
lost.

How much of the history of the cullud race is lost!

About the Chester Himes book I feel much as the NEGRO DIGEST
does this month or the New York POST today. The leading character just
doesn't have any sense hardly. And there is too much confusion between
what he thinks and what appear to be broad general statements of the
authors until one can't tell which is which and neither are sane to me.[1]

I've been asked to do the English commentary on a Jean Cocteau film
made in Africa.[2] I'm to see it today.

Sincerely,

Langston

---

1. *Blanche asked Hughes to do a blurb for* Lonely Crusade, *but he refused on the grounds
he outlines here.*
2. L'Amitié Noire.

LANGSTON HUGHES TO CARL VAN VECHTEN, SEPTEMBER 18, 1947

Dear Carlo,

Who is the nice looking cullud lady you sent me two or three times
now on a postal card, just a few days ago most recently. I already have her
in my album, but don't know who she is. . . . Enclosed a carbon of a letter
just sent to Blanche with the manuscript of a new book of Negro poems.[1]
I think I spoke to you about Jacob Lawrence as a possible illustrator.[2]
Blanche writes that she doesn't know who he is! So I am trying to tell her.
What do you think of the whole idea? . . . Jan Meyerowitz played some
more of his opera version of MULATTO to me the other night, which I
like.* He's about half done with the setting. The contracts came back
from Milan for the Italian production, too, of it as a play. . . . Handy's
bringing out musical setting of FREEDOM TRAIN poem in a couple of
weeks. . . . And I reckon I told you they asked me to do the English commentary of L'AMITIÉ NOIRE, the French short made in the Chad for
which Cocteau did the French commentary. Swell little picture with
some wonderful music and dancing—but the New York censors are making them cut out many of the best shots unfortunately. . . . I'm trying to
get off to Mexico or somewhere next week on a vacation before November lectures began. Have the proofs of STREET SCENE folio to correct

first, and a couple of other little things to do. Also, get vaccinated. . . .
Hello to Fania.

Sincerely,
Langston

*ORIGINAL version of MULATTO—NOT the Broadway one! So you won't suffer so.

1. *For the first time, Hughes did not send his manuscript to Van Vechten immediately. Instead he sent his new book of poems,* One-Way Ticket, *to Arna Bontemps first.*
2. *Hughes eventually had to pay Lawrence, a well-known black artist, six hundred dollars of his own money when Knopf refused to pay for the illustrations.*

*I*n June, the German composer Jan Meyerowitz, who was Jewish, contacted Hughes. He had set two of Hughes's blues poems to music and wanted to discuss the possibility of collaborating with Hughes on an opera. Mulatto spoke to him: "I had been very German in thought and every other way, and I had been forced out, rejected by my country. I knew what Mulatto was about. . . . Musically it is my and my people's story too."

CARL VAN VECHTEN TO LANGSTON HUGHES, SEPTEMBER 19, 1947
(POSTCARD)

Dear Langston, I like your letter to Blanche and the whole idea, but you would convince her more readily of Lawrence's ability by informing her there are thirty pictures by him in the Museum of Modern Art, just around her corner. I send out many postcards every day and "nice looking cullud lady" describes a good many of them. It would even fit Lena Horne! Why dont you send me the card and I'll return it to you properly identified. Even without the rape of the young lady I am most allergic to Mulatto. It's the young man whose manner is most offensive to me. Are you postponing my Yale column indefinitely again? I hope not. My hand in yours,

Carlo!

Friday

LOOK at Jackie Robinson on the cover of TIME and what a write-up!'

1. *The September 22, 1947, issue of* Time *devoted its cover and six pages to Robinson, his career and personal life. It also saluted his boss, the Brooklyn Dodgers' owner, Branch Rickey. The cover features a beaming Robinson surrounded by giant baseballs. Under Robinson's name the caption reads: "He and the boss took a chance."*

LANGSTON HUGHES TO CARL VAN VECHTEN, SEPTEMBER 22, 1947

September 22, 1947

Dear Carlo,

The nice looking colored lady has been returned to you for identification. . . . The young lady in MULATTO got raped only in the Broadway version, not in my original—which is being set to music. Nor does the young man behave so badly in the original either. He simply does not have much sense like Hamlet and Don Quixote and Chester Himes' heroes. Poor boy! And on Colonel Tom's plantation nobody thought of a psychiatrist. . . . The opera sounds like nothing I have ever heard before. The composer performs it in a German accent which adds to its unusualness and intrigues me no end. . . . I hope to go to Ted Ward's opening,¹ then go to where the summer has gone on a vacation. But first I shall send you a few more columns.

Sincerely,
Langston

1. *The black playwright Ted Ward wrote the Reconstruction Era drama* Our Lan'. *It opened at the Royale Theatre on Broadway on September 27, 1947.*

CARL VAN VECHTEN TO LANGSTON HUGHES, SEPTEMBER 22, 1947
(POSTCARD)

Dear Langston,

Thanks for two more "Here to Yonders." Where is "Frank's." Written up by Bill Chase.¹

What is "Skifferings" please?

Hearts and Flowers to you!
Carlo

Monday

1. *Bill Chase had a column in the* Amsterdam News *called "All Ears."*

September 23, 1947

Dear Carl:

Do you mean to tell me that you do not know where "Frank's" is! Or do I read your card wrong? Frank's is the large restaurant on the north side of West 125th Street, exactly 315 W. 125th Street. It is just about the oldest restaurant in Harlem and was, I understand, a solid and well known steak and fish place long before Harlem became colored. Many of the old waiters are still there, and some of the old patrons still come from other sections of the city to dine there occasionally.

"Skifferening" I am not sure about, but I rather imagine it derives from Dan Burley's Blues-Boogie-Woogie style of piano playing (Chicago style), which he calls, "Skiffle."

I trust you will send me soon a postcard picture of Nell Lutcher. Thanks immensely for the fine picture of Jacob Lawrence.[1] If you see Blanche please tell her what a good artist he is.

Sincerely,
Langston

1. *Van Vechten photographed the artist Jacob Lawrence on July 31, 1941.*

V *an Vechten wanted Hughes to organize his* Street Scene *material for Yale, but he had bigger problems. The FBI had removed Hughes's name from its "Key Figures" list in 1945, concluding that his Communist affiliations were relatively minor. But in June 1947, J. Edgar Hoover requested a report on Hughes that would prove conclusively that he was a Communist. Hughes faced the familiar accusations at every stop on his lecture tour.*

Meanwhile, he was moving from St. Nicholas Avenue to his very first real home, a house on East 127th Street, in the heart of Harlem. The property would be owned jointly by Emerson and Toy Harper, and Hughes.

March 5, 1948

Dear Carlo:

The Friendship Press, 156 Fifth Avenue, New York 10, N.Y., has published a quite colorful map of American Negro achievement designed by Lou Jefferson, priced at 50¢. In case you do not know about this, I imagine you would want it for your collection.

I had been hoping to get a chance to come down to arrange the STREET SCENE material this week, but the CHICAGO TRIBUNE, aided and abetted by the American Legion in Illinois, has started a terrific red-bating campaign against me, which has just caused the cancellation of three of my speaking engagements in Illinois next week under the threats of withdrawal of Community Chest sponsorship from the Urban League and other sponsoring organizations, and in Springfield actual threats of mob violence. This has piled up my correspondence so, and there has been so much writing and wiring back and forth that I have not yet been able to complete the arrangement of the Negro poetry anthology, which must be turned in on Monday before I leave for the West Coast. Also, I am moving from my studio to this apartment, with great piles of material and files to move and rearrange. Also, I have to work out my income tax report, so I do not see when I shall have an extra hour between now and when I get on the train. Thus I would suggest that you either send the STREET SCENE material to Yale as it is or else keep it until I return East in June. As I believe I told you, the complete score has just been published by Chappell.

It was certainly nice seeing you at the party the other evening, as well as several old friends I have not seen in a number of years. Lots of good wishes to you and I will be writing you shortly.

Sincerely,
Langston

Mr. Carl Van Vechten
101 Central Park West
New York, New York

*R*ED-TINGED POET TO SPEAK AT WINNETKA PRIVATE SCHOOL *was the headline of a March 1 article in the* Chicago Daily Tribune. *The newspaper notified readers that Hughes was scheduled to speak at the exclusive North Shore Country Day school on March 15, and suggested that the school had booked Hughes without full knowledge of his rap sheet with the House Committee on Un-American Activities, a document that had been growing steadily since 1938. The paper's strategy worked. The next day a story headlined* CALL ON SCHOOL TO CANCEL TALK BY POET HUGHES *reported: "Officials of North Shore Country Day school, an exclusive private school in Winnetka, called conferences yesterday to discuss demands that they cancel the scheduled appearance March 15 of Langston Hughes, Negro writer of revolutionary poetry and member of communist front organizations." Hughes was still fuming about the ordeal when he wrote about it in his May 15 "Here to Yonder" column: "Aided and abetted by the Hearst press and the Chicago Tribune, they have front-paged from Coast to Coast that I am a 'self-confessed card-carrying member of the Communist Party,' which is not now and has never been true," he told his readers.*

CARL VAN VECHTEN TO LANGSTON HUGHES, MARCH 9, 1948

Poor Langston, To mix metaphors the wages of writing controversially about politics is that you have to face the music. It will be worse, you know, before it is better, and if there is a war I dare say they'll pop you in a nice clean jail . . . Poor Langston!

Apparently you dont understand the Library situation. No library has sufficient funds to engage enough people to do all the work that has to be done. In any case libraries have great difficulty engaging anybody with sufficient background to do special organization work. The basements of the British Museum and the NY Public Library still have UNOPENED packages of letters and manuscripts dating back to the 18th century. I have tried therefore to send all the material for the Johnson Collection to Yale completely organized so that research workers could use it with ease. Street Scene is beyond me, however: I need your help. It can wait till June. As Is it is no good to anyone. I count on you in June, but you promised to write that article for the Defender in January (I have this in writing) and it hasn't appeared yet, so can I depend on you?

I also have material here, some for Helen Pollock's Northeastern Collection, for you to sign.

Also I discover from a letter you sent in that the original manuscript for Masters of the Dew went to Atlanta. Have other original manuscripts gone to other libraries? This should be noted in my descriptions of the Yale material.

What in the world are you moving to 634 for?[1] I thought you had bought a house at 20 East 127 Street . . . Are you moving TWICE? What wonderful ambition!

Hearts and flowers to you!
Carlo!

March 9, 1948

1. *Probably Hughes's constant wanderings had left Van Vechten confused. He had bought a house at 20 East 127th Street, and he was moving from 634 St. Nicholas Avenue to live there.*

LANGSTON HUGHES TO CARL VAN VECHTEN, APRIL 28, 1948
(POSTCARD)

Hollow Hills Farm
Monterey, California

April 28, 1948

Dear Carlo, I'm here for ten days or so catching my breath after an adventurous lecture tour . . . Carmel Valley is lovely as ever and Noel has three little deer. . . . Did you see Father Dunn's TRIAL BY FIRE when it was played in New York?[1] I saw it in Pasadena and found it hair-raising. I hope it will be performed many places since the rights are available to amateur and little threatre groups. . . . In June I will be your way.

Langston

1. *Hughes was so impressed with the play that he devoted his May 22 "Here to Yonder" column to it: "A young Catholic priest, Father George H. Dunn, has written one of the most effective, provocative, and moving plays on race relations in America that I have ever seen." The play was based on the real-life tragedy of a black family burned out of their home by white racists in a small town near Los Angeles.*

Hughes was driven back to Carmel by the hostility and threats he faced on his tour. He declared himself and his values intact in his May 15 Defender column: "Gerald L. K. Smith, the Klan and others who think like them, evidently want me to retire from the American lecture platform—but they have another want coming." Still, he agreed when his booking agent suggested he take a year off from the lecture circuit.

CARL VAN VECHTEN TO LANGSTON HUGHES, OCTOBER 11, 1948

Dear Langston, Last night I read Montage of a Dream Deferred[1] with mounting excitement and interest. It is one of your best and offers magnificent opportunities to the typographer: I long to see it in print. To all intents and purposes these poems have the intrinsic value of separate poems, but they are strung on an idea and phrases which hold them together more closely than the ordinary book of poems. Still any one can be removed from its setting without affecting its sense, and it is not essential to read the book in order, altho it probably reads better that way. The new group arrived this morning and I have not looked at that yet.

Meyerowitz plans are handsome.[2] He called me but he is going away (or perhaps has gone) and so nothing can be done by way of photography at present. I can do nothing about Piquion at the moment either as I have too much other work on hand. . . . A package from YOU goes to Yale today along with the Thurman letters. HE doesnt seem to have liked Louise much.

I am having my portrait painted (AGAIN) at midnight by a skater![3]

Hearts and Flowers

October 11, 1948

1. Hughes had written breathlessly to Bontemps about his new manuscript on September 14: "The new poem is what you might call a precedent shattering opus—also could be known as a tour de force." Montage was a book-length poem in five sections.
2. Meyerowitz was planning a student cast for Mulatto, something he could put together for $5,000. The black concert singer Muriel Rahn was interested in appearing as a guest star.
3. The skater was Harrison Thompson, who painted Van Vechten in the evenings after his show, Howdy, Mr. Ice.

A Negro History Week tour took Hughes to Black Mountain College, an experimental learning community in Black Mountain, North Carolina, founded in 1933 by the German emigré and Bauhaus artist Josef Albers.

LANGSTON HUGHES TO CARL VAN VECHTEN, FEBRUARY 11, 1949

Black Mountain College,
Negro History Week, 1949
Dear Carlo—
This is just about the most amazing campus I have ever seen in my natural life—and interracial, too! . . . I've invited one of their exchange students from Berlin—a former Nazi Hitler Youthite to spend a week with Aunt Toy in Harlem! Come June.
Langston

I n late February, Hughes assumed a three-month teaching position at the Laboratory School at the University of Chicago. As visiting lecturer on poetry, he taught students ranging in age from four to seventeen. He was popular among students and faculty alike.

LANGSTON HUGHES TO CARL VAN VECHTEN, APRIL 3, 1949
(ON THE UNIVERSITY OF CHICAGO LABORATORY SCHOOL STATIONERY)

April 3, 1949

Dear Carlo,
Thanks so much for your and Fania's wire.[1] And I wish I had seen you to invite you-all up to the house afterwards as we had an old bottle of

Haitian rum Mme. Jacques Romain² brought me a couple of years ago I had saved for the opera opening and Guillen³ brought Bola de Nieve⁴ along who played "out of this world." But I couldn't find you in the crowd.

The school loves the pictures of the poets and is having them mounted. You've probably had a note from the director by now.

See current (April) AMERICAN SCHOLAR, and HARPER'S for mentions of me for Yale. And I left a big box of proofs of POETRY OF NEGRO etc. in New York to be delivered to you this week.

That's a very nice review of your Stein book in the Sunday Herald Trib.⁵

What did you think of the op-pry? It was all new to me, too, never having heard or seen it in action before. I found it less grand and more amusing than I had expected it to be, but needing somwhere a really big musical moment.

Yours for perfect pitch,
Sincerely,
Langston

1. *Carl and Fania sent their traditional congratulatory wire at the New York City Center opening of Hughes's opera about Haiti's Jean-Jacques Dessalines, written with* Troubled Island *composer William Grant Still. This was the first opera written by blacks to be produced by a major American company. It had taken more than ten years to reach the stage.*
2. *Hughes had admired the radical poet Jacques Romain, who had died in Haiti in 1944. With Mercer Cook, Hughes translated Romain's novel* Gourverneurs de la Rosée, or Masters of the Dew. *It was published by Reynal and Hitchcock in June 1947.*
3. *Hughes met the Cuban poet Nicolás Guillén during a visit he made to Havana in February 1930. Hughes and his work would have a substantial impact on Guillén's poetic sensibility.*
4. *Bola de Nieve is a nickname for Ignacio Villa, a well-known Cuban musician.*
5. *In his April 3, 1949,* New York Herald-Tribune *review, W. G. Rogers praised* Last Operas and Plays, *the Gertrude Stein collection edited by Van Vechten, for "pointing out how diversified her creative endowment was." He also liked Van Vechten's introduction: "Readers prone to skip prefaces should start this book at the beginning."*

CARL VAN VECHTEN TO LANGSTON HUGHES, APRIL 5, 1949

Dear Langston, Toy said to Fania, "If I can get some people I'll ask you up after the opera tonight," but nothing more was heard of this, nor did we see her again. We looked for you seriously for ONE hour back stage after the opera. You were not to be found.* We saw Still, of course. We enjoyed Troubled Island a lot. The music is conventional (and so, to be frank, is the book) and rather lightoperaish, but it is tuneful and never dull. The direction was appallingly bad. With better direction the music and book would both be brightened considerably. The orchestral direction was brilliant. I found the best singers (and actors) the girl who sang the opening lullaby, Richard Charles, the tenor, and Natzka, tho Weede¹ was far from bad. Marie Powers, a great actress and singer in other roles was completely miscast and frankly pretty God-awful. More like a windmill than a Negro. The natural ending of the opera and a terrifically ironic and stunning one would have been the robbing of the body by the streetboys. What follows is completely anti-climactic. As it stands, the part of Azelia should have a more dramatic scene in the second act. The whole thing would be better done by Negroes, but it is very important to impress upon repertory musical theatres the idea that it is not necessary to engage a Negro company to give a Negro opera. I think more will be heard of this work.

Thanks for your column on the filibuster.²

The pictures of Guillen are sensational and he DID come back for color. Also Billie Fiesta³ (Guillen's name for her!) Did come and was an angel. I could talk about her for weeks and probably will when I see you. You mention a lot of magazines you are in but omit LIFE, and, Mr Hughes, how do you reconcile your poem on the Waldorf with the fact that this was the place chosen for the recent Russians to stage their show?⁴

I have tons of stuff for Yale from you, not organized yet. I have been too infernally busy. I am having another photograph show in a week⁵ and being Miss Stein's executor keeps me jumping. Yes is for a Very Young Man goes on in New York in June.⁶

You will scarcely credit this, but Mrs Bethune called me today and is coming down for photographs tomorrow night. And have you heard of Janet Collins,⁷ the Negro dancer from Los Angeles, who is the sensation of NY . . . ? More than that she is the TALK of New York. I will photograph her soon, but I am just recovering from Billie Holiday who was here° for WEEKS. We all loved her and will probably install reefers instead of Philip Morris cigarettes in the future.

I am speaking at Yale on the 26, to the Library staff and quantities of material from the JWJ Collection are to be exhibited in cases.

Hearts and flowers to you,

Carlo!

April 5, 1949

°at 101
*HUNDREDS were milling around trying to find you. Where WERE YOU? Did you see Polyna Stoska?

1. *The well-respected actor Robert Weede played the lead role of Jean-Jaques Dessalines.*
2. *In Hughes's March 19, 1949, "Here to Yonder" column in the* Chicago Defender, *Jesse B. Semple, a recurring everyman character invented by Hughes, pontificates on the sixteen-day Senate filibuster over President Truman's controversial civil rights program.*
3. *Billie Holiday.*
4. *An article in the April 4, 1949, issue of* Life *magazine denounced Langston Hughes, along with Albert Einstein, Paul Robeson, Leonard Bernstein, Dorothy Parker, and Arthur Miller, with the headline* RED VISITORS CAUSE RUMPUS: DUPES AND FELLOW TRAVELERS DRESS UP COMMUNIST FRONTS. *The "Communist front" organization in question was the National Council of the Arts, Sciences Professions, which had been targeted by the House Committee on Un-American Activities. The National Council was sponsoring an international cultural and scientific conference on which the article ostensibly was reporting and which Hughes attended. Van Vechten teases Hughes because the conference was held at the Waldorf-Astoria, the subject of Hughes's poetic scorn in his 1931 verse "Advertisement for the Waldorf-Astoria."*
5. *The show, called "Personalities of Our Times," was sponsored by an up-scale men's clothing store, Roger Kent, at Rockefeller Plaza, from April 11 until May 2.*
6. Yes Is for a Very Young Man *was a play by Gertrude Stein. Its New York premiere was on June 6, 1949, at the Cherry Lane Theatre.*
7. *Janet Collins was the first African American prima ballerina in the Metropolitan Opera Company. In 1949, the* New York Times *dance critic John Martin called her "the most exciting young dancer who has flashed across the current scene in a long time."*

O f all of the photography sessions Van Vechten conducted since he began taking pictures in the early 1930s, his time with Billie Holiday was among the most memorable. The session took an entire night and "seemed like a complete career," he reminisced in a December 1962 Esquire magazine essay about his photography career, called "Portraits of the Artists." She wasn't there for "weeks," as he claims in the letter above, but that was the impression she left. His close friend and lighting assistant, Saul Mauriber, was also present.

Holiday was indifferent to the session until Van Vechten showed her a photograph he had taken years before of her inspiration, Bessie Smith. Holiday wept and from that point on was "putty in my hands," Carl wrote in Esquire. After hours of photography, Holiday told Carl, Fania, and Saul her life story, "one no one could invent," Carl remembered. Everyone was moved to tears. Holiday stayed until 5 a.m. Van Vechten never saw her again.

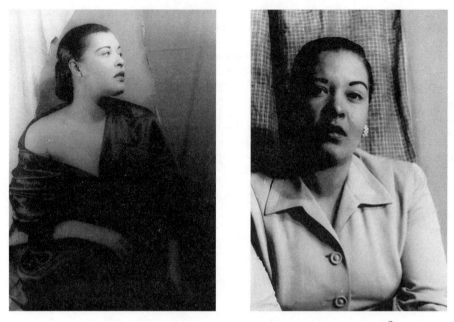

BILLIE HOLIDAY, PHOTOGRAPHS BY CARL VAN VECHTEN, MARCH 23, 1949

CARL VAN VECHTEN TO LANGSTON HUGHES, MAY 29, 1949

Dear Langston, I have had a pretty bad time for the past six weeks and the doctor says I must take it easy and not work so hard. I am giving up many of my activities and one of the things I must give up is the arrangement of YOUR material. Of course, I will finish up what I have on hand, but hereafter instruct your young man to send your material to Donald Gallup, Esq., The James Weldon Johnson Memorial Collection of Negro Arts and Letters, Yale University Library, New Haven, Connecticut. At the same time you should send a letter advising that you are shipping material.

When are you coming to New York and when do I see you?

My best to you,

Carlo

May 29, 1949

CARL VAN VECHTEN TO LANGSTON HUGHES, SEPTEMBER 21, 1949

Dear Langston, As I wrote you many months ago (you never answered the letter, although I wrote you I was sick at the time) please send material to Yale, in the future to Donald G Gallup, curator of the American Literature Collection (which includes the JWJ) in the Yale University Library: There will be some startling news about this soon.

Sincerely,

Carlo!

September 21, 1949

I hope you stayed till the end of that wonderful party the other night. Juanita Hall sang and Archie[1] danced.

1. *Archie Savage.*

LANGSTON HUGHES TO CARL VAN VECHTEN, SEPTEMBER 23, 1949

Dear Carlo,

Just a little note to wish Bon Voyage in air,[1] and to tell you that I found your note with directions as to where to send the Yale material, and Dorothy has given me instructions as to how to prepare it—put all Arna's and other known persons' letters in envelopes, etc. This I will do and will list the various envelopes and packets. I have a big box full ready to go now—a summer's collection.

Thanks immensely for the fine photos of Guillen, and for that wonderful postcard of Mary McLeod Bethune that came last week, with white hair like a celestial crown. A youngster from Berlin whose folks are all in the arts and theatre there was here last week and was entranced with your photographs I showed him. He's been a student at Black Mountain College.

The party was swell the other night! We want so much to have you and Fania up to our house when you come back. Mrs. Harper has spoken of it often, but hasn't been at all well this summer, up and down with arthritis-neuritis pains.

And I have been meaning to write or phone you all summer and see when I could come down to call and tell you about my stay at the University of Chicago, which was very pleasant indeed—except hard work with so many kids wanting to write. But I have been up to my neck meeting two deadlines—one on the Simon & Schuster SIMPLE book which was due in September 1,[2] and the other on the musical show lyrics which they wanted to start auditioning this month.[3] The book is in, and the show is coming along well, but still needs a lot of work. Maybe when you come you can hear some of the songs, if you'd like to do so.

Contracts have been signed for an off-Broadway production of the Meyerowitz opera, MULATTO which has a new scene in it—a memory-dream sequence which will partly dance and sounds quite nice to me musically.

Jimmy Davis (<u>Lover Man</u> composer) has been in Paris for more than a year: 1 Place Lucien Herr, Villa Pax, Paris 5e, and his songs are being played quite a little on the French radio, I hear. He was on the Chevalier[4] "This Is Paris" program last week.

Pleasant trip and Happy Landing! And come on time—not C.P.T.[5]

Yours,

Langston

MARY MCCLEOD BETHUNE,
PHOTOGRAPH BY CARL VAN
VECHTEN, APRIL 6, 1949

1. *Van Vechten was traveling to Paris to consult with Alice B. Toklas about more posthumous Stein publications.*
2. *Hughes fashioned* Simple Speaks His Mind *out of the nearly two hundred Jesse B. Semple sketches he had done over the years. He wrote to Bontemps on December 9, 1949, about the activities of Simon & Schuster: "They're checking all the blurb and advertising copy with me so as not to offend the race, and are most careful and cooperative about everything. A really fine office to deal with."*
3. *Hughes accepted an offer to compose the lyrics for a musical play about the Depression,* Just Around the Corner. *Joe Sherman provided the music and Abby Mann and Bernard Drew wrote the story.*
4. *French musical-comedy performer Maurice Chevalier.*
5. *C.P.T. is Colored People's Time, a joke among African Americans about their alleged habitual tardiness.*

LANGSTON HUGHES TO CARL VAN VECHTEN, NOVEMBER 6, 1949

November 6, 1949

Dear Carlo,

From the little echoes I've heard, you must have had a wonderful time in Europe. Of course, I want to hear all about it when you've gotten your breath back—and about Fisk, too.[1]

This is just to welcome you back! And to say that I phoned on Thursday when I thought you might be passing through, but got no answer, so I sent wires of greeting on down to Fisk to both you and Charles S. I wish I could have been there for the opening of the Gallery.

MULATTO (!) the Meyerowitz musical version, which had it's first audition at your house, goes into rehearsal at Columbia University next week (where the MEDIUM started out) to open January 18th for ten performances. So save that date for you and Fania, if you can bear to see Bert choke his papa again. We've changed some of the lines to make him less of a brat. And to music, maybe it is better. A kind of dreamdance sequence of the Colonel and Cora's love and youth has been added which has some lovely melodies and improves the second act greatly.

Stars and stripes to you,

Sincerely,

Langston

1. *Van Vechten was happy enough with Fisk's handling of the George Gershwin Collection to organize a second collection for them, a donation of work by Alfred Steiglitz from Gertrude Stein. The Steiglitz Collection would be housed in the Carl Van Vechten Gallery, which was established in 1949.*

LANGSTON HUGHES TO CARL VAN VECHTEN, NOVEMBER 25, 1949

Mr. Carl Van Vechten
101 Central Park West
New York, New York
Dear Carlo,

By express I am sending this week-end to Yale University the material listed on the enclosed sheet—quite a big box full, sorted as per your instructions, signed and dated.

Dorothy (and also Muriel Rahn) tells me that the Collection is to open January 7th. I'm delighted, and certainly I hope to be there.

I am saving (or have requested returned to me) all the draft of the special Negro Poets Issue of VOICES which I edited to appear in January,[1] with the various poets' own original manuscripts; also all the proofs on that as well as the manuscripts, drafts, and proofs of the book which Simon and Schuster is bringing out in March made from my Chicago Defender columns, "SIMPLE SPEAKS HIS MIND"; and all the drafts of the opera version of "MULATTO" now in rehearsal to open January 18th at Columbia University; also the drafts of my song in the forthcoming Dwight Wiman[2] revue, "DANCE ME A SONG." All of these things will go to the Collection as the projects see the light of day.

Maudell,[3] the African dancer (of the U.S.A.) and recent Diego Rivera model lately returned from Mexico, is living at our house. If you should want to photograph her, lemme know.

While you were in Europe I wrote about six hundred songs (drafts a foot high are in the Yale box mentioned above) some of which Burl Ives, Avon Long, and others are slated to record. Also wrote two ballets, and enough Defender columns to run until February; also a one-act opera libretto and a prologue for "MULATTO" which now seems about to be called, "THE BARRIER."

Here's hoping to see you soon.

Sincerely,
Langston

1. *The Winter 1950 issue of* Voices: A Quarterly of Poetry *featured work by Robert Hayden, Gwendolyn Brooks, Jessie Fauset, Georgia Douglas Johnson, and Melvin B. Tolson.*
2. *Dwight Deere Wiman was a major producer, a veteran of fifty shows.*
3. *Maudelle Bass.*

CARL VAN VECHTEN TO LANGSTON HUGHES, NOVEMBER 30, 1949

Dear Langston, Thanks for your letters and card. I have already photographed Maudell and would like to again but I am about 20 reels behind on photography, having just returned from abroad, and think I'd better go slow for a while. Of course I am saving the 18 January. You must know by now that the Yale Collection opens formally and officially on January 7.* Muriel Rahn will sing at that one too. The Fisk opening was very exciting, but I had a bad cold and was much run down, so that it practically finished me off. I am okay now. Come down to see me some time . . .

Hearty handshakes,
Carlo

November 30, 1949

*I hope you will come.

1950–1964

The ceremony marking the opening of the James Weldon Johnson Memorial Collection of American Negro Arts and Letters took place on January 7, 1950, at Yale University's Sterling Memorial Library. Carl, Fania, and Langston were in attendance, as were Charles S. Johnson and Mrs. James Weldon Johnson. The inaugural festivities included Muriel Rahn singing "The Awakening," by James Weldon Johnson, and an aria from The Barrier, with Jan Meyerowitz at the piano. Charles Johnson saluted Van Vechten as "the first white American to interpret objectively, with deftness and charm, the external features of the American Negro in a new age and setting." An exhibit of materials from the collection—including the work of the Boston artist Mary Bell—was open for public view at Sterling Memorial Library at Yale until February 15.

AT THE OPENING OF THE JAMES WELDON JOHNSON
MEMORIAL COLLECTION OF AMERICAN NEGRO ARTS
AND LETTERS, YALE UNIVERSITY, JANUARY 7, 1950.
CARL VAN VECHTEN IS PHOTOGRAPHING, FROM
LEFT TO RIGHT: ELLEN TUNNY, DONALD GALLUP,
MRS. CHARLES S. JOHNSON, LANGSTON HUGHES,
MRS. JAMES T. BABB, DR. CHARLES S. JOHNSON.
PHOTOGRAPH BY SAUL MAURIBER

LANGSTON HUGHES TO CARL VAN VECHTEN, JANUARY 15, 1950

Sunday, January 15, 1950

Dear Carlo,
    Thanks so much for the postcard of Ella. But the really wonderful one
is that full-faced African head at Yale. . . . The whole afternoon up there
was really great, and the exhibition is terrific! . . . Enclosed are front row
seats for "The Barrier" on Wednesday night. You'll find a prologue, and a
second act ballet memory-sequenced added since you heard the score.
And the whole orchestra is not as loud as was Meyerowitz piano. . . . I'll
be looking forward to seeing you and Fania then.

                              Sincerely,
                              Langston

The Barrier *was a critical success. Virgil Thomson's write-up in the January 19* New York Herald-Tribune *was typical: "There is strength in the music and at moments a great lyric charm." The* New York Times *singled out Hughes's libretto as "one of the strongest" the reviewer had ever seen. In the January 28* New Yorker, *the reviewer, Philip Hamburger, expressed awe: "Few musical events have stirred me quite so deeply."*

CARL VAN VECHTEN TO LANGSTON HUGHES, APRIL 15, 1950
(POSTCARD)

Dear Langston, Simple is a wonderful book, perhaps your most typical & best.[1] As I am reviewing it for the NY Times I need not repeat myself. Thanks for the warmly inscribed copy. I hope you will telephone & come in soon & inscribe my paper copy, & proofs for Yale. Spring to you & Toy.
April 15 Carlo

1. Simple Speaks His Mind *was published by Simon & Schuster in 1950.*

LANGSTON HUGHES TO CARL VAN VECHTEN, MAY 9, 1950

Dear Carlo,
I LOVED your review in the Sunday TIMES![1] And the phrase about "a sane approach to insanity" sent me! It's the first of my Sunday reviews, and a very nice one indeed.

I'm head over heels meeting a deadline on some book chapters[2]—as I have to start work on May 15th on a new show contracted.[3] And on the 18th out to Lincoln University, Missouri, for their new library opening. Arna will be there. Then to Chi for a Book Party the DEFENDER is giving. But will ring you before I leave and run down to sign your other book and see you, since it has been TOO long already.

Mrs. Harper is still out in Kansas City visiting her mother and enjoying herself. Been way up to Minneapolis driving with friends. Meanwhile, we have put in a new garden for her delectation when she returns—so she'll keep looking out the window and won't see the dust in the house.

SIMPLE is a best seller in two New York shops S.&S. tell me—the Concord Bookshop on Times Square and, of all places, the Barclay Hotel shop.

Sincerely,

Langston

1. *In his May 7, 1950,* New York Times *review, Carl Van Vechten called Hughes's treatment of "the race problem" as both serious and comical—"a sane approach to real insanity."*

2. *Hughes owed Simon & Schuster chapters of* Battle of Harlem, *a biography of Samuel Jesse Battle, a retired parole commissioner of New York who was the city's first black policeman. Eventually both Simon & Schuster and Blanche Knopf declined the book, which was never published.*

3. *The show was probably his Depression-era musical play* Just Around the Corner.

LANGSTON HUGHES TO CARL VAN VECHTEN, JUNE 21, 1950

(POSTCARD)

Greenwood Lake, N.Y.

June 21, 1950

Dear Carlo,

I loved your party the other day—like old times seeing Miguel and Blanche and all. And I liked the new people I met, particularly the actor boy and his wife and the Lawrenceville writer.[1] . . . So sorry to have to miss Dorothy's party. . . . About six people want to make a play out of "Simple." Should I let them, or try it myself. . . . Hy to Fania.

Langston

1. *The Lawrenceville writer was Frederick Buechner, whose first book,* A Long Day's Dying, *was published by Knopf in 1950. The party was for Van Vechten's seventieth birthday. He wrote to Donald Angus about the affair: "We had a terrific party and I wish you might have been here: garlic ice cream, Valencian rice, and two cakes in the shape of 70."*

CARL VAN VECHTEN TO LANGSTON HUGHES, FEBRUARY 1, 1951

Dear Langston, I remember reading Montage of a Dream Deferred years ago in manuscript and sending it on to Yale. I admire it immensely. It's a delightful book and I'm glad you got it published even if the Knopfs couldn't see it.[1] For your other communications I am also grateful. There will be a 25 cent edition of Nigger Heaven in a minute with a note, also by George Schuyler. I'll send you a copy.

I suppose you know that Dorothy has been very ill, is still very ill, in fact.[2]

Hands across the roofs,
Carlo!

February 1, 1951

1. *Blanche Knopf turned down* Montage of a Dream Deferred, *so Hughes published it with Henry Holt in 1951. Some reviewers were lukewarm while others were negative, like the poet Babette Deutsch in the* New York Times, *who declared that the book demonstrated "the limitations of folk art."*
2. *Dorothy Peterson suffered from arthritis.*

DOROTHY PETERSON, PHOTOGRAPH
BY CARL VAN VECHTEN,
MARCH 26, 1932

George Schuyler wrote an afterword to Nigger Heaven, *which he called "A Critical Commentary." He reflected on his 1926 Pittsburgh* Courier *review of* Nigger Heaven: *"I felt that it was 'good reporting about a certain side of Harlem life. What the author has seen he reports faithfully and truthfully. There lies the rub. Negroes, like other folk, don't like the truth. . . . Hence the howl.' "*

The 1951 resurrection of Nigger Heaven *did not last long. On November 7, 1951, Van Vechten wrote to Donald Gallup, curator of the Yale University Library: "Some Negro has objected to Nigger Heaven again and the cheap edition has been withdrawn by the publisher."*

CARL VAN VECHTEN TO LANGSTON HUGHES, NOVEMBER 4, 1951

Dear Langston,

Thanks for sending me the Gipsy ballads[1] which I am happy to read again: They are beautiful and gipsies have always fascinated me: I think there is something allied to Pushkin in these verses.

Have you heard that we have a room to ourselves at Yale? Have you heard how beautiful it is, how large the collection, and how you shine out in it? I wish you would go to see it. I wish you would write about it in its new home. It is a fine place for research now, with everything handy including chairs and tables.

Dorothy is bad again, with arthritis and I hope you will call her. She needs her friends. Fortunately she has plenty.

saluti,
Carlo

Sunday, November 4, 1951

Love to Toy!

---

1. *The gypsy ballads were translations by Hughes of fifteen of eighteen original ballads in* Romancero Gitano, *by the Spanish poet García Lorca.*

Carlo—Another race card for Yale. They're nicer than they used to be, lots of them.

Langston

POSTCARD SENT TO CARL VAN VECHTEN
BY LANGSTON HUGHES, NOVEMBER 20, 1951

LANGSTON HUGHES TO CARL VAN VECHTEN, APRIL 7, 1952

April 7, 1952

Mr. Carl Van Vechten
101 Central Park West
New York, New York
Dear Carlo,

Here's my new phone number (private, so please don't give it to ANY-one): Lehigh 4-2952. It kept ringing night and day so I had to have it changed.

I'd love to see you sometime soon, if you have a moment, to talk about what to do about the twenty years material in my basement that Yale ought to have soon. (We had three leaks and a flood down there this winter and I'm getting worried.) And I'd like to see you anyhow, not having laid eyes on you lately. So if you'll let me know what afternoon or evening, I'll run down.

I've just finished a children's book for Franklin Watts, Inc., which I let our leading Negro children's librarian read, with the enclosed gratifying comment.[1] Now I'm trying to finish the Battle book this month.

Best to Fania—who wrote me a lovely note about "Laughing."[2]

Sincerely,
Langston

1. The First Book of Negroes *appeared in December 1952 to generally good reviews.* Common Sense *judged:* "In this latest of Mr. Hughes' presentations of the many phases in approach to the race issue, the author shines more brilliant than ever." The Negro History Bulletin *called the book* "a stroke of rare genius." But the Boston Chronicle *found the omission of W. E. B. Du Bois and Paul Robeson* "indefensible": "Is this a concession to Senator Joseph McCarthy of Wisconsin, who will not read the book anyhow? If so, it indicates an intellectual dishonesty which I cannot associate with the forthright Langston Hughes, whose radical leftism used sometimes to shock readers into thinking about the underprivileged." The reviewer speculated correctly.
2. Laughing to Keep from Crying *was published by Henry Holt in 1952. It was Hughes's first collection of short stories since* The Ways of White Folks *appeared in 1934.*

CARL VAN VECHTEN TO LANGSTON HUGHES, AUGUST 14, 1952

Dear Langston. Thanks for Uncle Tom. I was delighted with your introduction. It has always seemed to me an abomination that a book which did so much good has become associated in the public mind (colored public mind at least) with the worst type of modern Negro. Your comparison with Christ then is very apt. Of course, I was touched too by your inscription and this of course will go to Yale along with the book.

Many warm greetings to you,

Carlo

August 14, 1952

H ughes had agreed to write an introduction to a special edition of Uncle Tom's Cabin *for Dodd, Mead. He wrote about the enormous impact that the book had had on the nation's conscience: "The truth of the matter is that* Uncle Tom's Cabin *in 1852 was not merely a book. It was a flash, as Frederick Douglass put it, to 'light a million camp fires in front of the embattled hosts of slavery.' It was an appeal to the consciences of all free men to look upon bondage as a crime. It was a call to action as timely as a newly printed handbill or a newspaper headline."*

CARL VAN VECHTEN TO LANGSTON HUGHES, SEPTEMBER 4, 1952

Dear Langston,

At last I have read all your back letters and arranged them chronologically, a terrific job, but one well worth the doing: they will go to Yale presently. They are among the most valuable lots in the Collection: warm (showing how colored and white get along on occasion), intimate, full of references to every living thing, and a mine of information about Negro habits and doings, full of enclosures, rich in folklore, and fabulous in friendship. There are hundreds of them. I have also done Nora's, almost as extensively, and now must tackle Dorothy's and Essie's, and Taylor's.[1] JWJ's, Nella's, A'Lelia's, Countee's, etc, also Ethel's, were done long ago and are at Yale.[2]

In spite of Ralph Ellison's professed distaste for the camera, his photographs continue to appear everywhere. Perhaps he has a distaste for me, or for YALE.[3]

Dorothy tells me you are doing an article for the Defender about the new room for the JWJ Collection.[4] I hope this is true, because it is a long time since the collection has had a boost, the new room has never been written about. The new COLORED cataloguer, Edna Lockheart, working on the collection began Sept. 2. There is so much material from modern writers we want!

We were happy to see you at the Warfield-Price nuptial party[5] and hope we see you again SOON.

Hands across the rooftops,

Carlo

September 4, 1952

Regards to Toy.

1. *Nora Holt, Dorothy Peterson, Essie Robeson, and Taylor Gordon all corresponded with Carl Van Vechten.*
2. *James Weldon Johnson had an extensive correspondence with Van Vechten until his death. Nella Larsen and her ex-husband, Elmer Imes, also exchanged letters with Van Vechten, as did A'Lelia Walker, Countee Cullen, and Ethel Waters.*
3. *Van Vechten was right; Ralph Ellison did not like him. "I despised his photography," he told Hughes biographer, Arnold Rampersad, in 1983. "In fact, I didn't care for the whole Van Vechten influence. It introduced a note of decadence into Afro-American literary matters which was not needed." Hughes never told Van Vechten how Ellison really felt.*
4. *Hughes never wrote this column.*
5. *The black soprano Leontyne Price was married to the baritone William Warfield from 1952 to 1972.*

V*an Vechten continued to build his collections at Yale, Fisk, and the New York Public Library. At the same time, Hughes was contending with accusations about his communist leanings from every corner. Finally, on March 23, 1953, he was served with a subpoena to appear before the Senate permanent investigations subcommittee, headed by Senator Joseph McCarthy.*

On March 26, Hughes traveled to Washington, D.C., accompanied by his lawyer, Frank Reeves, and armed with a prepared statement. During the interrogation, Hughes never denounced Communism, but he was careful to put his leftist beliefs into a historical context, saying that "roughly the beginnings of my sympathies with the Soviet ideology were coincident with the Scottsboro case, the American Depression, and . . . they ran through for some ten or twelve years or more, certainly up to the Nazi-Soviet Pact." These beliefs were now part of the past: "I would say a complete reorientation of my thinking and emotional feelings occurred roughly four or five years ago."

Hughes took to the road to escape these troubles. He spent ten days at Hollow Hill Farm with Noël Sullivan in June. He returned in late June and spent the summer working on Famous American Negroes, *a children's book, for Dodd, Mead. The persistent reactionary mood in the country forced Langston to leave out all famous blacks with radical leanings, including W. E. B. Du Bois.*

Hughes did not write to Van Vechten about his experience at the hearings.

September 20, 1953

Dear Carlo,

I'd be delighted to write Caroline Dudley's blues for her, please tell her.[1] And if you'll TYPE out her address for me, I'll write her myself. But not being familiar with her writing, I'm not sure I'd get it right from the top of her letter. I'll send her my new books, too, soon as I know where. Her letters to me care of Segers never arrived.[2] I don't believe they've published me since NOT WITHOUT LAUGHTER so they probably have an old Cleveland address or something.

I had two September deadlines to meet: a FIRST BOOK OF RHYTHMS for Franklin Watts, and a FAMOUS AMERICAN NEGROES book for Dodd, Mead, so had to work about 18 hours a day all summer since getting back from the Coast. Didn't hardly see the sun! But I've turned both in now, so have a breathing space, although exhausted. Watts says the RHYTHMS book is "great" and they hoping to find just the right artist for it. (I wish it could be Miguel.) At any rate, they've given me two more to do: GYPSIES and JAZZ,[3] so I guess I will turn into a writer for children.

Meanwhile, my mail has piled up to the ceiling. Also, many presents lately that I'm beginning to think September must be Christmas: a beautiful broacaded gold thread album from the biggest woman's magazine in Japan; a fine charcoal drawing of soldiers learning to read from a soldier down South; maple syrup from Vermont; handkerchiefs from Canada; and the reissues of Ma Rainey and Blind Lemon Jefferson; and Gwendolyn Brooks' new novel.[4] All still to be acknowledged, so I have to get to letter writing lest I acquire a rep like Marian Anderson. I had good Chinese assistant all summer,[5] but had to keep him busy typing the books, and now he's gone back to college in California yesterday. I heard an appeal last spring to help Chinese students stranded in this country by giving them work, so I called up the China Institute—and they sent me one BORN here whose parents own two big shops in San Francisco! And his uncle edits one of New York's Chinese dailies. But maybe because he didn't need work, he was most industrious.

It looks as if MULATTO is about to be done in Buenos Aires. And The BARRIER has a producer interested in London. (But he wants Marian Anderson!) Meyerowitz is in Italy. He writes that the Dutch radio production of the BARRIER was quite good, and he's bringing a tape recording of it back—in Dutch—so we can hear it.

I read TAKE A GIANT STEP[6] and liked it very much. I hope it goes well here, and maybe might get to the opening Thursday.

And most any time now, I'd be able to get out of Harlem and come down your way and sign that book. Sorry to be so long, but I've been a literary sharecropper all summer, having long ago taken the advances—and spent them! So I'll phone you and see when you're home. I haven't laid eyes on you for ages. And would love to see you.

Sincerely yours,

Langston

1. *Caroline Dudley Delteil had written to Hughes asking him to contribute some poetry to a book she was writing but never published. As Caroline Dudley Reagon, she had produced the* Revue Nègre *in Paris with Josephine Baker in 1925. Caroline and her sisters, Katherine and Dorothy, had been friends with Van Vechten since his college days in Chicago.*
2. *The progressive French publisher Pierre Seghers published translations of Hughes's poetry in his* Poètes d'Aujourd'hui *series. Editions Rieder, and not Editions Seghers, published the French translation of* Not Without Laughter *in 1934.*
3. The First Book of Jazz *was published by Franklin Watts in 1955. Hughes would abandon the other project,* First Book of Gypsies.
4. Maud Martha *was published by Harper in 1953.*
5. *Zeppelin Wong remembered his summer with Hughes in a 1980 conversation with Arnold Rampersad: "I was in New York for the summer only and was definitely committed to go home to San Francisco to attend law school in the fall. A friend of mine answered the phone at Columbia and she knew I wanted a job—so she sent me. By the time Langston discovered that I could not type, and knew nothing about short-hand, I had started giving lessons in Chinese cooking to Mrs. Harper. He threatened to fire me, but she warned him: if Zep goes, you go." Later he wrote nostalgically to Hughes about "the wonderful summer I spent with you."*
6. *An autobiographical play written by Louis Peterson about a young black man coming of age in white middle-class America. It opened on September 24, 1953, with Louis Gossett in the lead role.*

(POSTCARD)

3/6/54

Carlo-

The sun do move! I'm staying at a "white" hotel in St. Louis! Headed south on 3 weeks lecture tour. Spangled banners to you!

Langston

H ughes encountered virtually no antagonism on this tour, his first since his appearance before the Senate subcommittee on investigations. He had one adventure that he excitedly reported to Arna Bontemps in a June 30, 1954, letter. In Cairo, Illinois, an electric sign pointed toward the home of David Lansden, an often-harrassed white NAACP lawyer. "Some folks drove me by to see it," Hughes wrote, "and from another car a rock had just sailed through his window, so he came rushing out to shoot US! I was introduced to him in the street under rather distraught circumstances! No lie! I'm telling you, something happens everywhere I go. But I'm still here!"

LANGSTON HUGHES TO CARL VAN VECHTEN, APRIL 4, 1954

April 4, 1954

Dear Carlo,

I'm just back from my lecture tour—St. Louis, Southern Illinois University, Florida, Normal, and the 50th anniversary of Mrs. Bethune's school, whence I flew over to Nassau for a few days—where I wish I was again, as cold as it is here! . . . In St. Louis I came across about the most cullud colored paper I've ever seen, THE EVENING WHIRL, which I intended to pass along to Yale—but thought you might like to glance at it first before it reaches the archives.

When may I come down and see your new house?[1]

Conch shells and African daisies to you,

Sincerely,

Langston

1. In the fall of 1954, Fania and Carl moved to 146 Central Park West because the building at 101 Central Park West was going cooperative. In Carl Van Vechten and the Irreverent Decades, Bruce Kellner describes their successive Central Park West homes: "[They] always overflowed with 'things': dozens of glass and ceramic and china and porcelain cats, the inevitably useless and extravagant Christmas or glass paperweights; paintings and photographs on every wall, in every room; articulated, metal-linked, and glass-eyed silver fish in Chinese bowls on laquered tables; Venetian chandeliers; miniature orange trees; Polynesian shadow puppets; Oriental headdresses; hundreds of books, even after Carl's various collections had been established. Old 'things' simply made room for new ones."

*A*frica was on Hughes's mind these days. He was thrilled when Henry W. Nxumalo, the assistant editor of Drum, a South African arts magazine, asked him to be a judge for its third international short story competition. He had also learned from Lincoln University's president, Horace Mann Bond, that Prime Minister Kwame Nkrumah of Ghana, Africa's most famous political voice and a Lincoln alumnus, wanted Hughes to be his official biographer. As flattered as he was by this request, Hughes declined.

CARL VAN VECHTEN TO LANGSTON HUGHES, APRIL 6, 1954
(POSTCARD)

Dear Langston,

Thanks for letting me see The Whirl. Shall I pass it on to Yale or send it back to you? When you get ready to come down all you have to do is telephone. In the past, you have often promised us a sight of you that never materialized.

18 vestal virgins (housebroken) to you!¹
Carlo

Tuesday

1. *Van Vechten refers here to an oratorio written by Hughes, "The Five Foolish Virgins,"*
another collaboration with Jan Meyerowitz. It was staged at New York's Town Hall on
February 11, 1954. Hughes's libretto was based on the story in Matthew 25: 1–13 about five
wise virgins who waited for their bridegrooms and their foolish counterparts who failed to
do so.

LANGSTON HUGHES TO CARL VAN VECHTEN, JUNE 21, 1954

June 21, 1954

Dear Carlo,

This young Negro actor, Clayton Smeltz¹ (who was raised in a white orphanage in Seattle and never saw a Negro until he was nine when he had hysterics for three days) bids fair to become the Charles Gilpin and

Paul Robeson (plus maybe Ida Aldridge) rolled into one. He's really very talented. (Ask Harold Jackman or Ida Cullen about his recent dynamics at an Evening of Negro Playwrights at the Library). So maybe you'd like to photograph him before he gets too hard to get hold of. If so, let me know when (giving a couple of dates if you can) and I'll bring him down. Reason I say suggest more than one time is because "Mice and Men" failed to pay off,[2] having quit his job for it, he has to look for another right away as that group went broke, so he might go out of town for the summer shortly, having a possibility of doing Emperor Jones in summer theatre, or maybe waiting table at the same time.

At any rate, I want to see you my own self, and would love to come down, if I may, almost any late afternoon. I've been working like mad finishing up a book of jazz for kids that took more time than I thought, but now gone to press.[3]

Meanwhile, I've been going through material for the 2nd Big Sea I'm hoping to write this summer,[4] and have gotten a couple more big boxes ready for Yale, including all the letters of Jim Babb and Donald Gallup, which I guess they won't object to receiving back for the Collection.

Knopf sent me advance sheets of "Tell Freedom," which I think is a wonderful book. And recently I've had several nice letters from Peter Abrahams, who just sent me the English edition.[5] Funny how that incident of a Negro lad being whipped at the insistence of whites (whipped by parents) has turned up in three books lately, Abrahams, Killens,[6] and one other I can't remember—so it seems common to both Georgia and South Africa.

Summer solstices to you,

Langston

1. *Hughes first met Clayton Smeltz, who would become Clayton Corbin, on May 27, when he watched him and several other former Karamu House actors perform at a two-hour program on the history of Negro playwrights in Harlem. Corbin went on to perform in* The King and I, The Blacks, *and the 1967 revival of* Emperor Jones.
2. *Corbin played the role of Lenny in the 1954 off-Broadway production of* Of Mice and Men.
3. The First Book of Jazz *was published by Franklin Watts in 1955.*
4. *Hughes's second autobiographical volume,* I Wonder As I Wander, *was published by Rinehart & Company in 1956. He dedicated his book to Arthur and Marion Spingarn. He had gone immediately to Spingarn, his long-term legal consultant, when subpeonaed by the Senate subcommittee on investigations in 1953.*
5. *The autobiography of the South African writer Peter Abraham,* Tell Freedom: Memories of Africa, *was published by Knopf in 1954. Hughes wrote a blurb for the book, which included a reflection of Hughes's influence on the author's life and work.*
6. *John Oliver Killens's first novel,* Youngblood, *was published by the Dial Press in 1954.*

DEAR YARD DOG: You are invited to a repeat
                performance of our party—
                where last year we got to-
                gether and howled for our
                own amusement——on Monday,
                December 27, same back yard,
         guest of Edith Wilson, Toy and Geechie Harper,
         and Langston Hughes, at 20 East 127th Street,
         from 9:00 P. M. until ! ! !

Carlo and Fania — This was lots of fun last year — Edith Wilson's gathering of mostly old-time show folks. We're all in on it this time. Hope you can come.

Langston

LANGSTON HUGHES TO CARL VAN VECHTEN,
DECEMBER 16, 1954 (INVITATION)

LANGSTON HUGHES TO CARL VAN VECHTEN, APRIL 3, 1955

Dear Carlo,

Curiously enough, I was just on the verge of writing you a note when the postman brought that charmingly written little book about you yesterday[1]—so I stopped to read it, and find it delightfully warm and real and to be no bigger than it is, a pretty thorough coverage of your life, ways, and activities. And certainly your personality comes through. (Incidentally, I love Saul's picture of you—which I'd never seen before; and that beautiful one of you and Fania). And, naturally, I am DE-lighted to be referred to and quoted therein! (Who wouldn't be?) Thanks so very much for sending me a copy so far in advance of publication.

What I was about to write you about yesterday was (and is) to ask you if by any chance you've got a spare hundred lying around loose anywhere you could lend me for a month.

Brokeness suddenly descended upon me unawares and my stenographer's last check bounced. Turned out I was $1.48 short! (And I thought I was $37.00 ahead of that—but I'd neglected to make a deduct on my book). So I was shocked! I don't mind being broke myself, but typists live more hand to mouth than authors, and I don't want to get more than a week or two behind with her—since I've just recently been fortunate enough to find her, she's reliable and very good, and I've a mountain of manuscripts in final draft stage to get typed up and turned in this month: FAMOUS NEGRO MUSIC MAKERS (a juvenile) due at Dodd, Mead's on the 15th,[2] and the second volume of my autobiography (in which you figure again) due at Reinhart's early in May—on both of which I'll collect remaining advances due on delivery of manuscripts of almost a thousand bucks. But right now I don't have a thousand pennies—having awakened this week-end for the first time in a long time "cold in hand." (And the Harpers have had some enormous plumbing and heating bills this winter—old pipes bursting, etc.—and neither have been too well, either. Fortunately, nothing intended for Yale is under any pipes, and lately I've almost completed the basement sorting—four BIG boxes of letters alone from you, Walter, Du Bois, Zora, Arna, etc., mostly already filled under each name. But I want to list and sort them into years before boxing for shipment.)

Anyhow, if you're broke, too, don't worry about it. But if you aren't, and want to help ART and the RACE through the rainy month of April, I'll send it back to you when the sun shines in May and ASCAP and publishers pay off. What really broke me has been Africa—I've received almost two hundred manuscripts from there in answer to my letters for short stories to Azikiwe's paper,[3] DRUM, AFRICA, and the BANTU NEWS, as well as various writers. From which I garnered 56 that I think are good, some by African Negro writers—fiction, not folk, contemporary which Simon and Schuster are now considering. But what a mountain of typing I had to pay for, and air-mail postage for the past six months. But, aside from the manuscripts (some in long hand) I've gotten some fascinating letters, and think I've discovered two really talented writers in Cape Town, youngsters, one 23, one 24, the former I believe as talented as Peter Abrahams (TELL FREEDOM, etc.) who helped me on this project I started last year.*

Thanks again for C.V.V. AND THE 20s, and tulips and jonquils to you,

Langston

---

*Amos Tutuola[4] (the PALM WINE DRINKARD guy) sent a story from Nigeria—and very

wisely said, "I will send more when you send money." It's all in long hand and most fantastic, so I'm saving the script for Yale.

1. *Edward Lueders's* Carl Van Vechten and the Twenties *was published by the University of New Mexico Press in 1955. Lueders quoted Hughes on Van Vechten's parties during the twenties: "[He] moved about filling glasses and playing host with the greatest of zest." He took from* The Big Sea *Hughes's observations about Van Vechten's character: "He never talks grandiloquently about democracy and Americanism nor makes a fetish of those qualities. But he lives them with sincerity and humor. Perhaps that is why his parties were reported in the Harlem press."*
2. *Hughes amazed even himself by finishing this book in ten days. "Don't tell anybody," he begged Noël Sullivan in an April 8, 1955, letter. The pervasive and threatening anti-Communist spirit left Hughes no choice but to exclude Paul Robeson from* Famous Negro Music Makers, *which was published in 1955.*
3. *Nnamdi Azikiwe was the editor of the* West African Pilot.
4. *Amos Tutuola was the author of* The Palm-Wine Drinkard and His Dead Palm-Wine Tapster in the Dead's Town, *published by Faber & Faber in London in 1952.*

T*he invitation to judge short stories for* Drum *inspired Langston to assemble an anthology of short stories written by Africans. Despite his best efforts, Hughes could not interest a publisher in this collection or a similar collection intended for the juvenile market. In 1960, he was finally able to publish* An African Treasury: Articles, Essays, Stories, Poems by Black Africans *with Crown Publishers.*

CARL VAN VECHTEN TO LANGSTON HUGHES, APRIL 6, 1955

Of course, dear Langston.

Also I'm very excited about your African anthology. I pick up everything African I can find for Yale as I think that MAY be the coming continent. Anyway this book will fill an empty niche and it is clever of you to have thought of it.

Did you know that Fisk is giving me a doctor's degree to celebrate my 75 anniversary?[1]

fondly,
Carlo

April 6, 1955

1. *"Carl Van Vechten of New York, famous newspaper critic, author, collector, and photographer was in Nashville yesterday to receive an honorary doctor of letters degree from Fisk University, a university he has befriended more than once," announced the* Nashville Tennessean *on May 31, 1955. Van Vechten wrote excitedly to Bruce Kellner on May 29: "Tomorrow I become by magic an LLD — without writing a thesis."*

LANGSTON HUGHES TO CARL VAN VECHTEN, APRIL 7, 1955

Dear Carlo,

Thanks no end! I'll have it back to you in about a month. Saved again!

Fisk is a very intelligent school! Also, re: you, it's about time! Delighted!

A young man, David Hepburn, managing editor of OUR WORLD,[1] was just here gathering personal stories about Walter for a feature magazine piece they intend to run. He's talked with Gladys and Poppy,[2] and wishes to talk with you, so I took the liberty of giving him your address, but not the phone. You'll probably be getting a note from him. He's an O.K. newspaper man.

It seems that Simon and Schuster have taken the book of Roy de Carava's photographs for which I did a running text to be called THE SWEET FLY-PAPER OF LIFE.[3] They're working out format and printing costs before sending a contract. But the editor says it's 99% sure they'll do it, as it got 100% editorial board approval.

CARL VAN VECHTEN RECEIVES HIS
HONORARY DEGREE FROM FISK
UNIVERSITY PRESIDENT CHARLES
S. JOHNSON, MAY 30, 1955

And did I tell you Jack Robbins wants me to do an opera libretto from UNCLE TOM'S CABIN?[4] Which idea sort of intrigues me, as I love the book.

Best to you, and thanks again,

Sincerely,

Langston

---

1. Our World *was a large-format pictorial magazine about African American culture.*
2. *Walter White divorced his first wife, Gladys, in 1949 to marry the South African-born food writer, Poppy Cannon, the same year.*
3. The Sweet Flypaper of Life *appeared on November 1 to glowing reviews. A November 27* New York Times *review described it as "a delicate and lovely fiction-document of life in Harlem." On December 13, the* New York Herald-Tribune *concluded: "Langston Hughes' words and Roy DeCarava's photographs achieve a harmony which is more than poetry or photography alone, but its own kind of art."*
4. *Hughes never finished this libretto.*

June 14, 1955

Dear Carlo,

Thanks so much for sending the photos down to Dodd, Mead.[1] I know how difficult such seeming "little" things are when one is busy, so I doubly appreciate your doing so. But there really are no pictures of Bojangles or Bessie as alive as yours.

I had to miss the Public Library opening of your show—I was just on the last pages of the last draft of I WONDER AS I WANDER, my No. 2 autobiography just turned into the publishers yesterday. It's 583 pages, to date my biggest book! And only covers four years, from where THE BIG SEA ended to 1933, mostly concerning my trip around the world. But I will get down to the Library soon, and hope to see you at the Schomburg Monday.

Meanwhile I wish you the happiest birthday ever—75 years of such light and life-giving (and knowledge giving) deserves it! HAPPY BIRTH-DAY!

> Be seeing you soon,
> Sincerely,

1. *Van Vechten contributed several photographs to Hughes's book,* Famous Negro Music Makers, *published in 1956 by Dodd, Mead.*

AT THE COUNTEE CULLEN BRANCH OF THE NEW YORK PUBLIC LIBRARY, FROM LEFT TO RIGHT: THE LIBRARIAN REGINA ANDREWS, W. E. B. DU BOIS, THE NOVELIST GEORGE LAMMING, VAN VECHTEN, AND NORA HOLT. THE WOMAN SEATED IN FRONT IS UNIDENTIFIED. THIS PHOTOGRAPH APPEARED IN THE *AMSTERDAM NEWS* ON JULY 16, 1955

T*he exhibit of Van Vechten's photographs at the Countee Cullen branch of the New York Public Library, in honor of his seventy-fifth birthday, included portraits of Marian Anderson, Pearl Bailey, Josephine Baker, W. E. B. Du Bois, Billie Holiday, Langston Hughes, Harold Jackman, Leontyne Price, Paul Robeson, Ethel Waters, and Gertrude Stein, among others.*

CARL VAN VECHTEN TO LANGSTON HUGHES, JUNE 24, 1955

NORA HOLT AND CARL VAN VECHTEN
AT YALE, JUNE 22, 1955

Dear Langston,

I have to thank you for two fine letters, a Lorca layout (It was some-body else who wanted this list, not senile Dr. Carlo: so I will not accept your kind offer to loan them),[1] for your presence at the Schomburg show[2] and at the dinner chez Bon Soir, and for a wonderful recording of your poetry. I hope also you will take in the NY Public Library show and if barely possible the Yale show,[3] both of the latter are terrific and they are entirely different. I also took occasion to look in on the JWJ Collection and found it in apple-pie order, and O, so much bigger than when I last visited Yale. Thanks to my birthday, too, I have a lot more money to present to the endowment fund.[4]

Many happy returns of the DAYS (if the days DO return; do you know Emerson's poem about the DAYS?)

Carlo

June 24, 1955

1. *Hughes's second "fine" letter to Van Vechten, on June 15, was a list of his books by the Spanish poet Garcia Lorca, something Van Vechten had requested. He ended his letter with "So, questions answered! (About time!)"*
2. *The Schomburg Center for Research in Black Culture, a branch of the New York Public Library, sponsored an exhibition of Van Vechten's photographs of black notables such as Countee Cullen, W. E. B. Du Bois, James Weldon Johnson, Ann Petry, Walter White, and Richard Wright.*
3. *The Henry W. and Albert A. Berg Collection in the New York Public Library hosted another exhibition of Van Vechten's photographs, the first exhibition ever held at the library in honor of a living writer. At Yale, Donald Gallup, the curator of the Yale University Library, organized an exhibition of items from each of the collections Van Vechten had established at Yale.*
4. *Guests made contributions to the James Weldon Johnson Fund in lieu of birthday gifts.*

B*on Soir, Jimmie Daniels's nightclub in Harlem, was the site of Van Vechten's seventy-fifth birthday celebration. In his tribute, George Schuyler praised Van Vechten's commitments to black progress: "We, in our poor way, pay tribute tonight to our good friend who put the hex on jim crow, who has been tireless in his persistence, who has opened countless minds and hearts in circles where it has done incalculable good for all concerned."*

Van Vechten received several celebratory telegrams from friends and fans, but a birthday greeting from Roy Wilkins, executive secretary of the NAACP, was particularly gratifying. He thanked Wilkins in a June 28 letter: "Dear Mr. Wilkins, I have had a wonderful 75th birthday, but your letter, representing the NAACP, was the climax. Thank you!"

CARL VAN VECHTEN TO LANGSTON HUGHES, SEPTEMBER 11, 1956

Dear Langston,

Thanks for sending me the early copy of The First Book of the West Indies¹ which will presently adorn the JWJ Collection. I read it immediately with great pleasure and examined all the delightful pictures. I could have added a few names to our lists of celebrated West Indians, but probably you have all the names the publishers cared to use. However, I was amazed to find you omitting Edgar Mittelholzer, Destiné, and Josephine Premice, not to mention Geoffrey Holder, and Hugh Laing*[2] . . . Perhaps you are trying to do too much, always a bad idea. Your account of your activities really frightened me. Dorothy is back. Have you seen her? I love your West Indies book sufficiently so that I shall ask others to share my pleasure.

    Papa Drums to you and a barrel of Haitian Rum to you.

                    Carlo

                                    September 11, 1956

*Eusebia Cosmé?[3]

1. *Published by Franklin Watts.*
2. *Edgar Austin Mittelhölzer was a Guyanese novelist; Haiti-born Jean-Louis Destiné was a choreographer; Josephine Premice is a singer and actress of Haitian extraction; Geoffrey Holder, a dancer, choreographer, and actor, was born in Trinidad; and Hugh Laing was a Barbados-born ballet dancer and one of Van Vechten's favorite photographic subjects.*
3. *A Cuban actress.*

LANGSTON HUGHES TO CARL VAN VECHTEN, SEPTEMBER 16, 1956

Mr. Carl Van Vechten
146 Central Park West
New York 23, N.Y.
Dear Carlo,
    Tried to phone you awhile back, but no answer, so you're probably taking a nap, or out. So this is to let you know, sadly, that I've just gotten word from the Coast that Noel Sullivan died of a heart attack in San Francisco[1]—which, Noel-like, felled him on his way to the theatre. Funeral arrangements are as yet indefinite, but [if] you'd like to send condolences they would reach his neice at Carmel: Mrs. Brenda Ferrari, Hollow Hills Farm, Route 1, Box 775, Carmel, California. I've phoned Ethel, Barthe's studio (he's due in this weekend en route to Europe), and others of Noel's friends whom I know.

    I enjoyed your little note and what you say about WEST INDIES. I had a quite long list of famous West Indians, but space limitations caused it to be pared down to the few listed. Besides, kids' publishers are none too keen on mentioning living people for fear they might "cut a hog" before the book comes out. The dead are safely gone.

Did I tell you I've just finished a little novel called TAMBOURINES TO GLORY about the goings-on in gospel churches?[2] Also made a play of it with a Tambourine Chorus and two women preacher-songsters, one sweet, one naughty: Ethel Waters, Pearl Bailey would be ideal casting for them. If you know a producer who would like to do a big Negro singing show using gospel songs for the first time on Broadway pass the world along, please. Langston

1. *Hughes received a telegram that morning:* GOD CALLED NOEL SULLIVAN TO HIMSELF AT 7:30 THIS SATURDAY AFTER A CORONARY OCCLUSION. *It was Sullivan's second heart attack in a few days. Sullivan left Hughes $2,000 in his will.*
2. *Published by John Day in 1958.*

CARL VAN VECHTEN TO LANGSTON HUGHES, NOVEMBER 16, 1956

Dear Langston,

I, in having read I wonder as I wander, consider it one of your better jobs, written with a good deal of skill, well organized, indeed much better organized than the original book in this series, and invariably interesting, even to those who have heard some of this before, I am almost certain that the Russian section is not only the longest but also the best. Certainly you are not involved personally in the other sections to the degree that you were in Russia.

Will you telephone me please when you can come to inscribe this opus? I would telephone you, but I always discover this to be quite a chore, to find you in and not in bed, etc. etc.

My congratulations,
Carlo

November 16, 1956

Generally, reviewers greeted the second volume of Hughes's autobiography, I Wonder As I Wander, *warmly. In the* Saturday Review, *Roi Ottley called it "excellent fare" and the* Pittsburgh Courier *described it as "a yarn of bright, glittering texture." Writing in the* New York Herald-Tribune, J. Saunders Redding *was disappointed, calling the book "frank and charming, though neither events nor people are seen in depth. Mr. Hughes, it seems, did more wandering than wondering."*

LANGSTON HUGHES TO CARL VAN VECHTEN, FEBRUARY 5, 1957

Dear Carlo—

How sweet of you and Fania to send me those two <u>beautiful</u> boxes of wine jelly for my birthday! I never had any before, and both vintages are delicious. . . . I am working hard these days—trying as usual to meet delayed deadlines—two kid's books at the moment, a play, and the Gabriela Mistral translations.[1] Meanwhile, I've written a Calypso song— now being sung at the Le Cupidon—"Beat It Out, Mon." And Josh White has just recorded my "Red Sun Blues" beautifully. There'll be a new "Simple Stakes A Claim" book in the summer. . . . Hope to see you soon.

Sincerely yours truly—
Langston

1. *Hughes had been approached by the director of Indiana University Press in February 1956 to translate from Spanish a series of poems by Gabriela Mistral, a Chilean poet who won the Nobel Prize for Literature in 1945. Mistral died of cancer on January 10, 1957, before Hughes could meet her. The* Selected Poems of Gabriela Mistral *was published in January 1958.*

CARL VAN VECHTEN AND FANIA MARINOFF, 1955

CARL VAN VECHTEN TO LANGSTON HUGHES, MAY 28, 1957

Dear Langston,

I am back from the deep south after many adventures, scabrous and otherwise.[1] In one adventure I met Lizzie Miles[2] on the street of New

Orleans. I had not seen her since she lived in Harlem, a friend of Spencer Williams,[3] but she recognized me and I recognized her after 27 years of separation! I would LOVE to see Simply Heavenly,[4] but the FIRST row is obligatory on account of my hearing.[5] I will be glad to pay for the seats if you will send me two for Tuesday June 4. I could go other times too but this is the best in the coming week. I am happy you got off to a good start.

Did I tell you that The Tattooed Countess is being made into a musical, a fine one too?[6] The music is marvellous.

my greeting, my compliments, and my congratulations,
Carlo

May 28, 1957

1. *Van Vechten went to Richmond often during the twenties and thirties. On this trip, accompanied by Saul Mauriber, he decided to explore more of the South.*
2. *Lizzie Miles was a popular black singer.*
3. *Williams was a musician, writer, director, and actor.*
4. *Hughes's musical based upon his character Jesse B. Semple, born in the pages of the* Chicago Defender, *had its debut on May 21, 1957, in New York.*
5. *Van Vechten started losing his hearing in 1945. In 1957, he began wearing a hearing aid at the movies, surreptitiously attaching it after the lights went down and removing it shortly before they came up.*
6. *The show would not be produced until 1961.*

CARL VAN VECHTEN TO LANGSTON HUGHES, JUNE 5, 1957

Dear Langston,

I was delighted with Simply Heavenly, and I laughed so much and was so enthusiastic about some of the scenes and songs that I must have been even a better than average audience. It seems to me that with this character and the stories about him* you have more of less hit your stride. If you would add a dash or more of poetry (cf. Synge of Tennessee Williams in Orpheus Descending) you would be able to confuse a folk story with the classics. Who is David Martin?[1] Does he know how good he is? I liked ALL the actors and singers, but especially Claudia McNeill (I do not know any of the actors, but She came out front after the show and while she was talking to a friend I went straight over to her and kissed her), Ethel Ayler (who will have a career) and Melvin Stewart.[2] Perhaps I am greedy but I want to photograph these three and if they are interested ask them to call me (before noon if possible). Congratula-

tions and I am pretty sure, this time, that you have hit the bulls eye again.
Cornets to you, hot dogs, and the best of glory!

Carlo

Mildred loved it too!³

*and now with this play about him

1. *Martin composed the music for the show.*
2. *McNeill shone as Miss Mamie, a regular at Simple's favorite bar; Ayler was Zarita, Simple's girlfriend on the sly; and Melvin Stewart played Jesse B. Semple.*
3. *Mildred Thornton.*

D*espite lighting problems,* Simply Heavenly *opened to a packed and enthusiastic audience on May 21 at the 85th Street Playhouse. In the May 23* New York Times, *Brooks Atkinson wrote: "Mr. Hughes loves Harlem. He loves the humor, the quarrels, the intrigues, the crises and the native shrewdness that makes life possible from day to day. He has written 'Simply Heavenly' like a Harlem man. If it were a tidier show, it probably would be a good deal less enjoyable." On the same day, Walter Kerr of the* New York Journal-American *called it a "rambling, sometimes ramshackle, but always utterly delightful salute to Lenox Avenue."*

There were black critics who thought Simply Heavenly *did a disservice to the race by depicting blacks in Harlem as pleasure-seeking and living for the moment. The Communist party leader William Patterson told Hughes in a June 7 letter: "To me, Lang, the play was political. But the politics suited my enemy's — Simple's enemy's — aims and purposes in describing the Negro."*

LANGSTON HUGHES TO CARL VAN VECHTEN, JUNE 7, 1957

June 7, 1957

Dear Carl,

Thank you very much for you nice note about the show. I certainly regretted not being there on Friday, but I am very glad that you enjoyed it. I told Claudia McNeill of your desire to photograph her and she has promised to phone you. As soon as I see Melvin Stewart and Ethel Ayler I will give them your message and I'm sure they will be happy to have their pictures taken.

David Martin is the son of the founder of the old famous Harlem Martin-Smith Music School. He used to be in charge of the band at Cafe Society. He plays the piano very well and accompanies most of the record dates of Sammy Davis, Jr. and a number of other well-known entertainers. He did the music of my BALLADS IN BLUES suite of four songs that you no doubt have heard Juanita Hall sing in the night clubs. SIMPLY HEAVENLY is his first show.

We're putting another song in the show next week and since I would like very much for Fania to see the show when she returns,¹ I hope you will come again and bring her. I will reserve seats if you will let me know when.

Here's hoping you will have fun photographing the principals.

Sincerely yours,

Langston

1. *Van Vechten wrote to Bruce Kellner on May 2, 1957: "Fania sails on a cruise on the* Caronia *May 11 and will be gone until after my birthday."*

CARL VAN VECHTEN TO LANGSTON HUGHES, JUNE 26, 1957

Dear Langston,

It was a pleasure to have you here and it will always be a pleasure when you come on time,¹ but you wore away Bruce Kellner's jacket with his address book. He went home without a jacket and left yours HERE. So, if you will send one of your secretaries down pronto he can collect this. . . . I am expecting YOU, Claudia McNeill, Ethel Ayler, and Melvin Stewart here promptly at 5 on Tuesday July to see the color pictures. Better confirm this.

A professor in the University of New Mexico² is very interested in an undergraduate Negro writer who he thinks has genius. He wrote me about him and asked if there was any institution of foundation that would help care for such a boy. I recommended Guggenheim and Fulbright, but perhaps you know of some Negro foundation or an individual of either race who might be interested. He has to earn every cent he spends for college or otherwise. He has no dependents and he lives alone. May I suggest he write to YOU? I sent him a small amount of money to tide him over present responsibilities. His name is Lloyd Addison.

much affection to you, toujours,

Carlo

June 26, 1957

1. *Hughes attended a birthday party for Van Vechten on June 15 at Van Vechten's home.*
2. *Edward Lueders.*

LANGSTON HUGHES TO CARL VAN VECHTEN, JUNE 28, 1957

June 28, 1957

Dear Carl:

Concerning the young writer from the University of Mexico, A Whitney Fellowship might be easier for him to get as a beginner than the others you mention. Arna Bontemps is one of the judges and is always on the lookout for new young writers for them to consider. I suggest that you advise the young man to apply for a Whitney. The address is:

WHITNEY FOUNDATION
630 Fifth Avenue
New York, NY

Meanwhile, tell him to send you or me some samples of his work, and I in turn will let Arna read them when he comes to New York next month. I do not think it would be diplomatic for him to send work directly to Arna if he is applying for a fellowship, since in such an event the manuscript should go through proper channels.

My coat and everything in the pockets came back intact. What happened to Bruce Kellner's address book, I do not know since I found nothing at all in the pockets of his jacket. Please tell him how sorry I am to have mistakenly gone off with his coat and I do hope he finds his book.

I look forward to seeing you on Tuesday at 5 with the folks from the theatre.

Sincerely yours,
Langston

LANGSTON HUGHES TO CARL VAN VECHTEN, JULY 28, 1957

July 28, 1957

Dear Carlo,

Since Fania didn't get to see my show, please ask her if she would like to come to the Broadway opening, Tuesday, August 20th, at the Playhouse in West 48th Street. If so, I'd love to invite you both, and will reserve two front row seats. This time it will have a real folk guitarist, Brownie McGhee,[1] a new Zarita,[2] and a small off-stage band. But otherwise, I hope, just the same.

I've read Lloyd Addison's poems and found them a bit hard to keep my mind on. But some of them read aloud have an intriguing sound. From the enclosed carbon of my letter to him, you can see how they affected me. Certainly, they are different, and I hope he gets a little Fellowship encouragement. I'm holding the copies I have for Arna to see, awaiting his Wildwood, N.J. address, where he will be in August.[3] If you've seen none of his poetry, I'll lend them to you meanwhile. It seems a sort of cross between Gertrude Stein and e. e. cummings (plus Russell Atkins) in style.

I've just finished my Gabriela Mistral translations for the Indiana University Press, and the record NOTES for an interesting album of Haitian folks songs for Vanguard—all done by the hardest since something comes up every day concerning SIMPLY HEAVENLY that takes hours! Show are the <u>most</u> work! Which is why I like best the one in Los Angeles I haven't seen or read, A PART OF THE BLUES, based on my life, times, and poetry, that got good reviews last week, and on which I didn't have to work at all. But I wish I could fly out to see it.[4]

Cordial regards, as ever,

Langston

1. *McGhee was a well-known blues singer and folk guitarist.*
2. *Anna English replaced Ethel Ayler as Zarita when Ayler left to understudy Lena Horne in* Jamaica, *a musical.*
3. *Bontemps was also unmoved by Addison's poetry, as he told Hughes in a March 9, 1958, letter. Addison would publish a volume of poetry,* The Aura and the Umbra, *in 1970.*
4. *Walter Brough composed* A Part of the Blues, *a tribute to the life and work of Langston Hughes. The revue broke attendance records at the Stage Society Theatre, but its reviews were lukewarm. The Los Angeles* Herald & Express *praised the first act but called the second act "long, sketchy, and repetitious." The* Los Angeles Times *described it as "an interesting novelty, vaguely significant, and efficiently presented."*

LANGSTON HUGHES TO CARL VAN VECHTEN, AUGUST 23, 1957

August 23, 1957

Dear Carlo and Fania—

The champagne reached me just as I was about to enplane for Hollywood to see my other show playing out here, "A Part of the Blues." What a wonderful present! It's the biggest bottle of champagne I ever held in my hands. What happened was (although it had Playhouse on it) it was addressed to 137 West 28th Street, so it didn't get back to the theatre until yesterday. But it's in time to toast "Simple Stakes a Claim" out September 16th.[1] I'll be back in town 'ere then.

It's hotter out here than New York—96° this morning—and not noon yet!

Both your notes came before I left. Also a lovely one from Cornelia Otis Skinner.[2] I'm glad folks seem to like the show. Especially you-all.

Affectionately,
Langston

And gracias again!

1. *Published in 1957 by Rinehart.*
2. *Skinner was a well-known actress.*

CARL VAN VECHTEN TO LANGSTON HUGHES, SEPTEMBER 27, 1957

Dear Langston,

I am beginning to believe that you have finally arrived as a BIG Name and that you will soon be R I C H ! Hewes notice of the play in the Sat. Review was, of course, terrific.[1] And Orville Prescott's review of the new Simple book could hardly be more complimentary.[2] I have noticed many other evidences of your increasing popularity and I congratulate you. Unfortunately we can't attend your autograph party. Long ago we promised this Sunday to some nieces of Fania and their children, who live far out on Long Island, but we hope the party will be a huge success.

I want to remind you that Sidney Poitier asked you to call him in October re photographs. I hope, indeed, that something can be arranged now. He should surely be in the collection.

I send you my good wishes and my assured affection,
Carlo

September 27, 1957

1. *In the September 7* Saturday Review, *Henry Hewes wrote about* Simply Heavenly: *"Mr. Hughes has caught the spirit and truth of Harlem life so affectionately and with so much humor and compassion." He predicted that "some may complain that 'Simply Heavenly' insults Negroes by presenting them as semi-illiterate, undisciplined, and immoral, but it also reveals Harlem society as a widely differentiated group of human beings with the same desires and idiosyncracies as anyone else, but with a somewhat superior capacity to be practical about their situation and to joke at their own expense."*
2. *Orville Prescott regularly wrote reviews for the* New York Times, *but Nash Burger reviewed* Simple Stakes a Claim *for the September 17 issue of the* Times. *He called the book a "timely" one that "enlightens as well as entertains."*

S imply Heavenly, *which had opened on August 20 at the 48th Street Playhouse, closed on October 12, after sixty-two performances. Stella Holt, the show's resourceful producer, found another site, the Renata Theatre, at 144 Bleeker Street. A revised, leaner* Simply Heavenly *opened there on November 8.*

November 19, 1957

Dear Langston,

You sent me the enclosed postcards some time ago and the letter got mislaid and I forgot to return them. Anyhow, here they are.

Thanks for the news about the two books.[1] I will pass this on to Yale.

I hope you get your audiences at the Renata, but you must remember that the cast has lost two of its best members. And that most of the audiences so far speak of no one else but Claudia. It is not YOUR fault that you have lost her and I am happy she has a more remunerative job (Ethel Ayler got one first) but the result is the same.[2]

I am up to my neck working on my collections, photographs and two prefaces, but expect to emerge in time to go to heaven.

With the warmest possible greetings and cordial feelings (I wish to GOD you would stop signing yourself "sincerely". One is sincere with the butcher. It is taken for granted one is sincere with one's friends. Certainly I get letters from no one else in the world with such a conventional signing off.)

Carlo

November 19, 1957

1. *Hughes had told Van Vechten that he planned to deliver the manuscript for another juvenile book,* Famous Negro Heroes of America, *to Dodd, Mead in the coming winter and that he also had completed a volume of poems for children,* Year Round. *He did not find a publisher for this book.*
2. *Claudia McNeill consistently earned the best notices in the show. She took a part in a production of* Winesburg, Ohio, *based on the 1919 book by Sherwood Anderson, with Hughes's blessing. She was replaced by Marion Barton.*

LANGSTON HUGHES TO CARL VAN VECHTEN, NOVEMBER 30, 1957

November 30, 1957

Carlo:

I've been knocking myself out on three (3) very URGENT and long overdue book deadlines,[1] so I reckon <u>Sincerely</u> was about the limit of my vocabulary. But I want you to know I remain

Yours with pomegranates, sequins,
gold dust, and melon seed
from here on in unto the end,
Langston

P.S. And I guess you know Knopf is going to publish my SELECTED POEMS and I guess you know who I would want to do the Foreword or Introduction — most much want if such should be my honor.

---

1. *Hughes was also in the middle of selecting material for a* Langston Hughes Reader *proposed by the publisher George Braziller.*

CARL VAN VECHTEN TO LANGSTON HUGHES, NOVEMBER 30, 1957

Dear Langston,

Thanks for your letter, thanks for your new signature, and thanks for the invitation. I have two prefaces ahead of me which are driving me crazy, one of a Gershwin book, another for a Stein volume: these are due by March 1.[1] Naturally, I can't resist doing YOURS, and you are doing me a favor by asking me, BUT I HOPE IT DOEsn't have to be ready by March 1! And of course I'll have to see the contents of the book before I write the preface. Perhaps we can wait at least till the galleys, but I'd prefer the page proofs.

I too am extremely busy, mostly with dealing with my papers (an extenive series) before my obsequies. Fortunately my letters are almost all disposed of already and I only have to keep up with contemporary arrivals.

BUT I shall ALWAYS have time to send
AFFECTION to you and frequently even MORE,
Carlo

November 30, 1957

---

1. *Van Vechten was working on an introduction to* The Gershwin Years, *by Edward Jablonski and Lawrence D. Stewart, and "A Few Notes a propos of a 'Little' Novel of Thank You," an introduction for* A Novel of Thank You, *the last in a series of Stein's unpublished writings published by Yale University Press.*

December 3, 1957

Dear Carlo:

I wrote Herbert Weinstock at Knopf that I hope you'd do my Preface for the SELECTED POEMS, since you did it of my first, and this'll probably be my last—so we would have come full circle together, poetically speaking!

Re letters, I wish I had only "contemporary arrivals" to read and list. But I've STILL got TONS in the basement from years gone by.*

About the SELECTED POEMS, no publication date has been set yet, nor the final selection approved. So I reckon the time will probably be next fall, so there's no rush.

SIMPLY HEAVENLY in the Village (Which I finally saw last week) is being played like a road show—for laughs—real broad and noisy—but amusing, I thought, and the audience the night I was there seemed to love it. The new Miss Mamie (while no Claudia) gets just as much applause. And the new landlady (Lillian Hayman, formerly of PORGY AND BESS around-the-world company) is WONDERFUL in her brief bit. The Zarita has improved, and Simple is better than ever. He's a good and growing young actor.

Simple blessing to you in this sputnik world,

Langston

P.S. I spoke to Sidney Poitier again about being photographed. He is about the busiest boy in the world; had to fly then to West Indies for retakes or something; and expected to go to London again on return, so could not promise to make it soon.

*Sometimes I get more than 30 a day now—more than I can read, and answer, and work too.

February 18, 1958

Dear Carlo,

A note from Charles Enoch Wheeler today tells me that he has a considerable collection of old Bessie Smiths, Clara, Trixie, Blind Lemon, and Bert Williams which he wishes to give to Yale. I've written him suggesting he send you a list of them, in case of duplication. His address, if you'd like to write him, is 6327 Engleside Avenue, Chicago 37, Illinois.

Me, I've been in the hospital with flu, finished a book, and gone on a lecture tour since I've last written you. And still feel kinder achey from the flu.

MY SELECTED POEMS is so big that Herbert Weinstock does not think it needs an introduction, so he recently informed me, so I reckon you can count that off your writing schedule.[1] But I would have liked it.

My biggest volume to date is going to be the BIG Braziller book due out at the end of March, THE LANGSTON HUGHES READER, which has some of everything I ever wrote in it, including the entire playscript of SIMPLY HEAVENLY, and various hithero unpublished articles and speeches.

But an even bigger book is the next-fall BOOK OF NEGRO FOLK-LORE that Arna and I have compiled for Dodd, Mead, and which I've just arranged and turned in. The manuscript was a foot and a half tall nearly, and weighed some 10 pounds! Lots of Zora in it, and a section of Harlem jive and bop material that I think quite amusing, as well as the current folk lore of race relations. It runs from Br'er Rabbit to Bopster tales, spirituals to songs in the folk manner like Mae Barnes'[2] I AIN'T GONNA BE NO TOPSY, slave anecdotes and hoodoo to Jackie Mabley's HOW TO HIP A CHILD from one of her Apollo routines.

Dodd, Mead also has another book coming up which I suggested to them: a collection of Ollie Harrington's BOOTSIE cartoons for which I may do a foreword,[3] in case someone like Thurber is unavailable to discuss them for a draughtsman's viewpoint. Some of the original drawings are quite wonderful—in fact most are.

Best to Fania and all the moons (and coons) of the future to you,

Sincerely,

Langston

P.S. SIMPLY HEAVENLY opened in Los Angeles last week—and seems headed for closing this week: producers fell out, main backer withdrew, all kinds of fussing and fighting at the top. But the London Jack Hylton production seems assured for late Spring with Melvin going over to play Simple there. Garrick Theatre.

---

1. *In actuality, Weinstock, a senior Knopf editor, wrote to Hughes on December 17 about the Van Vechten introduction to his book: "I certainly do not think that at this time it would be a good idea to ask Carl Van Vechten to write one."*
2. *The black singer Mae Barnes was born Edith Mae Stith.*
3. *Hughes did write an introduction to* Bootsie and Others *(Dodd, Mead, 1958), a collection of the work of Ollie Harrington, a celebrated black cartoonist.*

CARL VAN VECHTEN TO LANGSTON HUGHES, FEBRUARY 19, 1958

Dear Langston, The Lord giveth and the Lord taketh away, but any writing is a chore for me now, so I am relieved at Weinstock's decision. I'm afraid Poitier will never be photographed by me until he is an old man if he is upset by his many occupations. He will constantly have more, not less. The Museum of the City of NY is doing a show about the Negro in the Theatre. I can scarcely keep out of THIS. Do you know any way of getting near to Johnnie Mathis. I want to photograph HIM too. On Saturday I photograph Gloria Davey in Aïda! Latin Hymns to you and a flute,
                                    Carlo
                                                        February 19

Your new book will add to your reputation.

CARL VAN VECHTEN TO LANGSTON HUGHES, APRIL 13, 1958

Dear Langston, The Langston Hughes omnibus' is HERE and I love it. I think it is the first appearance in print of Simply Heavenly and I was especially happy to find the chapter from the Big Sea with a description of MY Parties. All you have to do now is to walk in and inscribe this volume, which you have already promised to do.
    my compliments, my congratulations, my heart, and my soul!

Carlo
                                                        April 13, 1958

1. *The* Langston Hughes Reader *was published in 1958 by George Braziller. It includes short stories, poems, song lyrics, novel excerpts, plays, articles, and selections from Hughes's two autobiographies,* The Big Sea *(1940) and* I Wonder As I Wander *(1956). Here, Van Vechten refers to a chapter from* The Big Sea *called "Downtown," in which Hughes's description of several of Van Vechten's parties includes the observation: "Only Mr. Van Vechten's parties were so Negro that they were reported as a matter of course in the colored society columns, just as though they occurred in Harlem instead of West 55th Street."*

CARL VAN VECHTEN TO LANGSTON HUGHES, SEPTEMBER 16, 1958

Dear Langston, Bruce Kellner, who teaches at a college in Cedar Rapids, Iowa, won't be in NYC again for at least a year perhaps it will be convenient for you to get my letters to Yale before then, where it is MORE convenient for anybody writing about ME, or YOU, or Negroes, or whatever to examine them than it is chez vous. You are frequently sleeping, or out of town or not in. Yale NEVER sleeps. Let me know when you can send them. For Yale and my letters they can easily arrange them as soon as you have read them or whatever else you want to do. It would be a GREAT favor to me and Yale and Bruce, if you would get these to Yale as subito as possible. All of your letters to me got to Yale promptly and the old ones were in Yale ten years ago. You may not believe this but I am much busier than YOU, but by working steadily from dawn to midnight I manage to get things done. I am looking forward to Tambourines to Glory, Have you read A Place Without Twilight, by Peter Feibleman.[1] If you haven't, you'd better.

My compliments, my warm greetings, and my congratulations,

Carlo

Sept. 16

I hear the GREAT Bertice Reading played Mamie in London and Claudia McNeill writes me a love letter.[2]

I still have never got Poitier for photographs!

1. A Place Without Twilight *was published by the World Publishing Company in Cleveland in 1958. Van Vechten photographed Feibleman the same year.*
2. *McNeill wrote to Van Vechten in August 23, 1958: "You are such a fine person, that I most times feel your mother must have been an angel and you are her immortality on earth."*

LANGSTON HUGHES TO CARL VAN VECHTEN, SEPTEMBER 18, 1958

Carlo, mon cher:

Amigo mio:

Man: I got 30 letters today, which took me all day to read, answer, and get ready for Yale—which is why it is hard to go back 30 years and read mail—when I can't hardly keep ahead 30 minutes with contemporary correspondence! But I see in the papers where Mrs. Roosevelt answers 100 letters a day—so I am taking heart from that! You and she are human dynamos or something, I reckon—and not cullud. Anyhow, your letters will really go to Yale SUBITO if you say so. (I gather SUBITO means with "all deliberate speed"). But what I had actually rather do some day next week is have a drink with you one afternoon, rather than spend it looking for your letters still not unearthed in the basement! Or maybe I can do both.

What is PLACE WITHOUT TWILIGHT? And is it as good as PRANCING NIGGER¹ was? Which I still love.

We'll probably NEVER get ahold of Sidney Poitier now. But he told me he was going to do RAISIN IN THE SUN this winter in New York, so maybe then. Perhaps I'll see him on the Coast in October, as I head that way on lecture tour in a couple of weeks, and since Mr. Goldwyn invites me to dinner, I'll probably visit the PORGY AND-YOU-IS-MY-WOMAN-NOW set.²

Is Bruce Kellner the guy whose coat I wore off by mistake? And did you ever see or hear Bertice Redding? I didn't so far as I know, but she certainly stole the London show. It is now about to be done in Prague. Maybe it will have better luck there—in a state supported theatre. And the BARRIER is to [be] done on the Rome radio in November, with Meyerowitz flying over to assist in rehearsals. And MULATTO is now on the boards in Tokyo. And I'm still in Harlem un-caught-up with my mail.

Anyway, Lincoln 4¢ stamps to you! Langston

"TAMBOURINES TO GLORY"³ has a real lively black-yellow-red jacket (proofs)!

1. Prancing Nigger *was the title of a novel by Ronald Firbank that was published by Brentano in 1924. The original title was* Sorrow in Sunlight; *Van Vechten, who wrote the preface, was responsible for the new title, which is a phrase in the book.*
2. *Samuel Goldwyn was the producer of the 1959 musical* Porgy *and* Bess, *starring Poitier. Goldwyn had first contacted Hughes in the summer of 1957. As he wrote Arna Bontemps in a July 5 letter: "Did I tell you Sam Goldwyn (his own self) called me up from Hollywood Friday and asked for a script. Said he had only heard of me as a writer, but not a play writer. I started to tell him that I once wrote a play (Mulatto) that would make the hair curl on his haid. But didn't."*
3. *Hughes's novel* Tambourines to Glory *was published by the John Day Company in 1958. The novel is based on a play,* Tambourines to Glory: A Play with Spirituals, Jubilees, and Gospel Songs. *Both the play and the book are tributes to the black gospel tradition.*

CARL VAN VECHTEN TO LANGSTON HUGHES, SEPTEMBER 20, 1958

Dear Langston: You can have a drink whenever you desire one, or almost anything else. It is hard to believe that you still have me in the basement. I believed everything was being cleared out when somebody helped you at Yale's expense years ago. I don't know what to tell you about my letters except people who would write about you often want to see them and if they are not at Yale NOBODY CAN. Because, of course, nobody can see anything chez vous except letters on file. Anyway, please get the ones on file sent to Yale as soon as you can. Subito actually means immediately. ALL your letters to me except contemporary ones (and these go as they come) have been in Yale for YEARS.

A place without Twilight is not at all like Prancing Nigger, but it is a beautiful book and was so regarded by all reviewers when it appeared six months ago. I am meeting the author next week. The book is about New Orleans Negroes. Why is it that only cullud are so difficult to line up for photographs? I have spent more time on Althea Gibson already than she has spent on her tennis career and I am still working on her. Sidney Poitier ditto. Johnny Mathis ditto. Sugar Ray ditto.[1]

Bertice Reading is the best known Negro actress in London. She is American, but she has not worked here. She played Ethel Waters' part in The Member of the Wedding in London, and more recently in William Faulkner's Requiem for a Nun in which she is working with Zachary Scott and Ruth Ford. She will be seen as the "nun" in New York later this season. There are several photographs of her at Yale. I am mad to see Tambourines to Glory.

Considering your natural disposition you are pretty well organized. I was organized before I was permitted to have a disposition. In any case I draw distinctions and what e'er betides I get important things done.

You still haven't told me whether you have seen the WONDERFUL entertainers' show (Negro) at the Museum of the City of New York,[2] which probably means you haven't. This is really shameful and one of the reasons why cullud have such a low average for responsibility.

Many warm words to you, and a spray of muguet.

Carlo

September 20, 1958

1. *Van Vechten photographed the tennis champion Althea Gibson in 1958. He never photographed the actor Sidney Poitier, heavyweight champion Sugar Ray Robinson, or the singer Johnny Mathis.*

2. *The entertainers show was called "The Art of the Negro in Dance, Music and Drama." It opened at the Museum of the City of New York on June 18 and ran through September 29. It celebrated the achievements of black artists and included memorabilia, portraits, programs, and scenes from various stage productions. Van Vechten's portraits of Ella Fitzgerald, Eartha Kitt, Billie Holiday, Bessie Smith, Harry Belafonte, Earl Hyman, and Marian Anderson were part of the show.*

LANGSTON HUGHES TO CARL VAN VECHTEN, OCTOBER 5, 1958

Dear Carlo:

Cullud though I may be, the Lord cares about me, and has enabled me to find without too much delay a whole batch of your letters from 1925 on in the basement, and these are now all sorted out in folders by years right up to now—with some years missing—but no doubt in the basement somewhere still. So these latter I will send later. What with complications in page proofs regarding a Dorsey gospel song in both THE BOOK OF NEGRO FOLKLORE and TAMBOURINES TO GLORY, permission to use at last moment STILL not being forthcoming, and having to replace it with something else that fitted line for line, and other last minute details before flying off to Kansas City in a few hours to begin my fall lecture tour, I wasn't able to research my own materials any more this week. But soon as I come back, your letters, a considerable number of Arna's, and a sizable box of Countee and other literary and musical ones will go off to Yale. They are all sorted. My summer helper has returned to his Cleveland music school. He and various other helpers have long since absorbed the money Yale gave me originally to sort and classify material—but that is neither here nor there. Everything I have of literary research value will eventually be sorted and sent anyhow. But it was my impression these things were for posterity, not contemporary use, I proceeded at "all <u>deliberate</u> speed" rather than subito. Now that you have clarified me, SUbiTO! <u>subito</u>. No, unfortunately, I haven't see the Theatre show yet. Can't seem to get out of my house—always some imminent deadline looking me in the face, or unending proofs to read, or somebody who wants to know why I haven't sent their unsolicited manuscript back yet that they sent me to read and comment upon. Anyhow, tambourines to you! And to glory! . . . Sincerely,

Langston

CARL VAN VECHTEN TO LANGSTON HUGHES, OCTOBER 30, 1958

Dear Langston, Thanks for sending me Tambourines to Glory. It is quite a book and I read it at a single sitting with the greatest pleasure. It is more relaxed and spontaneous than your previous fiction and the mingling of the numbers racket with services in the Church of God is something that may actually have happened.

I am also grateful to you for sending 142 of my letters to Yale and doubtless you will dig the others out before too many months have passed. And for my sake you will somehow get (by motor-bus, taxi, helicopter, or ANGEL) to my show in the Museum of the City of New York.

Apparently I cannot cure you of your business signature of "sincerely." So I will take this the way I presume it is meant. At least it is unique, as no other of my numerous correspondents is so formal. Red roses to you and a hock of the best ham!

Carlo

October 30, 1958

CARL VAN VECHTEN TO LANGSTON HUGHES, OCTOBER 11, 1959

Dear Langston, I had no idea last night that you had given me a book.[1] Perhaps you had just left it without saying a word! At any rate, I am delighted to have it. It was an inspiration to bind these trombones in RED and as you take the jacket off you can actually hear them blowing out hallelujahs. THANK YOU.

Perhaps I did not make myself clear to you last night about the way I feel about the JWJ Memorial Collection of Negro Arts and Letters. For the past ten years I have devoted at least fifty per cent of my waking hours to this perpepuation of the fame of the Negro and it saddens me to real- ize how few Negroes realize this and how still fewer make any attempt to assist the collection. That was why I was so enchanted with Nora's effort. I know it is not easy to organize such a group, but she carried it off like a general. And with glorious results.

One of the most brilliant episodes in the Collection is my mounted photographs of Negroes prominent in the Arts and Sciences. It would seem a simple matter to permit oneself to be photographed for so good a cause and that is why it makes me very sad when some one like Sidney Poitier (who SHOULD know better) acts like a spoiled child when he is asked to pose. In the end of course it is his own loss. Also he is one Negro who has rebuffed me personally with exceptional rudeness. That has not been my experience with Marian Anderson or Joe Louis for that matter![2]

I am not running this show as a benefit for myself. It is even named for some one else. It is conducted solely to glorify the Negro and I hope that some day at least a majority of the race will begin to realize this fact.

yrs, with too much impatience and some faint hope!

Carlo, the Patriarch!

October 11, 1959

---

1. Tambourines to Glory.
2. *In a May 16, 2000, phone conversation, Sidney Poitier told me he had no recollection of these attempts to photograph him. He thought he might have resisted because the idea of being photographed simply did not appeal to him at the time. Hughes was one of his heroes, but he had no memory of Carl Van Vechten at all. Van Vechten photographed Mar- ian Anderson on January 14, 1940, and Joe Louis on September 15, 1941.*

October 12, 1959
Columbus Night

Dear Carlo: Unbearded Patriarch—

I haven't gotten such a long letter from you since the days of the Cullud Renaissance! And I would answer you in kind were it not that I have a toothache and have to get up early and go have it pulled out.

Of course, I understand how you feel about the JWJ Collection. I feel that way, too. But, in my long life, I have noticed no general excitement among large numbers of the colored race about ANY collection—from the Schomburg to the Metropolitan, JWJ to the Library of Congress, Cluny to the Cloisters. They are just not collection minded. And (as I have heard you say about other things many times)—"that's the way it is." So, those of us who do know and do care will just have to redouble our efforts, I reckon, and include in these efforts (as did Nora) the bestirring of others.

Concerning Sidney and the photos, he has never said he wouldn't be photographed. I've spoken to him both here, and on the Coast, and in Chicago about it, and each time he's said, "Soon as my next picture is over," or "Soon as the play settles down," or something like that. He is certainly a very busy (and very tense) young man and also very hard to get a hold of, or talk with quietly. And probably can't quite cope with all the things that go into career making with the success, say, of Miss Eartha Kitt. And he has no Essie to his Robeson, or Lennie to the Horne.[1] Or, so it seems to me "that's the way it is." About which I do not know what to do. He does not seem as yet to have managed to surround himself with efficient and helpful people—as Harry Belafonte and some of the other Negro stars seem to have achieved—which might leave him a little more time to be courteous and photographable.

Anyhow, have you photographed the colored beatnik poet of the Village, LeRoi Jones?[2] He seems to me to be talented. I've never met him. But when I first read his poems, I asked someone to find out for me if he was colored, and in some fashion the inquiry reached him. So he called me up to tell me he was. I wasn't home, but he left the message. (I thought he was colored anyway, named LeRoy). He edits a magazine called YUNGEN and, I believe, has his own print shop.[3]

Which is all my observations for the moment as I have to put a clove in my tooth and go to bed. But, so you can lament better the faults of the race.*

Sackcloth dipped in eau de Vie and just like a soupçon of ashes in

champagne—that wonderful big-bottle kind like you had at the party the
other night (which was a wonderful party)—
Langston

*We <u>both</u> should use a capital R—Race!

[*Handwritten on the back of the letter*] I was so glad to see you the other
night. I guess absence makes the heart grow fonder.

1. *Essie Robeson and Lennie Hayton were instrumental in building the careers of their
   spouses, Lena Horne and Paul Robeson, respectively.*
2. *The poet, playwright, and critic LeRoi Jones changed his name to Imamu Amiri Baraka in
   1966.*
3. *Hughes touted LeRoi Jones and his magazine,* Yugen *(which Hughes misspelled* Yungen*),
   in his* Defender *column: "LEROI JONES represents color within the Beat Generation
   very well because his poetry is good and the little magazine he publishes in the Village,
   'Yungen,' is quite worth reading."*

CARL VAN VECHTEN TO LANGSTON HUGHES, OCTOBER 16, 1959

Dear Langston, If you are having a time with a tooth I am having a session with two which will occupy me, off and on, all winter! Anyway I
don't recall that you have written me such a good letter since 1868. I will
be delighted to photograph Mr <u>LE</u>Roi Jones, when you or somebody
can arrange it. But if he doesn't like your poems he MAY NOT like my
photographs.[1]

It will amuse you to know that my hardest project has been Thurgood
Marshall! Both Roy Wilkins and Arthur Spingarn have worked on him
unsuccessfully. He doesn't even answer my letters.

I agree with you about a capital R for Race and I am having a wonder-
ful time with your BLUES.
My right ear to you, lambkin,
Carlo, the Patriarch
October 16, 1959

1. *Van Vechten photographed LeRoi Jones on January 3, 1962.*

LANGSTON HUGHES TO CARL VAN VECHTEN, OCTOBER 16, 1959

October 16, 1959

Well Carlo:
When I come back from Trinidad I will see what I can do about LEroI

Jones. Up til my departure I have to continue with dentists and deadlines. . . . Donald says he is sending the Yale truck down on October 28. I
have 13 boxes ready, each and all unique of its kind—orderly and non-
racial.

Tambourines—Langston

*H*ughes's visit to Trinidad in October 1959 was his second visit to the
Caribbean. After his first trip, in 1947, he came back and declared
"MY NEW LOVE IS JAMAICA!" in his November 29, 1947,
Chicago Defender *column. Hughes spent eleven days in early November 1959
giving lectures and readings in Trinidad. He also visited Anne Marie Coussey,
his Paris love from 1924. She was now happily married to the most prominent
black lawyer in Trinidad, H. O. B. Wooding, and was the mother of four grown
children. Still, she remembered "those carefree days" they had spent together in
Paris and, she told him in an October 19, 1959, letter, had "always treasured"
them. She bore him no ill will for his ambivalence thirty-five years earlier.
Instead, she was happy that he had become "such an outstanding success, and
[had] reached the top."*

LANGSTON HUGHES TO CARL VAN VECHTEN, FEBRUARY 1, 1960

Carlo—
For no good reason—just to say Hello on my birthday—and to wish
you neither a cool world nor a long dream. But 10 early asters.

Langston

P.S.S. I caught that California flu on the Coast. House bound for 10
days.

2nd P.S. I'm off, a three week lecture tour, to the cold old Middle West
tomorrow. . . . My "Shakespeare in Harlem"[1] opens while I'm gone, Tuesday, Feb. 9th, at the 41st St. Theatre off-Broadway.

---

1. *The one-act play* Shakespeare in Harlem, *by Robert Glenn, was a pastiche of vignettes
from Hughes's poetry, plays, and prose.*

Hughes had just seen the dramatic adaptations of both Richard Wright's 1958 novel, The Long Dream, and Warren Miller's 1959 novel, The Cool World. In both plays, he found the depictions of blacks deplorable. In his March 3, 1960, Chicago Defender column, he criticized The Long Dream: "Dear Lord! How long is the list of plays in which the Negro is defeated in the end!" In a January 21, 1960, letter to Arna Bontemps, he complained about The Cool World: "Am I becoming oversensitive racially, and NAACP-ish?" he asked Bontemps, after describing the play as "a holy horror with nobody at all sympathetic or likable." He concluded mordantly: "Oh, well, set back 50 years again!"

CARL VAN VECHTEN TO LANGSTON HUGHES, JUNE 24, 1960
(POSTCARD)

Dear Langston, A thousand thanks for your telegrams, letters & numerous messages. We missed you very much on Monday. Love to you from Carlo, happy octogenarian

I collected on my birthday over 2000 for the endowment fund of the JWJ Collection. Carlo

June 24, 1960

On June 20, eighty of Van Vechten's friends gathered to wish him a happy birthday at Jimmie (misspelled "Jimmy" in the newspaper caption) Daniel's Bon Soir, just as many of them had done five years earlier. Carl received a collective gift of two thousand dollars to contribute to the endowment fund of the James Weldon Johnson Memorial Collection of Negro Arts and Letters at Yale. He was genuinely surprised when Yale presented him *with a beautifully printed pamphlet called* 80, *a bibliographic compilation of the correspondence and published works of eighty writers whose materials Van Vechten had gathered for the library. The celebrations were topped off with a surprise gift from the New York Public Library. He described it to Alice B. Toklas in a May 31 letter: "My name is to be carved in stone letters, six inches high, on one of the four columns in the lobby of the Fifth Avenue entrance under the caption: Generous Donors to the Library. Most of the other donors are names like Rockefeller, Vanderbilt, Ford, Tilden, Lenox, and Astor, so Papa Woojums feels like a millionaire."*

RIGHT THIS WAY, FOLKS — Fania Matinoff (Mrs. Carl Van Vechten), former dancer, shows guests how to get off on the right foot at the birthday party honoring her distinguished husband on his 80th birthday at Jimmy Daniels' Bon Soir Monday evening. Left to right: Aileen Pringle, former movie star and one of the hostesses; Arthur Spingarn, philanthropist; Gladys Powell White, Miss Matinoff, Carmen de Lavallade, dancer of Metropolitan Opera Co., and Mr. Van Vechten, honoree, poet, music critic and philanthropist.

FROM THE *NEW YORK COURIER*, JULY 2, 1960

LANGSTON HUGHES TO CARL VAN VECHTEN, JUNE 26, 1960

Dear Carlo —

Riding out to the University Auditorium today with Arthur Spingarn to receive my Spingarn Medal, he told me how entertaining was your Bon Soir birthday dinner. I'm surely sorry the airlines strikes kept me in Puerto Rico so I couldn't be there.

Midwest maples and elms to you —

Langston

H ughes had gone to Puerto Rico for a vacation for two weeks in early June and was still there when he learned he would receive the forty-fifth annual Spingarn Medal. The finalists included Gwendolyn Brooks, Lorraine Hansberry, and four student civil rights activists in Greensboro, North Carolina. In his June 26, 1960, acceptance speech, Hughes accepted the award "in the name of the Negro people": "Without them, on my part, there would have been no poems; without their hopes and fears and dreams, no stories; without their struggles, no dramas; without their music, no songs."

LANGSTON HUGHES, RECEIVING THE 45TH ANNUAL
SPINGARN AWARD FROM ARTHUR SPINGARN, JUNE 26, 1960

CARL VAN VECHTEN TO LANGSTON HUGHES, JUNE 30, 1960
(TELEGRAM)

=DEAR LANGSTON CONGRATULATIONS BUT SHOULD HAVE
HAD THE SPINGARN MEDAL 26 YEARS AGO LOVE
=FANIA AND CARLO

Thanks so much to you and Fania for your congratulatory wire. I'm out here for filming of "Raisin in the Sun." Using my poem as a prologue. Met Zsa Zsa Gabor on location yesterday. Pork chops to you—
Langston

Columbia Pictures paid Hughes for a few days of publicity work for the movie Raisin in the Sun, *based on the play of the same name by Lorraine Hansberry. The title was borrowed from Hughes's poem "Harlem":*

What happens to a dream deferred?

Does it dry up
like a raisin in the sun?
Or fester like a sore—
And then run?
Does it stink like rotten meat?
Or crust and sugar over—
like a syrupy sweet?
Maybe it just sags
like a heavy load.

Or does it explode?

August 28, 1960

Dear Carlo:

I meant to write you last week (but in the swirl of rehearsals, I am not sure I did or didn't) to invite you and Fania to the opening of TAMBOURINES TO GLORY at Westport on Monday, September 5, in case you would like to travel that far. If you would, I'd do my best to get you FRONT ROW seats, so let me know, please soon.

If not the COUNTRY opening, then sure the next one—when (and if) it comes to Broadway.

Rehearsals seem to me to be going very well—and such an amiable cast:

> HAZEL SCOTT
> GEORGIA BURKE
> CLARA WARD
> NIPSEY RUSSELL
> JOE ATTLES

and Eva Jessye directing the Choir.

Me. I've been busy getting up every morning before day—to make a 10 o'clock rehearsal!

> Call Boards and Call Boys to you—
> Comme toujours,
> Langston

F*our years after Hughes had written* Tambourines to Glory: A Play with Spirituals, Jubilees, and Gospel Songs, *the play opened in Connecticut at the Westport Country Playhouse on September 5, 1960. The* Norwalk Hour *reported on September 9: "A packed theatre saw, applauded, and stomped and whistled at the final curtain Monday night at the Westport Country Playhouse where Hazel Scott and a cast of 25 gave a terrific performance of 'Tambourines to Glory,' written by Langston Hughes." Most reviews were favorable, but there were black patrons who felt that the show portrayed African Americans stereotypically: "I thought we'd gotten away from that kind of thing," one theatergoer told the* Amsterdam News.

CARL VAN VECHTEN TO LANGSTON HUGHES, OCTOBER 27, 1960

Dear Langston, THANKS for everything. I hope you haven't forgotten that Bessie Smith begins a week's engagement at the Museum of Modern

Art at Three o'clock on Sunday the six.¹ Congratulations on getting an apology from Time. Did you ever start that Columbia Interview with Bill Ingersoll? Mine is done now.

Love to you,

Carlo

October 27, 1960

1. *Van Vechten refers to a screening of the 1929 film short* St. Louis Blues, *starring Bessie Smith.*

V*an Vechten had accepted an invitation to record his reminiscences with William Ingersoll for the Columbia University Oral History Project. Over the course of several days, Van Vechten discussed his youth in Iowa ("I had a great ambition to be a writer very early, but my main interest was always to get out of Cedar Rapids"); his marriage ("We agree about few subjects, but Fania is a maid of many moods, and a few minutes after a violent discussion she is all smiles and charm. She is enchanting in this aspect and the other aspect is soon forgotten"); old age ("So many people think in old age you feel differently from what you were when you were young. That's not true at all. I feel exactly the same way I felt when I was eighteen years old"); pet peeves ("A dinner invitation is a sacred obligation; if you die, send your executor"); and his relationship to African Americans ("I never think of people as Negroes. I think of them as friends. If they're not friends, I'm not interested"); among many other subjects. The 366-page interview is housed at the New York Public Library. Ingersoll never conducted an interview with Hughes.*

LANGSTON HUGHES TO CARL VAN VECHTEN, DECEMBER 12, 1960
(CHRISTMAS CARD)

Dear Carl and Fania—Just back a few days ago from a wonderful week in Nigeria, home via Rome, Paris, London. Paris seemed to me as lovely as ever. I want to go right back. . . . I was with Dick Wright when he left for the hospital, seemingly not very ill—so I was his last visitor at home. In London I had a backstage hour with Eartha Kitt closing her 13th week of sold out tables; and I met the composer of "King Kong" who's coming over here next year.

Happy Holidays!

Hughes had accepted an invitation to attend the inauguration of Nnamdi Azikiwe as governor general and commander-in-chief of Nigeria, which had gained independence from Great Britain on October 1. Hughes was awed when Azikiwe, after taking the oath of office, recited his "Poem" from The Weary Blues, which begins: "We have tomorrow / Bright before us / Like a flame." Azikiwe was also an alumnus of Lincoln University. From Nigeria, Hughes traveled to Rome, a city he had never visited, and then on to Paris, his former home. He found an ill Richard Wright stretched out on his bed at home and couldn't stop himself from saying, "Man, you look like you are ready to go to glory!" Wright laughed and asked about Harlem. "I'd like to see it again," he said. He promised to write to Hughes, but never recovered from his illness. He died on November 28.

LANGSTON HUGHES TO CARL VAN VECHTEN, FEBRUARY 21, 1961

(TELEGRAM)

I SEE IN THE PRESS THAT YOU AND I ARE TO REPRESENT THE RACE IN THE NATIONAL INSTITUTE OF ARTS AND LETTERS WHICH DELIGHTS ME TO HAVE SUCH GENIAL COMPANY THEREIN I SALUTE YOU WITH SOMERSAULTS AND HANDSPRINGS LANGSTON

The National Institute of Arts and Letters, the honorary academy founded in 1898 in order to recognize American citizens of distinction in literature and the fine arts, had voted to admit both Hughes and Van Vechten into its ranks. Membership in the NIAL is limited to 250. Its headquarters are located in New York City.

LANGSTON HUGHES TO CARL VAN VECHTEN, MAY 3, 1961
(TELEGRAM)

C V V
MAY YOUR DELIGHTFUL COUNTESS COME TO LIFE ON STAGE
AS WONDERFULLY AS SHE LIVES BETWEEN COVERS
L

H*ughes cabled Van Vechten to congratulate him on the opening of a new musical adaptation of* The Tattooed Countess. *Coleman Dowell had approached Van Vechten in 1957 about making a musical based on his 1924 novel. Van Vechten had hated the 1925 movie version of his book, called* A Woman of the World, *and had rejected other offers to interpret the*

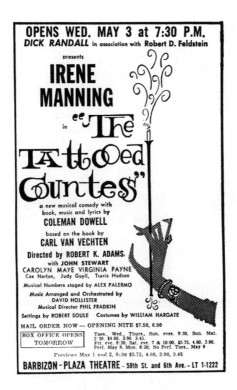

novel for the stage and screen. But he decided to take a chance on Dowell because his interpretation was "exactly the right mood," he told the New York Herald-Tribune *on May 6, 1961.*

When The Tattooed Countess *opened on May 3 the critical response was immediate and unforgiving. Judith Crist wrote in her "First Night Report" for the* New York Herald-Tribune: *"Suffice it to say that both book and lyrics are done in a leaden prose style and the music varies between the reminiscent and the monotonous." The musical closed on May 6, after four performances.*

July 18, 1961

Dear Carlo:

Would you happen to know where Edward Donahoe¹ is? If you do, please jot his address on a card and post it to me. Some two years ago now, I had a note from him, ill in a sanitorium in New Mexico, in which he mentioned hearing from you. His letter got buried in a big box of old mail unanswered, that I just now am finding time to go through carefully. I'd like to write Edward if I can learn his present whereabouts.

For the first time in the U.S. this Friday, July 21, THE BARRIER will be sung without Muriel Rahn who is, I hear, not well at all. The new CORA, Gwendolyn Walters, is wonderful, everybody who has heard a rehearsal, says. It will be sung again on Monday, July 24, both performances at the new NYU aircooled Student Center across Washington Square at 8:30 P.M. in case you'd like to hear it. Free. Conducted by Gordon Davidson. Meyerowitz, in the midst of rehearsals, fell down and broke his leg, so is off the scene. Peress² said, "God's will is sometimes best." I haven't been to rehearsals al all, so this will be a free-wheeling production uninhibited by composer or author. But I hear it so moving the singers cry. So we'll see on Friday.

I'm stuck on a deadline for a book for which the jacket is already made! I've got to write 200 pages in the next three weeks. Am trying.

Cordial regards to Fania and to you.

Kansas sun flowers—

Langston

---

1. *Donohoe had been an editor for Knopf during the 1920s. He was Edward IV among Van Vechten's Edwards.*
2. *Maurice Peress was a conductor who proposed this revival of* The Barrier *to Hughes.*

CARL VAN VECHTEN TO LANGSTON HUGHES, JULY 20, 1961

Dear Langston, I sympathize with you on your deadline. I have one with Esquire for an article and some photographs to be used in the Christmas number, but demanded in the middle of August.[1] This weather is not conducive to hard physical work.

Edward Donohoe may be reached at Nazareth Sanitarium, P.O. Box 270, Albuquerque, NM. His trouble is mental. Recently he was released on probation, but he has to report back to the Sanitarium on occasion, and this is the only address I have. I write him frequently and send him foolish presents.

Unfortunately I cannot visit The Barrier on either of the days mentioned. I am most sorry about Meyerowitz. That poor fellow is surfeited with bad luck. His notices for Esther,[2] that is his unpleasant notices, were undeserved. I found Esther much better on the whole than many a new opera at the Metropolitan. The performance was brilliant.

Hearts and Flowers!

Carlo

Give my regards to Mr Bass.

1. The article, "Portraits of the Artists," contained the caption: "A distinguished novelist-photographer remembers some friends, with and without a camera."
2. Based on the Bible story of Esther and her cousin Mordecai, the opera Esther was commissioned by the Fromm Foundation of Chicago and featured a score by Meyerowitz and a libretto by Hughes. It premiered in New York on April 27. The next morning, the New York Times called the music "more earnest than inspired."

George Houston Bass became Hughes's secretary in the summer of 1959 (Hughes's previous secretary, Raoul Abdul, had quit in order to study lieder and oratorio in Vienna). A math major at Fisk University, Bass had been recommended by Arna Bontemps, and he and Hughes became close. "Living and working with Langston Hughes revolutionized my life," Bass told Arnold Rampersad, Hughes's biographer, in a June 4, 1987 interview. He worked as Hughes's assistant until 1964, when he resigned to pursue his own career as a writer, despite Hughes's protective warnings. In his will, Hughes named Bass executor-trustee of his estate, along with Arna Bontemps.

July 21, 1961

Dear Carlo:

Thanks for Edward's address. And for the nice remarks about ESTHER which I phoned Meyerowitz to cheer him up, since he can't hear THE BARRIER tonight, but his doctor says he can go in a wheel chair on Monday.

Meanwhile, echoes of all beautiful music to you in your inner ear.

Comme toujours,

Langston

Dear Langston, We are just home after Black Nativity, thoroughly exhausted. What a marvellous piece it is and how Zora would love it. The jammed house today clapped all through it and one colored lady waved her arms and shouted and then got up and danced down the aisle, overcome by religious excitement. There is no sense in closing this rally round the cross. The audience adored it and so did Fania and

Carlo   Sunday night

Carlo—So glad you and Fania saw my show. I thought you'd like it. Con amore—Langston

Black Nativity *was a gospel Christmas drama commissioned by Gary Kramer, a music scholar and founder of a gospel management company. Like Kramer, Hughes believed gospel was poised for a breakthrough into mainstream music. Hughes began visiting storefront churches and temples in November 1961, and by December 6, he had finished the play, whose music was already in the public domain, with the exception of a few melodies set by Alex Bradford.*

When Black Nativity *opened on December 10, 1961, critics and audiences were enthralled.* The Daily Mirror *called it "an exciting blend of text, dance, spirituals, and hymns" as well as a "timely reminder of what Christmas really means."*

LANGSTON HUGHES TO CARL VAN VECHTEN, FEBRUARY 1, 1962

February 1, 1962
Midnight

Dear Carlo and Fania:

I've just finished the champagne[1]—a few friends dropped in—with Aunt Toy's cake, it was wonderful! And a real surprise when it came this afternoon. Thanks a million! Gracias!

Langston

1. *The champagne was a gift to celebrate Hughes's birthday on February 1.*

CARL VAN VECHTEN TO LANGSTON HUGHES, APRIL 13, 1963

Dear Langston,

I loved the Saturday Review, altho I disagreed with practically everything Jones said, but I love to have anything said by my people in a National Magazine. What a number!

Hearts and flowers,
Carlo

April 13, 1963

The editors of the Saturday Review *had invited LeRoi Jones, Langston Hughes, and the novelist John A. Williams to comment on the "Problems of the Negro Writer." Their responses ran in the April 20, 1963, issue. In his essay "The Myth of 'Negro Literature,'" Jones argues:*

The most persistent and aggravating reason for the absence of achievement among serious Negro artists is that generally the Negroes in a posi-

tion to pursue some art, especially the art of literature, have been members of the Negro middle class, a group that has always gone out of its way to cultivate any mediocrity.

Music, he believed, was the salvation of black culture:

There has never been an equivalent to Duke Ellington or Louis Armstrong in Negro writing; even the best of contemporary literature written by Negroes cannot yet be compared to the fantastic beauty of Charlie Parker's music.

In "The Bread and Butter Side," Hughes discussed the practical reality facing black writers. There were still too few blacks in publishing houses or in the radio, television, and movie industries, he argued. On top of job difficulties,

The Negro writer, of course, suffers from all the other prejudices color is heir to in our USA, depending on what part of the country he lives in or travels. In New York, a Negro going to a downtown cocktail party given for a white fellow-writer may be told by the apartment doorman, no matter how well dressed the guest may be, "The servants' entrance is around the corner." Such occurrences seem incredible in Manhattan today, but they are not. In the South, on the other hand, nothing boorish is incredible.

LANGSTON HUGHES TO CARL VAN VECHTEN, JUNE 17, 1963
(TELEGRAM)

WITH HAPPIEST OF MEMORIES OF ALL THE YEARS OF OUR
FRIENDSHIP I WISH YOU THE HAPPIEST OF DAYS TODAY
WITH ADMIRATION AND AFFECTION AND ONE DOZEN
DANCING HIPPOPOTAMI
LANGSTON

T*he artist Richard Banks hosted Van Vechten's eighty-third birthday party at Banks's apartment in New York City. The cabaret entertainer Mabel Mercer sang an unaccompanied rendition of "Sunday in Savan-*

nah," Carl's favorite from her repertoire. Mercer and Tallulah Bankhead led the entire party in "Happy Birthday." Van Vechten described the evening to his friend Paul Padgette: "Champagne flowed freely and several times during the evening the guests stood up in front of me and saluted me. Toasted me, that is. . . . What a party! I never had it so good!"

CARL VAN VECHTEN TO LANGSTON HUGHES, JUNE 18, 1963
(POSTCARD)

Dear Langston, Thank you for your good wishes. I had a wonderful day and actually felt about 16, ending up in the arms of Tallulah & Mabel! Love to you

Carlo

June 18

CARL VAN VECHTEN TO LANGSTON HUGHES, JUNE 19, 1963

Dear and friendly Doctor,
Now we are even![1]

1. On June 7, Howard University awarded Hughes his second honorary degree. Lincoln University had granted him his first in 1943. Van Vechten actually had only one honorary degree to Hughes's two. It was granted by Fisk University in 1955.

LANGSTON HUGHES TO CARL VAN VECHTEN, OCTOBER 6, 1963

October 6, 1963

Dear Carlo:

Greetings! I'm back from Europe and head-over-heels in rehearsals — of TWO shows.[1] BLACK NATIVITY opens its 40-week national tour in Boston at the Shubert on October 14, and is being redone a bit.

TAMBOURINES TO GLORY opens at the all-done-over and very pretty Little Theatre (next to Sardi's) on Saturday, November 2. I would be delighted if you and Fania would be my guests — and if you let me know soon, I'll get you FRONT ROW CENTER seats.

Hilda Simms and Lou Gossett with Clara Ward head the cast. So far, it looks good and the singing is 110 proof, with a new gospel singer named Dorothy Drake who bids fair to raise the roof.

Footballs and crysanthemums to you—

Sincerely,

Langston

1. *On July 2, Langston and his secretary, George Bass, had sailed for Europe on a two-month vacation.*

Black Nativity *did extremely well in Boston. The* Boston Globe *called it "a triumph of emotional experiences as well as a delight to the senses."*

Tambourines to Glory *did not fare as well. Howard Taubman of the* New York Times *wrote that the play had "the look of something slapped together." Still, "the singing and songs, particularly the gospel numbers" were "better than all right."*

LANGSTON HUGHES TO CARL VAN VECHTEN, JANUARY 13, 1964

January 13, 1964

Carlo—

It looks like "Jericho" is a little hit—says the "Times" and "Trib." I hope you can see (and HEAR) it. It's loud.

Langston

Jericho-Jim Crow, *Hughes's new gospel musical about the Civil Rights Movement, opened on January 2, 1946, in Greenwich Village in New York at the Sanctuary, a church that housed in its basement the Greenwich Mews Theater, which was run by Stella Holt, Hughes's producer. On January 13, the* New York Times*'s reviewer raved: "If the plaster didn't fall from the ceiling . . . it's a tribute to sturdy construction and not the fault of the ringing debut of Langston Hughes's 'Jericho Jim Crow.' " The* New York Herald-Tribune*'s reviewer agreed: "The somber yet optimistic tale is told poetically,* *powerfully, gloriously, enthusiastically and at times wittily. The tide of memory comes rushing through the sanctuary from the very first clash of the cymbals, and before the hour is over it has swept up everyone in its flood."*

CARL VAN VECHTEN TO LANGSTON HUGHES, JUNE 2, 1964

Dear Langston, You and I have been through so many new negroes that we are a little tired of it all. BUT I was really excited about the group you have brought together. Le Roi Jones who appears to be somebody, I photographed long since. I wonder when he & Baldwin will have a fight! It will be a big one. I am very happy to receive your book with its beautiful inscription.[1]

Much affection to you
Carlo

It was certainly old home night at Rita's. I had a really wonderful time.
June 2, 1964

1. *The book was either Hughes's 1963 short-story collection,* Something in Common and Other Stories, *published by Hill & Wang, or a 1964 collection he edited,* New Negro Poets: USA, *published by Indiana University Press.*

LEROI JONES, PHOTOGRAPH
BY CARL VAN VECHTEN, 1962

JAMES BALDWIN, PHOTOGRAPH
BY CARL VAN VECHTEN, 1955

H ughes received an invitation in the fall of 1964 to participate in the Berlin Folk Festival at the end of September. The theme of the festival was the impact of Africa on twentieth-century art and culture. Other participants included Wole Soyinka, Jorge Luis Borges, and Aimé Césaire. The festival provided an occasion for Hughes to take another long vacation in Europe. He returned to the United States on November 8.

LANGSTON HUGHES TO CARL VAN VECHTEN, DECEMBER 8, 1964

December 8, 1964

Dear Carlo:

I had a wonderful 8 weeks in Europe and came back loaded down with medals and books and records and things publishers and friends in Berlin, Paris, and London gave me. I'd love to come down and show you and Fania my Akademie medal and laurel wreath and all whenever you all will receive me, maybe next week if you're free. It's been much too long since I've seen you. . . . I felt fine when I got back to New York, but two days later came down with the flu and am just getting back to myself. You recall what Simple said: "White folks thrive on vacations, but they almost kill Negroes!" I'm afraid it's true. . . . Cherio,

Langston

LANGSTON HUGHES TO FANIA VAN VECHTEN, DECEMBER 21, 1964
(TELEGRAM)

ALL MY LOVE AND SYMPATHY TO YOU TODAY
LANGSTON HUGHES

H ughes never got to show Van Vechten his medal and wreath. On December 21 he received a telegram from the National Institute of Arts and Letters: HAVE YOU HEARD THAT CARL VAN VECHTEN

DIED THIS MORNING IN HIS SLEEP? He and Fania had just celebrated their fiftieth wedding anniversary on October 21. A memorial service was held on December 23. On June 17, 1966, which would have been his eighty-sixth birthday, Carl Van Vechten's ashes were scattered in the Shakespeare Gardens in Central Park, across the street from his home. Hughes's official tribute to Van Vechten, prepared for the National Institute of Arts and Letters, is printed as Appendix III, page 337.

LANGSTON HUGHES TO FANIA VAN VECHTEN, JANUARY 27, 1965

January 27, 1965

Dear Fania:

That you blessed <u>us</u> for coming to your house the other day was the sweetest thing you could have done because we didn't know what to say—except that we wanted to bless you and Carlo for blessing us all through so many wonderful years of knowing you both. Your sorrow radiated love. And you know that all your friends are at your command if there is anything helpful that we can do.

Affectionately ever,
Langston

LANGSTON HUGHES AND CARL VAN VECHTEN, NEW YORK CITY,
FEBRUARY 16, 1963. PHOTOGRAPH BY RICHARD AVEDON

INTRODUCING LANGSTON HUGHES
TO THE READER
by Carl Van Vechten

Published as the Introduction to Langston Hughes's The Weary Blues
(New York: Alfred A. Knopf, 1926)

I

At the moment I cannot recall the name of any other person whatever who, at the age of twenty-three, has enjoyed so picturesque and rambling an existence as Langston Hughes. Indeed, a complete account of his disorderly and delightfully fantastic career would make a fascinating picaresque romance which I hope this young Negro will write before so much more befalls him that he may find it difficult to capture all the salient episodes within the limits of a single volume.

Born on February 1, 1902, in Joplin, Missouri, he had lived, before his twelfth year, in the City of Mexico; Topeka, Kansas; Colorado Springs; Charlestown, Indiana; Kansas City; and Buffalo. He attended Central High School, from which he graduated, at Cleveland, Ohio, while in the summer, there and in Chicago, he worked as delivery- and dummy-boy in hat-stores. In his senior year he was elected class poet and editor of the Year Book.

After four years in Cleveland, he once more joined his father in Mexico, only to migrate to New York where he entered Columbia University. There, finding the environment distasteful, or worse, he remained till spring, when he quit, broke with his father and, with thirteen dollars in cash, went on his own. First, he worked for a truck-farmer on Staten Island; next, he delivered flowers for Thorley; at length he partially satisfied an insatiable craving to go to sea by signing up with an old ship anchored in the Hudson for the winter. His first real cruise as a sailor carried him to the Canary Islands, the Azores, and the West Coast of Africa, of which voyage he has written: "Oh, the sun in Dakar! Oh, the little black girls of Burutu! Oh, the blue, blue bay of

Loanda! Calabar, the city lost in a forest; the long, shining days at sea, the masts rock-ing against the stars at night; the black Kru-boy sailors, taken at Freetown, bathing on deck morning and evening; Tom Pey and Haneo, whose dangerous job it was to dive under the seven-ton mahogany logs floating and bobbing at the ship's side and fasten them to the chains of the crane; the vile houses of rotting women at Lagos; the desola-tion of the Congo; Johnny Walker, and the millions of whisky bottles buried in the sea along the West Coast; the daily fights on board, officers, sailors, everybody drunk; the timorous, frightened missionaries we carried as passengers; and George, the Kentucky colored boy, dancing and singing the Blues on the after-deck under the stars."

Returning to New York with plenty of money and a monkey, he presently shipped again—this time for Holland. Again he came back to New York and again he sailed—on his twenty-second birthday: February 1, 1924. Three weeks later he found himself in Paris with less than seven dollars. However, he was soon provided for: a woman of his own race engaged him as doorman at her *boîte de nuit.* Later he was employed, first as second cook, then as waiter, at the Grand Duc, where the Negro entertainer, Florence, sang at this epoch. Here he made friends with an Italian family who carried him off to their villa at Desenzano on Lago di Garda where he passed a happy month, followed by a night in Verona and a week in Venice. On his way back across Italy his passport was stolen and he became a beach-comber in Genoa. He has described his life there to me: "Wine and figs and pasta. And sunlight! And amusing companions, dozens of other beach-combers roving the dockyards and water-front streets, getting their heads whacked by the Fascisti, and breaking one loaf of bread into so many pieces that nobody got more than a crumb. I lived in the public gardens along the water-front and slept in the Albergo Populare for two lire a night amidst the snores of hundreds of other derelicts. . . . I painted my way home as a sailor. It seems that I must have painted the whole ship myself. We made a regular 'grand tour': Livorno, Napoli (we passed so close to Capri I could have cried). Then all around Sicily—Catania, Messina, Palermo—the Lipari Islands, miserable little peaks of pumice stone out in the sea; then across to Spain, divine Spain! My buddy and I went on a spree in Valencia for a night and a day. . . . Oh, the sweet wine of Valencia!"

He arrived in New York on November 10, 1924. That evening I attended a dance given in Harlem by the National Association for the Advancement of Colored People. Some time during the course of the night, Walter White asked me to meet two young Negro poets. He introduced me to Countée Cullen and Langston Hughes. Before that moment I had never heard of either of them.

II

I have merely sketched a primitive outline of a career as rich in adventures as a fruit-cake is full of raisins. I have already stated that I hope Langston Hughes may be per-suaded to set it down on paper in the minutest detail, for the bull-fights in Mexico, the drunken gaiety of the Grand Duc, the delicately exquisite grace of the little black girls at Burutu, the exotic languor of the Spanish women at Valencia, the barbaric jazz dances of the cabarets in New York's own Harlem, the companionship of sailors of many races and nationalities, all have stamped an indelible impression on the highly sensitized, poetic imagination of this young Negro, an impression which has found its initial expression in the poems assembled in this book.

And also herein may be discerned that nostalgia for color and warmth and beauty which explains this boy's nomadic instincts.

> "We should have a land of sun,
> Of gorgeous sun,
> And a land of fragrant water
> Where the twilight
> Is a soft bandanna handkerchief
> Of rose and gold,
> And not this land where life is cold,"

he sings. Again, he tells his dream:

> "To fling my arms wide
> In the face of the sun,
> Dance! whirl! whirl!
> Till the quick day is done.
> Rest at pale evening. . . .
> A tall, slim tree. . . .
> Night coming tenderly,
> Black like me."

More of this wistful longing may be discovered in the poems entitled "The South" and "As I Grew Older." His verses, however, are by no means limited to an exclusive mood; he writes caressingly of little black prostitutes in Harlem; his cabaret songs throb with the true jazz rhythm; his sea-pieces ache with a calm, melancholy lyricism; he cries bitterly from the heart of his race in "Cross" and "The Jester"; he sighs, in one of the most successful of his fragile poems, over the loss of a loved friend. Always, however, his stanzas are subjective, personal. They are the (I had almost said informal, for they have a highly deceptive air of spontaneous improvisation) expression of an essentially sensitive and subtly illusive nature, seeking always to break through the veil that obscures for him, at least in some degree, the ultimate needs of that nature.

To the Negro race in America, since the day when Phillis Wheatley indited lines to General George Washington and other aristocratic figures (for Phillis Wheatley never sang "My way's cloudy," or "By an' by, I'm goin' to lay down dis heavy load") there have been born many poets. Paul Laurence Dunbar, James Weldon Johnson, Claude McKay, Jean Toomer, Georgia Douglas Johnson, Countée Cullen, are a few of the more memorable names. Not the least of these names, I think, is that of Langston Hughes, and perhaps his adventures and personality offer the promise of as rich a fulfillment as has been the lot of any of the others.

CARL VAN VECHTEN
New York
August 3, 1925

TWO POEMS BY LANGSTON HUGHES

Advertisement for the Waldorf-Astoria

Fine living . . . à la carte??
Come to the Waldorf-Astoria!

        LISTEN, HUNGRY ONES!
Look! See what *Vanity Fair* says about the
    new Waldorf-Astoria:
    "All the luxuries of private home. . . ."
Now, won't that be charming when the last flop-house
    has turned you down this winter?
    Furthermore:
"It is far beyond anything hitherto attempted in the hotel
    world. . . ." It cost twenty-eight million dollars. The
    famous Oscar Tschirky is in charge of banqueting.
    Alexandre Gastaud is chef. It will be a distinguished
    background for society.
So when you've got no place else to go, homeless and hungry
    ones, choose the Waldorf as a background for your rags—
(Or do you still consider the subway after midnight good
    enough?)

        ROOMERS
Take a room at the new Waldorf, you down-and-outers—
    sleepers in charity's flop-houses where God pulls a
    long face, and you have to pray to get a bed.
They serve swell board at the Waldorf-Astoria. Look at this menu, will you:

        GUMBO CREOLE
        CRABMEAT IN CASSOLETTE
        BOILED BRISKET OF BEEF

SMALL ONIONS IN CREAM
WATERCRESS SALAD
PEACH MELBA

Have luncheon there this afternoon, all you jobless.
    Why not?
Dine with some of the men and women who got rich off of
    your labor, who clip coupons with clean white fingers
    because your hands dug coal, drilled stone, sewed gar-
    ments, poured steel to let other people draw dividends
    and live easy.
(Or haven't you had enough yet of the soup-lines and the
    bitter bread of charity?)
Walk through Peacock Alley tonight before dinner, and get
    warm, anyway. You've got nothing else to do.

EVICTED FAMILIES

All you families put out in the street:
    Apartments in the Towers are only $10,000 a year.
        (Three rooms and two baths.) Move in there until
        times get good, and you can do better. $10,000 and $1.00
        are about the same to you, aren't they?
    Who cares about money with a wife and kids homeless, and
    nobody in the family working? Wouldn't a duplex
    high above the street be grand, with a view of the rich-
    est city in the world at your nose?
"A lease, if you prefer, or an arrangement terminable at will."

NEGROES

Oh, Lawd, I done forgot Harlem!
Say, you colored folks, hungry a long time in 135th Street—
    they got swell music at the Waldorf-Astoria. It sure is a
    mighty nice place to shake hips in, too. There's dancing
    after supper in a big warm room. It's cold as hell
    on Lenox Avenue. All you've had all day is a cup of
    coffee. Your pawnshop overcoat's a ragged banner on
    your hungry frame. You know, downtown folks are just
    crazy about Paul Robeson! Maybe they'll like you, too,
    black mob from Harlem. Drop in at the Waldorf this
    afternoon for tea. Stay to dinner. Give Park Avenue a
    lot of darkie color—free for nothing! Ask the Junior
    Leaguers to sing a spiritual for you. They probably
    know 'em better than you do—and their lips won't be
    so chapped with cold after they step out of their closed
    cars in the undercover driveways.
        Hallelujah! Undercover driveways!
        Ma soul's a witness for de Waldorf-Astoria!
(A thousand nigger section-hands keep the roadbeds smooth,
    so investments in railroads pay ladies with diamond
    necklaces staring at Sert murals.)
        Thank God A-mighty!

(And a million niggers bend their backs on rubber
    plantations, for rich behinds to ride on thick tires to the
    Theatre Guild tonight.)
        Ma soul's a witness!
(And here we stand, shivering in the cold, in Harlem.)
        Glory be to God—
        De Waldorf-Astoria's open!

EVERYBODY

So get proud and rare back; everybody! The new Waldorf-Astoria's
    open!
(Special siding for private cars from the railroad yards.)
    You ain't been there yet?
(A thousand miles of carpet and a million bathrooms.)
    What's the matter?
You haven't seen the ads in the papers? Didn't you get a card?
    Don't you know they specialize in American cooking?
    Ankle on down to 49th Street at Park Avenue. Get up
    off that subway bench tonight with the evening POST
    for cover! Come on out o' that flop-house! Stop shivering
    your guts out all day on street corners under the El.
Jesus, ain't you tired yet?

CHRISTMAS CARD

Hail Mary, Mother of God!
    the new Christ child of the Revolution's about to be
    born.
(Kick hard, red baby, in the bitter womb of the mob.)
Somebody, put an ad in *Vanity Fair* quick!
Call Oscar of the Waldorf—for Christ's sake!!
    It's almost Christmas, and that little girl—turned whore
    because her belly was too hungry to stand it anymore—
    wants a nice clean bed for the Immaculate Conception.
Listen, Mary, Mother of God, wrap your new born babe in
    the red flag of Revolution: the Waldorf-Astoria's the
    best manger we've got. For reservations: Telephone EL.
    5-3000.

Goodbye Christ

Listen, Christ,
You did alright in your day, I reckon—
But that day's gone now.
They ghosted you up a swell story, too,
Called it Bible—
But it's dead now,
The popes and the preachers've
Made too much money from it.
They've sold you to too many

Kings, generals, robbers, and killers—
Even to the Tzar and the Cossacks,
Even to Rockefeller's Church,
Even to THE SATURDAY EVENING POST.
You ain't no good no more.
They've pawned you
Till you've done wore out.

Goodbye,
Christ Jesus Lord God Jehova,
Beat it on away from here now.
Make way for a new guy with no religion at all—
A real guy named
Marx Communist Lenin Peasant Stalin Worker ME—

I said, ME!
Go ahead on now,
You're getting in the way of things, Lord.
And please take Saint Ghandi with you when you go,
And Saint Pope Pius,
And Saint Aimee McPherson,
And big black Saint Becton
Of the Consecrated Dime.
And step on the gas, Christ!
Move!

Don't be so slow about movin'!
The world is mine from now on—
And nobody's gonna sell ME
To a king, or a general,
Or a millionaire.

CARL VAN VECHTEN
1880–1964

*Address by Langston Hughes to the National Institute of Arts and Letters,
New York, January 8, 1965*

A sure sign of old age is when a man begins to disapprove of the young. At the age of 84, Carl Van Vechten had not yet grown old. His enthusiasm for youth in the arts, and his quest for new talent, remained until the end unabated in music, in theatre, in writing and in painting. His tastes continued as catholic as ever. Despite Carl Van Vechten's long-known deep interest in the creativity of the Negro people, and the immense amount of time he devoted to Negro activities, his concerns were by no means limited to darker Americans. James Purdy is a recent example of Van Vechten discovery and interest from manuscript to final printed page. In music from blues to bop and beyond, from Yvette Guilbert to Mahalia Jackson, from the long ago Mary Garden to the contemporary Leontyne Price, from George Gershwin of the twenties to Charlie Mingus of the sixties, Carl Van Vechten kept a listening ear as to the grace notes, and a listening heart as to the meanings of the music of each generation — in spite of the fact that he gave up professional music criticism at the age of forty because, he said, "intellectual hardening of the arteries" made one unreceptive to innovations. As subsequent enthusiasms indicated, however, he must have found this statement untrue during the decades that followed.

Almost always Carl Van Vechten was ahead of his times insofar as public taste and the canons of publicity went. The times had to catch up with him. In 1924, when most "cultured" people ignored America's basic Negro music, Carl Van Vechten wrote, "Jazz may not be the last hope of American music, nor yet the best hope, but at present, I am convinced, it is its only hope." In 1942, when he founded the James Weldon Johnson Memorial Collection of Negro Arts and Letters at Yale University, he presented it his enormous collection of recordings, jazz and otherwise, by colored composers and artists, as well as his many letters and manuscripts from Negro writers, painters and

337

theatre people. Dr. Charles S. Johnson, then president of Fisk University, termed Carl Van Vechten "the first white American to interpret objectively, with deftness and charm, the external features of the American Negro in a new age and setting."

Deftness and charm were so much a part of Carl Van Vechten's articles and critiques hailing his various enthusiasms, that some, accustomed to more ponderous academic criticism, felt that the Van Vechten personality consisted mostly of fanfare and fun. It did possess these attributes. But behind the fanfare lay genuine critical acumen, often of a highly prophetic nature. And humor, wit, and sophistication in the best sense gave yeast to all the fun Van Vechten found in writing and living. He might be called both a hedonist and a humanist. In New York, Hollywood and Paris, he had a wide circle of lively, intelligent and decorative friends, particularly in the arts. There were no ethnic or religious barriers to his friendships. For many years on June 17 the joint birthdays of James Weldon Johnson, Negro, Alfred A. Knopf, Jr., Jewish, and himself were celebrated together with the three colors of our flag—red, white and blue—on the cakes at dinner, presided over by his charming wife, Fania Marinoff.

When, late in life, he became a serious photographer, Van Vechten photographed not only his friends, but hundreds of valued and celebrated personalities, to the extent of some 15,000 negatives. Steichen termed his photography "darned good." On the shelves of the world's libraries, Van Vechten leaves for the pleasure of future readers who will discover him seven novels, numerous critiques, essays and memoirs, and three charming books about cats. He established the Anna Marble Pollack Memorial Library of Books About Cats at Yale. Fisk University has the George Gershwin Memorial Collection of Music and Musical Literature, as well as his gift of the Florine Stettheimer Memorial Collection of Books About the Fine Arts. The New York Public Library possesses his personal papers, letters and manuscripts. And, of his long and happy sojourn among us, his friends possess a rainbow of memories.

TRIBUTE TO CARL VAN VECHTEN
by Langston Hughes

Delivered at the November 20, 1942, dinner in honor of Carl Van Vechten, reprinted with permission from Bruce Kellner.

Greetings for Mr. Canada Lee to deliver to Mr. Carl Van Vechten by Mr. Langston Hughes:

> Hey, now!
> Some skin, Gate!
> I can't make a speech
> Cause it's getting late.
> And not having heard
> What's gone on before,
> I might be repeating
> What you already know.
> You're a mellow fellow,
> And I guess they've told you so—
> Then on the compliments,
> I'm gonna take it slow.
> Being a writer yourself,
> You can write your own autobiography—
> But I'm just gonna picture you
> As you appear to me:
> You've got a little bit of colored
> Mixed up in you—
> Cause you like the blues
> Just like colored folks do.
> You've got a lot of Harlem, too,
> In your smile,
> Cause you can laugh at simple things
> Like a wise child.

I don't know whether
Your strain runs back to Africa or not,
But there's something like a tom-tom
In that rhythm that you've got.
You know, I'm not talking
About your *physical* being.
I'm talking about the spirit
That's in you pressing.
To tell you the truth,
Your outsides is kinder battered and beat—
But there's something in your heart
That's mighty sweet.
You always wish all gamblers
Would throw a lucky seven—
And you've done your best to bring my people
Out of their—peanut gallery!
You know, I mean that old
Segregated heaven—away from it all—
That you and I know
Ain't no heaven a-tall.
You've got room
In your democracy
For all kind of folks,
Including me.
You're not only mellow
And a righteous man,
You're also a real, good old
Honest-to-God American.
But as I said before,
The hour's growing late.
You don't need no speech nohow.
Take it easy, Gate!
(EXIT)

NOTE: This little monologue to be delivered as though extemporaneous, in character, one hep cat to another, more or less.

                                          L . H .

SELECTED
BIBLIOGRAPHY

Bass, George Houston, and Henry Louis Gates, Jr., eds. *Mule Bone: A Comedy of Negro Life by Langston Hughes and Zora Neale Hurston.* New York: HarperPerennial, 1991.

Chauncey, George. *Gay New York: Gender, Urban Culture, and the Making of the Gay Male World, 1890–1940.* New York: Basic Books, 1994.

Denning, Michael. *The Cultural Front: The Laboring of American Culture in the Twentieth Century.* London: Verso, 1996.

Douglas, Ann. *Terrible Honesty: Mongrel Manhattan in the 1920s.* New York: Farrar, Straus & Giroux, 1995.

Duberman, Martin. *Paul Robeson: A Biography.* New York: The New Press, 1989.

Hemenway, Robert. *Zora Neale Hurston: A Literary Biography.* Urbana: University of Illinois Press, 1977.

Huggins, Nathan Irvin. *Harlem Renaissance.* New York: Oxford University Press, 1971.

Hughes, Langston. *The Big Sea.* New York: Knopf, 1940.

——. *I Wonder As I Wander.* New York: Rinehart & Co., 1956.

Hutchinson, George. *The Harlem Renaissance in Black and White.* Cambridge: Harvard University Press, 1995.

Kellner, Bruce. *Carl Van Vechten and the Irreverent Decades.* Oklahoma: Oklahoma University Press, 1968.

——. *The Harlem Renaissance: A Historical Dictionary for the Era.* New York: Methuen, 1987.

——, ed. *"Keep A-Inchin' Along": Selected Writings of Carl Van Vechten about Black Art and Letters.* Westport, Connecticut: Greenwood Press, 1979.

——, ed. *Letters of Carl Van Vechten.* New Haven: Yale University Press, 1987.

Lewis, David Levering, ed. *The Portable Harlem Renaissance Reader.* New York: Viking Penguin, 1994.

——. *When Harlem Was In Vogue.* New York: Oxford University Press, 1979.

Nichols, Charles H., ed. *Arna Bontemps–Langston Hughes: Letters.* New York: Paragon House, 1990.

Rampersad, Arnold. *The Life of Langston Hughes, Vol. 1, 1902–1941: I, Too, Sing America.* New York: Oxford University Press, 1986.

——. *The Life of Langston Hughes, Vol. 2, 1941–1967: I Dream a World.* New York: Oxford University Press, 1988.

Rampersad, Arnold, and David Roessel, eds. *The Collected Poems of Langston Hughes.* New York: Knopf, 1998.

Watson, Steven. *The Harlem Renaissance: Hub of African-American Culture, 1920–1930.* New York: Pantheon Books, 1995.

INDEX

cummings, e. e., 293
Cunard, Nancy, xxxii, 111, 112*n*, 227
Cutting, Bronson, 169, 170*n*

Dali, Salvador, 129, 212*n*
D'Alvarez, Marguerite, 41*n*, 154, 155*n*, 159
Dance Index, 212, 214
Dance Me a Song (revue), 263
Dancer, Earl, 56*n*, 60, 61*n*
Daniels, Jimmie, 157, 169 *and illus.,* 174,
    219, 221, 285, 308
Dark People of the Soviets (Hughes), 102
Darrow, Clarence, 56*n*
Daughters of the American Revolution
    (DAR), 146
Davey, Gloria, 299
Davidson, Gerald, 139
Davidson, Gordon, 316
Davis, Allison, 62, 63
Davis, Arthur, 191*n*
Davis, Jimmy, 206, *illus. 207,* 207*n,* 208,
    215, 228, 262
Davis, Sammy, Jr., 291
Dawson, William, 210
Day, John, 287*n*
Dear Lovely Death (Hughes), 90, 93
Death in Venice (Mann), 24
DeCarava, Roy, 282
Decker, Caroline, 109, 117*n*
Deep Are the Roots (d'Usseau and Gow),
    236, 237*n*
Deeter, Jasper, 67, 68
Delany, Hubert, 146
De Priest, Oscar, 93, 94*n*
d'Erlanger, Baron Leo, 164*n*
d'Erlanger, Baroness Edwina, 163, 164*n,*
    185
Dessalines, Jean-Jacques, 141*n,* 257*n,* 259*n*
Destiné, Jean-Louis, 286
Deutsch, Babette, 269*n*
Devil's Disciple, The (Shaw), 68
Diaghileff, Serge, 196
Dial, 37
Dismond, Geraldyn, 153, 155*n*
Divine, Father, 129, 130*n,* 195
Dodd, Mead, 272, 274, 280, 283, 295*n,* 298
Dodge, Mabel, *see* Luhan, Mabel Dodge
Dodson, Owen, 163, 164*n*
Don't You Want to Be Free (Hughes), 141,
    142*n,* 145, 183

Donahoe, Edward, 219, 316–18
Doro, Maria, 32, 33*n*
Dos Passos, John, 117
Doubleday Publishers, 243–4
Douglas, Aaron, xxxii, 25, 35, *illus. 42, 46,*
    56, 117
Douglass, Frederick, 195, 210, 272
Dowell, Coleman, 315–16
Dramatists Guild, 71, 139, 189
Draper, Muriel, xxxii–xxxiii, 66, 100, 101*n,*
    109, 152
Dreiser, Theodore, 133, 110, 117
Drew, Bernard, 262*n*
Du Bois, W. E. B., xvi, xxi, xxii, xxxiii,
    xxxvi, 8*n,* 15*n,* 35, 52, 60*n,* 63, 114*n,* 163,
    195, 246*n,* 271*n,* 274, 280, *illus. 283, 284,*
    285*n*
Du Bois, Yolande, 60*n,* 239
Dudley, Caroline, 63, 274, 275*n*
Dudley, Katherine, 275*n*
Dulaney, Princess, 218
Dunbar, Paul Lawrence, 192, 193*n,* 331
Duncan, Isadora, 160, 161*n*
Dunham, Katherine, 175*n,* 185, 189, 190,
    191*n,* 195, 199, 201
Dunne, George H., 254
Durant, Kenneth, 208
Durland, Addison, 88
d'Usseau, Arnaud, 237*n*
Dust Tracks on a Road (Hurston), xxxiv,
    213

Egor Bulachev and Others (Gorky), 102
Einstein, Albert, 259*n*
Elder, Paul, 124
Ellington, Duke, 189, 197, 199, 221, 222*n,*
    223, 320
Elliott, Jimmy, 218, 219
Ellison, Ralph, xxv, 230, 231, 272, 273*n*
Emperor Jones, The (O'Neill), xxxviii, 68,
    112*n,* 114, 115
Esquire, 110, 117, 118, 125*n,* 129, 183, 259
Epstein, Jacob, 158
Ernst, Max, 117
Ernst, Morris, 146
Esther (Hughes and Meyerowitz), 317, 318
Evans, Bobby, 187
Evans, John, 109, 111*n,* 116, 117
Ewing, Max, xxxiii, 107, 112, 114, 207
Excavations (Van Vechten), 27

A NOTE ABOUT THE EDITOR

Emily Bernard was born in Nashville, Tennessee, in 1967. She attended Yale University, receiving a B.A. in 1989 and a Ph.D. in 1998; both degrees are in American Studies. She is currently an assistant professor of African American Studies at Smith College. She is the recipient of a Dorothy Danforth Compton Fellowship, a Ford Foundation Fellowship, an NEH Fellowship, and a W. E. B. Du Bois Resident Fellowship at Harvard University. This is her first book.

A NOTE ON THE TYPE

The text of this book was set in a face named Didot, considered by many to be the first modern typeface. The Didot family of Paris was involved in many aspects of printing and publishing, but the most important member of the family in the field of type design was Firmin Didot (1764–1836), grandson of the founder, who produced the typeface in 1784.

Composed by North Market Street Graphics, Lancaster, Pennsylvania

Printed and bound by Quebecor Printing, Fairfield, Pennsylvania

Designed by Iris Weinstein

tulips and jonquils to yo

Dear Carlo,
Have been laying off to
write you for weeks, but
we've been moving so fast
and rough that I haven't
had a chance, but at last
we come to a stopping place
with the sight of the Citadel
20 miles away on a mountain
top. We came across Cuba in old
cars that continually broke down,
and camions full of
peasants and chickens, took
deck passage on a French ship
for East au Prince and rode
in the open for three days with
the sugar-cane workers coming
home, while the boat went
all around Southern Haiti picking up cargo. The last night a
storm came up and we slept
in the...

Dear Langston, Will you
come to a Buffet supper
We are giving in honor of
Dorothy Peterson on
Saturday Oct. 10 at
6.30? Nous esperons
que oui.
Love
Carlo The Patriard,
September 25, 1939

WESTERN UNION

Received at 2040 East 9th St. Cleveland, Ohio
NB208 11=NEWYORK NY 1 116P
1931 FEB 1 PM 1 56
LANGSTON HUGHES=/
$800 CARNEGIE AVE CLEVELAND OHIO=;
FOURTEEN GOLD AND SILVER STALLIONS WITH SAPPHIRE NAMES TO YOU
TODAY=
CARLO.

Thanks also for your letters
contained. Col Bousfield of
I have written Lt Davis to a
I have contacted all and sur
I am very excited about your
surprise me with my pents d
through some way.   Can yo
what number of the New Repu
show in Harlem was most suc
marvellously displayed which
THAT of a High School...So

In the meantime four red r

April 28. [1944]

Last night I attended the
fun and inconceivably gr
are obliged to POSE to di
honeys.   I still havent
along gran

In the meantime four red ros

The Defender though
terrible....I'm anxious to hear
about Nora and Santa Fe and
Hollywood....and the director you
might meet when he
comes   engaged
in getting educated
term papers, graphs, and all
that sort of thing......I hope
I get smart sometime.
Sincerely,
Langston